ALIENATION: FROM MARX TO MODERN SOCIOLOGY

ALIENATION
FROM MARX
TO MODERN SOCIOLOGY

A Macrosociological Analysis by
JOACHIM ISRAEL, University of Copenhagen

Consulting Editor: Amitai Etzioni

NEW JERSEY: HUMANITIES PRESS
SUSSEX: HARVESTER PRESS

Reprinted in 1979 by Humanities Press in the United States of America and by Harvester Press in Great Britain by arrangement with the author.

(U.S.A.)   ISBN 0-391-00903-6
(England)   ISBN 0 85527 854 6

The original edition of this book appeared in Swedish under the title *Alienation: från Marx till modern sociologi* (Stockholm: Rabén & Sjögren, 1968).

CONTENTS

*Science should not be an egoistic pleasure.
Those who are fortunate enough to be able
to devote themselves to scientific work
should be the first to apply their knowledge
in the service of humanity.*

KARL MARX

PREFACE

This book was first published in Swedish in 1968. Since I agreed to carry out the translation into English myself, I had the unusual opportunity not only to revise it, but also to add new chapters and to rewrite several of the old.

The idea of analyzing the concept of "alienation" grew out of an empirical study at a mental hospital. One of the variables used in this study was the subjects' degree of alienation, measured in the now-usual way: psychological dimensions, like the experience of powerlessness, meaninglessness, etc., were operationalized in attitude scales. When analyzing the concept of "alienation," I was struck by how often references were made to Karl Marx, especially in American studies. However, his theories usually were not presented in a very detailed way. At the same time it became clear that the use of the term differed considerably from the way Marx originally had developed it. Whereas in Marx's writings "alienation" refers to social processes, the term in empirical social science has been changed into a psychological concept.

Therefore, I started to read Marx again after a twenty-year break. I must confess that it became fascinating reading, much more fascinating than when I had read him the first time. It became clear to me that Marx's interest in the concept of "alienation" was a consequence of his intellectual attachment to Hegelian philosophy, an attachment which was not uncritical. To the contrary, Marx took the "materialist" position in the old philosophical and epistemological issue concerning the nature of the world about which we have knowledge. This issue, idealism vs. materialism, is in my opinion now only of historical interest.

After analyzing Marx's use of the concept, I tried to explicate the way similar ideas were treated in other classics of sociology. Simmel, using the concept of "objectification," becomes most similar to Marx, whereas Durkheim takes a quite different stand, emphasizing moral problems and consensus when he talks about "anomy." Most conspicuous, however, is the absence of such a concept in Max Weber's work in spite of the fact that he, like Marx, deals with the problem of capitalist institutions.

The analysis of the concept of alienation indicated that, if one uses the term, one has to ask: "From what is it that man is alienated?" One answer is: From his "true nature," which means from "the nature of man" as postulated by a certain author. In other words, theories of alienation presuppose postulated notions concerning "the nature of man" and "the nature of society." These problems are taken up in chapter 1, which at the same time tries to present a theoretical frame for the analysis of this concept. It can also be shown that postulated or normative notions concerning man's nature and the nature of society are brought in, though often implicitly, when "alienation" is used in empirical theories. In fact, one can assert that all sociological and psychological theories of an empirical kind are implicitly or explicitly based upon postulated, normative notions which precede and therefore delimit the content of empirical theories. (This idea has been further developed in a coming publication.[1])

Chapter 2 presents some of the ideas upon which Marx based his own theories or from which he received inspiration. This chapter, however, has been kept deliberately short in order to avoid getting involved in problems of the history of ideas.

In chapter 3 Marx's own ideas are presented and analyzed, and an explication of the alienation concept is attempted. There it is also shown that Marx quite early abandoned the concept and its philosophical background for another concept, which one of his most interesting interpreters, Georg Lukács, termed "reification," implying that man is transformed into a passive object, a thing.

In chapter 4 some problems related to the idea of alienation in the writings of Marx are taken up. It is shown that one interpretation of Marxism not unusual even among Marxists—namely, to understand Marx's theories as an economic determinism—is wrong and that Marx's epistemological position in this aspect is quite different: Man is not only a product of his circumstances—economical as well as others—but he is also the creator of these circumstances. Thus a dialectical relationship—between man as a creating subject and an object influenced by the world he has created—is the basis for Marx's theories, resembling to a certain extent some of the premises of general systems theory. In this chapter, also, the problem of "false consciousness" is analyzed and an explication of the term attempted.

In chapter 5 the theories of Weber, Simmel, and Durkheim are analyzed with regard to one point of view: their analysis and criticism of capitalism and the industrialized society. For Marx, capitalist society and its economic institutions stand out as the example of an irrational use of resources. Weber, on the other hand, develops the concept of "formal

[1] Joachim Israel, "Postulates and Construction in the Social Sciences," in *The Context of Social Psychology*, ed. J. Israel and H. Tajfel (forthcoming).

rationality" when characterizing the same economic system. Therefore, this concept is dealt with in detail and some of its consequences critically analyzed. I hope that this will throw light on Weber from an angle which is not very usual when his theories are treated in American studies.

Since in chapter 1 it is maintained that one should find out which implicit notions about man's nature and man's relation to society are the basis for theories of modern society, an attempt is made to bring out this aspect.

This holds also for the authors who are treated in chapter 6, exemplifying modern macrosociological and social-psychological thinking in this area. One section each is devoted to Erich Fromm, Herbert Marcuse, and C. W. Mills, who have in common the level of analysis, though diverging on basic issues in spite of the fact that they built their theories on Marxist lines. It is also attempted to show how they differ from, and stand in opposition to, Marx. The criticism has been especially elaborated with regard to Marcuse's writings.

In chapter 7 current positivistic sociology and its empirical theories concerning alienation are reviewed. There the following are analyzed: Seeman, who has done important work in making "alienation" available in empirical theories; Blauner, who has applied it; and Mizruchi, who goes a different road by basing his theories on the concept of "anomie." In addition, the theory developed by the Finnish sociologist Erik Allardt (probably unknown to an American audience, since he writes in Finnish and Swedish) is presented.

Chapter 8 reviews the discussion of the problem of alienation in socialist societies, building on the debate which was quite lively in some of these countries before the invasion of Czechoslovakia.

In the final chapter, 9, I try to develop my own theoretical outline, relating it to recent developments in the most highly industrialized societies, such as the U.S. and the Soviet Union. In order to connect this theoretical outline with the situation and present crisis of what may be termed "modern man," the suggestion is made that the concept of alienation and its theoretical foundation should be abandoned in favor of the concept of "reification." Such an approach can, if one wishes, be defended by referring to the development in Marx's own writings. The young Marx, basing his notions heavily on philosophical theories and on a strong normative, humanistic approach, becomes the economist and sociologist Marx in the writings of his mature years. In this chapter especially, some theories developed in the heavy volume *Grundrisse der Kritik der Politischen Ökonomie (Rohentwurf)*, which contains studies for *Capital* and which was published the first time in German in 1953, are used. However, I do not consider myself to be an orthodox Marxist. I am not orthodox in any aspect; I have tried to develop my own lines.

The basic idea in this chapter is the fact that a market economy has a tendency to transform everything into commodities—a tendency that Marx called the "fetishism of commodities." One central aspect concerns how man is transformed into a commodity. That occurs in a dual way. First, he becomes labor power or a production factor, to use the language of modern economics. As labor power he is a seller on the market, but the tendency is to treat him as an object as labor power, no more, no less. The second way in which man becomes an object is by his being transformed into a consumer. When his basic needs are satisfied, new ones are created; and he is steadily exposed to propaganda and advertising to buy and to consume, since high consumption has become an important precondition for high production in those parts of the industrialized world which produce for each other. Finally, technological development leads to the creation of bureaucratic structures in which man again becomes an object, a small cogwheel in an immense machinery. Thus "blind" forces in a market economy determine his life, whereas his own possibilities to determine and to control his life in a conscious and intended way become diminished.

This book was written to satisfy demands on a graduate level for courses in theory of society in sociology and political science and is used as a text in the Scandinavian countries.

I wish to express my thanks to my colleagues and friends who contributed highly valuable criticism. I also want to thank Mrs. Patricia Howard, who corrected the errors in my English text. Translations from non-English sources are my own except where a translator is cited.

1
A FRAME OF REFERENCE

INTRODUCTION

"The period comprises the most motley mixture of crying contradictions:
. . . passions without truth, truths without passion." The words, written
by Karl Marx, are quoted from his long essay "The Eighteenth Brumaire
of Louis Bonaparte," published in the magazine *Die Revolution*, 1852.
They contain a concentrated criticism of the epoch and are at the same
time a condensed description of the phenomenon Marx called "human
self-alienation."

One possible interpretation of the quoted lines is that the individual is
split, that his capacities for intellectual and for emotional experiences have
become separated from each other. The intellectual interests are not integrated with emotional involvement, with passion. Instead the intellect
becomes detached, and the involved person often a "poseur." He lacks
awareness of facts and of his own motives. He lacks the self-awareness
which is a guarantee of the genuiness of his passions.

I am not sure that Marx would have accepted such an interpretation.
Probably it is too "psychologizing" to fit into his thinking, and probably
he would have objected to this interpretation by wanting to go one step
further, posing the following question: How is it that such a split between
intellectual and emotional capacities is common in the described period?
He would then have tried to analyze those social conditions which in his
view gave rise to the described psychological phenomena (which, in
fact, he does in the essay mentioned above). In general, Marx would have
considered the problem primarily from a *sociological* point of view.

Thus we may conclude that the problem of alienation can be analyzed
from two points of departure, or on two different levels. It can be con-

sidered as a psychological problem and it can be analyzed as a sociological issue.

THE CONCEPT OF ALIENATION IN THE WRITINGS OF THE YOUNG MARX

In Marx's early writings (especially in one of the two most important works from that period), theories about human alienation assume a prominent place. The volume—written in 1844 in Paris—was discovered in the twenties and published for the first time in 1932 under the title *Economic and Philosophical Manuscripts.*[1] In this work he develops the theory of *Entfremdung* (usually translated as "alienation"). However, this concept is used only once in his second important work of that period, which bears the title *The German Ideology.*[2] Marx wrote it with Friedrich Engels during a stay in Brussels in 1845–46. In this volume, which contains the first outline of "historical materialism," the only time when alienation is mentioned it occurs in a somewhat derogatory way. Marx and Engels say, somewhat contemptuously, that they employ the term *alienation* for one reason only: that philosophers may understand what they are talking about. Their appreciation of "philosophers" is given in one of the eleven theses introducing *The German Ideology*: "The philosophers have only *interpreted* the world in different ways; the point is to *change* it."[3]

However, in the writings of the mature Marx, especially in the heavy volume *Grundrisse der Kritik der Politischen Ökonomie (Rohentwurf)* [*Outline for a Critical Analysis of Political Economy (Raw Sketch)*][4] written in 1857, he returns to the concept, though using it in a different

---

[1] References to Marx's early writings are usually made citing the *Marx-Engels Gesamtausgabe* with the usual abbreviation *Mega* used. The complete edition of Marx and Engels's writings was started in 1927 by the Marx-Engels Institute in Moscow under the direction of D. Riazanow. He became a victim of the purges during the Stalin period and was succeeded by Adoratsky. Only twelve volumes appeared before the outbreak of the Second World War. They were subsequently published in German under the complete title *Karl Marx, Friedrich Engels: Historisch-Kritische Gesamtausgabe, Marx-Engels Verlag Berlin.* The edition was divided into sections, each section containing several volumes. In the first volume of *Mega* some of Marx's early writings were published the first time.

A new complete edition of Marx and Engels's works is now prepared by the Institute for Marxism-Leninism in Moscow.

Economic and Philosophical Manuscripts are published in Section I, Volume 3, of *Mega.* Our reference will be *Mega I.3.*

[2] *Mega I.5.*

[3] Ibid., p. 535.

[4] (Berlin: Dietz Verlag, 1953).

and more sociological way. In *Capital*, Marx's most important work—for which the previously mentioned book was an outline—he finally changes his theory of alienation into the theory of "fetishism of commodities,"[5] though even there the term *alienation* appears.

It is my opinion that the important problem is not whether Marx uses the same or a different concept, but whether there exist different theories of alienation in his writings and whether there is a continuity in Marx's thinking. The question has been posed, Is there one Marx or two?—the young and philosophically oriented, and the mature Marx, mainly concerned with sociological and economical problems.[6] Did the young Marx deal with alienation and the emancipation of the individual, whereas the mature Marx dealt with the analysis of the sociological problems and the economic structure of capitalist society?

In answering the question of whether or not there is a continuity in the writings of Karl Marx, I would definitely say yes. This, however, does not imply that the direction of his thinking did not change. Marx's theorizing starts with a critical survey of Hegel's thought. His theory of human alienation as presented in *Manuscripts* is an attempt to differentiate his own thinking from Hegel's, but he still uses the same terminology. In addition, and more important, his theory of alienation is rooted in a philosophical-anthropological theory of human nature, whereas his later development of the theory of alienation is based on a much more sociological concept of human nature.

After this introduction we will present a short summary of the process of alienation as it is sketched in *The German Ideology*. "The social power, i.e., the multiplied productive force, which results from the cooperation of different individuals as it is determined by the division of labor, appears to these individuals, since their cooperation is not voluntary but natural, not as their united power, but as an alien force existing outside them, of whose origin and purpose they are ignorant, and which they therefore cannot control, but which on the contrary, passes through its own power-series of phases and stages, independent of the will and the action of man, even appearing to govern his will and action."[7, 8]

The main ideas of the theory of alienation and the first beginnings of

---

[5] For a discussion of the theory of fetishism of commodities, see the last chapter of this book.

[6] L. R. Langslet, "Young Marx and Alienation in Western Debate," *Inquiry* VI (1963), 3–17. One of the most intriguing analyses of this problem is undertaken by the French philosopher Louis Althusser in his book *Pour Marx*. He denies that the theory of alienation has any continuation in Marx's later works. I do not agree with Althusser on the point.

[7] *Mega I.5*, pp. 23–24.

[8] Marx uses the term "natural" equivalent to "governed by objective laws," i.e., "the natural laws" of society and its process of social production.

the theory of fetishism of commodities and the social consequences of this fetishism are present in a concentrated form in this quotation. In a social system with a certain mode of production—namely the capitalist one—the productive forces, for example, modern technology, will be experienced by human beings as controlling them instead of being under their control. This is mainly due to the social institutions created by men to organize and to govern the process of social production. Marx does not see the development of productive forces *as such* as the bases for the development of alienation. Were that the case, his criticism would be directed against the process of industrialization.

Marx makes a distinction between the *productive forces*, i.e., the forces available to man for producing the goods he needs and the *social relation* which occurs in the process of production and which organizes this process. "By social is meant the cooperation of several individuals, no matter under what conditions, in what matter or to what end. It follows from this, that a determinate mode of production, or industrial stage, is always bound up with a determinate mode of cooperation, or social stage, and this mode of cooperation is itself a "productive force."[9]

Since cooperation is itself a productive force, it should be organized so that it is in agreement with the other productive forces. Marx develops a special type of "cultural lag" theory when he asserts that the productive forces have reached a developmental stage where they should no longer be organized so that they can be controlled by special individuals, but should be under societal control. The productive forces demand a special type of human cooperation. This can be achieved only when production is organized in a way that makes this type of cooperation possible.[10]

Another idea contained in the description of alienation is that the "relations of production" force upon the individual a division of labor, which he cannot control himself. When Marx speaks about "division of labor," he refers not only to the division of jobs within industrial production, but also to more general social processes: the division between manual and intellectual work; the division between commerce and industrial production. The division between manual and intellectual work is of particular importance: "The division of labor only becomes a real division from the moment when the distinction between material and mental labor appears."[11] The explanation given by Marx is: "For as soon as the division of labor begins, each man has a particular, exclusive sphere of activity, which is forced upon him and from which he cannot escape."[12]

[9] *Mega I.5*, pp. 18–19.
[10] See chapter 3.
[11] *Mega I.5*, p. 21.
[12] Ibid., p. 22.

Of central concern in Marx's theory of alienation is the human being and the chances he has of controlling his social and natural environment, rather than being a victim of uncontrollable forces. Thus we can say that the problem of alienation introduces a special aspect into the analysis of social processes: the concern with the fate of human beings. This humanistic aspect—the emancipation of man, his self-realization—remains in the writings of Marx, although the emphasis shifts. This is due to the change in his ideas concerning human nature. Whereas Marx's first concept of man leads him to an individualistic, humanistic attitude, he shifts later to a sociological concept: "Man is in the most literal sense a *zoon politicon*, not merely a political animal, but an animal which can develop into an individual only in society."[13] One hint with regard to the goal of this development is given when Marx later on in the same volume maintains that working hours should be reduced to a minimum in order to make possible free development and schooling in such areas as art and science.[14] The human being and his social role lie at the nucleus of Marx's thinking.

A THEORETICAL FRAME OF REFERENCE

THE USE OF THE TERM "ALIENATION"

Since Marx was the first to introduce the concept of alienation into sociological theory—in other fields it had been used a long time before Marx—we have given a short introductory account of his ideas in this area. Before we can continue to analyze the use of this concept and its development, we will start with some remarks, outlining some theoretical problems.

As we will see, the term *alienation* has been employed in very different ways. However, two usages are especially predominant: one referring to *sociological processes* and one to *psychological states*.

In a modern Marxist representation the Soviet Russian philosopher Ogurzov[15] maintains that alienation is a philosophical-sociological concept. It refers to a sociological process characterized by the fact that the individual's productive activity, his work, and the results of his activity have become independent and have gained command over the human being. According to this presentation, "bourgeois sociology" can be criticized for its tendency to psychologize "alienation" and transform it into a psychological category.

[13] *Grundrisse*, p. 5.
[14] Ibid., p. 593.
[15] D. Ogurzov, mimeographed chapter on "Alienation" (n.d.). To appear in *Societ Philosophical Encyclopedia*.

An analysis of the definition of alienation as used, for example, by Seeman[16] gives some justification for this assertion. Seeman defines alienation in terms of psychological states experienced by an individual. He distinguishes between five states, namely "powerlessness," "meaninglessness," "normlessness," "isolation," and "self-estrangement." All five categories refer to psychological states experienced subjectively. They do not refer to sociological processes. The ways in which Seeman and others have measured these concepts confirm the impression of a psychologizing of alienation.

However, it is by no means difficult to combine both approaches to alienation. On a *sociological* level one can attempt to describe and analyze the economic-sociological processes which affect the individual and his role in society. Given a certain social structure, one important task will be to study processes which affect the individual's relation to his work, his social relations, and the relations he establishes to nonhuman objects. On a *psychological* level one can attempt to describe and to analyze those psychological experiences which are a consequence of the individual's relations to persons and objects. One can also study the individual's perception of his own conditions in a society characterized by sociological processes of alienation. In the first case we study estranging processes. In the second case we study states of estrangement.

The double meaning of the concept of alienation—its reference both to sociological processes and psychological states—is one of the reasons for the confusion prevailing in the literature. However, it is not unusual for concepts in sociology or social psychology to have a double meaning. Take, for example, another much-used concept, *frustration*. Here we find the same tendency. It refers both to those processes which block need-satisfaction and to the state of deprivation which is a consequence of blocked need-satisfaction. A similar situation is found in the use of the concept of *anomie*.

Another distinction should be mentioned. On an empirical level a distinction can be made between alienation as a *subjective* and as an *objective* phenomenon.[17] To study alienation as a subjective phenomenon implies that one studies the individual's own experiences and the verbalizations of these experiences. Alienation as a *subjective* phenomenon therefore concerns social psychological conditions.

Alienation as an objective phenomenon may refer to at least two things. It can, as distinguished from subjective experiences, imply the study of

---

[16] M. Seeman, "On the Meaning of Alienation," *American Sociological Review* XXVI (1961), 753-58.

[17] For a discussion of the distinction see J. Israel, *Socialpsykologi* (Stockholm: Svenska Bokförlaget, 1963), p. 185 ff.; and E. H. Mizruchi, *Success and Opportunity* (New York: The Free Press, 1964).

objectively *observable behavior.* Behavior is conceived as objectively observable when a psychologically or sociologically trained observer can demonstrate the occurrence of the phenomenon called alienation. In that case it also concerns psychological conditions. But, as distinguished from the subjective state, the observations of the phenomena are independent of the subject's verbal report of his experiences. Therefore an agreement may, but not necessarily does, exist between the data a neutral observer can demonstrate and the experience which the individual himself can report. This has a certain bearing upon a problem which we are going to discuss later on, namely, whether a person can be so alienated that he is unable to experience his alienation.

But alienation as an objective phenomenon can also refer to social conditions of a certain type, in which case the objective phenomenon is a sociological and not a psychological variable. *Objective* in this sense coincides with, or is similar to, a definition of alienation in terms of social processes.

It is not unusual that in empirically oriented sociological literature the subjective individual states are defined as *alienation,* whereas the objective social conditions or processes are labeled *anomia,* in the sense in which Durkheim[18] used the concept and which has been further developed in the theories of Merton.[19] For that reason and because there are interesting attempts to develop theories in which both the concepts of alienation and of anomia are contained,[20] we will also try to analyze the concept of anomia as it relates to the concept of alienation.

SOME PRECONDITIONS FOR A THEORY OF ALIENATION

Macrosociological theories concerning societies and large social structures, as well as more limited theories of "the middle range,"[21] usually make assumptions of three different types, though they may be related to each other. These assumptions concern (1) conceptions of *human nature,* (2) conceptions of the *nature of society,* and (3) visions concerning *developmental trends and the formation of future societies.*

[18] E. Durkheim, *The Division of Labor in Society,* trans. G. Simpson (New York: The Free Press, 1964). See also the discussion of Durkheim's theory in chapter 5. To increase the conceptual confusion, "anomie" is sometimes used in the subjective sense, i.e., to denote an individual experience of a psychological state. Attitude scales to measure "subjective anomie" have been developed by, e.g., L. Srole, "Social Integration and Certain Corollaries," *American Sociological Review* XXI (1956), 709–16.
[19] R. Merton, *Social Theory and Social Structure* (Glencoe, Ill.: The Free Press, 1957).
[20] E. Allardt, *Samhällsstruktur och sociala spänningar* (Helsingfors: Söderströms & Co., 1965). See also the discussion of Allardt's theories in chapter 8.
[21] Merton, *Social Theory.*

Theories do not always comprise all three classes of conceptions. The last one, in fact, has been looked upon as undesirable by social scientists, trained in a positivist tradition. It involves speculative arguments which usually have reference to the author's "philosophy of life" and often contain statements of certain goals, which in turn are built upon normative systems, e.g., special ethics.[22]

The assumptions introduced concerning human nature and the nature of society need not necessarily be expressed as *explicit* postulates or hypotheses. Very often they are *implicit* and can be discovered only through a scrutinizing analysis of theoretical statements.

Finally they can be expressed on different levels of abstraction. Take, for example, theories concerning human nature. These may be formulated in a very general way and contain statements about "man"—which abilities and capacities are typical of him, which attributes differentiate man from other animals, which are the motivating forces with which he is endowed.

On a more concrete level statements about "human nature" may refer, for example, to motivational structures in more limited situations. One example is the theories concerning human behavior within an organizational frame. Questions such as "What motivates man to work?" may be answered by theories as distinct as "scientific management"[23] (where the label "scientific" in our opinion is completely unjustified) and "human relations."[24]

We will look very briefly at the three classes of assumptions.

Theories about *human nature* can be of various kinds. They can be *scientific*, i.e., contain propositions which can be empirically tested. They can be *philosophical-anthropological* theories, which usually contain propositions about the properties which make up the human being or speak about "the essence" of man. Propositions containing statements about "essence" are usually rejected as metaphysical by scientists trained in the tradition of logical empiricism and its philosophy of science.[25]

Lastly, theories about man can be *normative*, containing sentences stating how man *ought* to be formed or which goals he ought to strive for.

---

[22] Also great physicists like Albert Einstein and Niels Bohr developed their own "philosophy of nature." Speculative reasoning, therefore, seems not to be restricted to outstanding representatives of social science.

[23] F. W. Taylor, *Scientific Management* (New York: Harper, 1911).

[24] R. Lickert, *New Patterns of Management* (New York: McGraw-Hill Book Company, 1961).

[25] For an interesting analysis of metatheories developed by logical expiricism and by other schools, e.g., in Germany, see G. Radnitzki, *Contemporary Schools of Metascience*, Vol. I, *Anglo-Saxon Schools of Metascience* (Göteborg: Akademiförlaget, 1968).

Philosophical-anthropological sentences are neither empirical nor normative sentences, but they can be easily integrated within empirical theories or ethical systems. Theories presented as scientific often contain normative elements, for instance, theories about mental health. These are often presented as scientific–empirical. But they usually make assumptions about certain goals a person should achieve, or about the ways in which he should realize himself in order to be classified as "mentally healthy."[26]

Scientific theories about human nature can be *biological*, e.g., genetic theories. If one equates "human nature" with inherited traits, it is reasonable to state that "human nature" is contained in forty-six chromosomes.

Other scientific theories about man may be psychological or sociological. A common psychological theory makes assumptions about genetic dispositions and about the individual's anatomic and physiological structure; on this basis it assumes certain instincts or needs and innate reflexes. Everything else is then considered to be the product of a continuous process of learning.

A sociological theory of "human nature" may build upon assumptions concerning the effect of social conditions on man's behavior. He is considered to be influenced by the groups, class, or other social categories to which he is thought to belong. Social roles form his personality, and internalized expectations are the nucleus of this personality.[27] Interaction with other human beings influences his self-image and his self-evaluation, and that in turn is of great importance for the further development of his social interaction.

Later we will have more to say about *homo sociologicus*. Generally speaking, theories about human nature may discuss problems concerning the relative influence of inheritance and environment, whether man is oriented toward individualistic or collectivistic goals, or whether he is basically social, asocial, or neither.

Theories concerning the *nature of society* will be treated very briefly here as we will discuss them in the next section. According to Coser,[28] theories about society can be roughly classified into two categories: (1) Theories which take as their point of departure the necessity of consensus and assume a state of balance or equilibrium to be the "normal" or "natural" one. Conflicts in these theories are usually considered to be disturbing factors. (2) Theories which take as their point of departure the existence of conflicting interests and other types of antagonistic

---

[26] M. Jahoda, *Current Concepts of Positive Mental Health* (New York: Basic Books, 1958); and K. Håkansson, *Psykisk Sjukdom* [*Psychic Sickness*], Research Reports from the Dept. of Sociology, Uppsala University, No. 26, 1968 (mimeo).

[27] Israel, *Socialpsykologi*.

[28] L. Coser, *The Functions of Social Conflict* (Glencoe, Ill.: The Free Press, 1956).

tendencies. States of balance or equilibrium are in this case usually considered to be nonachievable or, if achieved, will immediately be abolished. In these theories conflicting states are considered to be the "normal" or "natural" ones, whereas states of equilibrium are short-lived or are the exception to the rule.

Theories about the nature of society differ concerning assumptions regarding the role of consensus and conflict, concerning the need for integration or the lack of such a tendency, concerning the desirability of conformity or the innovating function of deviancy, concerning the functional necessity of stratification or the desirability of equality, concerning matters of stability or social change and whether a society is basically a mass-society[29] or a pluralistic one composed of countervailing powers,[30] etc.

One important fact should be pointed out. The question on which theories about societies diverge are usually not scientific questions as such. Even if the arguments about the relative importance of certain factors are posed in a scientific language, the decision to include certain factors into a theory about society and the importance attributed to them is usually dependent on value-judgments. In other words, they are normative and reveal (or more often conceal) either the scientist's private biases or the ideological[31] influences to which he may be exposed in his social role as scientist and member of the scientific community.

INDIVIDUAL-ORIENTED AND SOCIETY-ORIENTED THEORIES

The period after the Second World War has been a revival of the discussion about the young Marx and his theories of alienation. The discussion, as the Norwegian philosopher Langslet[32] aptly demonstrates, has developed in two directions. One is based on the conception of alienation as an *"ontological-ethical"* problem, as Langslet calls it. The other direction the debate has taken deals with alienation as a *"psychological-sociological"* problem. The first-mentioned orientation is represented by existential philosophy and by such theologians as Paul Tillich.[33] There the discussion centers around the rootlessness of man in modern society. In this debate the conception that alienation is a constitutive element in all

[29] C. W. Mills, *The Power Elite* (New York: Oxford University Press, 1959).

[30] D. Riesman, *The Lonely Crowd* (Garden City: Doubleday Anchor, 1953.)

[31] G. Myrdal has taken up the problem of values on several occasions. See, e.g., *Value in Social Theory* (London: Routledge & Kegan Paul, 1958) or *Asian Drama* (New York: Twentieth Century Fund and Pantheon Books, 1968).

[32] Langslet, "Young Marx and Alienation."

[33] Ibid., p. 13.

human existence often comes to the fore. That is to say, alienation will be found everywhere, in all periods, completely independent of the social conditions which distinguish a given society. In our discussion we will totally ignore this problem-complex as it is located outside the framework of this book. However, Langslet does hold that those who take up the debate about alienation from an existentialist point of view can link their discussions to the writings of the young Marx.

Marx's theories about alienation are to a large degree, and as I see it even primarily, sociological theories. Therefore, those who take a psychological-sociological starting point can also and without difficulties link their analyses to the writings of the young Marx, especially since he is the first to present a sociological theory of alienation. Assumptions about "human nature" and about "the nature of society" enter into theories of alienation. If one declares that an *individual is alienated, it is implied that he must be alienated from something.* Even if not made explicit in theories of alienation, the very term refers to a state or a process which deviates from a state considered to be *normal*. The normal state referred to may be "normal" in two ways. It may be thought to be an *ideal* state, which it is desirable to achieve. In this case one builds upon certain value assumptions which in turn define certain goals. But "normal" can also refer to a state which is common in a statistical sense. An alienated subject may, then, be nothing more than a deviating individual.

Theories of alienation usually build implicitly or explicitly upon certain assumptions and conceptions: (1) They make *certain assumptions about human nature.* Marx has two theories of alienation. The first one (developed in his *Economic and Philosophical Manuscripts*) builds upon a philosophical-anthropological theory of human nature in which are contained normative propositions referring to a humanistic, ethical system. One of our tasks will be to show that this is the case.

His second theory of alienation, however, is based upon a sociological theory of man. This theory, too, contains normative ethical aspects.

Therefore, our first task in analyzing theories of alienation will be to uncover the type of theory about man which is implicit. We will find that the conception of man plays an important role in the formulation of the theory. (2) Theories of alienation are based not only upon certain images concerning the nature of society but also upon the *relationship between the individual and society.* Usually the notions concerning the relationship between the individual and society presuppose, *first,* theories or ideas about conflicts or antagonisms between the individual on the one hand and the society on the other. These conflicts or antagonisms are considered to be caused by assumed demands which are made by both the individual and the society, but which are incompatible with each other. The idea of incompatible demands is in turn based upon another, usually *implicit,* supposition, i.e., the assumption that either the individual or the society or both are striving for certain relatively constant states. One example of such assumptions is the notion concerning balance and equilibrium, either within the human organism or within the societal mechanism (generally this assumption is built upon some kind of mechanistic or organic model). The states of balance are steadily disturbed, but at the same time there are built-in mechanisms or strivings to restore the balanced state.

Disturbances of the balanced states of societal organisms can be caused, for instance, by behavior deviating from social norms. Therefore, lasting, "harmonious," social conditions cannot be achieved unless individuals exhibit conforming behavior.

Sigmund Freud's[34] theory of the social necessity of the repression of human instincts is another example of notions concerning the incompatible and antagonistic states supposed to exist between the individual and society. Freud asserts that human instincts have a basically asocial orientation (a notion also taken up by Marcuse).[35] Only the repression of instincts and the sublimation of their energy makes possible the individual's social adjustment.

Balanced states in the individual can be disturbed by demands made by society, which prevent need-satisfaction or a "harmonious" development, or which affect the chances of self-realization. The social structure of society prevents the individual from reaching desired states of satisfaction, balance, etc.

Taking the notion of incompatible demands as the point of departure, theories of human alienation can be divided into two classes. If the theory assumes that it is mainly the individual who strives for the achievement of his demands but is prevented from attaining these demands by society, the ensuing discussion often concerns the problem of how to *change society* in order to make it possible for the individual to reach his goals. Within sociology the emphasis in this context is usually on problems of social change and its consequences.

If, however, the emphasis is put upon social demands which cannot be achieved due to the fact that norm-deviating behavior creates lack of consensus or conformity, which are considered as functional prerequisites for society to reach a balanced state (or something similar), then the question centers around problems of individual *social adjustment.*

In the first type of theory social processes create alienation. In the second type of theory, alienation is created by human behavior and be-

[34] S. Freud, *An Outline of Psychoanalysis* (New York: Norton, 1949).
[35] H. Marcuse, *Eros and Civilization* (New York: Vintage Books, 1955).

comes a problem of social adjustment or—more accurately—of lack of such adjustment. Sociological theories which deal with problems of social adjustment sometimes make assumptions concerning certain conditions which have to be fulfilled in order that a society can function "normally." These assumptions are of a normative kind since all functional theories presuppose values. One example is the hypothesis that there must exist a certain number of common goals for *all* members of the society, otherwise processes of disorganization might take place. Therefore such theories place strong emphasis on problems which concern the process of socialization, and on conforming behavior, as these are the means for producing consensus with regard to values and goals.

I will call the two classes of theories *individual-oriented* and *society-oriented*, respectively.

An interesting problem for a metatheory of sociology would be to examine the kinds of value-judgments, or biases, which are implicit in such theories. A reasonable assumption is that *individual-oriented* theories build upon liberal or humanistic values, whereas the latter often have a socialist orientation.[36]

Society-oriented hypotheses, on the other hand, with their notions of social balance and equilibrium, are hypothesized to rest upon conservative values. As a consequence, their interest for problems of social change is limited. Society-oriented theories, however, can also be compatible with authoritarian values. In the latter case collectivistic values of a certain kind enter into the theory. Such collectivist notions may assert that the individual should subordinate his own interests to the interest of the society and thus further "greater" and "higher" social goals. But an important observation should be made concerning certain distinctions about collectivistic values. Not all value systems which demand that individual goals should be subsumed to collectives ones are necessarily authoritarian in their orientation. The decisive factor in our view is the way collective goals are formulated. If they mean a glorification of the "state," of "power" and "power symbols," or of the "greatness of the member group," they are usually authoritarian in their objectives.[37] In contrast, nonauthoritarian collectivistic value systems often formulate social goals as messianic states in which want is abolished and material affluence prevails, where there is a state of equality between individuals and freedom for all. The subordination of the individual's own goals

---

[36] Marx's theory of alienation as developed in *Manuscripts* is built upon, as we intend to show, assumptions of a humanistic-ethical type.

[37] For a discussion of authoritarianism see T. W. Adorno, E. Frenkel-Brunswik, D. J. Levinson, and R. N. Sanford, *The Authoritarian Personality* (New York: Harper, 1950).

(frequently conceived of as egoistic ones) to collective goals is often considered to be a temporary condition. Its aim is to facilitate the necessary social changes, which in turn will enable individual "self-realization" for as many as possible.[38]

Let us for a moment return to our distinction between individual- and society-oriented theories. They all presume a conflict between the individual and society, yet there is a third type of theory which does not assume such a conflict. In his second theory of alienation, Marx develops a notion which has a different starting point. He assumes that society is nothing other than the sum total of its individuals organized within a special social system. There exists a continuous struggle between man and "nature." Man tries to extend his mastery over nature. He develops new productive forces, new techniques, and new scientific methods. In his attempt to master nature and to transform its objects into means for need-satisfaction, there arise antagonistic conflicts between men due to the existing power conditions and property relations. Thus in this Marxian theory the struggle between the individual and society is situated *within* society and is between groups or classes of the society.

As the emphasis is on the change of social conditions, this third type of theory can be seen as a special case of the class of individual-oriented theories. I have mentioned it because the formulation of the basic conflict is of great importance to the development of a theory of alienation. There the central theme is whether man is dominated by the forces he has created himself or whether he is able to master these social forces.

In summary: We can now divide theories of alienation according to two criteria: (1) the type of theory concerning human nature which is presupposed, (2) the type of solution for basically existing conflicts which is proposed. If the theories are oriented toward social change and assume alienation to be a consequence of the organization of society, we call them individual-oriented. If they place the emphasis on the individual and suggest changes in his social adjustment, we call them society-oriented.

If we assume that our first criterion can be divided into two types, sociological-psychological theories vs. philosophical-anthropological and normative theories of human nature (a dichotomy which sometimes is difficult to apply since scientific theories often implicitly incorporate value-judgments),[39] we get the table shown in Figure 1:

---

[38] Differences in societal goals between "rightist" and "leftist" dictatorial regimes are often disregarded when one discusses conditions of life under such regimes. If there are similarities, they usually are limited to certain methods. A dictatorial regime can have *authoritarian goals* and apply *authoritarian means* to reach them. However, it can also have *nonauthoritarian goals* but still use authoritarian methods to reach them. Similarly, societies with democratic goals often use authoritarian means.

[39] Myrdal, *Value in Social Theory.*

Theories about the cause of alienation	Theory about human nature	
	Sociological-psychological	Philosophical-anthropological
I. Society-oriented (conflict: man-society)	Weber Durkheim	Rousseau
IIa. Individual-oriented (conflict: man-society)	Simmel Fromm	Rousseau Marx's first theory Marcuse
IIb. (conflict within society)	Marx's second theory Mills	

Figure 1. Classification of theories of alienation.

ALIENATION—A PRELIMINARY ANALYSIS

There are both simple and more complicated theories of alienation. The more simple ("simple" does not imply a value-judgment) theories are those which do not develop special theories concerning human nature, but which generally utilize a psychological or sociological concept. These theories are often *discrepancy-theories*. They maintain that there exists a discrepancy between learned expectations, values, or goals and a difficulty or an impossibility in a given social system to realize these values or goals. The consequence of this discrepancy is a psychological state of alienation.[40]

The more complex theories concerning alienation, e.g., those developed by Marx, contain a series of elements. In order to clarify the meaning of these theories, we will try to present a preliminary explication. We distinguish *five* different elements, and these elements and their relationship are presented diagrammatically in Figure 2.

First, we distinguish certain sociological conditions. *Second*, we deal with certain psychological conditions. *Third*, we have a series of social processes, e.g., social relations between individuals. These relations present a link between the sociological and the psychological conditions.

Let us take an example. Marx asserts that property-relations are one of the causes of a certain type of human experience. Private ownership of

[40] Discrepancy theories are represented in this book by theories developed, e.g., by E. Allardt (see chapter 7) and by C. W. Mills (see chapter 6).

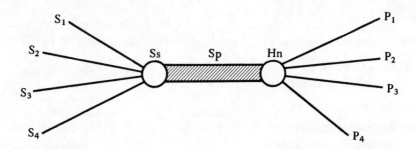

Figure 2. A preliminary diagrammatic representation of alienation.

means of production causes the individual to experience his work as something which does not belong to him. The result is that he becomes alien to his own activity. Property-relations are sociological phenomena and therefore belong to our first category. The individual's experience is a psychological condition and therefore belongs to our second category.

The sociological conditions in turn give rise to a certain social structure in the society in which they occur. This social structure is the *fourth element* in our model.

Notions about the relationship between sociological and psychological conditions, i.e., the way in which people react to certain social conditions, presuppose a theory about man, his needs, and his "nature." The concept of human nature is our *fifth* element.

Theories of alienation usually assume a lack of agreement between the actual psychological states in the human being and his "real needs." These needs are considered to be an expression of "human nature." As previously mentioned, to be alienated implies alienation from something, e.g., from one's "real needs." In individual-oriented theories the aim is to analyze how the discrepancy between actual psychological conditions or states and the demands of "human nature" can be abolished. This is achieved by a change in those sociological conditions which create the discrepancy. In society-oriented theories one can assume by analogy a discrepancy between actual social conditions and an "ideal" social structure, which has been created by means of deviating or asocial behavior.

Let us now for a moment return to Figure 2 and explain the symbols and their relationships.

$S_1, S_2, \ldots, S_n$ refer to different *social conditions*, our first category. $P_1, P_2, \ldots, P_n$ refer to different *psychological conditions* or states. Ss denotes a certain *social structure*; Hn refers to a special concept of *"human nature"* (we do not assume *one* human nature). Finally, Sp refers to *social processes*, e.g., relations between individuals.

As we pointed out earlier, "alienation" is used in two different senses. It refers partly to P_1, i.e., a certain psychological state, and partly to Sp_1, i.e., certain social processes which causes P_1. Later we will return to a more detailed analysis in connection with the discussion of Marx's theories of alienation.[41]

The way causal relations are explained largely depends on the type of theory applied. In individual-oriented theories social conditions are usually considered to be independent variables and the psychological conditions to be dependent. In society-oriented theories psychological conditions are used as causal variables, whereas the social conditions are seen as effect-variables. Finally, one may reasonably assume a feedback mechanism, in which social conditions affect psychological states, which in turn influence social conditions.

[41] See chapter 3.

2

CONCEPTS OF ALIENATION
BEFORE MARX

INTRODUCTION

The concept of alienation has a long past in the history of ideas. We are
not trying to give a systematic account of the use of alienation prior to
Marx, but rather attempting to summarize the accounts of those authors
and those ideological currents which affected the thought of Karl Marx.
We have selected three: First, Rousseau, from whom Marx quotes in
his early works and whom, to judge from his notes,[1] he has read very
carefully. The second source of influence over Marx is the criticism of
the period launched by the German romanticist writers. The attack was
directed against the social change which occurred as a consequence of
the earliest period of the process of industrialization. In his early writings
Marx quite often uses the terminology of the German romanticist writers.
Finally we will offer a short account of Hegel's treatment of alienation,
as he was the philosopher having the most profound influence on the
thinking of Marx, and it is his terminology that Marx uses in both his
earlier and his later works. Though he criticized Hegel very stringently
and rejected his idealistic philosophy, he admitted his admiration for him.
In a early work, *Economic and Philosophical Manuscripts*, Marx writes:
"The *Phenomenology* [written by Hegel] is a concealed, unclear and
mystifying criticism, but in so far as it grasps the *alienation* of man . . .
all the elements of criticism are contained in it. . . ."[2]

The account of the history of the alienation concept is short and often

---

[1] *Mega I.2.*
[2] *Mega I.3*, p. 156.

based on secondhand analyses. The reader not interested in the historical background of this concept is asked to turn directly to chapter 3.

ALIENATION IN ROUSSEAU'S WRITINGS

ROUSSEAU'S INDIVIDUAL-ORIENTED THEORY

In Rousseau's writings are found theories of alienation containing both individual-oriented and society-oriented elements. The former are present in his earlier writings, where he takes as his point of departure the human being in a natural state. Later he changes his emphasis to the actions of individuals existing within a social system.

Rousseau does not have *one* single conception of the human being. Instead he deals with different theories in which various stages of development can be differentiated. He starts with an assumption about the human being in a natural state.[3] This state is characterized by the fact that the human being lives in isolation, as a fisherman or a hunter, maintaining himself by using the products nature presents to him. In this stage man needs no other human beings for his livelihood and can satisfy his needs without encroaching upon the interests of others. In this stage of development man is neither good nor bad. He lacks moral judgment or ideas, since he is living independently and without social relations with other human beings.

In this phase man is characterized by owning a *free will*, and by this characteristic he can be differentiated from animals. The free will of man is free because it is affected only by his own needs, not by social relations with other people. Man's free will enables him to become a perfect and total being.

Therefore the other basic trait of the human being in a natural state is called by Rousseau *perfectibilité*. In addition to these two basic characteristics, man is also endowed with two elementary instincts, manifesting themselves as emotional forces: one is *amour de soi*, or self-love, being a kind of instinct for self-preservation; the second—*commisération*, or sympathy—is the source of the reproduction of the species.

The dependence on nature does not, according to Rousseau, prevent man from being free. It is the dependence on other people which creates all vice. The transition from the natural state to the socialized one, a state in which man has learned social interaction, is among other things a consequence of the increase in population. Another factor is natural

[3] J. J. Rousseau, *The Political Writings of Jean Jacques Rousseau*, ed. C. E. Vaugh, 3 vols. (Cambridge: The University Press, 1915).

catastrophies, which force men to interact with each other. This interaction in turn furthers the development of language.[4]

It is when continuous relations between people lead to the development
of more complicated social systems that the decisive break occurs. In
these systems the division of labor takes place and private ownership
develops. Consequently, lack of equality is created and man's freedom
diminishes. (As pointed out in chapter 1, Marx develops in *The German
Ideology* similar ideas concerning the historic development of man. In his
thinking, too, the division of labor, enforced work, and private ownership
play an important role in the alienation of man.[5])

Inherited differences between people now become noticeable. These
differences lead to social differentiation, to the division of men into rich
and poor. As a result class-antagonism grows up (to use one of Marx's
concepts). Men become greedy, egoistic, and bad.[6] *Amour de soi* changes
into *amour propre*, i.e., egoistic self-love, which means that man strives
for the satisfaction of his own interests and needs at the expense of others'
needs. Man is no longer free and self-sufficient. Competition and antagonistic interests arise. Everyone tries to surpass the other and pretends to
be superior. A discrepancy is created between *être* and *paraitre*, between
man's factual being, his "true" personality so to speak, and the image of
himself he tries to create. This chaotic state can be altered to a state of
order by means of a social contract. Nevertheless, such an agreement is
only a partial solution because, as Rousseau says, the vices which make
necessary the creation of social institutions are the same ones which
make misuse of the same institutions unavoidable.[7]

To prevent selfishness—*amour propre*—and the need for power, which
springs from it, from spreading and in order to bridle the need to outdo
and dominate others and strive for purely egoistic goals, the individual
must subordinate himself to a *volonté générale*, a common will. This
common will is not only the sum of all individual wills, but moreover
as an entity is something different, superordinate to the sum of all individual wills. This *volonté générale* manifests itself in a social order to
which the individual subject subordinates himself and in which he is
willing to abstain from his own desires. However, since at the same time
he is a member of this social system, he has an opportunity of influencing
it.

Rousseau does not develop a special theory of alienation: "We find in
Rousseau's work neither a philosophical nor a sociological theory of

---

[4] Rousseau, Vol. I, p. 173.

[5] *Mega I.5*, p. 39 ff.

[6] Rousseau, Vol. I, p. 180.

[7] Rousseau, Vol. I, p. 190

alienation. On the contrary we find a *phenomenological description of perception* and of a *living experience* of the social world as alienated, and reified, and of how inauthentic human existence is in such a world, "says the Polish philosopher Baczko in an analysis of Rousseau's theories.[8] The change from *amour de soi* to *amour propre*, from self-love to selfishness, is the reason why the individual wants to "pretend" to be someone else than he really "is." As a consequence his life becomes "inauthentic," and this is the nucleus of human alienation. Interpreted in that way Rousseau's ideas may be categorized as belonging to the class of individual-oriented theories. He makes assumptions concerning human nature, which, through the process of socialization and as a consequence of societal demands, cannot express itself but gives rise to conduct and traits which are alien to this very "human nature."

THE TRANSITION TO A SOCIETY-ORIENTED THEORY

At this point a dilemma arises for Rousseau. How can the conflict between individual and society be solved? He admits that a return to the natural state is no longer possible. Instead he maintains that the process of socialization must teach the individual to submit to the demands of society. These demands ought to be shaped in such a way that they are able to provide a new form of freedom on a higher level of development.[9]

Rousseau pictures the subordination of man in the following way: He speaks of a total alienation of each person associated with the social system and the transmission of all his rights to the community. In this context Rousseau uses the term *alienation* in a different, but for his epoch common, usage. Here *alienation* means "detachment," as the term is used in theories of natural law.[10]

In a later section of his book *Contrat social*, Rousseau describes the process of detachment by alleging that those who have the courage to give the people a legal order must be able to alter human nature, to transform each individual. This individual, himself a totality and as such closed up in his own isolation, must be brought at least in part to integrate himself into a higher order of totality. It is from this totality that the individual then obtains his life and his being. This in turn will lead to the substitution of his physical and independent existence for a partial and moral existence. Those who dare to change an individual will take away man's power in order to endow him with those powers which he can use only when cooperating with other people.

[8] B. Baczko," Rousseau et l'aliénation sociale," *Annales J. J. Rousseau* XXXV (1963), 223–37.

[9] J. Wössner, *Sozialnatur und Sozialstruktur* (Berlin: Duncker & Humblot, 1965).

[10] Baczko, "Rousseau," p. 223.

Rousseau suggests the substitution of the individualistic competitive subject with a person for whom cooperation with others becomes a natural need. Marx read Rousseau and quotes his passages on this subject in one of his earliest essays, "Zur Judenfrage" ("On the Jewish Question").[11] Marx makes a distinction between the *individual subject* and the *cooperating citizen*—in fact he distinguishes between *l'homme* and *le citoyen*. Later, this problem concerning the dilemma between individual freedom and cooperation with others through subordination of personal needs is constantly taken up. In the essay mentioned, Marx discusses man's situation in bourgeois society. He contends that in this society the individual with all his selfishness is considered to be the *real* human being, whereas the citizen with all his moral capacities is only an *abstract* person. Marx therefore adds:

> Political emancipation is a reduction of man, on the one hand to a member of civil society, an *independent* and *egoistic* individual, and on the other hand to a *citizen*, to a moral person.
> Human emancipation will only be complete when the real, individual man has absorbed into himself the abstract citizen; when as an individual man, in his everyday life, in his work, and in his relationships, he has become a *species-being*; and when he has recognized and organized his own powers (*forces propres*) as *social* powers so that he no longer separates this social power from himself as *political* power.[12]

In the quoted lines we find one of the most important ideas which the young Marx has concerning the emancipation of man. For him, man is a totality, characterized among other things by basic *social capacities*. These capacities are a part of the "essence" of the human species. Therefore Marx also uses the term *species-being*, which he took from Hegelian philosophy, but the term is given various meanings by Marx.[13] One of these is that if one abstracts from the individual and looks at him as one specimen of the human species, then one can consider him as endowed with potential social powers. Those will come into operation more and more when society is created in such a way that it liberates these powers instead of preventing them from being expressed. As previously pointed out, Marx perceived the societal order of his time as one which prevented this emancipation by dividing man into a private person and a citizen, by separating his private and his public—Marx uses the term *political*—interests. This separation also isolates man from other men, and this isolation furthers selfishness.

[11] *Mega I.1*, p. 599.
[12] Ibid.
[13] See chapter 4.

Whereas Rousseau's idea concerning a social contract and the subordination of man is, generally speaking, an example of a society-oriented theory, Marx's theory at that stage of the development of his thinking is still individual-oriented. He criticizes Rousseau for his concept of forcing man into a society by means of a social contract.[14] For Marx the socialized human being is "the natural man," at least in the theories of man he developed in *The German Ideology* and later.

For Marx it is important to create such social conditions that allow "natural man" to realize himself. Man as a social being is a part of the human species and therefore contains in himself all the potentialities of the species. When man comes to realize this, then he will turn into "an universal and therefore free being."[15]

THE CRITICISM OF THE EPOCH IN GERMAN ROMANTICISM

The Norwegian philosopher Langslet points out in his book about Marx and alienation[16] that there are two terms in German language, both of which are translated as "alienation." In German a distinction is made between *Entfremdung* and *Entäusserung*. The latter term is used in theories concerning natural law and in economics. It means that something which is a part of man has been disengaged or detached from him. The first term refers to estrangement.

In theories of natural law and in the ideas developed by Rousseau the concept *alienation* is used in the sense of a human being's having been exposed to this disengagement or detachment. Rousseau, for example, speaks of man's being disengaged from his original, natural freedom by entering into social contract.

In German philosophy the terms *Entfremdung* and *Entäusserung* receive another meaning. One point of departure in German idealistic philosophy is the division between "spirit" and "materia," which in turn creates different kinds of antagonism. According to Tucker[17] the division between man's "true ego" and his "phenomenal" ego (which plays an important role in the moral philosophy of Kant) has been instrumental in changing the meaning of the concept of *alienation*. The individual is conceived of as having a double nature, as being composed of two parts. One is, from an ethical point of view, the perfect being. The

[14] *Mega I.5*, p. 64.
[15] *Mega I.3*, p. 87.
[16] L. R. Langslet, *Den unge Marx og menneskets "fremmedgjörelse"* [*Young Marx and Man's "Alienation"*] (Oslo: Johan Grundt Tanum Forlag, 1963).
[17] R. Tucker, *Philosophy and Myth in Karl Marx* (Cambridge: At the University Press, 1961).

other, the factual being, is directed by the senses and therefore has many shortcomings. This ego, characterized by its shortcomings, is experienced as something alien to the "real and perfect" ego.[18] Fichte, one exponent of German romantic philosophy, also divides the ego. Going to the extreme he talks about the ego's *Entäusserung*—its detachment from itself into another entity called "non-ego."

These speculations about the individual and his divided self form a part of the criticism against the social and economic development in this period, characterized by the beginnings of industrialization. German romantic philosophy developed out of "the discrepancy between the historical reality and the humanistic, romantic and political ideals of harmony and the demands that these ideals should be realized as the basis of man's emancipation."[19]

German romantic philosophy experienced the period as one characterized by "decay." It tried to find solutions which might save man from his predicament. One of those who treated the problem is Schiller, a leading figure in German romantic literature and philosophy.

Schiller[20] builds his reasoning on a idea developed by Kant, who thought that human nature could reach perfection only through long and specific experience and practice. It is impossible for one human being to achieve perfection because his life span is too short. Human nature can be realized only in the long chain of generations. There is no possibility of individual self-realization, only of the realization of the human species, which as a species can achieve new heights of development toward perfection. As we already have seen, this idea is adopted by Marx, although he gives it a special meaning, which will be discussed later.

Schiller assumes that the development toward higher stages of realization would not occur, were it not for the antagonism existing between the individual's strivings for individual perfection and his need for social adjustment. It is this antagonism which becomes the driving force toward the self-realization of human nature.

In addition, Schiller has anthropological conceptions concerning the antagonistic forces within human nature: there is a dualism between emotion and reason, between fantasy and analytical capacity. Schiller conceives of an ideal stage in which these basic capacities are integrated into a harmonic synthesis. However, this harmony is prevented by factual conditions in which emotion dominates reason (or vice versa) or in

---

[18] Ibid., p. 34.

[19] H. Popitz, *Der entfremdete Mensch* (Basel: Verlag für Recht und Gesellschaft, 1953), p. 12.

[20] Ibid., p. 16 ff.

which the two are separate.[21] Unlike the harmonious man of classical Greece, Schiller asserts that his period is dominated by the lack of harmony and antagonistic strivings which exist within the individual, though without these antagonisms the human species would not be able to reach higher stages of development. Therefore the antagonisms are necessary, although they prevent perfection in the current epoch.

Schiller also presents some "sociological" theories to explain the lack of harmony among his contemporary fellow citizens. One of the basic reasons for the lack of harmony is the division of labor, the specialization of man, and the division of science into different branches. The human being in classical Greece was not yet specialized; philosophy embraced all sciences. He represented a totality, which can now be reached only if individuals join forces and become integrated into a larger community.

As long as such integration fails to occur, the individual will be bound to only a fraction of totality, and Schiller maintains that a human being bound only to a fraction himself becomes a fraction. He adds that the individual who listens only to the monotonous sound of the machine he tends can never achieve harmony within his being. The person who strives to achieve a position in bourgeois society will not strive for culture, but will rather experience knowledge and culture as obstacles to his strivings.

The young Marx also considered the division of labor to be an important obstacle to the development of universal man with many capacities, and he saw it, therefore, as conducive to the creation of alienation. He criticized bourgeois society for developing those traits in man which would deepen his alienation.

Another idea which Schiller puts forwards is that social and economic development creates new needs in man, but does not increase his freedom. The increased opportunity to master nature and its forces can lead to a greater dependence. It is interesting to see how Schiller's ideas are to be found once again in the criticism directed against "consumption-society" by such authors as Marcuse.[22]

Marx has some similar ideas, although he does not come to the same negative conclusions as Schiller. In the third volume of *Capital* he writes:

> The realm of freedom only begins, in fact, where that labor which is determined by need and external purposes ceases; it is therefore, by its very nature, outside the sphere of material production proper. Just as the savage must wrestle with nature in order to satisfy his wants, to maintain and reproduce his life, so also must civilized man, and he

[21] Compare the quotation from Marx's essay "The Eighteenth Brumaire" on page 1.
[22] See chapter 6.

must do it in all forms of society and under any possible mode of production. With his development the realm of natural necessity expands, because his wants increase, but at the same time the forces of production, by which these wants are satisfied, also increase.[23]

Part of the criticism of society which lies in Schiller's ideas, and in the romantic period in general, builds upon philosophical-anthropological theories of harmonious states in the human being, as a result of harmonious relations between man and his environment. Such theories presuppose ideas about dualism and antagonistic forces within human nature, forces which can be united only under certain social conditions. The early process of industrialization is experienced as a threat to this harmony; therefore the criticism is directed against industrialization and its feared consequences. In this respect Marx's theory deviates from those put forward by the German romantic thinkers.

One basic tendency in all these romantic theories is that concepts of antagonism between individual and society are basic conditions for theories about alienation. In this case they are supplemented by a dualistic anthropological, philosophical thesis, which places the conflicts within the individual, but does it as a consequence of social pressure.

ALIENATION IN HEGEL'S PHILOSOPHY

The meaning given to *alienation* in the writings of the young Marx (where he uses the term in the sense of "estrangement" as well as in the sense of "detachment") is closely related to Hegel's use of the concept in his philosophy. Yet at the same time the development of the theory of alienation in *Economic and Philosophical Manuscripts* is a critical attempt to distinguish himself from Hegel and his philosophy, which nevertheless greatly influenced Marx.

A theory of alienation, as Marcuse[24] indicates, is already apparent in one of Hegel's earliest works *Theologische Jugendschriften*. The alienation of man is here seen as a consequence of private ownership as a social institution. Man, according to Hegel, lives in a world which is shaped by his work and by his knowledge, but it is a world in which man feels himself alien, a world whose laws prevent basic need-satisfaction.

Later, beginning with the so-called *Jenenser Vorlesungen*, Hegel starts to analyze the problem of work as a process of detachment (*Entäus-*

---

[23] K. Marx, *Capital*, German edition (Berlin: Dietz Verlag, 1965) Vol. III, p. 828.
[24] H. Marcuse, *Reason and Revolution* (Boston: Beacon Press, 1960).

serung).[25] Work has a mediating function between man and that part of his world which is "nature." To satisfy his needs, man through his own work changes nature and nature's objects into objects for his own needs. But work has an additional function. Hegel distinguishes between the objective and the subjective world. Through his work man overcomes the alienation which the objective world presents. Through work, nature is transformed into a medium of man's development, his subjective world is enlarged, and the alienated world is diminished.[26] The self-realizing function of work, however, is threatened by the machine. The more mechanized work becomes, the less value it has as an expression of man's abilities and capacities. The more work is transformed into a mechanical process, the more it becomes labor and toil. In addition, work is no longer a means for need-satisfaction but is transformed into coercive activity. The products of work no longer have a use-value for the man who produces them, but become commodities.

The mechanization of work is closely related to the division of labor and to specialization, which in turn creates monotony. Marcuse[27] points out that Hegel often uses his metaphysical theories in order to describe social conditions typical of a given society. The description Hegel gives of work and its consequences resembles that given by Marx in *Capital*, in which he analyzes the production of commodities and the effect of the laws of the commodity-market on the individual and his work.

The central discussion of alienation appears, however, in Hegel's ontology. For Hegel, history is the march of the spirit toward freedom. Freedom can be found only in self-consciousness. God is absolute self-consciousness. History therefore is the autobiography of God. This is a short and concentrated description of Hegel's ontology, as presented by Sidney Hook.[28] For Hegel, God is an absolute and infinite being. He is the total reality. This reality is equated with *der Weltgeist*—the world-spirit. This spirit, which comprises everything, is reality and is alone reality. "It is the inner essence of the world, that which is essential and is per se," Hegel declares in his *Phänomenologie des Geistes*.

The world-spirit is driven by a need for self-consciousness, and, in order to be able to reach this self-consciousness, the spirit must assume concrete and objective shapes. It must become concrete, because only as a concrete

---

[25] K. Löwith, *Von Hegel zu Nietzsche* (Stuttgart: W. Kohlhammer Verlag, 1953), and Popitz, *Der entfremdete Mensch*, p. 117 ff. See also the discussion in the next chapter, where *Entäusserung* has been translated into *exteriorization* and where the term is explained.

[26] Marcuse, *Reason and Revolution*, p. 77.

[27] Ibid.

[28] S. Hook, *From Hegel to Marx* (Ann Arbor: University of Michigan Press, 1962).

substance will it attain self-consciousness. The world-spirit also has a creative ability which shows itself in all the objects in which the spirit expresses itself. The essence of the spirit is activity, and by activity it realizes itself. It becomes itself an object—its own object.

The self-realization occurs within time and space, i.e., in history and in nature. The transformation of the world-spirit into outer objects is called by Hegel the "self-detachment" (*Selbstentäusserung*) of the spirit. The creative activity of the spirit causes parts of its essence to be detached from itself. The detached part becomes objects outside the spirit.

What role does man play in Hegel's ontology? Nature and man are two different aspects of the spirit. Nature is that part of the spirit which has detached itself from the totality. But this detached part is not conscious about itself as being a part of the totality. Man, however, is that part of the spirit which is gaining self-consciousness through thinking and through reason.[29] The spirit which manifests itself in man becomes self-conscious through thinking, and as a consequence the state of self-alienation (in which all objects detached from the total spirit are ensnared) is overcome.

This kind of reasoning presupposes a distinction between subject and object and the relation between them. The self-conscious subject is seen as distinct from the alienated "outer" object, both, however, being ways in which the spirit has expressed itself in its creative activity. One problem is why the self-conscious spirit should experience the objective world as something alienated. Why does the spirit conceive the experience of that which occurs outside itself as something which is alien and directed against the spirit?[30]

Hegel develops a theory concerning the image, the notion which the spirit has of itself. The spirit is identical with God. It is total and infinite. It comprises the whole reality. But the totality is disturbed by the fact that something appears as an object and as detached from the spirit. For that reason the spirit must consider the object as something which is alienated and detached. The existence of objects contradicts the self-perception of the spirit as something absolute. The objects are barriers which threaten to obliterate the experience of totality and of absoluteness.

However, self-detachment and the subsequent alienation are necessary if the spirit is to achieve self-consciousness. The demand for totality is contradictory to the existence of subject-object relations. But without this distinction the spirit—and man as a part of the spirit which becomes self-conscious—cannot achieve self-consciousness. But without self-consciousness there is no perfection. Yet the spirit wants to have perfec-

---

[29] Tucker, *Philosophy and Myth*, p. 48.
[30] Ibid., p. 52.

tion as well as absoluteness, though these two properties are opposed to each other. For that reason a dialectical process is always continuing. The spirit must detach itself from its totality and create objects in order to reach self-consciousness and hence perfection. However, the self-detachment, also called self-objectivation, is at the same time negated by the spirit because it threatens its totality. The negation of the object-state is abolished by the creation of new objects. Thus the negation is negated—a central state in a dialectical process.

The alienation of the spirit from itself through the creation of objects has a central function for the strivings of the spirit after self-realization. Alienation is the necessary consequence of the antagonism between totality and self-consciousness: the demand for totality causes objects to appear as something alienated, but without objects no self-consciousness can develop. The spirit needs the objects to be able to reflect itself. The dialectic process is a constant shifting between strivings for totality and for self-consciousness.

Undoubtedly there is some brilliance in these metaphysical speculations which later became the basis of Marx's critical analyses.

3

KARL MARX'S THEORIES OF ALIENATION

INTRODUCTION

In 1836 Karl Marx came to Berlin, at the age of eighteen, with the intention of studying law. At that time the University of Berlin was a center of German idealistic philosophy. Hegel, who had held the chair in philosophy, had died five years earlier; but his spirit and his thinking still dominated the philosophical discussions and teaching at the university. His students had divided themselves in two groups: one, which was politically conservative, called itself the Old Hegelians; the other group, politically on the left, was known as the Young Hegelians.[1]

Marx studied law for two years but became interested in philosophy in his second term. In a letter in 1837 to his father, who had urged him to concentrate on his law studies, he wrote that he intended to write a doctoral dissertation in the field of the philosophy of law. The first part, for which he had already assembled notes, he intended to call "The Metaphysics of Law."[2]

In the course of his studies he came into contact with a group which assembled regularly to discuss problems of Hegel's philosophical writings. In this group, called the Doctors' Club, Marx became more and more interested in philosophy. His father wrote him one letter after the other, telling him to continue his studies of the law. However, when his father died in 1838, Marx immediately decided to finish with law and to concentrate on his studies of philosophy.[3]

---

[1] For a detailed description of Marx's life, see A Cornu, *Karl Marx und Friedrich Engels* (Berlin: Dietz Verlag, 1954).

[2] *Mega I.2*, p. 213 ff.

[3] Cornu, *Karl Marx*.

Among the Young Hegelians Marx met a young philosopher by the name of Feuerbach, whose criticism of Hegel's philosophy of religion and whose materialistic-philosophical orientation made a deep impression on Marx. Feuerbach's anthropology, i.e., his philosophy concerning human nature, also influenced Marx greatly, and traces of it can be found in Marx's *Economic and Philosophical Manuscripts*. In 1839 Marx started to write his doctoral thesis, which was published two years later. In it he discussed differences in the philosophy of nature between the Greek philosophical schools called Democritian and Epicurean. In the preface to his thesis Marx acknowledged the influence of Hegel on his own thinking, but even at this stage his thesis contains a criticism of Hegel's philosophy. The same tendency can be found in most of his early writings: the attachment to Hegel's philosophy was combined with a sharp criticism of it. The criticism also concerns theories of alienation, in spite of the fact that Marx uses Hegel's terminology.

Young Marx's analysis of alienation comprises three aspects.[4] (1) Religious alienation, which is analyzed in connection with a critical discussion of Feuerbach's philosophy of religion. (2) Political alienation, a theory which contains a sharp criticism of Hegel's philosophy of the state. In his analysis, at least to a certain extent, Marx is attached to Rousseau's ideas. (3) Economic alienation, rooted in the alienation from labor. This is the main theme of the Marxian theory of alienation, and it contains his first articulated attempt to analyze and criticize the economic and social conditions of "bourgeois society." Economic alienation for Marx is the most basic alienation. Religion and the state he does not consider as independent variables. According to Marx the form they take is dependent on the existing economic conditions, especially the mode of production. This forms the basis on which the organization of the state, religion, law, etc., constitute a superstructure.

RELIGIOUS ALIENATION

Marx accepts Feuerbach's thesis, that it is man who has created God, not the opposite. In 1841 Feuerbach published a book entitled *The Essence of Christianity*. In this work he maintains that man ascribes to God all the best qualities of his own, while he experiences himself as sinful and wretched. This erroneous "self-evaluation" in connection with a projection of the best of human qualities onto God, creates alienation. Man, declares Feuerbach, becomes alien to his own essence, because it is projected onto God, and therefore alien to himself.

[4] L. R. Langslet, *Den unge Karl Marx og menneskets "fremmedgjörelse,"* [*Young Karl Marx and Man's "Alienation"*] (Oslo: Johan Grundt Tanum Forlag, 1963).

Marx, however, is not content with this psychological explanation. Instead he asks the following question: How is it that religion is able to play this alienating role? The answer Marx gives is that the alienation which apparently originates in religion is only a reflection of a more basic phenomenon, i.e., that the economic and social destitution in which many people are condemned to live creates a feeling of powerlessness, of nothingness, of misery. Religion merely reflects man's own wretchedness.

This is a sociological hypothesis that Marx submits. His analysis is found in one of his earliest essays "Zur Kritik der Hegelschen Rechts-philosophie" ("A Criticism of Hegel's Philosophy of Law"), written in 1843. There he states: "The basis of irreligious criticism is this: *man makes religion*; religion does not make man. Religion is indeed man's self-consciousness and self-awareness so long as he has not found himself or has lost himself again. But *man* is not an abstract being, squatting out-side the world. Man is the *human world*, the state, society. This state, this society, produce religion which is the *consciousness* of an *inverted world* because it is an *inverted world*."[5]

Thus, Marx attacks abstract ideas about the state and society, which were common in the German thought of his epoch, and substitutes for them a sociological analysis. In society are found intolerable social conditions which affect the attitude toward religion. Marx continues his analysis, using the metaphorical language of German romanticism: "*Religious* suffering is at the same time an *expression* of real suffering and a *protest* against real suffering. Religion is the sigh of the oppressed creature, the sentiment of a heartless world, and the soul of soulless conditions. It is the *opium* of the people.

The abolition of religion as the *illusory* happiness of men, is a demand for their *real* hapiness."[6]

The much-quoted phrase referring to religion as "opium of the people" gains quite a different meaning when read in context. It refers to a sociological hypothesis concerning the role of religion for people living under miserable social and economic conditions.

Marx later asserts that the criticism of religion is necessary as part of the criticism of societal conditions in general. This "criticism," he says, "has plucked the imaginary flowers from the chain, not in order that man shall bear the chain without caprice or consolation but so that he shall cast off the chain and pluck the living flower. The criticism of religion disillusions man so that he will think, act and fashion his reality as a man who has lost his illusions and regained his reason; so that he will revolve about himself as his own true sun. Religion is only the illusory

---

[5] *Mega I.2*, p. 607.
[6] Ibid.

sun about which man revolves so long as he does not revolve about himself."[7]

The criticism of religion is a precondition necessary to reveal the foundation of man's alienation. According to Marx, it is the task of philosophy to do that: "The immediate *task of philosophy*, which is in the service of history, is to unmask human self-alienation in its *secular form* now that it has been unmasked in its *sacred form*."[8]

Marx tried to undertake this task the year after he wrote these lines. In *Economic and Philosophical Manuscripts* he presents a sociological analysis of those social conditions, which create the type of alienation basic to Marx's thinking. Before we discuss this analysis, we shall very briefly consider the notion of political alienation.

POLITICAL ALIENATION

The point of departure in Marx's analysis is Hegel's theory of the state and his philosophy of law. Hegel deified the state and saw in the existing Prussian state the highest peak in historical development. As Bottomore and Rubel aptly summarize: "According to Hegel abstract right is sublimated in morality, morality is sublimated in the family, the family is sublimated in civil society, civil society is sublimated in the State, and finally the State is sublimated in world history."[9]

Hegel drew a distinction between the state and society. In Hegel's opinion the state was God's spirit as it is expressed on earth. Therefore, it was the individual's duty to worship the state as a manifestation of the spirit of God. Man must also remember that if it is difficult to understand nature, it is still more difficult to understand the essence of the state.[10]

Marx asserted that this concept of the state had the same function as religion, being a projection of human power into an abstract idea which in turn makes man feel the more powerless. Again Marx poses the same question as when he analyzed the social function of religion: "How is it that human beings project onto outside objects, onto reified abstractions, those powers which are truly their own?"[11]

Once again the answer he gave was a sociological explanation unlike

---

[7] Ibid., p. 608.

[8] Ibid.

[9] T. B. Bottomore and M. Rubel, Introduction to *Karl Marx: Selected Writings in Sociology and Social Philosophy*, (New York: McGraw-Hill Book Company, 1964), p. 6.

[10] Quoted after K. Popper, *The Open Society and Its Enemies* (London: George Routledge & Sons, 1945), Vol. II, p. 28.

[11] Bottomore and Rubel, *Karl Marx: Selected Writings*, p. 5.

Hegel's metaphysical speculations: "The *State* and the *structure of society* are not, from the standpoint of *politics, two* different things. The state is the structure of society."[12] Today such a statement would probably be considered as trivial. When Marx wrote these lines in 1844, they must have appeared to many as courageous and original thinking.

Marx also made clear the alienating function of the attempt to attribute divine properties to the state. In this case the existence of social problems could not be attributed to the state and its organization: "The more powerful the State, and therefore the more *political* a country is, the less likely it is to seek the basis of *social evils* and to grasp the *general* explanation of them, in the *principle of the State* itself, that is in the *structure of society,* of which the State is the active, conscious and official expression."[13]

Hegel's notions about the state and its authority, as Popper remarks, have a clearly totalitarian stamp.[14] Popper, who is somewhat hostile to Marxism, suggests that Marxists should have revealed Hegel's theory of the state as dictated by his class-interests, which aimed at protecting the dominance of the Prussian state. Thus Hegel's theories could be considered not only as an expression of his metaphysical philosophy but also as an attempt to contribute to the restoration of Prussia and the reign of King Friedrich Wilhelm.

The authoritarian character of Hegel's ideas is also revealed in his demand that the individual should subordinate himself to the state. In fact, it is the subject's duty to do so. As Marcuse observes,[15] the state thereby acquires disciplinarian traits.

The bourgeois society is seen by Hegel as a negation of a natural and more original social community, as a change from *Gemeinschaft* to *Gesellschaft,* to use Tönnies's terminology. The bourgeois society is an alienated form of the original community. It results in individualization, which in turn creates antagonism of interest. The negation is again negated by a synthesis between community and individualism. This synthesis is the "state," which realizes the world-spirit.

In his criticism of the Hegelian philosophy of the state Marx also takes up another theme.[16] He develops a detailed analysis of bureaucracy. According to Hegel the members of the bureaucracy, the German *Beamte,* have an important mediating function. We have already mentioned that Hegel distinguishes between civil society and the state, which

[12] *Mega I.3,* p. 14.

[13] Ibid., p. 15.

[14] Popper, *The Open Society.*

[15] H. Marcuse, *Reason and Revolution* (Boston: Beacon Press, 1960), p. 175.

[16] *Mega I.1,* p. 401 ff.

represents the general interests. The civil society is made up of families, the estates, and other classlike groupings. The task of the bureaucracy is to mediate the general interest to these groups caught in antagonisms of interests.

Marx criticizes this view.[17] He points out that bureaucratic organizations are formalistic ones, which soon come into conflict with the individuals they should serve. However, another point is also taken up by Marx. The division between civil society and the state assumes that a subject as a *private person* belongs to the civil society. As a citizen he should belong to the state.

But according to Hegel civil society and state are separated. Thus the private person and the citizen are also separated from each other. The distinction which Marx draws once again is that previously referred to as the distinction between *l'homme* and *le citoyen* (see p. 22).

If we analyze Hegel's theory of the state and Marx's criticism of it in terms of our previous distinction, it can be said that Hegel's theory is society-oriented. In the totalitarian state he looks for opportunity to overcome the conflicts of interests between groups and between the individual as private person and as citizen. Marx, on the other hand—by taking as his starting point an individual-oriented theory—experiences the state and its bureaucracy as (to quote Langslet) "isolated and alien to the individual. The state does not care about the individual's existence in a society without communion between people and the individual in his relation to such a state does not experience a feeling of solidarity; he is only able to relate himself to it as an isolated monad, an *Individual*. Man's inner life is divided in a world split up in such a way."[18]

The final point we wish to mention is Marx's attack on Hegel's dialectics of history, whereby the state becomes the final realization of the spirit. Marx contends that it is in this metaphysical thought that the mystery of Hegel's philosophy of the state is concentrated. The solution to the existing division and the ensuing alienation cannot be a totalitarian state, but a democratic order. Marx says that democracy starts with man. Just as religion does not create man, but rather man creates religion, so the constitution does not create man, but rather man creates the constitution."[19]

Marx speaks of democracy, but democracy without a state, for in a true democracy[20] the state will vanish. Under such conditions man's political alienation can be overcome. Man as a social being can realize

[17] Ibid., p. 247 ff.
[18] Langslet, p. 83.
[19] *Mega I.1*, p. 434.
[20] Ibid., p. 435.

himself in a social order which corresponds to man's social nature: "*Every* emancipation is a *restoration* of the human world and of human relationships to *man himself.*"[21]

Political alienation can first be overcome when the more basic alienation, the economic one, is overcome. Thus Marx deals first with religious alienation, revealing the theology of his time. He then continues with political alienation by criticizing the theories of state. In both cases he hypothesizes similar social functions for both religion and the state. Religion is used to conceal secular misery, while submission to a totalitarian state is in order to hide existing social evils. It also attempts to create an imaginary community to divert attention from existing conflicts of interest. Which are, then, the central factors affecting the individual's life? Marx summarizes them and states their relationship to the state: "The material life of individuals, which certainly does not depend on their mere "will," but on their mode of production and their form of intercourse, which reciprocally influence each other, are the real basis of the State. The material life is, at every stage in which the division of labor and private property are still necessary, quite independent of the *will* of individuals. These real conditions are not created by State power; they are rather the power which creates them."[22]

ECONOMIC ALIENATION

MAN AND WORK

In 1923 the Hungarian philosopher and literary historian Georg Lukács published a book entitled *History and Class-Consciousness.* The book, with its central essay ("The Reification and the Consciousness of the Proletariat"), is noteworthy from several points of view. For one thing Lukács, partly under strong pressure, later repudiated most of the ideas in this very scholarly book.[23] Still more noteworthy, however, is that in this book Lukács presents Marx's theory concerning economic alienation not only as this theory was developed in its second version (among other places in *Capital*) but also in the shape it was given by the young Marx. This former version, developed in the *Manuscripts*, was published

[21] Ibid., p. 599.

[22] *Mega I.5*, p. 307.

[23] Concerning Lukács and his work see I. Mészaros, "Philosophie des 'tertium datur' und des Koexstienz-dialogs," *Festschrift zum achtzigsten Geburtstag von Georg Lukács*, ed. F. Benseler (Neuwied: Hermann Luchterhand Verlag, 1965); and M. Watnik, "Relativism and Class Consciousness: Georg Lukács," in *Revisionism*, ed. L. Labedz (London: George Allen and Unwin, 1962).

Back by Popular Demand

Sistah to Sistah

Presented by:
The lovely ladies of the Lambda Kappa Chapter

Come join us on Monday, November 13
in room 2080 of the Russell Student Union
at 7:30 p.m. for a

fun

and **informative**

discussion of women's issues
by women
for women Come join us on Monday, November 13
in room 2080 of the Russell Student Union
at 7:30 p.m. for a
from one *sistah* to another.

We can't wait to see you there!

Sponsored by: *Alpha Kappa Alpha Sorority, Incorporated*

for the first time about ten years after Lukács's book appeared, in the aforementioned edition of *Mega*.

How was Lukács able to reconstruct the theories developed by the young Marx? Lukács had studied Hegel as thoroughly as Marx had. He was very well acquainted with Hegel's theory of alienation and could therefore guess the way in which the thinking of young Marx developed. But Lukács was also influenced by the writings of Georg Simmel, who had been his teacher. In addition he had a very friendly relationship with Max Weber, with whom he often had discussions.

By taking *Capital* as his point of departure, Lukács was able to develop by the deductive method the theories which had been worked out by the young Marx. At the same time he incorporated in his analysis Max Weber's ideas concerning the role of rationality in industrialized society, especially with regard to the development of capitalism. In view of this we do not consider it an exaggeration to state that Lukács's book constitutes a bridge between Marx and other leading figures in classical German sociology. Yet it is also a support for those who assert that there is a continuity in the thinking of Marx as opposed to those who want to construct a breach beginning with the publication of *The German Ideology*. Had this continuity not existed, it would have been difficult or impossible for Lukács to deduce from *Capital* ideas which the young Marx developed.

To understand the problem of economic alienation, it is necessary to understand the role which Marx attributes to labor. In Marx's opinion labor constitutes man's most important activity—in fact, he calls it "life-activity." Through work man creates his world, and as a consequence he creates himself. This process of self-creation, seen in a historical perspective (also called by Marx *praxis*), was understood by Hegel. Marx adopted the concept of self-creation from Hegel: "The outstanding thing in Hegel's *Phenomenology* is that Hegel grasps the self-creation of man as a process . . . and that he, therefore, grasps the nature of *labor*, and conceives objective man (true, because real man) as the result of his *own labor*."[24]

A special explanation perhaps is warranted for the term "objective man." A basic idea in Marx's conception of labor is that man "objectifies" himself, which means that through creative activity man, by using his capacities in working up raw materials, transforms them into objects. Accordingly, these objects reflect his abilities.

By means of his own work, man also experiences himself as an active, conscious being, as an active *subject* as opposed to a passive *object*. Since the objects of his work reflect his own "nature," he can evaluate

[24] *Mega I.3*, p. 156.

himself through his activity. By this self-evaluation man also becomes an *object* for himself, for his own perception. There is reciprocal interaction between the acting subject and the self-evaluating object. The activity and the objects which are produced are used as the basis for self-evaluation, and in turn this evaluation influences the individual's activity. However, this occurs only if his labor is free and not enforced.

Marx's ideas, as we have tried to interpret them, recall to a high degree the theories developed by G. H. Mead and other interactionists.[25] Both have a process-theory of the "creation of man." This is especially interesting since Marx, through his anthropological ideas about human nature, differentiates himself from Mead.

Labor in Marx's philosophical anthropology plays a central role. In fact it is the way in which man realizes his own nature, his *Gattungswesen*, i.e., the essence of the human species. Through work man creates a world of *objects*. He molds and transforms nature and produces objects for his own need-satisfaction. But the world of objects in Marx's theories also includes social institutions through which the process of production is regulated and controlled.

Let us quote Marx to see from his own words the relation between work and the essence of man: "It is just in his work upon the objective world that man really proves himself as a species-being. This production is his active species-life. By means of it nature appears as his work and his reality. The function of labor is, therefore, the *objectification of man's species-life;* for he no longer reproduces himself merely intellectually, as in his consciousness, but actively and in a real sense, and he sees his own reflection in a world he has constructed."[26]

Man produces his own life. Through creative work man achieves self-realization, i.e., he realizes the potentialities of the species and at the same time gives expression to his basic social nature. In the concept of "species-life" there is contained not only the notion of the potentialities common to all men, but also the notion of man as basically social, i.e., *cooperative.*

We can now attempt a summary. The basic process existing in all societies is "objectification," man's conscious attempt to create objects for his need-satisfaction, and the social institutions through which production occurs. (Marx later speaks less of objectification and more of "social" or "total" production.)

However, not every process of objectification is considered "normal," i.e., an expression of human life-activity and a realization of the species. This is the case only under certain conditions, namely, when work is

25 G. H. Mead, *The Social Psychology of George Herbert Mead*, ed. and with an introduction by Anselm Strauss (Chicago: University of Chicago Press, 1956).

26 *Mega I.3*, pp. 88–89.

creative. Work is creative (1) if man makes "his life activity itself an object of his *will and consciousness*,"[27] (my italics), (2) if man through work can express his *capabilities* in a *comprehensive way*, (3) if through this work he can express his *social nature*, (4) if work is not simply *a means* for maintaining man's subsistence, i.e., if it is not purely instrumental.

Thus the *ideal of labor is represented by the active, consciously willing, self-realizing man in a social process of production*, where in addition the *activity is a goal in itself*.

Any other kind of labor is an alienated activity. Its characteristics are presented by Marx as follows: "Just as alienated labor transforms free and self-directed activity into a means, so it transforms the species-life of man into a means of physical existence."[28] The process of objectification, then, which is alienated, is a special case of the general process occurring in all societies and in all periods marked by different levels of development of the productive forces.

Thus Marx's theory of alienated labor presupposes a certain theory of human nature and a certain ideal of work, this ideal being a part of the theory of human nature. If this basic point is not understood, one cannot understand Marx's *first* theory of alienation as presented in *Manuscripts*.

This theory contains several elements: philosophical ideas, as well as normative–ethical ones, also a sociological and economical analysis within a historical perspective. In the theory can be found: (1) the dependence on Hegel's philosophy and at the same time its repudiation; (2) the dependence on Feuerbach's philosophical anthropology, which influences Marx's view about human nature (in his next work, *The German Ideology*, Marx first refutes Feuerbach's anthropology); (3) the dependence on German romanticism and its criticism of the process of industrialization;[29] (4) the dependence on the humanistic ethics of the period.

We will briefly elaborate the last two points. The description of the function of labor to a certain extent fits the artisan's activity in preindustrialized society: the artisan's shaping every product in an individual way, making of it an expression of his personality and being attached to it. The artisan's work may thus appear as goal-directed. In addition the artisan, determining his own working conditions, is a "free" man.

The normative-ethical elements concerning the function of labor are contained in Marx's ideal of work. Why, one could ask, should a man consciously produce and direct his activity? Why should his work-activity be a means for self-realization? This can be understood only if

[27] Ibid., p. 88.

[28] Ibid., p. 89.

[29] Concerning the influence of German romanticism on Marx's thinking, see M. Lifschitz, *Karl Marx und die Ästhetik* (Dresden, 1961).

these elements are introduced as *normative* ones, as goals which man *ought* to strive for, as desired ends and not as a descriptive analysis. As normative elements they are integrated parts of a humanistic-ethical system. We will discuss this hypothesis in the next chapter.

Marx now asks: How is it that labor has become alienated? The answer is in his own words: "Production is the acquisition of nature by the individual within and through a certain social structure."[30] If this is so, then one has to study and to analyze the social structure of an existing society. The social structure in turn is dependent on the level of development of the means of production of a given society, e.g., the level of technology. But a still more important feature of the social structure, according to Marx, is the social relations within which the process of social production occurs. He is especially concerned with property- and power-relations.

The new elements which distinguish Marx from his predecessors and the school of thought by which he was influenced are his *sociological orientation* and his *critical* analysis of economic theories. This analysis, the outstanding hallmark of Marx's method, aims at the criticism of economics and its theories. Marx wished to reveal that these laws, which are considered to be *general* laws of economics, are dependent upon a definite social and political structure. Thus he writes in *Manuscripts*: "Political economics begins with the fact of private property; it does not explain it. It conceived the *material* process of private property, as this occurs in reality, in general and abstract formulas, which then serve it as laws; it does not *comprehend* these laws; it does not show how they arise out of the nature of private property."[31] (My italics)

What Marx attempts, from his earliest writings to *Capital*, is to show how economic laws are dependent on certain social conditions, on the social structure of the society to which they apply. Thus Marx tries to show that economic theories are "ideologies," which are based on existing conditions, but which never question the conditions or discuss the consequences of changed conditions. Modern sociology has very often followed the path of economics and all too often rejected what is the main task of a sociology of knowledge (a statement which naturally expresses my own value-judgments).

Let us return to Marx. According to his analysis in *Manuscripts*, there are three conditions in capitalist society which cause profound changes in the work-situation and in the individual's social relations. These conditions, which transform labor into an alienated condition, are: first, the

---

[30] K. Marx, *Grundrisse der Kritik der Politischen Ökonomie (Rohentwurf)* (Berlin: Dietz Verlag, 1953), p. 9.
[31] *Mega I.3*, p. 81.

fact of private property and, especially, of private ownership of means of production; second, the process of division of labor, which in turn is a consequence of the development of "productive forces," particularly of technology and the use of machines. The third condition is that human labor is changed into a commodity on par with all other commodities. For that reason, labor is subordinated to the market-laws of capitalist society. The latter condition is a part of the process which Marx in *Capital* subsequently calls "fetishism of commodities."[32]

THE MARKET IN CAPITALIST SOCIETY

In all Marx's writings on economic processes, from *Manuscripts* to *Capital*, he tries to develop a model, which can be used as a frame for the analysis of different economic systems appearing in history, but he concentrates mainly on capitalist society.[33] This model contains a number of analytical categories such as "mode of production," "productive forces," "relations of production," and so on. In this model also are found a number of methodological rules as to how society should be analyzed. For instance, Marx emphasized the role of social conflicts, especially class conflicts, in the analysis of the social structure of a society. He emphasized the importance of the ways in which the total social process of production is organized for the understanding of other societal phenomena, e.g., the legal order, the organization of the state, ethics, etc.

Using Marx's own model we can now try to describe some of his points of view which are necessary for the understanding of alienation. Marx starts his analysis with a classical problem in economics, namely, the theory of value. He takes as his starting point the traditional distinction between a product's *use-value* and its *exchange-value*. A product's use-value can vary, but it is always defined by the value it has to satisfy persistent needs. Thus use-value is an instrumental value. The use-value of water, e.g., is dependent on how thirsty a person is.

In order to have an *exchange-value* or "to be" an exchange value, as Marx sometimes says, a product has to be changed into a commodity. How does a product become a commodity? It is not the fact that a thing is a product of work which makes it into a commodity, because "natural things" too, e.g., precious stones, can be commodities. So can water if, for example, a person in a desert controls the only available well.

A product becomes a commodity only when it has been related to other products, e.g., when it can be exchanged against the other product. This exchange relationship is quantified in the exchange-value of a prod-

[32] *Capital*, Vol. I, p. 85 ff.
[33] C. W. Mills, *The Marxists* (New York: Dell Books, 1962), p. 36.

uct. "The property to function as exchange-value characterizes the commodity-property of a product."[34]

Since money is the general exchange-value—it can be exchanged for every product—Marx in his *Manuscripts* also analyzes the role of money. When a product has been changed into a commodity, use-value and exchange-value are separated. Independent of the use-value of a product, its exchange-value is determined by the laws of the capitalistic market system. Later when analyzing these laws in *Capital*, Marx uses his method to describe "the fetishism of commodities," which is the central aspect of his *second* theory of alienation. Briefly his reasoning is as follows: A product becomes a commodity by the establishment of an exchange relationship to another product. However, products cannot establish relationship by themselves. The *abstract* relationship quantified in the exchange-value in fact veils the social relationship of their owners, defined among other things by the power they possess. But in a capitalistic market system, the producers of commodities are independent of each other. That is, they produce privately but not for private use. Instead they produce for the satisfaction of the total need of society, i.e., for a social goal. "Through the *exchange* of products the *social integration* in society, split into atoms by private ownership and division of labor, is established. The commodity thus is an *economic* token, i.e. *the token for social relations between independent producers*, as far as these relations are mediated by products."[35]

In summary, the capitalistic market covers social relations by commodity relations. These commodities are produced for a social goal but are owned privately. Since the ownership of commodities carries with it power, everything is gradually changed into commodities.

In precapitalistic societies there also existed an exchange of products, but there the exchange was regulated by the products' immediate use-value. Production was oriented toward consumption. One produced as much as one could consume, and only the surplus was exchanged. However, the important point is that as long as products were exchanged on the basis of their use-value, they were not transformed into commodities.[36]

It is first in the capitalist society and through its market-structure that commodities have come to play such a dominant role. Not only can the products acquire exchange-value and be sold as commodities, but also that which produces them, namely human labor and therefore also the worker himself. According to Marx, the worker in capitalist society is forced to sell his working capacity to be able to exist. Work is no longer

[34] R. Hilferding, "Böhm-Bawerks Marx-Kritik," in *Der Marxismus—Seine Geschichte in Dokumenten*, ed. I. Fetscher (Munich: R. Piper & Co. Verlag, 1964) Vol. II, p. 227.
[35] Ibid.
[36] *Grundrisse*, p. 63 ff.

an expression of his personality and his needs, but something which has been forced upon him. His working capacity, being transformed into a thing, a commodity to be bought and sold, is no longer experienced as his life-power. The consequence is that the worker becomes alien to his own activity and alien to the products he produces. His own activity is no longer perceived as his own, and the products of his work no longer belong to him. Let us quote Marx, when he analyzes this aspect of alienation: "This fact simply implies that the object produced by labor, its product, now stands opposed to it as an *alien being*, as a *power independent* of the producer. The product of labor is labor which has been embodied in an. object and turned into a physical thing; . . . . . All these consequences follow from the fact that the worker is related to the *product of his labor* as to an *alien* object. For it is clear on this presupposition that the more the worker extends himself in work the more powerful becomes the world of objects which he creates in face of himself, the poorer he becomes in his inner life, and the less he belongs to himself."[37]

The wage which the worker receives is the exchange-value which his working capacity has for the time being. The individual produces commodities, but he does not own them. Instead he, too, has been degraded to a commodity. The more complicated and the more successful the capitalistic system of production becomes, the more unfree becomes the individual, the more he is transformed into a serf in the process of production, and the more he becomes a cog in a large, inanimate machinery. "The worker becomes poorer the more wealth he produces and the more his production increases in power and extent. The worker becomes an ever cheaper commodity the more goods he creates. The *devaluation* of the human world increases in direct relation with the *increase in value* of the world of things,"[38] Marx asserts in his analysis.

When Marx speaks of the worker becoming the poorer, the more he produces, he refers to the society which he himself witnessed. But it would be too one-sided to assume that "poverty" is used by Marx in a strictly economic sense. Bearing in mind his theory of work, we can safely assume that he uses the term in a wider sense. He also refers to psychological and mental impoverishment, as a consequence of the production process.

Against "the world of things" Marx places "the human world," the influence of which decreases. One interpretation of this idea is that "objects," "things" produced, become more and more important. The value of these things increases, whereas human interaction (based upon the valuation of man's talents, knowledge, and capabilities, considered

[38] Ibid., p. 82.
[37] *Mega 1.3*, p. 83.

desirable within Marx's normative framework) decreases. This tendency to objectification in which things are transformed from means for need-satisfaction to goals (commodities), from use-value to exchange-value, is in *Manuscripts* called *Entäusserung*—detachment. Lukács calls it *reification.*

But Marx proceeds one step further. He maintains that it is not only the products of labor and the workers' working capacity which are transformed into commodities. The capitalistic society is depicted as the epoch in history in which

> everything, which up to now has been considered as inalienable, is sold as objects of exchange, of chaffering. It is the time in which objects, which earlier have been conveyed, but never exchanged, have been given away but never offered for sale, have been acquired but never been bought: virtue, love, conviction, knowledge, consciousness and so on, the time which, in a word, everything has been transformed into a commercial commodity. It is the time of general corruption, of universal bribery or, in the language of economics, it is the time when each object, physical as well as moral, is put on the market as an object of exchange to be taxed at its correct value.[39]

It is with moral indignation that Marx lashes out at the tendency to transform everything into a commodity. What are the consequences for the individual of this tendency? Disregarding the moral aspects for the moment, there are some important social ones. In earlier periods with different types of social structure it was possible for the individual to understand economic relations and the context in which they occurred. He had insight into the way things were produced, used, and exchanged. In addition, the individual had a definite idea of his own role within the total process of production and distribution.

However, the market system of capitalistic society is governed by economic laws which appear as impersonal and objective and therefore as beyond influence. The individual does not understand them, and he feels that he is able neither to influence nor to rule economic conditions. Instead he perceives himself as a thing, an object which must surrender to these "iron laws." To express it in a different way, the individual no longer perceives himself as an active, industrious *subject* but as a passive object without a will of his own. The individual conceives himself as powerless, as an object for powers which he does not know and therefore cannot understand or influence.

There is another factor of importance. The division of labor places the subject so that he can make use of only a small part of his capacities.

[39] "The Poverty of Philosophy," *Mega I.6.*

His work is either manual or intellectual. Very often manual work can be carried out in a routine matter and becomes monotonous. In the process of social production man is ascribed to a limited role in which only a fraction of his knowledge and capabilities are brought to use. In addition, the individual usually has no comprehensive grasp of the process of production and therefore lacks insight into it. He becomes alien to his activity and to the products of his activity, for he is not concerned with them. They become objects belonging to others and are sold by others. It is those others—usually the owners of capital and the means of production—who can appropriate the profits of the sold products, a profit, which in accordance with Marx's theory of value, constitutes *surplus-value*. According to this theory of value, the only activity which can create new values is human work. The following question from Marx describe how surplus-value is created:

> The value of a commodity is determined by the *total quantity of labor* contained in it. But part of the quantity of labor is realized in a value, for which an equivalent has been paid in the form of wages; part of it is realized in a value for which *no* equivalent has been paid. Part of the labor contained in the commodity is *paid labor*; part is unpaid labor. Therefore by selling the commodity at *its value*, that is the crystallization of the *total quantity of labor* bestowed upon it, the capitalist must necessarily sell it at a profit. He sells not only what has cost him an equivalent, but he sells also what has cost him nothing, although it has cost his workman labor.[40]

This is, in Marx's own words, a concentrate of his theory of surplus-value, which has been a very controversial point in economic theory.[41]

THE PROCESS OF DIVISION OF LABOR

As previously stated, Marx's theory of alienation assumes three conditions, which cause the phenomena representing economic alienation. We have discussed the problem of commodities and will now take up the division of labor, the second condition referred to by Marx. When he considers this factor to be a causal one, he once again starts from his notion of labor as creative activity. In work man's potentialities for self-realization exist in a latent form. However, Marx conceived of self-realization not as an individualistic act alone. It is not only the question of an individual's

[40] K. Marx, *Wage, Price and Profit* (Moscow: Foreign Language Publishing House, n.d.).

[41] For a discussion see, e.g., Fetscher, *Der Marxismus—Seine Geschichte in Dokumenten*, Vol. II; and E. Heiman, *History of Economic Doctrines* (New York: Oxford University Press, 1964).

giving expression to his own capabilities. Self-realization, to Marx's way of thinking, is just as much a social activity. Man, participating in the social or total process of production, realizes by his activities the potentialities of the whole species to create a world shaped according to principles which agree with normative concepts of self-realization.

When work is no longer a spontaneous activity, when it is experienced as something enforced, it will be experienced as alien to "man's nature." It is partly the division of labor which causes labor to become coercive activity.

Marx describes the division of labor as a process in a historical perspective in the second of the two most important early works, *The German Ideology*.[42] "The production of life, both one's own by labor and new life by procreation, appears at once as double relationship, on the one hand as a natural, on the other as a social relationship."

Marx defines "social relationship" as "the cooperation of several individuals, no matter under what conditions, in what manner or to what end. It follows from this, that the determinate mode of production, or industrial stage, is always bound up with a determinate mode of cooperation, or social stage, and this mode of cooperation is itself a 'productive force.' "[43]

The way in which people create the means for the satisfaction of their needs depends on existing means of their disposal. In the early stages the mode of production depends to a high degree on geographical and climatic conditions. The more man develops special tools, the more complex becomes the mode of production. The more complicated the production, the greater the division of labor. The division of labor in the lowest stages of social development is dependent mainly on biological conditions, exemplified by the different roles played by men and women in the act of procreation. Division of labor at that stage is also based upon natural differences, for example, bodily powers.

The division of labor first becomes a real division when manual and intellectual work become differentiated. "For as soon as the division of labor begins, each man has a particular, exclusive sphere of activity, which is forced upon him and from which he cannot escape. He is a hunter, a fisherman, a shepherd, or critical critic, and must remain so if he does not want to loose his means of livelihood."[44]

Thus, division of labor not only enforces upon man the activity which he is to undertake, and which therefore is outside his own control, but

---

[42] *Mega I.5*, p. 19.

[43] Ibid.

[44] Ibid., p. 22. The expression "critical critic" is a reference to the Young Hegelians against whom Marx and Engels wrote a polemic book, *The Holy Family*, with the subtitle *Criticism of the Critical Criticism*.

also introduces class differences or, as Marx puts it, "*division of labor* implies the possibility, indeed the fact, that intellectual and material activity—enjoyment and labor, production and consumption—devolve on different individuals."[45]

This in its turn will lead to antagonism and conflict. Social contradictions and antagonism of interests increase with the increased division of labor. In the next stage of this process comes the differentiation between countryside and urban areas. Cities develop; food is produced in the countryside, other necessities of life in towns. The inhabitants of towns acquire economic interests—e.g., in low-priced foodstuff—which are contrary to the farmers' interest.

In towns the division of labor took place among various guilds. A person could become a member of these guilds only if he had learned his trade, so the artisans of the Middle Ages cherished a special interest for their work. They strove after real skill, which in turn sometimes developed into true artistic talent. In this way the artisan of the Middle Ages was also totally absorbed in his work. This is the somewhat idyllic and idealized description which Marx bestows upon artisanship.

During the next stage of development in the division of labor, a differentiation occurs between production and communication or commerce, which leads to the creation of a class of merchants. As communications became more developed, towns would start to compete with each other, and a division of labor between different towns and cities came about. The competition in turn contributed to the origin of manufactured goods in a preindustrial setting. Such production demanded capital; and, as a consequence of the accumulation of capital, property relations changed. When the means of production become privately owned, capital and labor are differentiated and separated.

"The division of labor implies from the outset the division of the *prerequisite of labor*, tools and materials, and thus the partitioning of accumulated capital among different owners. This also involves the separation of capital and labor and the different forms of property itself. The more the division of labor develops and accumulation increases, the more sharply this differentiation emerges."[46]

Let us summarize: The process of the division of labor intrudes upon the individual's freedom for the following reasons:

(1) It brings about a separation between the manual and intellectual aspects of the work and, therefore, prevents the individual from using all his capacities. During the development of industrialization manual skills become devaluated at the expense of intellectual skills.

[45] *Mega I.5*, p. 21.
[46] *Ibid.*, p. 41.

(2) Later manual skills become subordinated to the machine, as the process of mechanization proceeds. As a result, the individual no longer has his own abilities at his disposal. It is the machine which determines, e.g., how fast he should work. This second point concerns division of labor as a consequence of the level of technology.

(3) Division of labor—to return to the societal level—is followed by class conflicts resulting from the acquisition of the means of production by a limited group of persons.

The consequence of this latter condition, according to Marx, is mainly that the productive forces appear as independent forces severed from the individual's. "The reason for this is that the individuals, whose forces they are, themselves exist separated and in opposition to one another, while on the other hand these forces are the only real forces in the intercourse and association of these individuals."[47]

Marx's theory of "cultural lag," previously referred to, is in these lines. According to this theory, the productive forces, e.g., technology, are social forces in the sense that they presuppose cooperative action within the total process of production. However, since these forces are controlled by a minority, they can be used in the interests of this minority. This creates potential social conflict which prevents cooperative action. Whereas the level of development of productive forces should presuppose cooperative action and should make such action possible, the social relations—especially ownership relations—according to which social production is organized, prevent, or at least make difficult, cooperative action.

PRIVATE PROPERTY

From our discussion of the development of the division of labor, the relationship between this process and private property has emerged. In fact, Marx goes so far as to indicate that both division of labor and private property are identical phenomena. The first, says Marx, states a certain relationship between the individual and the *process of production*. Private property states the relationship between the individual and the product: he is detached from both.[48]

Private property has a double function: it is a product of alienation and in turn creates further alienation. Marx develops this early "system-theory" with built-in feedback mechanisms in the following way.

Private property is created through the alienated labor carried out by the worker. One reason for which labor becomes alienated (namely, the fact that the product of labor is not owned by those who produce it)

[47] Ibid., p. 56.
[48] Ibid., p. 22.

is also the reason for the creation of private property: *"Private property is, therefore, the product, the necessary result of alienated labor.*[49]

The existence then of private property accelerates and deepens the process of alienation within society. Thus private property becomes also the cause of alienation: "Only in the final stage of the development of private property is its secret revealed, namely, that it is on the one hand the *product* of alienated labor, and on the other hand the *means* by which labor is alienated, *the realization of this alienation.*"[50]

In this theory the kernel of the later theory of the exploitation of the worker is contained. It is not private property as such, but the private ownership of means of production which creates the process of exploitation. Through his work and the creation of surplus-value, the theory goes, the worker makes possible the accumulation of capital. The accumulated capital is then invested and in this way increases the possibilities of new exploitation, i.e., the creation of surplus-value, which the owner of the means of production can appropriate for himself. The relationship between alienated labor and exploitation becomes clear. Alienated labor is the labor by which man creates something that is detached from him and that is taken over by others who do not work, but who own the means of production and therefore control the process of production.

Marx depicts the symptoms of alienation as a consequence of private property in the following way: "The only connection which they (the workers) still have with the productive forces and with their own existence, labor, has lost for them any semblance of personal activity and sustains their life only while stunting it."[51]

How does Marx think the problem of private property can be solved? Since in his *Manuscripts* Marx conceives of property as the opposite of labor, its abolition is necessary in order to abolish at the same time human self-alienation and make possible "the real *appropriation* of human *nature* through and for man."[52] The abolition of private property will create a communist society, in which, as a consequence of the abolition of private property, the division of labor will also be removed. That in turn "makes it possible for me to perform one thing today, something else tomorrow, to hunt in the morning, to fish in the afternoon, to attend cattle in the evening and to criticize after the evening meal, all as I wish, without for that reason ever becoming a hunter, fisherman, shepherd or critic."[53]

For the young Marx the future communist society still appears as one

[49] *Mega 1.3*, p. 91.
[50] Ibid., p. 92.
[51] *Mega 1.5*, p. 57.
[52] *Mega 1.3*, pp. 83–85.
[53] *Mega 1.5*, p. 22.

populated by the hunters and fishermen of classical economics, but this vision is very quickly changed, especially when he starts to analyze the problems of economics in a more detailed fashion.

Finally in *Capital* he takes a totally different approach. Certainly private property, especially private ownership of the means of production, should be abolished, but division of labor will continue to exist. The emphasis is now on the organization of the process of social production in order to bring it under the conscious control of the individual. This will not abolish the division of labor but will make possible a considerable shortening of the working day, which is presented as an alternative to the abolition of one-sided division of labor: Regarding the process of social production, Marx states in the third volume of *Capital*: "Freedom in this field cannot consist of anything else but the fact that socialized mankind, the associated producers, regulate their interchange with Nature rationally, bring it under their common control, instead of being ruled by it as by some blind power, and accomplish their task with the least expenditure of energy and under such conditions as are proper and worthy for human beings. Nevertheless this always remains a realm of necessity. Beyond it begins that development of human potentialities for its own sake, the true realm of freedom, which, however, can only flourish upon that realm of necessity as its basis. The shortening of the working day is its fundamental prerequisite."[54]

So the notion of alienated work has been abandoned. Instead the emphasis is placed on the need for man actively to regulate and control his "life-activity," the process of social production. This will always necessitate labor, but the "realm of necessity" can be limited by a shortening of the working day. Thereafter begin the opportunities for human self-development and realization. However, there is one phrase in the quoted sentences which should be observed. Marx speaks about working conditions which are *"proper and worthy for human nature."* Even if the concept of alienated work no longer appears in the later writings of Marx, the quotation indicates that there still exist—implicitly or explicity —normative ideas in his sociological and economical theories. We will discuss this problem in the next chapter.

ALIENATION: A SUMMARY AND AN ELABORATION

We will now attempt a summary of the first theory of alienation and also try to elaborate our explication further. Finally, we will indicate the further development of the theory of alienated labor.

[54] *Capital*, Vol. III, pp. 873–74.

We begin with the process of objectification. The process leads to the "humanization of nature." "Man can transform the whole of nature to his 'inorganic body,' because he can objectify himself in nature (which is equal to saying that he humanizes nature)."[55] This humanization of nature, by the attempt to transform its objects into means of need-satisfaction, is prevented by the development of alienation.

Alienation is thus conceived of as a *social process* occurring under certain conditions. The *process of alienation* can be divided into two subprocesses. One of them, the more important one, is called *Entäusserung*, here translated to "exteriorization."[56] The concept indicates the young Marx's dependence on Hegel's terminology. The second process is called *Veräusserung*, to be translated as "disposing of."

Exteriorization means that something—in this case labor—which is considered to be a part of human nature is detached from man. Exteriorization occurs when man can no longer produce in cooperation with other men, due to his need to appropriate nature, to control it, and to humanize it in the aforementioned sense. To cite Marx's own definition of exteriorization: "What constitutes this exteriorization of labor? First that the work is *external* to the worker, that it is not part of his nature; and that, consequently, he does not fulfill himself in his work, but denies himself, has a feeling of misery rather than well-being, does not develop freely his mental and physical energies but is physically exhausted and mentally debased. The worker, therefore, feels himself at home only during his leisure time, whereas at work he feels homeless. His work is not voluntary but imposed, forced labor."[57]

The process of detachment leads to the psychological experience of labor as something *exterior* to man, being instrumental, but not a goal in itself or—as Marx would have said—a part of human essence.

The first aspect of exteriorization refers to the type of work, but Marx also gives the concept another meaning. The other aspect of exteriorization refers to the worker's relation to the products of his labor. "The worker puts his life into the object, and his life then no longer belongs to himself but to the object. . . . The greater this product is, therefore, the more he is diminished. The *exteriorization* of the worker into his product means not only that his labor becomes an object, assumes an *external* existence, but that it exists independently, *outside himself*, and alien to him, and that it stands opposed to him as an autonomous

---

[55] *Mega I.3*, p. 114.

[56] The German word *Äusserlich* has a double meaning. It refers partly to something which is "external," partly to something which is "not essential."

[57] *Mega I.3*, p. 85.

power. The life which he has given to the object sets itself against him as an alien and hostile force."[58]

This idea of the exteriorization of work into the product, making the product into a thing which gains control over the human being, is important because it already contains the notion of "reification." As we will later show, the concept of reification is most important for a modern, sociological version of the theory of alienation.

The second process, which we called "disposing of," is simpler to explain. It means that the worker disposes of his working power when he sells it as a commodity. Marx says, "Disposing-of, is the practice of exteriorization," and continues, "just as man, so long as he is engrossed in religion, can only objectify his essence by an *alien* and fantastic being; so under the sway of egoistic need, he can only affirm himself and produce objects in practice by subordinating his products and his own activity to the domination of an alien entity, and by attributing to them the significance of an alien entity, namely money."[59]

Another concept used in Marx's later theory, namely, "the fetishism of commodity," is hinted at in these lines. When money becomes the universal exchange object, it becomes a commodity and as such it often acquires a value independent of that which it represents. It also becomes a symbol of power.

We have now briefly described and analyzed the two sociological processes, *exteriorization* and *disposing of*, which can be subsumed to alienation. One problem arises. If alienation is a social process, created under certain social conditions, then all affected by these conditions should experience the consequences of alienation. Marx, however, speaks mainly of the consequences which alienation has for the worker. What about the consequences of alienation for other social classes or groupings? Marx can provide an answer. In his book *The Holy Family* he writes: "The possessing class and the proletarian class express the same human alienation. But the former is satisfied with its situation, feels itself well established in it, recognizes this self-alienation as its *own* power, and thus has the *appearance* of a human existence. The latter feels itself crushed by this *self-alienation*, sees in it its own impotence and the reality of an inhuman situation."[60]

Thus, according to Marx, the process of alienation affects all, but the alienating process is experienced in different ways, depending on the class to which the individual belongs.

[58] Ibid., p. 83.
[59] *Mega I.1*, p. 605.
[60] *Mega I.3*, p. 206.

In Marx's view the process of alienation is created by the following three *social conditions*: (1) the fact that man and his working power is transformed into a commodity, (2) division of labor, (3) private property. The *social conditions* and the *process of alienation* give rise to certain psychological consequences or *states of alienation*. The following can be distinguished:

(1) The worker becomes alien to his own *activity*. It is no longer perceived as a personal need, but as enforced. "It is not the satisfaction of a need, but only a *means* for satisfying other needs. Its alien character is clearly shown by the fact that as soon as there is no physical or other compulsion it is avoided like the plague."[61] (2) The individual experiences estrangement with regard to the *result* of his own activity. "The object produced by labor, its product, now stands opposed to it as an *alien being*, as a *power independent* of the producer."[62] Marx also points out that the more the individual tries to realize himself through his work, the more unreal this activity appears to him. The consequence of this is that the relationship of the individual to the product of his work also becomes "the relationship to the sensuous external world, to natural objects, as an alien and hostile world."[63]

(3) The worker not only becomes alien to the physical world in which he lives but also to his social world. He becomes estranged from the human species itself. He loses his own humanity. Therefore, he also becomes estranged in his social relations and in experiencing other human beings as subjects of cooperation. "When man confronts himself he also confronts *other* men. What is true of man's relationship to his work, to the product of his work and to himself, is also true of his relationship to other men. . . . In general, the statement that man is alienated from his species-life means that each man is alienated from others, and that each of the others is likewise alienated from human life."[64]

In chapter 1 we tried with the help of a diagram to explain the alienation concept. We have now described and analyzed Marx's theory of alienation. In the light of the preceding discussion, we will construct a new diagram.

The point of departure in this diagram is the process of production or objectification (PP). In the theory of Marx this is the basic social process. Through this process the material conditions for human life are created. Under "normal" conditions the process of objectification (according to

[61] Ibid., p. 85.
[62] Ibid., p. 83.
[63] Ibid., p. 86.
[64] Ibid., p. 89.

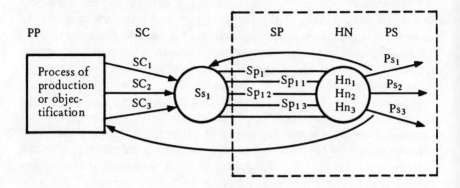

Figure 3. Diagrammatic representation of man's theory of alienation.

Marx) is an expression of the life-activity of the human species whose potential capabilities are realized at the same time.

The social process of production gives rise to special social conditions (SC). Of special interest for a theory of alienation are those social conditions according to which social production is organized. Marx considers that three of these conditions are of special importance for the origin of the sociological process of alienation. In our diagram these conditions are denoted Sc_1, Sc_2, Sc_3. Sc_1 refers to the social condition that working power is a commodity. Sc_2 denotes the social condition of private ownership of means of production. Sc_3 refers to the social condition of a special type of division of labor.

These three conditions among others characterize the social structure of the capitalistic society (SS). This is the third factor. From the theories of Marx it is not completely clear whether Sc_1, Sc_2, and Sc_3 are necessary and/or sufficient conditions to describe the social structure of the capitalistic society and as a consequence, alienation. Sometimes the impression is received that he considers them to be both necessary and sufficient conditions. If this is the case, it has important consequences for conceptions concerning the ways in which alienation can be overcome. (See chapter 8.)

The social structure of capitalistic society gives rise to a series of sociological processes (SP). One of them is alienation, Sp_1. This can be subdivided into three partial processes: Sp_{11} in our diagram refers to *exteriorization*; Sp_{12} refers to *disposing of*. Finally we have Sp_{13} denoting *reification* (this concept is discussed in more detail in the next section of this chapter). Are those three processes the only subprocesses of alienation or are there more? Can each appear in isolation or must they occur together in order that one can speak of alienation? One answer to this question is that it depends on the definition of alienation and of the theory developed. The quotations from the works of Marx, presented in the previous section, show that Marx himself considers *exteriorization* and *disposing of* as closely tied to each other. These concepts, however, play an insignificant role in his later work. In fact, they are rarely used. In the later works of Marx the phenomenon denoted as *reification* plays a dominant role. This holds especially for the phenomenon which Marx calls "fetishism of commodities."

The sociological, alienating processes operate in turn on human nature (HN) and the needs and capacities which characterize it. In Marx's theory of human nature three factors again play a significant role. Hn_1 refers to what Marx calls "the social being," Hn_2 denotes what is termed as "total being," and Hn_3 refers to the "creative being." These three concepts form the nucleus of Marx's view of human nature. His ideas will be discussed in more detail in the next chapter.

Since the alienating processes prevent human nature from acting according to its basic needs and capacities, psychological states (PS) are created. These are the alienated states of man. Once again, in our interpretation of Marx's theory there are three such states. Ps_1 refers to the fact that man experiences himself as alien in relation to his activity. Ps_2 denotes the fact that man is alien to the products of his working activity, and Ps_3 denotes his alienation from his species-being and therefore estrangement in his relations to other men.

In our diagram we have delimited an area by broken lines. This area comprises three of our variables, namely, SP, HN, and PS. It is these three variables that, according to my interpretation of Marxian theories, form the basis for alienation: Given a certain theory concerning human nature, certain sociological processes will create certain psychological states.

Finally, I have marked certain types of feedback mechanisms with the help of arrows connecting certain variables. The psychological states in which man is caught up have repercussions on the social structure of society, as well as on the basic social process of production. According to Marx, the individual's consciousness, his apperception of reality, is influenced by his social position within the structure of society. Accordingly, the causal influence in our diagram goes from left to right. At the same time it is the individual who creates and changes the basic social process of production and the resulting social structure of society. As we will show later, Marx does not have a one-sided social and economical deterministic theory. Instead he has the concept of a "dialectical" relationship, in which influences are going in both directions (in fact, certain of Marx's ideas concerning dialectical relations can be interpreted in terms of modern system theory).

The theory of alienation presented here is an attempt to explicate the theories developed in *Economic and Philosophical Manuscripts*. However, as early as in *The German Ideology* his view changes, basically because he renounces important parts of the theory of human nature, borrowed from Feuerbach.

THE TRANSITION FROM ALIENATION TO REIFICATION

One of our central hypotheses assumes that each theory of alienation is dependent upon a certain theory or view of man and "human nature." If the hypothesis is correct, a change in the theory of man would lead to a change in the theory of alienation.

The introduction to *The German Ideology* contains the so-called "eleven theses about Feuerbach." In these eleven theses Marx repudiates the materialistic philosophy and the philosophical anthropology of Feuerbach and presents his own position in outline.

In the sixth thesis Marx takes up the problem of human nature. He accuses Feuerbach of having reduced the essence of religion to the essence of man, and as a consequence that he must postulate the existence of an "abstract essence" of human nature. But, Marx points out, "the essence of man is not an abstraction inherent in each particular individual. The real nature of man is the totality of social relations."[65]

Marx presents here an explicit definition of the "nature of man," and it is a *sociological* definition. It can be interpreted in at least two ways. The *first* interpretation is that man is the totality of *his* social relations. This interpretation would be in accordance with the image of man in modern sociology—*homo sociologicus*: Man is the occupant of certain positions connected with certain roles. Roles are learned through social interaction and internalized. The internalized roles, constituting dispositions to act, form man's personality. This is, in a very condensed way, the image of *homo sociologicus*, and in this sense man is the totality of his social relations.[66] But is this the correct interpretation of Marx's definition? Hardly, because it would imply that Marx now conceives of man as a passive subject on which "society" stamps its mark, e.g., in the process of socialization and role-learning.

Marx still considers man as an active, creative being. Not only is he the sum of his social relations but also it is man himself who creates the

---

[65] *Mega I.5*, p. 534.

[66] R. Dahrendorf, *Homo Sociologicus* (Cologne: Westdeutscher Verlag, 1967).

conditions for his social relations. In the third of the eleven theses about Feuerbach, Marx thus asserts: "The materialistic doctrine concerning the changing of circumstances and education forgets that circumstances are changed by men and that the educator must himself be educated."[67]

Now let us go back to the definition of man. The second interpretation would then read in something like the following way: Man is the totality of social relations seen in a historical perspective.[68] His social relations are changed through the development of the productive forces, which alter the existing structure of a society, which in turn changes his social relations.

To make this statement less abstract, let us use an example. The alienation of man is created by special social conditions. These social conditions, however, are the result of human activity, so man creates alienation and by his own activity he can also overcome it. Alienated man is, then, the product of special conditions and corresponds to man's nature in a definite historical period. In this way Marx can differentiate between (1) "human nature at a given historical period" being a consequence of man's existing social relations and (2) man's "general human nature as it is changed in the historical process," though always being a consequence of the social relations he has created himself.

Human nature can be conceived of, on the one hand, as the *potentialities* which mankind has and, on the other hand, as the *existing* human being seen as a consequence of a certain social structure.[69] (We will have more to say about this problem in the next chapter.)

This definition of man leads Marx away from philosophical speculations. He deals with existing economic and social conditions and how these conditions affect man. In my opinion it is the change from the *problem of alienation* to the *problem of reification*.[70]

We will conclude this chapter with a short analysis of reification; the bulk of the problem, however, will be treated in the final chapter.

From a sociological point of view the concept of reification (the word was coined by Lukács[71] and not by Marx) is a very interesting one. As we will show, it has been dealt with in one way or another by many authors.

The Marxian theory of reification takes the commodity relationship as its starting point. A commodity, as discussed earlier, is characterized by its exchange-value. An object which is only a means for need-satisfaction

[67] *Mega 1.5*, p. 533.

[68] G. Hartfiel, *Wirtschaftliche und soziala Rationalität* (Stuttgart: Ferdinand Enke Verlag, 1968), p. 161.

[69] Ibid.

[70] See chapter 9.

[71] G. Lukács, *Geschichte und Klassenbewusstsein* (Berlin: Karl Dietz Verlag, 1923).

is not a commodity but has a use-value. The value of a commodity is determined by the chances of exchanging it for another commodity or for the "universal commodity"—money.

When an object has been transformed into a commodity, it loses, according to Marx, its "concrete meaning." A pair of shoes are no longer shoes in the sense "shoes which can be used for walking." As a commodity they are simply an object that can be exchanged, the value of which is determined not by need, but by the impersonal laws of the market. This contributes to the object's detachment from the original function or aims for which it was produced.

Implicit in the analysis of the commodity and its characteristics there appear to be at least two different ideas. Marx seems to have a notion of the *function* of every object. "Function" means, in this context, the objectives for which a thing is created. These objectives are usually, or often, that the object be a *means for need-satisfaction* or be used in a definite *social context*.

When an object is transformed into a commodity, it is no longer used for its original purpose (though later it may once again become a means for need-satisfaction). It becomes a *thing* with a certain exchange-value. As a thing it can become independent of the goals for which it was created and, moreover, can even thwart these goals. (The same holds for social organizations. They are reified when they acquire new goals, which may be turned against the creators of these organizations.)

It can be seen that the idea of a commodity-relationship presupposes, *first*, a notion of the "proper function" of an object. It is not clear whether "proper function," as Marx uses it, is a descriptive or a normative notion, i.e., whether he thinks there is one function it *has* or it *ought* to have in accordance with the intentions of its producers. In my opinion it is clearly a *normative notion*, or at least it implies normative preconditions, i.e., values (as concepts of "function" usually do).

The *second* idea implicit in the notion of commodity-relationship is related to the first. It implies that the value which a thing has as a commodity is not determined by its property of being a means for need-satisfaction, but by market laws. This means that its value is dependent on supply and demand and on those power-relations which may influence these factors. The exchange-value which has been put on an object causes its "original function" to be found only in a "latent" way. Thus the change in function about which we spoke previously is correlated with the transformation from use-value to exchange-value.

It is possible to think of different kinds of change in function. One such change would be that something which is a means for a certain goal becomes a means for an entirely different goal. A second type of change would occur if something which has been a means turns into a goal. Money, for example, is often exposed to such a displacement.

These kinds of ideas that are found in Marx's descriptions of economic processes[72] resemble theories put forward in modern sociology. The analysis of bureaucracy by Merton,[73] for example, can be translated into terms of the theory of reification. An organization of a social system is altered in such a way that its means are changed and become autonomous goals. "Ritualization" in a bureaucratic organization exemplifies this process, and also what Etzioni[74] calls "goal displacement."

Another example is Veblen's[75] concept of "conspicuous consumption." An object is used in such a way that it gives its owner the ability to demonstrate his social status. A Cadillac, for example, can primarily be used not as a means of transportation but as a status symbol. The tendency to acquire possessions and to evaluate oneself with the help of these possessions becomes another aspect of a sociological theory of reification.

A final example concerns the individuals and their relations to each other. Marx points out how individuals in precapitalist society were dependent on each other, how production was social production in the sense that producers were reciprocally dependent on each other. "The transformation of all products and activities into exchange-values presupposes the dissolution of all firm personal relations of dependence in production as well as the reciprocal dependence of producers."[76]

The capitalist market-system with its commodity structure transforms social relations between people into the relationship between things, to quote Lukács. The relations acquire "a ghostlike state of being things which in its strict, apparently totally closed conformity to law, covers the trace of its original essence—namely to be a relation between human beings."[77]

According to this conception, the individuals lose their capacity for spontaneous contact. Their relations acquire a calculating character. Men evaluate each other as objects, in the same way as they evaluate a commodity. Human beings become means for each other, means which can be exploited for achieving certain ends. But—and this is one of the central points in Marxist thinking concerning reification—the very phenomenon

---

[72] Grundrisse, pp. 33–148.

[73] R. Merton, *Social Theory and Social Structure* (Glencoe, Ill.: The Free Press, 1957).

[74] A. Etzioni, *A Comparative Analysis of Complex Organizations* (New York: The Free Press, 1961).

[75] T. Veblen, *The Theory of the Leisure Class* (New York: Macmillan, 1899).

[76] *Grundrisse*, p. 74.

[77] Lukács, *Geschichte*, p. 94.

does not appear to the individual as something abnormal, as something "alien to his nature." Instead, the process of reification acquires the characteristic of a "natural" relationship. Marx himself, for instance, indicates this condition when he says that the mysterious character of the commodity structure does not depend so much on the fact that the social character of work appears as a nonsocial property of the products of work. Still more important is the fact that this phenomenon is held out to the individual as something which can be characterized as a natural condition of the social system.

Therefore it is difficult for the individual to question reification. Instead he accepts the process as something natural. Lukács maintains[78] that the more capitalism develops, the more deeply and fatally is reification embedded into the consciousness of man.

It is not only the worker but also the whole society and its structure which become affected by this process. In order to find support for this thesis, Lukács refers to Max Weber and his principle of rationality. Weber asserted that modern industry, in the way in which it has been shaped in capitalistic society, must function in a rational way. This means that, given a certain goal, all means to this goal must be chosen in such a way that they can bring about its realization in the economically most effective way. Irrational and magical elements must be removed. Production must be built upon accurate computations, which in turn facilitate cost-accounting. This attitude, which in Weber's sense is rational and calculating, must encompass all areas of life: "The modern capitalist enterprise depends in its essence on calculation. It needs for its existence a legislation and administration, the functioning of which at least in principle can be computed in a rational way with the help of norms as firm and general as the ones with the help of which one can calculate the probable performance of a machine."[79]

One may question whether or not this tendency ascribed to capitalism has been strengthened under those conditions of production which are a consequence of modern technology. It is not merely that in mechanized production the individual is often transformed into a cog in a large machine. The form of social control within the industrial enterprise has also changed. Bureaucractic administration has replaced the authoritarian exercise of power.

Psychological knowledge is utilized to make more effective the changed power-forms. The manipulative aspects of "human engineering" and "human relations" have probably been conducive to the tendency to transform individuals into things.

---

[78]Ibid., p. 105.
[79] M. Weber, *Gesammelte Politische Schriften* (Munich: Drei Masken Verlag, 1921), p. 491.

Another social phenomenon which possibly contributes to the development of this aspect of reification is the dominant social value concerning *success*, which stresses the desirability of making a career and climbing the social ladder. This value presupposes an emphasis on status, an orientation towards competition and careerism. In a social situation in which this value is dominant, other people are often perceived either as obstacles to one's own strivings or as means for the realization of one's own goals. This form of reified attitude would then mean that human beings are evaluated from a certain point of view. Can they be the *means* of furthering one's own aspirations or do they constitute obstacles to them?

If reification is considered against this briefly sketched background, the possibilities of using the concept become clearer. It refers to such essential social phenomena that it is, not surprisingly, one of the most important aspects of modern social life.

In addition it appears to me as a fruitful starting point on the creation of a bridge between the sociological theories of Marx and "modern" sociological theorizing.

The analysis of reification restricts our discussion mainly to *sociological processes*, if in accordance with our explication in Figure 3, we conceive of "reification" as a partial process in the general process of alienation. Thus, with the transition from alienation to reification, comes a concentration on sociological phenomena.

In modern Marxist theory, too, there seems to be a tendency to restrict the discussion of alienation to processes which can be termed reification, although the concept is not always used.[80]

In an interesting essay, the Polish philosopher Adam Schaff defines the process of alienation as reification of the basic process of social production. He writes that "the products of human activity under certain social conditions function not only self-dependently (i.e., *independent* of the will and *intentions* of their creators), but even *against their will and intentions*, thwarting their plans and even one way or another threatening them."[81] (My italics.)

The description fits the characteristics of bureaucratic organization in the socialist countries as well as it fits any other process. Thus the concept of reification can be used, independently of the social structure of a society, to describe social processes.

We will now replace the description with a diagram.

HI stands for "human intentions." PP again represents the social process of production. In our diagram PP is influenced by HI. PP leads to the

---

[80] D. Ogurzov, chapter on "Alienation" in *Soviet Philosophical Encyclopedia*, Moscow (I have used a mimeographed version of the chapter, received by the author).

[81] A. Schaff, "Alienation och social verksamhet" ["Alienation and Social Activity"], *Bonniers Litterära Månadsskrift* 36 (1967), 609.

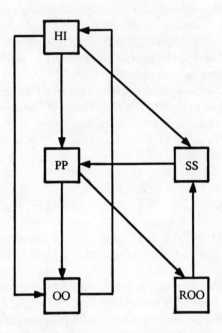

Figure 4.   Diagrammatic representation of reification process.

creation of objects and organizations, within which framework the process
of production occurs. The box OO denotes objects and organizations.
They also are influenced by the intentions of man (*nota bene*) if there
are no reification processes. OO influences HI. In addition we have one
box SS referring to the social system, which is created by HI and which
in turn affects PP. A "normal" nonreified system would consist of boxes
HI, PP, OO, and SS forming a system, in which all boxes are related to
each other as the arrows indicate.

When under given social conditions the process of reification is insti-
tuted, objects and organizations become independent of HI. We add a
new box labeled ROO, i.e., reified objects and organizations. We are now
in a position to construct another system PP—ROO—SS, a closed system,
which functions independently of HI, i.e., of human will and intentions.

4
SOME ADDITIONAL PROBLEMS OF MARXIAN THEORIES

INTRODUCTION

We have previously put forward the hypothesis that the first theory of alienation developed by Marx in *Manuscripts* is built upon a philosophical-anthropological theory of man and has strong normative elements, which in their turn are part of a humanistic-ethical system.

In this chapter we will try to analyze in greater detail the theory of man held by the young Marx. In addition we will show how the normative notion in general came into his scientific approach.

We will also attempt to present our argument in more detail than was possible in the previous chapter and to analyze the picture of man which Marx held after his break with the traditions of Hegel and Feuerbach. Despite contrary interpretations[1] we maintain that important humanistic elements are also contained in Marx's later theories.

However, the term *humanism* is not unambiguous and unproblematic. Therefore it seems desirable to attempt a semantic analysis of the ways in which Marx uses the term. This will be our third task.

Finally there is a special problem connected with the theory of man, which we intend to elaborate (to some extent). Its point of departure is Marx's sociological hypothesis concerning the relationship between social existence—the individual's social position—and consciousness, i.e., his perception of reality. One of the concepts developed in this context is "false consciousness," and we will analyze its meaning.

[1] L. Althusser, *Pour Marx* (Paris: Librairie Maspero S.A., 1965).

MARX'S THEORY OF HUMAN NATURE

SOME ASSUMPTIONS

How are the philosophical-anthropological notions related to the normative-ethical ones? We will present a number of hypotheses concerning the background of the young Marx's theory of man.

After considering his description of the different states of alienation in which man is to be found, it may be asked: Why should man experience himself as alienated when his daily activity is no longer perceived as creative? Why should he feel alienated when he cannot appropriate the products of his work? Why does his daily activity estrange him from mankind or from the essence of species?

The answer is that assumptions must be made concerning the "normal" or "ideal" type of work-activity, concerning man's "natural" relationship to the products of his work, and concerning the nature or the essence of the species, in order to hypothesize that under given social conditions man will feel alienated.

It follows, then, that what is required is (1) a theory of man, (2) a theory of the ideal type of work-activity (which could be a separate theory or an integrate part of the theory of man).

However, there is an further aspect. Marx often speaks about the "dehumanizing" effect which the conditions of capitalistic society have on man. But all assumptions concerning "dehumanization" presuppose the acceptance of certain normative-ethical standards of what constitutes "a humanized life."

This emerges clearly when comparing Marx's analysis of capitalistic society with that of Max Weber.[2] He, too, analyzes the conditions of capitalistic production in a very detailed way, but by strictly applying his thesis concerning value-free science (in itself a value!) he reaches completely different conclusions from those reached by Marx. He starts from the criteria of effectiveness and efficiency (these criteria also being built upon value judgments) with regard to a specific goal, namely, the maximation of profit; and he analyzes bureaucracy as the most effective method of administration. Only occasionally does he express his uneasiness about the consequences for men of this effective system. "At times he expressed profound antipathy for the standardization and devaluation of life by the bureaucratic machinery, but he was unable to reconcile the determinism of his theoretical system with this."[3]

[2] M. Weber, *Economy and Society*, ed. G. Roth and C. Wittich (New York: Bedminster Press, 1968). See also the next chapter.

[3] G. Kolko, "A Critique of Max Weber's Philosophy of History," *Ethics LXX*, No. 1 (1959), 29.

As a result, the problem of dehumanization is not salient in his writings. Marx, too, has a deterministic theoretical system, but he never dissociates himself from his value premises.

Now let us formulate a few hypotheses.

In Marx's theory concerning human nature, man is always portrayed as an *active* being, as a subject in the historical process, creating history and, by means of the basic process of social production, *creating himself*. The basic process of production is also referred to as *praxis*. In Marx's earlier works it is used as the opposite of philosophical speculation.

"All social life is essentially *practical*. All the mysteries which lead theory towards mysticism find their rational solution in human practice and in the comprehension of this practice,"[4] says Marx in the eight of his theses about Feuerbach with his fierce rejection of German speculative, idealistic philosophy.

Thus three concepts are essential: (1) the active subject, which by (2) *social practice* originates (3) the process of *self-creation* of man.

All human activity is goal-directed. If one does not confine oneself to establishing this fact, but, as Marx does, wants to participate in the setting up of goals, one has to introduce values, i.e., normative standards.

Our *first hypothesis* can be formulated as follows: Marx's view of man as an active, creating being leads him to analyze the goals of this activity, and in this way normative (ethical) standards are introduced into his theory.

However, praxis has yet another function in Marx's thinking: "Man must prove the truth, i.e., the reality and power, the 'this-sidedness' of his thinking in practice. The dispute over the reality of or nonreality of thinking that is isolated from practice is a purely *scholastic* question."[5]

From this quotation it becomes clear that *practice* is used as an important criteria, *the important* criteria in the epistemological theory, which Marx develops.

In an interesting analysis the Polish philosopher Kolakowski[6] compares Marx's epistemology to that developed by pragmatism. According to Kolakowski the epistemology of Marx starts from the practical activity of man which, being instrumental behavior, is thus goal-directed. Practical activity or praxis is an important criteria for knowledge.

In the first place it functions as a *selective factor* which orients man's interest toward certain objects. In the *second* place it is used as a *criterion to validate* knowledge obtained. In the third place it furnishes the *tools*

[4] *Mega I.5*, p. 534.

[5] Ibid., p. 533.

[6] L. Kolakowski, *Traktat über die Unsterblichkeit der Vernuft* (Munich: R. Piper & Co. Verlag, 1967).

with the help of which man can *organize* his knowledge within a certain system of intellectual organization.[7]

The theory of knowledge as developed by Marx and interpreted by Kolakowski corresponds very highly to the strategy employed in scientific activity: selection of certain problems, their organization into a theoretical system, and their testing against reality.

For our reasoning it is important to underline the fact that in Marx's epistemology *praxis* functions as a selective factor, an assumption which is in agreement with theories concerning selectivity in perception.[8] "The things which constitute our world are selected things," says Kolakowski.[9]

Selection, however, means choice, i.e., the establishment of preferences; but preferences can be established only with the help of value-premises.

Therefore the testing of reality and its organization into theoretical categories presupposes *value-standards*.

Our *second hypothesis*, then, states that the role played by praxis in the epistemology of Marx introduces normative elements in his theory.

In Marx's thinking there is a certain dialectic relationship between theory and praxis. If praxis is used as a truth-criterion, it influences theory, while theory, i.e., the intellectual organization of sense-data, influences praxis. Thus there exists a continuous interplay between theory and praxis, where theory determines praxis and praxis corrects and reorganizes theory. There is a steady interplay between theoretical and normative elements: praxis defines preferences and choices and so directs the search for knowledge into a certain direction. This interplay between theory and praxis is expressed by Marx in the following terms: "The philosophers have only *interpreted* the world in different ways; the point is to change it."[10]

Change, however, means change in a given direction, and this is determined by certain goals and values. Two aspects can be differentiated in Marx's theory. One is the sociological-economical analysis of capitalist society. The other side is the development of a messianic vision concerning a future society which is characterized by man's mastery of nature, his own included.[11]

Thus our *third hypothesis* assumes that the goal of creating an ideal "classless" society also introduces values into the theory and that these values are part of a humanistic ethic.

Messianic visions can contain notions on two levels. One is the *societal*

---

[7] Ibid., p. 68.

[8] See, e.g., J. Israel, *Socialpsykologi* (Stockholm: Svenska Bokförlaget, 1963).

[9] Kolakowski, *Traktat*, p. 76.

[10] *Mega I.5*, p. 535.

[11] K. Lichtheim, *Marxism* (London: Routledge and Kegan Paul, 1961).

level, where the creation of an ideal society is put forward, and where certain social values, such as equality, social justice, and liberty, are realized. However, notions of a messianic state can also include ideas about *individual self-realization.*

To the extent that Marx's messianic visions contain notions of the realization not only of social, but also of individual goals, another normative aspect is introduced. Theories about human self-realization implicitly presuppose normative notions. These concern those aspects of "human nature" which a man *ought* to realize and those which should be repressed.

Assume that one defines "self-realization" as "the individual's chances of expressing its talents and capacities and of acting according to his needs." This is a fairly common definition of "self-realization" and appears reasonable, at least at first sight.

But it is easy to show that this is too broad a definition. It fails to clarify which talents and capacities should be expressed and which needs should be satisfied. It is impossible to maintain that this should be true for *all* talents, capacities, and needs. A person with strong sadistic needs would certainly not be permitted to "realize himself" in most societies, given certain values. In another words, when speaking about self-realization, restrictions have to be introduced which are based on a set of values. Otherwise self-realization would mean the right for everyone to act in accordance with his strivings, and this is not possible.

We would like to illustrate this with an example given by the Hungarian philosopher Almasi who, in an essay about problems of alienation in socialist societies, refers to bureaucratic tendencies. He characterizes the behavior of a bureaucrat toward his clients as follows: "He finds pleasure in self-expression, such as exact and flowery composition and inhuman formalities. . . ."[12]

Our conclusion that theories concerning individual self-realization are based upon value-judgments leads us to formulate our *fourth hypothesis.*

To the extent that Marx includes individual self-realization in his goals, once again normative assumptions are injected into his theory. (A special problem is whether Marx considers individual self-realization independently of his social goals. In fact, he sees individual self-realization as possible only within and through society.)

We have given, in the form of hypotheses, four reasons which lead one to expect normative elements in Marx's theories: (1) his image of man as an active, goal-directed being, (2) his epistemology and the interplay of theory and praxis, (3) his messianic vision concerning future society, and finally (4) his notion of human self-realization.

[12] M. Almasi, "Alienation and Socialism," in *Marxism and Alienation,* ed. H. Aptheker (New York: Humanities Press, 1965).

A particular difficulty here is the role of values in social science, but a discussion of this problem will be deferred until the end of the final chapter.

THE ROLE OF DETERMINISM IN MARX'S THEORY OF MAN

A central notion in Marx's theory of man is the dependence of man's consciousness, his perception of reality, on his social position. As early as in *The German Ideology* he says: "The production of ideas, conceptions in short of consciousness, is at first directly interwoven with the material activity and material intercourse of men. . . ."[13]

Here Marx develops an empirical hypothesis with a clearly sociological content. He is aware of his empirical position because in the continuation of the quoted lines he declares that, unlike German idealistic philosophy which descends from heaven to earth, he wishes to move in the opposite direction. His point of departure is not taken from a notion about man nor from a human ideal type. Rather he tries to start from "real man." Real man is active man involved in his life-process, i.e., the basic social production of material life. "Life is not determined by consciousness, but consciousness by life."[14]

It has been often asserted that Marx's theory about man's activity, and especially of human cognitive processes, is a sociological-deterministic one. Man is the product of his social relations, which in turn are dependent on the mode of production. Thus man is shaped by social, particularly economic, conditions. He is the product of an economic determinism.

This is a false picture, though it is not unusual in vulgar interpretations of Marxism, even those of Marxists[15] themselves. Man *is* certainly a product of social, especially economic, conditions, but it is man himself who creates and changes these conditions. There exists a dialectic interplay, seen in a historical perspective, between man as active, self-creating subject and man as an object of the conditions he has created.

Marx does not conceive of history as a force striving relentlessly in a certain direction. On the contrary, he makes it perfectly clear that this is not the case. Very expressively he says: "*History* does *nothing*; it 'does

---

[13] *Mega I.5*, p. 15.

[14] Ibid., p. 16.

[15] During the Stalin-period this was the usual interpretation of Marxism. It has been pictured as a one-sided, economical, deterministic theory considering man as the product of social pressures to which he is exposed. In attempts to counterbalance this Stalinist interpretation of Marxism, anti-Stalinist Marxists have tried to emphasize the humanistic aspects of Marxism and to develop a "humanistic Marxism." This emphasis has played an important role in the discussion in Poland, Yugoslavia, etc. (See, e.g., *Socialist Humanism*, ed. E. Fromm (Garden City: Doubleday & Co., 1965.)

not possess immenses riches,' it 'does *not* fight battles.' It is *men*, real, living men, who do all this, who possess things and fight battles. It is not 'history' which uses men as a means of achieving—as it were an individual person—*its* own ends. History is *nothing* but the activity of men in pursuits of their ends."[16]

Therefore we can reject the interpretation of economic determinism, a rejection which should already have become clear when we discuss Marx's notion of "self-creation": "Men are the producers of their conceptions, ideas, etc.—real, active men, as they are conditioned by a determinate development of their productive forces."[17] In a condensed way this is the content of Marx's sociological thesis.

Another common error should also be corrected. As Erich Fromm[18] and others have several times pointed out, there is a psychological interpretation of Marx's "historical materialism." This is a grave misinterpretation. Its content is that Marx's theory of historical materialism is really a theory about human motivation. According to this interpretation, the driving forces of human behavior are individuals' desires to satisfy material needs, to strive for property and things to own, and for a high standard of living, etc. In general, the craving to own things, man's greed, is the central motivating force. Such needs can be used to explain individual behavior and the development of society, but nothing could be more erroneous than such an interpretation of Marx's materialism.

Marx refuses to use psychological explanations for social phenomena. If he speaks of greed, he attributes this motive to the prevailing conditions in capitalistic society, especially to the existence of private property.

Karl Popper, who is generally critical of Marx and his theories, points out as a great asset this *anti-psychologism* of Marx.[19] By "psychologism"

---

[16] *Mega I.3*, p. 265.

[17] *Mega I.5*, p. 17.

[18] E. Fromm, "Problems of Interpreting Marx," in *The New Sociology*, ed. I. L. Horowitz (New York: Oxford University Press, 1965). Fromm gives an interesting example of a false interpretation of Marx through an incorrect translation of *Economic and Philosophical Manuscripts*. There is found a sentence in which Marx asserts that the only wheel which political economy sets in motion is greed. In other words, Marx asserts that the economical theories of his time motivated man to develop greed. In a book by Robert Tucker (*Philosophy and Myth in Karl Marx*, Cambridge: At the University Press, 1961) the sentence is translated in the following way: "The only wheels that set political economy in motion are greed and the war between the greedy." Whereas in Marx's original sentence political economy is the *subject*, in this translation "greed" has become the subject. Therefore, Tucker asserts that "Marx believed that greed, a passion much more profound than the calculating self-interest of the classical economist 'economic man' was a maniacal obsession of man" (Fromm, "Problems," p. 190). Fromm adds that an error in translation easily can occur, but the meaning of Marx's text is clear and unequivocal.

[19] K. Popper, *The Open Society and Its Enemies*, Vol. II (London: George Routledge & Sons, 1946).

Popper means the tendency to explain sociological phenomena in terms
of psychological mechanisms, e.g., individual motivation. Such a procedure
implies the attempt to reduce sociological laws to psychological ones.
Marx never shows any inclination for this type of reductionism. He has a
sociological point of departure, and his level of explanation is always a
sociological one. According to him, social phenomena must be explained
with reference to social institutions, to the social structure of society, to
the mode of production, to the level of development of productive forces,
and to existing social relations within the sphere of the process of social
production.

SOME GENERAL ELEMENTS IN YOUNG MARX'S THEORY OF MAN

The rejection of psychologism and the use of a sociological level of explanation for social phenomena does not exclude a theory of human
nature. Social conditions affect man and his basic nature, but human nature
is used to explain existing social conditions. A theory of human nature,
on the other hand, can be used to postulate how society ought to develop
in order that this human nature can be realized.

Among Marxists the need for a theory of human nature has sometimes
been denied. Schaff, for example, discusses a thesis first suggested by
Lukács.[20] The rejection of psychologism has been formulated in this thesis
in the following way. It is impossible to understand or to explain the
individual if one considers him as an isolated being. Instead one should
consider him in terms of the network of social relations of which he is a
part, and of his "situation" in general.[21] Therefore accepting this thesis,
it has been asserted that a theory about the individual and his nature is
unnecessary from a Marxist point of view.

Schaff objects to this assumption by declaring that, on the one hand,
human behavior can be *explained* in terms of the individual's social relations; and, on the other hand, it can be asked: How is this individual,
shaped by his social relations, made up?[22]

Naturally this argument could also be objected to by contending that
from an "interactionist" point of view an individual's psychological make-
up, his personality, is shaped by the evaluations which others make of his
behavior; and so human behavior can be fully explained in terms of social

[20] A. Schaff, *Marxismus und das menschliche Individuum* (Vienna, Frankfurt, Zürich:
Europa Verlag, 1965).

[21] The idea of a "situational approach," which would enable sociology to develop an
"autonomous theory" without risks for reductionism, has been put forward by Karl
Popper in "Die Logik der Sozialwissenschaften," *Kölner Zeitschrift für Soziologie
und Sozialpsychologie* XIV (1962), 232–48.

[22] Schaff, *Marxismus*, p. 94.

interaction, the evaluation of the individual's behavior by others and his perception of the judgments of others—especially "significant others." (However, even a theory like this *is* a theory about "human nature.")

One could progress a step further and discuss the problem of how an individual ought to be shaped in order to reach certain goals or to realize certain values. Thus, for the discussion of a future society or "self-realized" man, a theory about man is still required.[23]

To understand the theories about man developed by the young Marx, one must understand the climate of thought in which he lived and which he tried to criticize. A large part of his early work is dedicated to polemics against German idealistic philosophy, especially against Hegel and the "Young Hegelians." Their speculations about man were often so fantastic that to Marx it must have been like a revelation when Feuerbach pointed out that man, too, was an object in the sensuous world, not only a spiritual thing. Schaff makes the comment that the thesis developed by Feuerbach —that philosophy's starting point should be the living being "the man consisting of blood and bones"—today seems self-evident and common-place, but in Marx's youth it was a discovery with a revolutionary meaning.[24]

Marx opposed speculative philosophy, though he made use of its terminology, and this has to be taken into consideration when discussing his theory of man. It is the terminology which sometimes creates the difficulties and problems of interpretations.

The *first element* in Marx's view of man is the notion that man is a *natural being*. This means, as we have intimated, that man is an active and acting being: "As a natural being, and as a living natural being he is, on the one hand, endowed with *natural powers* and *faculties*, which exists in him as tendencies and abilities, as *drives*. On the other hand, as a natural, embodied sentient, objective being he is a *suffering*, conditioned and limited being."[25]

Man is conceived of both as a biological and a social being, endowed with drives, whose objects are other beings or nature. This makes man work in order to transform nature into objects of need-satisfaction.

As Baczko[26] points out in an interesting analysis, the term *need* is used by Marx in a broad sense and includes biological needs as well as acquired

---

[23] D. Bell in his book *The End of Ideology* (Glencoe, Ill.: The Free Press, 1960) has discussed the problem of an ideal human being as a prerequisite for an ideal society in connection with Marx's theory of alienation.

[24] Schaff, *Marximus*, p. 37.

[25] *Mega I.3*, p. 160.

[26] B. Baczko, "Marx and the Idea of the Universality of Man," in *Socialist Humanism*, ed. E. Fromm (Garden City: Doubleday & Co., 1965).

ones. These latter are a consequence of man's basic activity, which both creates and satisfies needs, the satisfaction inducing a search for new needs.

The *second element* in Marx's view about human nature concerns man's basically social character. Man cannot exist without social relations. Therefore society is a consequence of man's basic social character. As early as in *Manuscripts* he develops the following idea, which he continuously returns to: "It is above all necessary to avoid postulating 'society' once again as an abstraction confronting the individual. The individual is the *social being*. The manifestations of his life—even when it does not appear directly in the form of a social manifestation, accomplished in association with other men—is, therefore, a manifestation and affirmation of *social life*."[27]

It is worthwhile to observe that in this quotation Marx not only underlines the social character of man, but also refutes the idea of a conflict between the individual and an "abstract" "entity" society. For Marx society is the sum total of all human relations.[28]

In the first chapter we postulated that the idea of a conflict between the individual and society is usually implicit in theories of alienation, but that Marx rejects such a view and places the conflict *within* society— between social classes whose interests clash with each other. Therefore the notion of a class conflict in Marx's theory can be derived from his sociological analysis as well as from his image of man.

We come now to the *third element* in Marx's view of man. Marx asks himself: Is there anything which is typical for the human species, something by which man can be characterized and at the same time be differentiated from the animal? He offers this answer: "Men can be distinguished from animals by consciousness, by religion, or by anything one likes. They themselves begin to distinguish themselves from animals as soon as they begin to *produce* their means of subsistence, a step which is determined by their physical constitution. In producing their means of subsistence men produce their actual material life."[29]

Marx is here speaking of what we have discussed several times earlier: the *role of labor* in the context of material production as a means for the

---

[27] *Mega I.3*, p. 117.

[28] Schaff, *Marxismus*, p. 94.

[29] *Mega I.5*, p. 10. Marx has taken over this idea from Hegel. He says, referring to Hegel's *Phenomenology*, that its outstanding achievement is the fact that "Hegel grasps the self-creation of man as a process . . . and that he, therefore, grasps the nature of *labor* and conceives objective man (true, because real man) as the result of his *own labor*" (*Mega I.3*, p. 16). Hannah Arendt in her book *The Human Condition* (Chicago: University of Chicago Press, 1958) points out that the same idea is found in the writings of Hume, which repeatedly say that it is neither thought nor reason which differentiates man from the animal, but labor (p. 86).

self-creation of man, i.e., the role of praxis. If labor is the characteristic which differentiates the human species from other animals, the problem arises that even animals work and at least partly produce their means of subsistence. Marx's reply to this objection is that man's work-activity differs from animal-activity[30] in *five ways*:

(a) When animals build nests and dwellings, they produce what is "strictly necessary for themselves or their young"; man, however, produces with a broader perspective and produces objects which are not, or not immediately, necessary for need-satisfaction. In Marx's terms man produces in a *universal way*.

(b) The only motive which activates animals is that created by need-tensions. Their activity is compulsive. Man, however, produces independent of actual physical needs and "only truly produces in freedom from such needs."

(c) Animal produces and reproduces only itself. Man, however, produces by changing and "humanizing" all nature. Thus by his production he broadens his life-sphere and creates new needs, which in turn become motives to enlarge his activity and to include still larger parts of nature in these activities.

(d) The products which an animal can create are completely dependent on a given anatomical and physiological structure. But for his part man stands "free in the face of his products." He develops and uses the most complicated means of production.

(e) Finally, the animal can produce only in the way which is typical for its species. Man, however, "knows how to produce in accordance with the standards of every species." Thus man can produce according to any standards, e.g., those of esthetics.

In summary, man's life-activity is characterized by producing within a universal perspective and independent of immediate needs. Furthermore, by so doing, man extends the area of activity and humanizes nature. He uses complex tools and diverse standards in his production.

There is a *fourth and final element* in Marx's thinking about the nature of man. "Though man is a unique individual—and it is just his particularity which makes him an individual, a really individual communial being—he is equally the *totality*, the ideal totality. . . . He exists in reality as the representation and the real mind of social existence, and as the sum of human manifestations of life."[31]

The fourth element, therefore, is man's totality. What does the concept mean? Marx seems to use it in at least two senses. He speaks about man

---

[30] *Mega I.3*, p. 88.
[31] Ibid., p. 117.

as an "ideal totality," which can be interpreted: "man being an ideal type is endowed with all the potentialities which characterize the species and which can be increasingly manifested as society and its productive forces develop. He represents all possible manifestation of human activity within society. He represents 'society as thought and experienced.' "[32]

The other meaning of "totality" refers to the individual and his chances of realizing *all his capacities and talents* under given social conditions. According to Marx, it is primarily the existence of private property that prevents man's comprehensive realization. "Private property has made us so stupid and partial that an object is only *ours* when we have it, when it exists for us as capital or when it is directly eaten, drunk, worn, inhabited, etc., in short, *utilized* in some way."[33]

The quotation not only represents a clear refutation of the psychologistic interpretation of Marx's theory (see the discussion on page 69), but also gives an inkling of man's possibilities for "total appropriation" of that which surrounds him, when he no longer has a instrumental relation to his surroundings. Thus, according to Marx, the abolition of private property should extend man's chances of total realization. Marx expresses this idea in the following way: "Man appropriates his manifold being in an all-inclusive way, and thus as a whole man. All his *human* ways of relating himself to the world—seeing, hearing, smelling, tasting, touching, thinking, observing, feeling, desiring, acting, loving—in short all the organs of his individuality, like the organs which are directly social in form, are in their objective action (their *action in relation to the object*) the appropriation of this object, the appropriation of human reality."[34]

Thus notion of the "total human being" coincides to a certain extent with the first element in Marx's theory about man, namely man as a "natural being." Total man in the second sense is man using all his senses, his perception, thinking, and motivation in order to "appropriate the world" and to make it his own. In the notion of "total man" as presented here, there is a clear attachment to German romanticism.

The two notions of "totality" contained in Marx's thinking seem to have a certain relationship to each other. "Total man as an ideal type" as the "essence of the species" is approached by individual man in his historical process of development. When he can "appropriate his world" in the total way described by Marx, he coincides with the ideal type. This is possible only under certain social conditions because "appropriation" is not dependent on psychological conditions, but on the *social conditions* which emancipate man and all his potentialities.

[32] Ibid.
[33] Ibid., p. 118.
[34] Ibid.

MAN AS "SPECIES-BEING"

If we synthesize the first and fourth element in Marx's theory about man, three aspects remain: man is a *social* being, a *universally creative* being, and a *total* being.

The social nature of man is often equated in the works of the young Marx with his "species-being" or "essence." This ambiguous term requires some explanation.

In the following we will equate the term *being* and *essence*, since the German term *Wesen* implies both. Without doubt the term has a metaphysical connotation. All propositions containing the expression *essence* can be classified as metaphysical. However, the term *species-being* also has sociological denotations.

Adam Schaff[35] attempts a semantic analysis of the term and holds that Marx uses it in at least four different ways:

(1) *Man as a social being*. Marx asserts that man is basically a social, i.e., cooperative being. However, under certain social conditions there exists a split between the individual's private life and his social existence. As a private person, man has only his egoistic needs as a motivating force. As a citizen, as a member of society, he should have as his motivating force goals which are common for all.[36] By living under certain social conditions man has been conditioned to experience competitive motives as the dominant one. It is first when social conditions allow him to act according to his cooperative motives that he is a social being, i.e., species-being. This presupposes the abolition of alienation.

(2) *Man as a specimen of mankind*. At an early stage of his development man was part of large tribes or hordes without being really social. Later man became an individual and so the preconditions for social action were created. This interpretation of species-being, used by Marx in *Grundrisse*,[37] is not the most common.

(3) *Man as a consciously acting being*, i.e., as an individual who plans his activity and tries to organize the social process of production.

(4) *Man as an ideal type, social, self-creating, and productive*. Marx makes the distinction between a man's *factual*, i.e., empirical way of being and his "ideal species-being." His factual being is man shaped and influenced by the developmental level of productive forces at given historical periods. Thus a man living in the Middle Ages is different from a man living in a society dominated by modern technology. The ideal type is

[35] Schaff, *Marxismus*, p. 199.
[36] R. Fjellström, "Marx's människosyn" ["Marx's View of Human Nature"], in *Marxism*, ed. Vänsterns Ungdomsförbund (Stockholm, 1967).
[37] Karl Marx, *Grundrisse der Kritik der Politischen Ökonomie* (Rohentwurf) (Berlin: Dietz Verlag, 1953), p. 395.

what man could be if, according to certain normative standards, all his "natural" capabilities and potentialities could be used to the maximum extent. Such an ideal man is a consciously producing individual who rules the productive forces instead of being ruled by them: an individual who is not only active in the satisfaction of his own needs, but who experiences himself as free only when he can create and produce independent of his immediate needs, and who, finally, is a man who produces in cooperation with others and who realizes himself through his contribution to the achievement of common goals.

If "species-being" is this ideal type, it is possible to analyze the "average man" at a given historical stage and thus determine the distance between factual and ideal man.

Marx uses the term *essence* and *species-being* more especially in his early writing, where he is still strongly influenced by Hegelian philosophy and its terminology.

Therefore Marx's concept of man contains metaphysical notions concerning the characteristics which comprise man's essence.

The change occurs when he formulates the previously quoted theses about Feuerbach. As we have indicated, man is there defined as the sum of his social relations, and society as the totality of human relations. In the *Grundrisse*,[38] Marx says, "Society is not comprised of individuals, but expresses the sum of relations in which individuals stand to each other." He further explains by saying that it is senseless to assert that from society's standpoint there is no difference between serf and master, because both are individuals. To be a serf and to be a master expresses social relations. To paraphrase in terms of modern sociology, Marx is here maintaining that society is the sum total of its role-relations. Consequently *Theses about Feuerbach* and *The German Ideology* mark the transition from the philosophical-anthropological to the sociological theory of man. However, as we have already indicated, Marx's sociological theory of man is not restricted to the concept of *homo sociologicus*, i.e., man as the sum of his role-relations. It is supplemented by the notion of historical-developmental states of human nature and by normative notions concerning how man ought to be. These normative notions, both before and after the introduction of the sociological theory of man, are part of a humanistic theory. However, since the term *humanism* is used in many different ways, we must analyze this special meaning with which it is endowed.

HUMANISM IN MARX'S THEORIES

For many people socialism means a social structure with strict centralization and expanded control over the life of the individual. We agree with

[38] Ibid., p. 176.

Erich Fromm when he says, "The goal of socialism for Marx was man's emancipation."[39]

Emancipation means changing those social conditions which, according to Marx, create private property. A society without private property is described in the following manner: "Only then is nature the *basis* of his own *human* experience and a vital element of human reality. The *natural* existence of man has here become his *human* existence and nature itself has become human for him. *The society* is the accomplished union of man with nature, the veritable resurrection of nature, the realized naturalism of man and the realized humanism of nature."[40]

Marx sets up *humanism* and *naturalism* against each other and joins them in a synthesis in which man is united with nature. In order to understand the rather difficult text, and especially the meaning of *naturalism* and *humanism*, we can link the analysis to our previous discussion. When analyzing the criteria concerning the differentiation of human work-activity from the animal one, Marx spoke of the "humanization of nature." This is accomplished by man continuously extending his sphere of productive activity, to include larger and larger parts of "nature."

In this instance man and his activity are placed as opposites to "nature." *Nature* here means *everything which is external to man and those products created by him and to social organizations.* In other words, nature is equated to everything not created by man. We will designate this meaning of nature *external nature.*

However, in another context Marx emphasized that man is a part of nature. "The statement that the physical and mental life of man, and nature, are interdependent means simply that nature is interdependent with itself, for man is a part of nature."[41]

Here "nature" is used with a different meaning, namely *everything organic within the universe, which is not created by man.* In this sense man is a part of nature. We will call this *nature in general.*

But Marx uses the term *nature* in at least a third sense, when he speaks of "human nature." In this instance nature is the same as man's being or essence. "Nature in general" is the widest use. Thereafter comes "external nature," and finally "human nature" is the most restricted sense of the term.

When in the previously quoted lines Marx speaks about "naturalism," I suggest that he refers to the realization of human nature made possible by certain social conditions. In this case "the *natural* existence of man becomes his human existence," i.e., when social conditions allow the realization of "human nature." If "naturalism" means the realization of

---

[39] E. Fromm, *Marx's Concept of Man* (New York: Frederick Ungar Publishing, 1961).
[40] *Mega I,3*, p. 116.
[41] Ibid., p. 87.

human nature, then "humanism" refers to the humanization of *external nature*. If the process of production is organized so that it allows man to realize himself, then external nature can be humanized, i.e., be systematically transferred into the sphere of human need-satisfaction, which in turn facilitates human self-realization. According to this interpretation, the expression in the quotation, "the realized naturalism of man," is equal to "man's nature realized by his own activity." The expression "the realized humanism of nature" is equal to "humanization of external nature in a way which makes possible human self-realization." "Humanism" therefore has to be defined—in this context—in terms of "naturalism."

Through the creation of communist society the synthesis between naturalism and humanism is first accomplished. In this society, too, other dialectic opposites are united into a synthetic whole. There the conflict between man's essence and his actual being, i.e., what he could be and what he actually is in a given historical period is done away with.

We reproduce the magnificent messianic vision which Marx describes: "Communism as a fully developed naturalism is humanism, and as a fully developed humanism is naturalism. It is the *definitive* resolution of the antagonism between man and nature, and between man and man. It is the true solution of the conflict between existence and essence, between objectification and self-affirmation, between freedom and necessity, between individual and species. It is the solution of the riddle of history and knows itself to be this solution."[42]

To summarize: in *Manuscripts* Marx uses the term *humanism* to describe the self-realization of man through his productive activity. Thus we can find three normative aspects in his humanism: (1) a philosophical-anthropological theory with strong normative aspects, (2) notions concerning the importance of creative activity, (3) notions concerning the way man ought to relate himself to this activity as a value in itself. These three normative elements function as a precondition for the notion of alienated labor. Therefore we agree with the Soviet philosopher Dawydow when he remarks that "alienated work consequently turns out to be alienation from the *ideal* of work."[43]

Our next problem is whether the change from an anthropological-philosophical to a sociological theory of man leads to the elimination of normative, and especially humanistic, aspects in Marx's second theory of alienation. Our previous discussion has indicated that we do not think such is the case, but let us analyze it and demonstrate what kinds of humanistic aspects Marx later emphasizes.

We have earlier (see p. 50) quoted from the third volume of Marx's

---

[42] Ibid., p. 114.

[43] J. M. Dawydow, *Freiheit und Entfremdung* (Berlin: VEB Deutscher Verlag der Wissenschaften, 1964).

Capital in which he writes about the necessity of arranging social production in a way that is *"proper and worthy for human nature."*

What does this expression mean? "Proper" and "worthy" cannot be explained by reference to his definition of man. If man is the sum total of his social relations and if this *sum* is human nature, then a sentence referring to "conditions which are proper and worthy for human nature" is nothing more than a tautology. If man is the result of his social relations and this result is equal to human nature, then conditions which are proper and worthy for human nature are nothing other than the same conditions of which man is the result. But I do not think that Marx used a tautology.

He went beyond his definition in using the quoted phrase. In addition to his definition of human nature as resulting from social interaction, he conceives of future man in a future society and of how this man *ought* to function. What is this man like?

We can glean one hint from Marx's theory of value. As mentioned earlier, Marx maintains that the only way to create values is by human work. He dedicates his analysis in *Capital* to demonstrating that value-creating activity is organized so that the products of work become commodities, and that man is ruled by the laws of the commodity market. "Conditions proper and worthy for human nature" would then be those conditions whereby man plans production *rationally* and keeps social and economic processes under his conscious control. If this interpretation is correct (and reference to a great number of Marx's own writings supports such an interpretation), then Marx has a strong rationalistic ethical system: Man should be an active, planning individual who is aware of the consequences of his action, not blindly exposed to them. This type of rationality in which society is controlled by the *conscious intentions* of man is an old humanistic ideal.

There is an alternative interpretation, which nevertheless does not necessarily exclude the first. Marx had a messianic vision concerning future society. "Proper" and "worthy" should then refer to those conditions which make possible the realization of future society: a classless society, i.e., one in which there exists equality among men and where man is not exploited by man. Again, these ideas are traditional elements of a humanistical-ethical system.

Thus, contrary to such authors as Althusser,[44] we reach the conclusion that Marx's theories contain normative elements even after he rejected the philosophical ideas which mark his earliest works.

Adam Schaff[45] points out that each humanistic system has its own theory

[44] Althusser, *Pour Marx.*
[45] Schaff, *Marxismus*, p. 219 ff.

of happiness. Such a theory may be developed in two ways: either in a *positive* way, by describing the preconditions for human happiness; or in a *negative* way, by indicating the conditions for the abolishment of man's unhappiness. Contained in Marx's theories are both the positive and the negative elements. But, more than that, there is a mixture of sociological-economical analysis and of normative-ethical discourse.

Thus Marx has two intentions: (1) the description and analysis of society and its conditions, and (2) the specific goal of creating critical knowledge as a means of freedom and emancipation. In its eagerness to be considered as science and to create a self-image of strictly scientific orientation, sociology in its modern version has abandoned the second task. It is the price paid for being "scientific." The question is whether the results are worth the costs.

"FALSE CONSCIOUSNESS"

SUBJECTIVE EXPERIENCE OF OBJECTIVE ALIENATION PROCESSES

We will now discuss the following interesting theoretical problem: To what degree do objective alienating processes which we have defined as alienation coincide with psychological experiences in the individual, i.e., with the experience of being alienated? Is it so, for example, that people who carry out monotonous work due to the process of the division of labor experience alienation of the type described by Marx? We shall briefly summarize the problem.

Let us make the following assumption: we study a society and find the existence of such alienating processes as Marx described. We interview individuals and find two types of reaction. A certain number of individuals have no experience whatsoever of alienation. Other individuals, though they experience the usual psychological state of alienation, do not consider this psychological state to be something extraordinary. Either they have not thought about it, or they may consider this state as "normal." At the most they may think that something is wrong without their being able to do anything about it.

One interpretation of these psychological states—an interpretation which is in agreement with Marx's theory—is that the sociological alienating processes are either so effective, or have been going on continuously for such a long period, that one no longer experiences them on a cognitive level. Under such conditions they might not appear as "alien to human nature" and its central needs. The lack of insight into one's own situation —for example, the fact that psychological experiences of alienation are not understood as such—should then be interpreted as an additional stage of psychological alienation.[46] This stage could be defined as one in which the individual is so alienated that he no longer experiences his alienation. The psychological state of being alienated could therefore lead to a split between the experience of it, and the analysis of his own situation which the individual carries out and by means of which he becomes aware of it. The result would then be that the subject either does not experience the psychological state of alienation at all, or that he experiences something about which he lacks insight on a cognitive level. This situation could be compared to a situation where a person is mentally sick but lacks insight into his illness. Such ideas concerning the lack of insight into one's own sickness play, as we know, an important role within psychiatry. As an illustration we will quote for a report written by a Swedish State Committee on the problems of mental illness: "A part of the ability to evaluate reality is the capacity to adopt a position with regard to the symptoms of sickness and its consequences, that is to say, to have an insight into one's own sickness. It is possible to achieve such insight only if the individual is capable of treating psychologically his own symptoms and of taking up a position with regard to them and to the measures which it may be necessary to take for their removal."[47]

Lack of insight into one's own sickness means that the subject himself cannot experience symptoms which have been observed by an expert and/or he cannot understand which measures are to be taken to change the situation. In serious cases of lack of insight into his sickness, the individual may be taken into a mental hospital without his consent: "Independently of his own consent and according to rules given below, a mentally sick person may be given care in a mental hospital if such care is necessary with regard to the kind or the degree of sickness."[48]

The comparison between mental illness and the psychological state of alienation is by no means far-fetched. In fact, the term *alienation* is also used in a psychiatric context.[49] In both cases a precondition is that there exist objective or normative criteria (or a mixture of both), according to which it is possible to decide whether a subject lacks insight into his own state. "Unconscious" psychological alienation can have profound consequences for the social action of the individual. If he experiences his situation as "normal," he will rarely reflect on the social conditions which create alienation. Instead he will consider them as normal. He cannot see

[46] P. Berger and S. Pullberg, "The Concept of Reification," *New Left Review* No. 35 (1966), 50–71.

[47] Statens Offentliga Utredningar, *Mentalsjukvården*, Stockholm 1964: 40 [Public Investigations of the Swedish Government], p. 178.

[48] Ibid., p. 14.

[49] J. Gabel, *Ideologie und Schizophrenie* (Frankfurt: S. Fischer, 1967).

them as a cause of his own psychological situation. In such a case the individual is, to use a concept from Marxian theory, in a state where he lacks "class consciousness." In this particular case the lack of class consciousness depends on the fact that the sociological processes of alienation create a state in the individual in which he is able to analyze neither his own psychological problems nor social problems in general.

The mechanism which we have tried to describe can be considered as a special case of the class of phenomena termed "false consciousness"[50] by Marx and Engels.

The point of departure is a well-known thesis of Marx: "Life is not determined by consciousness but consciousness by life."[51] This sociological hypothesis is reformulated later in Marx's famous "Preface to a Contribution to the Critique of Political Economy," in which he says, "It is not the consciousness of man that determines his being, but on the contrary his social being determines his consciousness."[52]

The sentence can be interpreted in different ways. It can be interpreted as a metaphysical proposition or as a sociological hypothesis, depending on the interpretation which one wants to give to the expression *social being*. One reasonable sociological interpretation is that the individual's social background (and, for Marx, his class-belongingness especially) determines his consciousness. The term *consciousness* has a somewhat broader meaning in Marx's theory than as used in psychology.

On the one hand, it refers to the forms of our thinking. In this respect it can be equated to cognitive analytical processes. On the other hand, it refers to the product of our thinking such as ideas, beliefs, and so on.

For Marx the process of thinking and the development of ideas, and therefore of consciousness, is intimately connected with the process of social production, i.e., of material production. In *The German Ideology* he writes thus: "The production of ideas, conceptions and consciousness, is at first directly interwoven with the material activities and the material intercourse of men, the language of real life." Later in the same chapter he says: "Men are the producers of their conceptions, ideas etc.,—real, active men, as they are conditioned by a determinate development of their productive forces and of the intercourse which corresponds to these, up to its most extensive forms. Consciousness can never be anything else but conscious existence, and the existence of man is the actual life process."[53]

50 K. Marx and F. Engels, *Selected Works* in two volumes (Moscow: Foreign Language Publishing House, 1949), Vol. II, p. 451. [Engels's letter to F. Mehring.]
51 *Mega I.5*, pp. 15–16.
52 Marx and Engels, "Preface to a Contribution to the Critique of Political Economy," *Selected Works*, Vol. I, p. 332.
53 *Mega I.5*, pp. 15–16.

It is an interesting fact that Marx has a genetic-developmental theory about consciousness. In many ways this theory reminds one of the theories developed by George Herbert Mead. Marx underlines the importance of language and social interaction for the consciousness of man and also for his self-consciousness.

He also stresses the fact that the awareness of other human beings and of the existence of objects outside man is the first step in the development of self-consciousness. I would like to quote a few lines from his theory of the development of consciousness: "Consciousness is at first, of course, merely an awareness of the immediate sensible environment and of the limited connection with other persons and things outside the individual, who is becoming self-conscious."[54] Further on, Marx continues to talk about the role of language in the development of consciousness, and says: "Language is as old as consciousness, language is practical consciousness, as it exists for other men, and thus as it first really exists for myself as well. Language, like consciousness, only arises from the need, the necessity, of intercourse with other men."[55] Thus the quoted lines reveal the "interactionist" theories which Marx embraced.

If one accepts that the individual's social background determines his ideas and beliefs, i.e., his consciousness, one important question is the following: How is it, for example, that many workers have the same opinions as persons belonging to other social classes, especially in a society which is marked by class antagonism? One possible Marxist explanation is that those people who have opinions which correspond to the opinions of persons belonging to an opposite class have a "false consciousness" which can be defined as "thought that is alienated from the real social being of the thinker."[56]

"False consciousness" is an extremely complicated concept. *One* interpretation may be that a person thinks and has opinions, beliefs, and values, which are not in agreement with his "social existence." Not only are they not in agreement with his social existence, they may even be to the disadvantage of his "real interests" as these are determined by his social position. Assume that the capacity to be creative is part of human "nature." A person who performs work through which he is unable to express his creative abilities ought, in that case—if he feels and thinks in agreement with his "nature"—to experience his work as "unnatural" and react against it. His social position, for example as a low-paid worker in a capitalist enterprise, should determine his consciousness in such a way that he opposes his work and the conditions of his work.

[54] *Mega I.5*, p. 27.
[55] *Mega I.5*, pp. 19–20.
[56] P. Berger and T. Luckman, *The Social Construction of Reality* (Garden City: Doubleday & Co., 1966).

If he fails to do this because he does not consider his work to be something unnatural, and if in addition he does not understand the content or the meaning of his own behavior, he has a "false consciousness." This means that he thinks in an alienated way. He lacks "insight into his own sickness" because he does not experience his own state of alienation.

The theory of "false consciousness," as it has been interpreted here, presupposes in the first place sociological assumptions concerning the relationship between "social existence" and "consciousness." In the second place it presupposes anthropological assumptions about human nature. Those two types of assumptions can be used to make predictions concerning the behavior of a human being or concerning the way he ought to behave in a certain situation.

We will now summarize our reasoning in a number of points:

(1) "Human nature" gives rise to a number of primary needs, N_1, $N_2 \ldots$, N_n, which are common for the human "species." Other needs are learned. We will call them NL_1, $NL_2 \ldots$, NL_n. Finally, as a part of "human nature" there exist certain cognitive processes such as the ability to think, the ability to form a picture of one's environment, and the ability to become conscious of the environment, other people, and oneself. These cognitive processes we will call C_1, $C_2 \ldots$, C_n.

(2) The individual has a certain social position which is a part of the social structure of society.

(3) The content of the cognitive processes is determined by the individual's social position. The content concerns among other things the image of oneself and the image one has concerning one's social environment.

(4) The social structure of society determines the individual's activity, especially that concerning his work as a part of the total processes of social production.

(5) When the individual's activity is not in agreement with N_1, $N_2 \ldots$, N_n, alienation, is created. This gives rise to learned needs, NL_{n+1}, $NL_{n+2} \ldots$, NL_{n+o}.

(6) NL_{n+1}, $NL_{n+2} \ldots$, NL_{n+o} influence the consciousness of the individual in such a way that the content of his cognitive processes become false. Among other things, this means that the individual does not understand that his activity does not satisfy B_1, $B_2 \ldots$, B_n. Neither does he understand that it is the social structure of society which is the main cause of his lack of understanding.

(7) The individual has a "false consciousness," which means a consciousness that is alienated and that therefore prevents the individual from having "insight into his own sickness," both with regard to himself and to the social structure which creates his alienation.

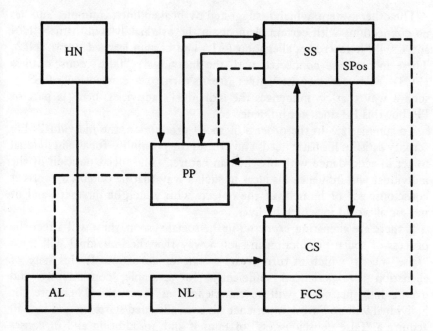

Figure 5. Diagrammatic representation of processes leading to "false consciousness."

Figure 5 illustrates the process which has been described and includes some "feedback mechanisms."[57]

The diagram suggests two systems. Each element or box in the system stands in relation to at least one other element. The one system in which the elements are connected with straight lines is, so to speak, the "normal" system. The social process of production (PP), or the "life activity" of human beings, is partly influenced by human nature (HN) and the needs which are part of it, and partly influenced by the social structure of society (SS). The individual's social position (SPos) influences his consciousness (CS), which in turn creates a picture of PP and SS. In this way PP can affect SS. In this system, with built in feedback mechanisms, the influence occurs most often in two directions.

[57] The idea of depicting the described processes as systems with built-in feedback mechanisms has been inspired by attempts to apply modern system-theory to sociology (see, e.g., W. Buckley, *Sociology and Modern Systems Theory*, Englewood Cliffs: Prentice-Hall, 1967).

The application of system-theory for the interpretation of Marxist theories is facilitated by modern Marxist accounts in which the term *dialectical* sometimes refers to processes which correspond to feedback mechanisms.

The other system, which is suggested by broken lines, is simpler and has no connections with certain elements in the original system, namely HN and Cs. PP here creates alienation (AL) and certain learned needs (NL). These in turn are connected with the individual's "false" consciousness (FCS). False consciousness gives rise in turn to a conception of SS in such a way that SS influences the individual's activities, being a part of PP, but this PP does not influence SS.

To summarize: In the process of social production, the individual's life activity satisfies his basic needs and creates the possibility for the individual to act in accordance with his "human nature." The social position of the individual will influence his ideas in such a way that he obtains a "correct consciousness" of himself, of the objects with which he interacts, and of the social world in which he lives.

If there are alienating *processes* in the social system, they will affect the process of social production in such a way that the individual will learn "false" needs, which in turn create a *state* of alienation. If this state of alienation is experienced sufficiently, for example, continuously and over a long period, it will be experienced as "normal." Therefore the individual will no longer experience his own alienated state. Instead he will acquire a "false consciousness" of himself and, in addition and in consequence of this, false beliefs about his social environment.

Clearly this theory presupposes certain assumptions about the relationship between the individual's social life and his "consciousness." It also presupposes assumptions of a certain *normative* kind about human nature. In this respect, however, there are no differences between the psychiatric theories concerning mental illness and this theory, especially since in theories concerning mental illness normative elements are usually presupposed.

FALSE CONSCIOUSNESS AND INTERESTS

We shall now attempt to give another interpretation of the concept of "false consciousness," although this interpretation is of a sociological-social-psychological type. It presupposes a series of assumptions:

(1) Man strives to act in accordance with his interests.

(2) His "real" or "true" interests are determined by his class belongingness.

(3) Through "scientific" analyses of the social situation of a given class it is possible to determine what, objectively seen, are the "true" interests of man (belonging to a given class).

(4) Not all people are able to carry out such an analysis. This is due to the fact that an analysis of the factual social situation demands a certain minimum amount of knowledge of social, economic, and sociological facts.

For that reason those who cannot analyze the situation cannot know whether they act in accordance with their "true" interests, or against them.

(5) When the knowledge is of such a type that they believe they act in accordance with their "real" interests, but if in fact they act against them, then they have a "false consciousness."

(6) A whole class which has a "false consciousness" can be said to "lack class consciousness." "Class consciousness" can be compared to that consciousness which makes it possible for a certain class and its members to act in accordance with their "real" interests.

This interpretation of "false consciousness" carries with it several interesting problems. Let us accept the first assumption as a postulate, because it can be said to be in agreement with common psychological theories concerning human behavior which is goal-oriented. Such assumptions assert that goals must be seen in relation to the needs and interests, etc., of the individual. The difficulty begins with the second assumption. Assume that a person is given the choice of acting in such a way that he can satisfy his own and his family's (wife and children's) interests or the interests which are determined by his class membership. Take, for example, the situation in which a worker must decide whether to go on strike or to continue his work and thereby take care of his family's needs. What are his "real" interests? Are the interests of his family more "real" than his class interests?

One way of solving the problem is to differentiate between short-term and long-term interests. By making such a distinction one could assert that a decision not to go on strike may possibly satisfy short-term interests, whereas participation in a strike may "in the long run" further the interests of his class and therefore also of the worker and his family. The distinction between short- and long-term interests introduces new difficulties. From a psychological point of view it may be that a person with a given level of knowledge has difficulties in analyzing long-term interests, and would therefore seek the satisfaction of his short-term interests. A further problem which enters in is that social norms in our society often demand identification with the family, with a concrete number of persons, rather than identification with a "class" which consists of a large number of individuals with whom the individual has no direct contact and who are unknown to him. But assume that both the level of knowledge and the possibility of identifying oneself with a class can be found to a sufficient extent. In this case new difficulties may arise. In order to maintain that the "real" interests of an individual are his class interests, it is necessary to define "class" in such a way that the definition makes it possible precisely to define "class interest." If, as is usually the case in Marx's theory, one defines class on the basis of the individual's position in the process of production, two classes result—that which owns the means of production, and the working class, the proletariat. According to such a definition of class, there exist only two types of class interests.

However, social reality is such that "classes" can be constituted on the basis of a greater number of criteria than position in the process of production. For instance, class can be defined with regard to the share of the total social product which the individual receives, i.e., with regard to his income and his standard of living. It can be shown that groups which hold the same position in the production process, who do not own the means of production, have totally different shares in the social product— different levels of income and varying privileges. It seems reasonable to assume that the interests of these groups must force them to defend their own standard of living and their own privileges in relation to other persons who, though they occupy the same position in the process of production, have a lower standard of living. At least, that would be the case in a society characterized by a competitive attitude.

As social reality is much more complicated than is admitted in Marxian class theory, it is very difficult to determine what is "correct" class consciousness and what are the "real interests" of a given class. This is especially true if one disregards long-term developmental tendencies, i.e., if one disregards long-term interests and has to take up a position with regard to a given concrete political question. Take, for example, the fact that in recent years strikes in Sweden have become very rare. Typical exceptions are strikes organized by airline pilots and by university professors; both groups are among the highest paid in Swedish society. The question is: Is it in the interests of the working class to support a strike which would give groups that are already privileged, additional privileges, or would it be in the interests of the working class to counteract this?

What, in this case, become the "true interests of the working class" can very often be equated with the taking up of definite tactical political stands.

Thus it is difficult to decide what the "real interests of the working class" are. They may be determined by at least two types of consideration. One type would be short-term political decisions, sometimes of a tactical nature related to the existing political, social, and economic conditions in a given society. The other type of consideration would take into account long-term goals, e.g., the creation of a socialist society.

Thus, political parties building their activity on Marxist theory are often faced with the dilemma of deciding which concrete decisions should be made in a given situation. As these decisions are complicated and since it is often assumed that workers may have a "false consciousness," it is easy to develop an elite-theory. According to such a theory there exists an avant-garde within the working class which is able to analyze a given situation and which has knowledge of "the true interests of the working class." The people belonging to this elite are usually intellectuals, not workers, and form the leadership of the Communist party. The idea of an elite which is in possession of the knowledge necessary—"the true consciousness"—to decide what is in the "interests of the working class" leads to certain consequences. One of them is the belief that "the authentic consciousness (i.e., the proletarian class consciousness) . . . is nothing more than the totality of reality-adequate theories which are constructed by intellectuals with a non-proletarian background, under the leadership of the working class, represented by the Communist Party."[58]

"The true consciousness" is therefore brought into the working class from outside by the ideologists of the party, who are capable of carrying out necessary "scientific" analyses and of drawing the correct conclusions. Such an illusion can hardly be sustained today when not only is the working class split politically in almost all Western European countries, but also when the world Communist movement no longer consists of one unitarian movement. What for one group may be a theory representing the "real needs of the working class" may for another group or faction appear as "contemptible revisionism," i.e., as an example of "false consciousness."

Let us summarize the second interpretation of "false consciousness." We began with a few psychological and sociological postulates and hypotheses respectively. One of them maintained that the individual's behavior is guided by his interests. Another made a distinction between short-term and long-term interests. Short-term interests are those which arise out of actual needs. Long-term interests are usually those which are related to the achievement of future goals. A third postulate asserted that an individual's "true" interests are those which are based upon his class membership. Thus, the "true" interests of a worker are the interests of the whole working class. The long-term goal of the working class is the overthrow of the capitalist and the creation of the socialist society, because, according to Marxist theory, this goal is a "historical necessity." It is the historical role of the working class to achieve this, just as it was the historical role of the bourgeoisie to overthrow feudal society and to create the bourgeois society. Therefore, all interests the fulfillment of which will facilitate the achievement of the ultimate goal are true interests.

A central problem arises. According to Marx, it is the social position of a man which determines his consciousness. Since Marx takes a rationalistic approach to human behavior, the consciousness of man should determine his interests and therefore his behavior. However, empirical facts indicate that many workers do not act in accordance with their "true" interests.

[58] Gabel, *Ideologie*, p. 9.

These facts can be explained in two ways. First, man is guided by short-term interests more than by long-term interests, partly because short-term interests are often associated with pressing, actual needs. Second, in order to understand long-term interests one requires a certain amount of knowledge, or, in Marx's language, a certain level of consciousness.

For several reasons members of the working class are not always able to acquire a level of consciousness which makes it possible to explain a given situation correctly and to determine what action is adequate, i.e., pursue long-term interests. Instead, they have a "false consciousness." The explanations they use in a given situation lead them to act in a way which is detrimental to the long-term goals of their own class. Therefore, intellectuals who have freed themselves from the fetters of their own social background form an elite. The most "advanced members" of this elite form the collective leadership of the political organizations which represent the "true" interests of the working class. Their day-to-day decisions are conceived of as being built upon a correct analysis and with regard to the long-term interests of the working class.

This presentation of the problems creates not only political problems, as we tried to show, but also a series of theoretical ones which we will try to analyze in the next section.

IDEOLOGY AND FALSE CONSCIOUSNESS

The concept "false consciousness" plays an important role in Marxist reasoning. However, there are very few attempts to analyze it in a more comprehensive way.[59]

In 1893 Engels, in a letter to Franz Mehring, wrote: "Ideology is a process which, by the so-called thinker, is, without doubt, carried out consciously, but with a false consciousness."[60]

This is probably the first time that the term "false consciousness" is used in the works of Marx and Engels. But long before that, both had written about the phenomenon itself, though not using the term.

The concept "false consciousness" is clearly very intimately related to another concept—namely, "ideology." It is therefore necessary to analyze in some detail the meaning of both concepts.

In order to understand the meaning of "ideology" and of "false consciousness" we must state some of the basic theoretical ideas of Marxist philosophy. (In this context it is possible only in a very brief, and therefore limited and superficial, way.) A distinction is usually made be-

---

[59] See, e.g., Gabel, *Ideologie*; and J. Szacki, "Remarks on the Marxian Concept of 'False Consciousness,'" *The Polish Sociological Bulletin* No. 2(14) (1966), 30–39.
[60] Marx and Engels, *Selected Works*, Vol. II, p. 451.

tween "dialectical materialism" and "historical materialism." The former is concerned with problems of epistemology, the latter with sociological-economic problems seen in a historical perspective. Therefore, "dialectical materialism" is mainly concerned with philosophical problems regarding the process of knowledge, whereas "historical materialism" deals with problems belonging to the social sciences.

One basic question in "dialectical materialism" concerns the way in which knowledge comes about. Engels, for example, writes in his main philosophical work[61] that thinking and consciousness are products of the human brain. Since man is a "product of nature," the products of the human brain are also "natural products." The next question becomes; What is "nature"? In one sense "nature" is "materia." Thus the problem concerning the creation and development of knowledge may be reduced to the problem of the relationship between "materia" and "ideas." Several solutions have been discussed. One maintains that ideas merely "reflect" materia and that correct knowledge is possible as a process by which nature is reflected in ideas, as in a mirror. This "mirror-theory" has been criticized severely. In fact, the whole problem of the relationship between "materia" and "thinking" can be refuted as a metaphysical one.

The idea of a mere reflection does not agree with another idea which is central to "historical materialism." This second idea is the previously stated hypothesis concerning the relationship between the individual's social position and his thinking, or consciousness. The Marxian hypothesis implies that consciousness is *influenced* by social conditions. Thus, this hypothesis refutes the idea of the "mirror-theory." Instead, it brings forward the important problem, which is not metaphysical, but empirical, of how social position—for example, class-belongingness—affects consciousness.

Now the relationship between social position and consciousness is in its turn only a special case of a much more general problem. This concerns the relationship between the process of social production (or "material production") and systems of ideas and knowledge, such as science, the legal system, morals, the arts, etc. As we will deal with this problem in the final chapter, at this point we will only mention the basic Marxian formulation of the problem. Marx considered the social process of production —the way in which people produce and reproduce the material conditions of their life—as a basic determining process. He calls it the *material basis*. The systems of ideas and knowledge, then, are considered to constitute the "ideological superstructure." Thus, in this sense, *ideology* means the total superstructure of ideas and knowledge related to the material basis. Again, a problem is the type of relationship between "material" basis and

[61] Marx and Engels, *Selected Works*, Vol. II, pp. 86–142.

"ideological superstructure." It could be a "mirror-image relationship," i.e., the superstructure only means a reflection of the material basis. It could, however, be a different relationship, in which "ideology" in turn may influence the "material conditions."[62] We will return to these problems in the final chapter.

To summarize: "Ideology" in its first sense can be equated with the system of ideas and knowledge forming the superstructure and being related by a certain (here unspecified) relationship to the material basis of the process of social production.

In this definition nothing is said about the problem of whether the systems of knowledge defined as ideology represent true or false knowledge, and thus no evaluation of the truth-value of an ideology is made.

However, "ideology" has also acquired another meaning in Marxist theorizing. Building on the principle that the social situation of a man determines his systems of ideas, i.e., his consciousness, one tries to find out in what way this influence works. "This means that opinions, statements, propositions and systems of ideas are not taken at their face value but are interpreted in the light of the life situation of the one expressing them. It further signifies that the specific character and life situation of the subject influences his opinions, perceptions and interpretations."[63]

Thus, an "ideology" is a system of thought developed by an individual against the background of his social position and general life-situation. Mannheim calls this the "particular conception" of ideology as opposed to the total conception.[64] The latter refers to the ideology of a historical epoch, or of a whole group or class within a given historical period.

With regard to the analysis of *total ideologies*, Mannheim makes a distinction between the approach characterized by freedom from value-judgments, and a second approach which is normatively oriented.

The first approach is characterized by Mannheim in the following way: "The non-evaluative general total conception of ideology is to be found primarily in those historical investigations, where provisionally for the sake of the simplification of the problem, no judgments are pronounced as to the correctness of the ideas to be treated. This approach confines itself to discovering the relations between certain mental structures and the life-situation in which they exist. We must constantly ask ourselves how it comes about that a given type of social situation gives rise to a given interpretation. Thus the ideological element is human thought,

---

[62] A typical example is Max Weber's theory concerning the effect of Protestant puritanism on the development of the capitalistic mode of production (see chapter 5).
[63] K. Mannheim, *Ideology and Utopia* (London: Routledge & Kegan Paul, 1954), pp. 50, 49, 71, 38, 85. Copyright © 1954 by Routledge & Kegan Paul, Ltd. Reprinted by permission of Routledge & Kegan Paul, Ltd. and Harcourt Brace Jovanovich, Inc.
[64] Ibid., p. 49 ff.

viewed at this level, and is always bound up with the existing life-situations of the thinker. According to this view human thought arises, and operates, not in a social vacuum but in a definite social milieu."[65]

The non-evaluative approach is mainly a methodological orientation, the aim of which is to discover relations between social conditions and the experience of reality as expressed in systems of knowledge.

When undertaking this analysis, however, one may find that distortions of reality occur. These distortions have a certain social function. They operate as "rationalizations" in the psycholoanalytical sense. They provide scientific, or quasi-scientific, explanations for existing social and economic conditions in order to defend certain basic interests.

Thus, Mannheim goes a step further. The thought system used by a ruling class is defined as "ideology," whereas the thought systems of oppressed groups, sketching a social change, are labeled "utopias." Mannheim writes:

The concept "ideology" reflects the one discovery which emerged from political conflict, namely that ruling groups can in their thinking become so intensively interest-bound to a situation that they are simply no longer able to see certain facts which would undermine their sense of domination. There is implicit in this word "ideology" the insight that in certain situations the collective unconsciousness of certain groups obscures the real condition of society, both to itself and to others, and thereby stabilises it.

The concept of *utopian* thinking reflects the opposite discovery of the political struggle, namely that certain oppressed groups are intellectually so strongly interested in the destruction and transformation of a given condition of society that they unwittingly see only those elements in the situation which tend to negate it. Their thinking is incapable of correctly diagnosing an existing condition of society. They are not at all concerned with what really exists; rather, in their thinking they already seek to change the situation that exists. Their thought is never a diagnosis of the situation, it can be used only as a direction for action.[66]

Thus "ideology" in this sense has a conserving function, whereas thought systems abstracting from existing conditions are defined as "utopias."

Our next step is to establish the relationship between "ideology" and "false consciousness." A person can be said to have a false consciousness when he is in a state of alienation, especially of self-alienation. This state prevents him from acquiring knowledge which is congruent with the

[65] Ibid., p. 71.
[66] Ibid., p. 38.

interest developed out of his social situation. Instead he accepts ideologies in the sense of "distorted thought systems." This in turn prevents him from certain types of social action, for example, action aimed at changing existing social conditions.

This concept of false consciousness presupposes certain assumptions in addition to those presented in previous sections. First, it requires a conflict theory concerning society. It particularly presupposes the existence of class antagonism based upon incompatible interests. Second, it presupposes a normative approach to the analysis of ideology. A system of thought, a theory in this case, is true only in relationship to certain practical consequences. "A theory then is wrong if in a given practical situation it uses concepts and categories, which if taken seriously would prevent man from adjusting to himself at that historical stage," says Mannheim.[67] So the concept of false consciousness has to be related to the Marxian concept of praxis and the pragmatist theory of knowledge in the Marxist version (see the discussion on pages 65–66).

The evaluative approach to ideology as compared with the non-evaluative wants to establish not only relationships between a social situation and a certain individual or common interests, but also certain future goals and certain thought systems or theories. Only those theories which help to create social action in accordance with certain well-defined basic interests toward certain goals are then defined as "true" ones.

A person who has a "false consciousness," i.e., who accepts ideologies, may do so either because he does not understand his "true interests" or because he does not accept certain goals which, from the point of view of a given normative system, he should accept. Therefore, false consciousness refers either to "incorrect knowledge" or to "incorrect preconditions" preventing the acquisition of knowledge. This theory of false consciousness also presupposes certain criteria as to what can be judged as false or correct. These criteria are normative ones, and truth is seen in relation to consequence or praxis.

Finally, we should remind ourselves of the distinction made by Mannheim between particular and total ideologies, the former being the incorrect knowledge systems of an individual, the latter being of a totality, for example, of a whole historical period. Thus, we can also differentiate between individual and collective false consciousness, depending on the level of abstraction we use.

One can imagine and describe "reality" on different levels of abstraction. One level is a description of concrete conditions or events; for example, the description and analysis of a strike in a given firm.[68] Another type of

[67] Ibid., p. 85.

[68] See, e.g., J. Israel, *Den vilda strejken* [*The Wild-cat Strike*] (Stockholm: Bokförlaget Aldus/Bonniers, 1964).

description is used on a higher level of abstraction; for instance, an analysis of "the conditions of production in capitalist society." Such a general analysis on an ideal-typical level, to use Weber's term, abstracts from details. It considers social phenomena as totalities and relates them to other totalities, for example in a description in which "conditions of production" are put in relation to "the legal system." When Marx in his analysis is not concerned with concrete conditions (as in *Capital*), we often find his reasoning to be carried out on such a high level of abstraction that he uses categories which describe totalities.

"It is not the dominance of economic motives in the explanation of history which in a basic way differentiates Marxism from the bourgeois science, but the totality view," says Georg Lukács.[69] Among the imimportant "totalities" utilized by Marx is the term *class*, especially one class, the *proletariat*.

Its historical task as a totality is to overthrow the capitalist society—another totality of which the proletariat is a part—and to create the socialist society. If one considers and analyzes social conditions as totalities, the problem of "false consciousness" becomes quite a different one. It is no longer a problem of individual consciousness. "In the fully developed proletariat," Marx says, "everything human is taken away, even the *appearance* of human. In the conditions of existence of the proletariat are contained, in the most inhuman form, all the conditions of existence of present-day society." For that reason Marx maintains: "It is not a matter of knowing what this or that proletarian, or even the proletariat as a whole, *conceives* of its aim at any particular moment. It is a question of knowing *what* the proletariat *is* and what it must historically accomplish in accordance with its *nature*. Its aim and its historical activities are ordained for it in a tangible and irrevocable way, by its own situation as well as by the whole organization of present-day civil society."[70]

From this quotation it becomes clear that the factual idea which a certain class holds, or the majority of its members hold, and which could be measured in an empirical way, may be defined as "class consciousness" if these ideas are related to a certain interpretation of history and to the role of this class in history. According to the Polish sociologist Szacki,[71] Marxist analyses of "false consciousness" on a high level of abstraction concern three types of "illusions." The first of these is what can be described as the "false consciousness" of the *age*.[72] This means that dominant ideas of a given period can be conceived of as "false" in the light

[69] G. Lukács, *Geschichte und Klassenbewusstsein* (Berlin: Karl Dietz Verlag, 1923).
[70] *Mega I.3*, p. 207.
[71] Szacki, "Remarks," p. 35.
[72] Ibid.

of what actually happened during this period. Secondly, a whole *class* can have a "false consciousness," for example, if it cannot analyze its role within a given society. Marx says of the petite bourgeoisie that as a class they have a tendency to imagine themselves as "elevated above class antagonism in general."[73] From this quotation it becomes clear that "false consciousness" must be related to a certain theory concerning society and conflicts within this society.

"Finally there is the "false consciousness" of the *ideologists*," says Szacki.[74] This problem concerns among other things those intellectuals who deliver the ideologies for the "ruling class," i.e., scientists, writers, and others forming public opinion through mass media. According to Marx, the important task is to counteract this influence by reforming consciousness: "The reform of consciousness is only a question of the world observing its own activities; the object is to make it stop dreaming about itself, and explain to it its own activity . . . our motto therefore should be: reform of consciousness, not by dogma but through an analysis of mystical consciousness which is obscure to itself . . . it will then become obvious that the world has long dreamt of things it has yet to realise in order really to possess them. It will be so obvious that what is involved is not to draw a demarcation line between the past and the future but to *fulfil* the ideas of the past. Finally it will become obvious that mankind is not beginning some *new* work, but is consciously completing his old work."[75]

In this vision Marx sees the abolition of "false consciousness" as the means of realizing dreams which mankind has always had. For Marx the creation of a correct consciousness through the scientific analysis of existing conditions is an important means for the creation of a new society. The realization of goals presupposes values and goal-oriented behavior derived from these values and consistent with them. "Obscure ideas" will then become such ideas that either take their point of departure from "false" values or that use values which may be "correct" ones, but which are not relevant in relation to the goal to be achieved.

[73] Marx and Engels, "The Eighteenth Brumaire of Louis Bonaparte," *Selected Works*, Vol. I, p. 250.

[74] Szacki, p. 36.

[75] *Mega I.1*, p. 575.

5

THE PROBLEM OF ALIENATION IN WEBER'S, SIMMEL'S, AND DURKHEIM'S THEORIES

INTRODUCTION

In an ideas-historical analysis of the work of classic sociologists and their theoretical systems, R. A. Nisbet chooses five unit ideas, as he calls them, i.e., themes which in a systematic way are taken up in different theoretical systems and by different theoreticians. These five themes, which he considers important because of their generality, their continuity, and their specifically sociological characteristics, are concentrated around five concepts, namely, *community, authority, status, the sacred*, and, finally, *alienation*.

One of his various explanations for the fact that it is just these concepts, and the theories developed around them that have attracted classical sociologists, is the moral ambitions of these scientists. "They did not arise out of the simple and morally uncommitted reasonings of pure science. There is no detraction from scientific greatness when we emphasize that such men as Weber and Durkheim were working with intellectual materials—values, concepts and theories—that could never have come into their possession apart from persisting moral conflicts in the nineteenth century. . . . The moral texture of these ideas is never wholly lost. Even in the scientific writings of Weber and Durkheim, a full century after these ideas had made their first appearance, the moral element remains vivid. The great sociologists never ceased to be moral philosophers."[1]

They were involved in society and in the deep-rooted changes taking place as a result of the industrial revolution, which meant the dissolution of the traditional social order. There are five problems which the industrial

[1] R. A. Nisbet, *The Sociological Tradition* (New York: Basic Books, 1966), p. 18.

revolution made actual and with which Weber is concerned, as are Marx, Simmel, and Durkheim: the situation of the working class, technical development, the development of the factory system with a system of division of labor as its main characteristics, property relations, and the problem of urbanization. The situation of the working class and the conditions of labor in general are related very closely to each other, and also to the problems of technical development, leading to the rise of the factory system. It is those five problems which are related to the theory of alienation. In other words, alienation and the industrial society are related in a causal relationship. It is the latter which gives rise to the former.

Nisbet also asserts that the idea of alienation is based on conceptions of the process of industrialization, the development of which is threatening progress and individualism. For that reason alienation can, according to Nisbet, be conceived of as an antithesis to the ideas of progress and individualism which flourished in the period characterized by the rise of industrialization. These conceptions comprise ideas concerning the continuous development of society toward higher levels of social organization and the continuously increasing chances of individuals to achieve self-realization. Conceptions concerning alienation, therefore, are often related to a pessimistic view of the future if, as in the theories of Marx, they are not changed and complemented by the messianic ideas of a future and better society.

MAX WEBER AND RATIONALITY

FORMAL AND MATERIAL RATIONALITY

When Georg Lukács[2] analyzed and reconstructed Marx's theory of alienation and tried to describe that social system within which capitalism can function, he used a long quotation from Max Weber's *Gesammelte Politische Schriften*[3] (*Collected Political Works*). The quotation Lukács used refers to the relationship between the mode of production within capitalist society and the type of legal practice which Weber considered to be typical of such a society. Weber asserts that aspects of capitalistic enterprise had been found earlier in different types of society. "However, the specific features of modern capitalism, in contrast to these ancient forms of capitalist acquisition, the strictly rational organization of work embedded in rational technology, nowhere developed in such irrationally constructed states, and could never have arisen within them, because these

---

[2] G. Lukács, *Geschichte und Klassenbewusstsein* (Berlin: Karl Dietz Verlag, 1923).

[3] M. Weber, *Gesammelte Politische Schriften* (Munich: Drei Masken Verlag, 1921).

modern organizations, with their fixed capital and precise calculations, are much too vulnerable to irrationalities of law and administration."[4]

Weber then describes the development of legal practice in England where the development of the law was carried out by lawyers serving their capitalist clients. They invented rational forms of business transactions making calculations possible. These transactions were then guaranteed by legal rules. The other example referred to by Weber concerns the role of the judge in a bureaucratic society. Circumstances were created "where the judge, as in the bureaucratic state, with its rational laws, is more or less an automaton of paragraphs: the legal documents, together with the costs and fees, are dropped in at the top with the expectation that the judgment will emerge at the bottom, together with more or less sound arguments—an apparatus, accordingly whose functioning is by and large *calculable* or predictable."[5]

For Lukács this was an excellent description of the process of reification. It means the transformation of society into a robot system which, according to him, was the consequence of capitalism and one of the preconditions for its prosperity. However, is the same critical analysis of society also be found in Weber's description? Is that a sign of alienation for him, too? By no means. On the contrary, the principle of rationality is, for Weber, the precondition for the functioning of the modern system of industrial enterprise, independent of the social system in which it develops. "Though by no means alone, the capitalist system has undeniably played a major role in the development of bureaucracy. Indeed, without it capitalistic production could not continue, and any rational type of socialism would have simply to take it over and increase its importance. Its development, largely under capitalist auspices, has created an urgent need for stable, strict, intensive and calculable administration. It is this need which is so fateful to any kind of large-scale administration."[6]

Rationality, the possibility of accounting for the effect of one's actions, and bureaucracy, which is a consequence of this principle of rationality, have certainly been created by the capitalist development, as this development goes hand in hand with industrial and technical development. But a socialist system, which produces under the same technical preconditions on the same level of development of productive forces, cannot, according to Weber, change the principle; neither, therefore, can it change the forms of organization which are built upon it. The development in the Soviet Union seems to have supported Weber's ideas. In dealing with this problem, the difference between the conception of the problem held by

[4] M. Weber, *Economy and Society*, ed. G. Roth and C. Wittich (New York: Bedminster Press, 1968), p. 1395.

[5] Ibid.

[6] Ibid., p. 224.

Marx and the point of view which Weber represents clearly emerges. The difference between Marx and Weber lies in their different conceptions of "rationality." For Marx, rational behavior is always seen in relation to certain social goals. Therefore, in his analysis of capitalist society, Marx bases his theoretical reasoning on values and evaluations. Weber, however, when he describes capitalism, tries to be value-free, both in description and in the taking up of a position.[7] To what extent he is successful we shall discuss later. But there is another difference between Marx and Weber, which concerns the meaning of rationality.

Therefore we must first analyze the principle of rationality as it is defined by Weber. He speaks first of economic action. His definition is very broad and general. "Action will be said to be 'economically oriented' so far as, according to its subjective meaning, it is concerned with the satisfaction of a desire for 'utilities' (*Nutzleistungen*)."[8] With regard to economic action Weber distinguishes between *formal* and *substantive* rationality.[9] *Formal* rationality with regard to economic action is defined as "the extent of quantitative calculation or accounting which is technically possible and which is actually applied."[10] In other words, an economic system is formally rational to the extent to which all actions within the system can be expressed in an quantitative way. This means that they can be accounted for and computed and preferably can be expressed in money value. "From a purely technical point of view, money is the most 'perfect' means of economic calculation. That is, it is formally the most rational means of orienting economic activity. Calculation in terms of money, not its actual use, is thus the specific means of rational, economic provision."[11] Formal rationality is independent of outside values and is related only to one main goal, namely, the central striving within the capitalistic system to achieve *Erwerben*, i.e., to receive profit. All such action which can be calculated and quantified and which leads to the achievement of this goal is, then, effective.

Formal rational behavior thus needs no goals and values external to the social system of capitalism. It refers only to *one goal's* being internal to the system. In the use of the concept of formal rationality lies one of the main differences between Marx and Max Weber. Marx, in his analysis of capitalistic society, mainly uses the other type of rationality, namely, substantive rationality. Let us now define what Weber means by *substantive*

---

[7] *From Max Weber, Essays in Sociology*, trans., ed., and with an introduction by H. H. Gerth and C. W. Mills (London: Routledge & Kegan Paul, 1948), p. 49.

[8] M. Weber, *Economy and Society*, p. 63.

[9] Ibid., p. 85.

[10] Ibid.

[11] Ibid., p. 86.

rationality. Substantive rationality concerns the distribution of products and refers to the degree to which a given number of persons can be provided with products in an adequate way. We will give Weber's own definition. "The 'substantive rationality,' on the other hand, is the degree to which the provisioning of given groups of persons (no matter how delimited) with goods is shaped by economically oriented social action under some criterion (past, present or potential) of ultimate values (*Wertende Postulate*), regardless of the nature of these ends."[12]

Formal rationality, considered as a technical problem, concerns the question of effectivity of calculations and computations. It does, therefore, not presuppose any external values. That economic behavior, however, which is characterized by substantive rationality builds on values concerning the distribution of goods and privileges. These values can be of a different and greatly varying kind, including, as Weber emphasizes, the values inherent in socialism and communism.

To quote: "The concept of 'substantive rationality' . . . is full of ambiguities. It conveys only one element common to all 'substantive' analyses: Namely, that they do not restrict themselves to note the purely formal and (relatively) unambiguous fact that action is based on 'goal-oriented' rational calculation with the technically most adequate available methods, but apply certain criteria of ultimate ends, whether they be ethical, political, utilitarian, hedonistic, concerned with status, egalitarian, or whatever. . . ."[13] Substantive rationality accordingly refers to the purpose or to goals for which effective technique is used as means. According to Weber the first type of rationality is value-free, at least free from values external to the system, while the latter builds on external values.

Much of the political debate of today, for example in Sweden, refers to the question of whether formal rationality, with its demands for effectivity, or substantive rationality, with its emphasis on a just distribution of the social product, shall receive priority in social and economic planning. This seems to be one of the central problems in any society characterized as a "welfare state" today.

The distinction between formal and substantive rationality should be seen against the background of another distinction which Weber makes when he speaks of different ways of orienting social action in general. He differentiates between "instrumentally rational" (*zweckrational*) and "value-rational" (*wertrational*) action.[14] He defines social action as such

[12] Ibid., p. 85.
[13] Ibid.
[14] Ibid., p. 24.

action to which an individual attaches a subjective meaning, and in which he takes account of the behavior of other people. Instrumentally rational behavior, then, is behavior which takes its point of reference in the expectations that a person has concerning the behavior of others. These expectations assume that one's own behavior will elicit a certain type of reaction in others, so that one is able to reach certain goals. If, for example, one gives an order, one assumes that it will lead to a certain effect, in relation to a certain goal.

In the case of value-rational action, one sets up certain absolute goals. Then one orients one's action with regard to the goals in such a way that all action contributes to the achievement of the goal. The difference between the two orientations seems to be that the first concentrates on the means to variable goals, while the second refers to certain absolute goals. "Examples of pure value-rational orientations," says Weber, "would be the actions of persons who, regardless of possible cost to themselves, act to put into practice their convictions of what seems to them to be required by duty, honour, the pursuit of beauty, a religious call, personal loyalty, or the importance of some 'cause' no matter in what it consists."[15]

Instrumentally rational behavior involves the analysis of existing means and also the taking into account of alternative means for reaching a certain goal. Weber asserts that instrumentally rational behavior excludes behavior which is traditional, i.e., guided by habit. Economic action is always a rational way of acting. It presupposes "deliberate planning" with regard to certain economic ends.[16] Thus, it appears that economic action which is called "formally rational" is a specific type of the general category of instrumentally rational behavior, namely, economically instrumental action. Substantive rational behavior in turn, then, is a specific type of value-rational action, namely, economically value-rational behavior.

The relationship between the general types of rational behavior and the specific types of economic rational behavior, however, may be somewhat more complicated, since Weber himself seems to use the concepts ambiguously. At least this is what Parsons maintains in a footnote to his English translation of *Wirtschaft und Gesellschaft*."[17]

Rational calculation is a precondition for the capitalistic mode of production, and formal rationality is in general one of its most important characteristics. According to Weber, four phenomena can be derived from this principle of rationality. We shall briefly deal with these four phenomena: (1) "the spirit of capitalism," (2) the technical means with which an enterprise is managed, (3) the system of authority which is a

[15] Ibid., p. 25.

[16] Ibid., p. 65.

[17] M. Weber, *The Theory of Social and Economic Organization*, trans. and ed. A. M. Henderson and T. Parsons (New York: Oxford University Press, 1947), p. 115.

consequence of the capitalist mode of production, namely, bureaucracy, (4) the social system.

"THE SPIRIT OF CAPITALISM"

Each highly developed system of production needs a working class for which work is more than something that is carried out by the sweat of one's brow. Work has to be established as a self-evident activity. In fact, it must be more than that. It must be experienced as a moral duty. "It is a duty which the individual ought to feel and feels with regard to the content of his 'occupational' activity independently of the fact of which it consists."[18] Expressed in current sociological terminology, Weber's thesis can be rephrased thus: the Protestant ethic has functioned as a norm-source in the process of socialization, which has led to the acceptance of "work as a moral duty."[19] In any case, one can assume that it was this ethic which was used by the owners of capital as an argument to create a "work moral." They themselves lived in what Weber termed an "intrawordly asceticism" in which economy and thrift were virtues. Instead of lavish consumption it was necessary to reinvest every penny one could save.[20] The moral of work and ascetic puritanism are two aspects which supplement each other. The moral of work is especially demanded of the worker even if it can be found in the employer. The puritan asceticism is mainly the contribution of the owners of capital. These orientations are probably necessary in all societies which find themselves at the beginning of the industrialization process. At this stage, it is necessary to have a rapid accumulation of capital. To the extent to which capital cannot be imported from outside, only one alternative exists: hard exploitation of

[18] M. Weber, *Gesammelte Aufsätze zur Religionssoziologie* (Tübingen: Mohr, 1920), Vol. I, p. 36.

[19] S. Johansson, "Max Weber—en mjukdatasociolog" ["A Soft-Data-Sociologist"], *Sociologisk Forskning* III (1966), 185–99, has made an interesting analysis of the assertions that Weber's purpose was to establish a causal relationship between Protestantism and the development of capitalism, which Weber himself has denied. He called this idea doctrinary (*Gesammelte Aufsätze zur Religionssoziologie*, Vol. I, p. 83). Another interesting hypothesis has been presented by J. Asplund, "En fri tolkning av Max Webers tes om protestantism och kapitalism" ["A Free Interpretation of Max Weber's Thesis Concerning Protestantism and Capitalism"], *Sociologisk Forskning III* (1966), 200–13. Asplund tries to establish a synthesis between the "intrawordly asceticism" and profit-making as an explanation for the development of the "spirit of capitalism."

[20] H. Marcuse points out in his book *Kultur und Gesellschaft* (Frankfurt: Edition Suhrkamp, 1965) that saving and asceticism no longer are driving forces in late capitalism, but that, on the contrary, they can be a hindrance. Since high comsumption is a precondition for effective production in the affluent, industrialized society, the puritan asceticism is replaced by another mentality, the goal of which is to own a multitude of consumption- and capital-commodities.

human labor power. The moral of work, and asceticism, therefore can be found in early capitalism in the Western world as well as in the Soviet Union during the twenties and in China of today. The striving for profit is also a part of "the spirit of capitalism." It is "activity which is oriented to opportunities for seeking new powers of control over goods, on a single occasion, repeatedly or continuously."[21] However, striving for profit also occurs outside the capitalistic rational system of enterprise. Weber says that it is found in "waiters, doctors, coachmen, cocottes, functionaries who allow themselves to be bribed, soldiers, robbers, crusaders, those who visit gambling halls, and beggars."[22] However, capitalism is, according to Weber, identical with striving for "renewed profit, for 'profitability,' because it must be so. Within a capitalist social order any given capitalist enterprise which does not orient itself towards the chances to achieve 'profitability' would be doomed."[23]

CALCULATION

The "spirit of capitalism," characterized by the work moral, ascetic puritanism, and the striving after profit, is a precondition for formal rationality. Its tools, or techniques, are systematic accounting and calculation, among other things with the help of capital accounting, which is a special form of monetary accounting. "Capital accounting is the valuation and verification of opportunities for profit and of the success of profit-making by means of a valuation of the total assets (goods and money) of the enterprise at the beginning of a profit-making venture, and the comparison of this with a similar valuation of the assets still present and newly acquired, at the end of the process."[24] Calculation, the use of statistics, the use of mathematical models, the description of experience in mathematical terms, prediction through accounting of "profitability" thus forms the kernel of formal rational behavior. Weber goes on to describe how in rational activity, which is built on capital accounting, "profitability" becomes dependent on prices, and how these in their turn are affected by competition. The consequence is that "capital accounting in its formally most rational shape thus presupposes *the battle of man with man*."[25] This factual statement does not elicit any comments by Weber, quite in accordance with his attempts to describe and not to value.

21 Weber, *Economy and Society*, p. 90.
22 Weber, *Gesammelte Aufsätze zur Religionssoziologie*, Vol. I, p. 4.
23 Ibid.
24 Weber, *Economy and Society*, p. 91.
25 Ibid., p. 93.

BUREAUCRATIC ORGANIZATION

A rational system which uses effective means of computation also presupposes a rational system of power. One has to make people accept the demands of the system. They must be able to subordinate themselves and carry out the duties which have been placed upon them. In other words, such a system needs a system of authority which is shaped in such a way that the demands of power are experienced as legitimate by those affected by it.

According to Weber, there are three principles involved in legitimate authority. The first builds on *tradition*; the second on *charisma*; the third is the *rational* type, which builds upon "a belief in the legality of enacted rules and the right of those elevated to authority under such rules to issue commands (legal authority)."[26]

Legal authority is found in its purest form in the bureaucratic administration. But not only that. Bureaucratic organization is "from a purely technical point of view, capable of attaining the highest degree of efficiency and is in this sense formally the most rationally known means of exercising authority over human beings. It is superior to any other form in precision, stability, in the stringency of its discipline and in its reliability. It thus makes possible a particularly high degree of calculability of results, for the heads of the organization and for those acting in relation to it. It is finally superior both in intensive efficiency and in the scope of its operation, and is formally capable of application to all kinds of administrative tasks."[27] The quotation indicates that Weber has great admiration for bureaucratic organization. Interesting in this connection is his emphasis on "stringency of discipline." One may ask whether the ideal type of bureaucracy, being the most efficient type of organization, is dependent on special cultural conditions. In particular, one may think of the authoritarian social structure of German culture in which Weber lived. Bendix, for example, has suggested that the ideal type of bureaucracy, which Weber praises so much, is able to function only within an authoritarian culture.[28]

An individual within a bureaucratic organization is free as a *person*, i.e., the authority of the system relates only to his work-task. He is part of a definite hierarchical order, which delimits the area of competence of each incumbent of a given position. Employment is based on certain methods of selection, which in turn relate to the technical qualifications of the applicant. Appointment is in the form of a contract which guar-

[26] Ibid., p. 215.

[27] Ibid., p. 223.

[28] R. Bendix, "Bureaucracy, the Problem and Its Setting," *American Sociological Review* 12 (1947), 493–507.

antees definite privileges to the incumbent of a given position. One of these is predetermined and secure salary. The incumbent of a position is placed within a career system. Promotion occurs on the basis of certain predetermined principles. One of the criteria of promotion, for example, is seniority. The incumbent of a given position does not own his means of production—a fact which, for Weber, is one of the most important preconditions for the functioning of a rationally ruled system. Those who are members of this system become dependent on those who own, or have at their disposal, the means of production.[29] If an employee did not lack the right of ownership of means of production, it would be impossible to maintain discipline and control. In fact, Weber maintains that the *power* which private ownership of the means of production gives rise to constitutes the special social importance of private ownership. Therefore, he adds, "from this life-situation out of this discipline of the enterprise, modern socialism has been born."[30] Unlike Marx, Weber here supports private ownership of means of production from a purely technical point of efficiency. Even if he sees the rise of socialism as a consequence of these conditions, he neither supports nor condemns them. He consequently uses formal rationality as the main criterion for his reasoning.

The fact that the bureaucratic, capitalistic apparatus of production functions well depends in turn on the fact that the whole society has been bureaucratized. *Das Beamtentum*, i.e., the system of civil servants and officials, is the cornerstone of a rational state administration. The fact that the acts of civil servants are predictable makes rational calculation possible. It frees private enterprise from arbitrariness and irrational acts, i.e., those acts which do not take into account the goals of formal rationality. The means and conditions of production of private capitalism rest upon the bureaucratic society, which in turn has been imbued by, and has accepted, capitalism. Weber asserts that this concerns the legal system as well as general administration, military organization as well as research. Ownership of the means of production gives power, political as well as military and economic: "The hierarchically built system of dependence is based on the fact that the tools which are indispensable for the enterprise and its economic existence—supplies and funds of capital—can be disposed of on the one hand by the employer, on the other hand by the holder of political power. The worker, the sales-clerk, the technician, the university assistant and every state official and soldier are in just the same way in this dependent position."[31] In fact, from a sociological point of view one can consider the state as an enterprise. Similar power and authority rela-

[29] Weber, *Gesammelte Politische Schriften*, p. 141.

[30] M. Weber, *Gesammelte Aufsätze zur Soziologie und Sozialpolitik* (Tübingen: Mohr, 1924), p. 501.

[31] Weber, *Gesammelte Politische Schriften*, p. 141.

tions prevail in the state administration, the army, the legal system, within the private enterprise. Here, Weber expresses a Marxist thesis; the development of the social organs and institutions is a consequence of the capitalist mode of production and its development.[32] This is an idea similar to that expressed by Marx, where he differentiated between the material base, consisting of the conditions of production, and the "ideological super-structure."

The phenomenon which Weber calls the "spirit of capitalism," i.e., the values and attitudes of life, being interwoven with the bureaucratic system of power and authority, with the "mathematizing" of decision-making processes both in private enterprises and in the public administration, and privately owned means of production, control over the money and trade systems—all this Weber subsumes under the principle of formal rationality.[33] The modern society is a rational society. Rationality has made capitalism possible, and capitalism builds upon it.

RATIONALITY AND THE INDIVIDUAL

A series of questions arise when one reads Weber's dispassionate description, which at least with regard to formal rationality should be value-free, as it is a *description* and analysis of social conditions and their function within a given social system. Such a description and analysis can, at least formally, be rendered value-free. The rationality of the capitalistic society has, as we know, been questioned by socialists. In fact, one of the most important points in socialism's attack on the capitalist mode of production is the anarchy which is said to characterize it, its lack of planning and coordination of production, and its dependence on the market system with its capricious laws. We will save this discussion until the final chapter. Here we will concentrate on some other problems.

What effects does Weber think that the rationalization of life has had on the lives of private individuals? Is the problem of alienation to be found within his theory? The development of formal rationality has been called "the demystification of social life."[34] Does this attempt to free social phenomena from mystifying beliefs and to make use of rational, mathematically formulated criteria for action, lead to undesirable consequences as far as the human being is concerned? To have these questions answered, it is necessary to clarify the image of man held by Weber and his beliefs as to how man functions in the rationalized society. However, before

[32] Ibid., p. 140.
[33] Weber, *Economy and Society.*
[34] K. Löwith, *Gesammelte Abhandlungen* (Stuttgart: W. Kohlhammer Verlag, 1960), p. 18.

taking up these problems for discussion, we shall briefly analyze the question of the relationship between formal and substantial rationality.

Why do people work? asks Weber. Those who own nothing do so in order to support themselves and their dependents. At best, they do it because they see work as a duty. Weber seems to attribute greater importance to the first motive. For those who are privileged to own property and who, in addition, are educated, other motives exist, for example, opportunities to receive high incomes. Their ambitions and the value they give to privileged work—for example, of an intellectual, scientific, and artistic nature—are also factors which must be taken into account. Finally, for those people who themselves take part in the acquisition of profit, their motivation to work is the capital which they risk, and the profits they can be expected to make.[35]

A planned economy, oriented to the satisfaction of certain minimum needs—for example, as it has developed in the Swedish welfare state, with its emphasis on basic economic security—in Weber's view leads to a reduction of formal rationality. If society guarantees a minimum of security for all, the most important motive to work for those who do not own anything disappears, i.e., the risk that their dependents will suffer when they themselves do not work hard. Weber concludes therefore: "A planned economy oriented to want satisfaction must, in proportion as it is radically carried through, weaken the incentive to labor so far as the risk of lack of support is involved. For it would, at least so far as there is a rational system of provision for wants, be impossible to allow a worker's dependents to suffer the full consequences of his lack of efficiency in production."[36] From these and other examples Weber concludes that "substantive and formal (in the sense of *exact calculation*) rationality are, it should be stated again, after all, largely distinct problems. This fundamental and, in the last analysis unavoidable, element of irrationality in economic systems is one of the important sources of all "social" problems and, above all, of the problems of socialism."[37] The experience gained from modern welfare societies, and also from the so-called consumption society, has proved that Weber was wrong in his assumption. The need to work, to be able to provide for one's own life and the lives of one's dependents, has been substituted by ambitions and aspirations to achieve a higher standard than that which has already been achieved. In the highly industrialized societies, when the basic needs are satisfied and when people have achieved a basic social security, they start striving for other material goals. Thus, there seems to be a lack in the psychological theory which

[35] Weber, *Economy and Society*, p. 110.
[36] Ibid.
[37] Ibid., p. 111.

Weber develops concerning the motivation to work. There remains the other problem of the mixture of formal and substantive rationality.

Weber correctly asserted that the principle of formal rationality, which builds upon economic calculation, is not itself able to formulate principles concerning the distribution of the social product.[38]

He seems to mean that material rationality is a disturbing element in an otherwise perfectly functioning, formally rational form of action. However, it seems that no society exists in which certain political, moral, or other kinds of values do not enter into play, thus affecting the purely technical idea of effectivity. To put effectiveness and technical perfection as a main goal is certainly a tendency among those who belong to the group which Galbraith termed the "technostructure."[39] The actual social conditions, and especially social problems such as may arise in any industrial society, however, seem to make it impossible to neglect problems of substantive rationality. In any case, the production of goods certainly is not a goal in itself. Production "ought" to be directed toward consumption. In highly industrialized societies, however, a reversal seems to occur: consumption sometimes appears to be a necessary condition for effective production. Thus, one could assert that principles of substantive rationality have become guiding principles for formal rationality.

In any case, one must ask for what a completely formal, rational form of acting is to be used? As we have pointed out, it could be seen as a goal in itself—and many technicians, economists, and other experts seem to develop this tendency to evaluate effectivity for its own sake. But it should be made clear that Weber does not hold this view. When he discusses "the spirit of capitalism," he maintains that those who make the acquisition of money into an end in itself are acting in an irrational manner.[40]

In a polemic against Brentano, who had pointed out that in these lines Weber admitted that rationality—formal rationality, naturally—could be used in an irrational way of life, Weber answered as follows: "Irrationality is not something in itself. It is something which must be judged as such from a definite rational point of view. For the non-religious, every religious way of life is an irrational. For the hedonist, every ascetic way of life is 'irrational,' even if measured by its own *ultimate value* [my italics] it is "rational."[41]

In my opinion this quotation can be interpreted only as stating that the formal rationality of calculation is rational only with regard to an ulti-

[38] Ibid., p. 109.
[39] J. K. Galbraith, *The New Industrial State* (London: Hamish Hamilton, 1967).
[40] Weber, *Gesammelte Aufsätze zur Religionssoziologie*, Vol. I, p. 35.
[41] Ibid., footnote 1.

mate value of its own. According to Weber the goal of all economic action is the maintainance of man's livelihood or, to use his own words, "the satisfaction of a desire for 'utilities' [*Nutzleitstungen*]."[42] Providing for man's needs, the satisfying of his desire for utilities concerns two aspects: (1) *production* of these utilities (2) the *distribution* of them. According to Weber's statement previously quoted, the second problem is determined by the principle of substantive rationality. These often interfere with the carrying through of the principle of formal rationality, which seems to concentrate on the most effective ways of producing utilities. In this attitude lies the most important difference between Weber and Marx: for Marx, the social production of utilities is subordinated to principles of distribution, according to definite political-economic evaluations, for example, social justice (however that term can be interpreted). For Weber, the social distribution of utilities is, at worst, a disturbing element in an effective process of production, where "effective" is equated with "the greatest possible profit."[43]

For that reason Marcuse[44] asks if the concept "formal rationality" is part of a value system, an "ideology."

Formal rational behavior tends to spread from the process of production into all areas of social life. This process of extension, which can be called "rationalization," turns modern technique and its application into a system of power, a system of dominating man in the name of formal rationality. Marcuse goes one step further and asks whether the idea of formal rationality in itself includes certain values and therefore becomes an ideology, i.e., a way of justifying the action of power-elites, dominating groups, a ruling class. Modern technology itself, not only its application, is a way of exerting power: "methodical, scientific, calculating and calculated power. Definite purposes and interests are not 'a posteriori' and from outside forced upon modern technique—they are an integral part of the construction of the technical apparatus."[45] Political action and social goals, then, can be defended on the grounds that they are necessary because of the existing technology, i.e., they are forced upon man and society as a consequence of the state of development of modern technology. Undesired consequences become unavoidable; the development of technique has its own inner dynamic. The theories of Galbraith,[46] for example, display such an attitude by asserting the fateful character of modern technology and its continuous development. The acceptance of

[42] Weber, *Economy and Society*, p. 63.
[43] Ibid., p. 90.
[44] Marcuse, *Kultur und Gesellschaft*, Vol. II.
[45] Ibid., p. 126.
[46] Galbraith, *The New Industrial State*.

"technical necessity" is facilitated because, as Habermas points out,[47] it appears that formal rationality is concerned with "the correct choice between strategies, the relevant use of technologies and the purposive shaping of systems (given definite goals in certain situations)." This, in consequence, leads to the fact that one does not analyze formal rational actions within the framework of the interests and broader goals of society, and that they are not scrutinized and "exposed to reflection and to reasonable reconstruction."[48]

Marcuse accuses Weber of having developed the ideological weapons for the defense of an irrational social system by concentrating on the descriptive aspects of formal rationality, rather than on a critical analysis, pointing out the consequences of the process of "rationalization." He therefore concludes—and in this is supported by others, e.g., Mommsen[49] —that Weber's description builds upon the value-system of the capitalist society and that consequently he can be considered to be "the classical exponent of bourgeois, individualistic capitalism," as Mommsen puts it.[50]

THE CONSEQUENCES OF RATIONALITY

It remains for us to discuss Weber's image of man. Is the process of rationalization, which in a total sense affects the industrial society, the bureaucratization of organizations and social systems, a danger to man? The question is important, since Weber considers formal rationality the most effective way of behavior and bureaucracy the most efficient system of authority distribution. Does Weber consider the problem of the consequences for mankind of this development, or does he abstain from dealing with it, and also abstain from a discussion touching on the central issues of the alienation complex?

To quote two of Weber's statements: "A lifeless machine is *petrified* spirit. Only because it is so, does it have the power to force man into its service and to determine in a dominating way his working day in the factory. *Petrified* spirit is also the living machine constituted by the bureaucratic organization, with its specialization of trained experts, its demarcation of competence, its rules and hierarchically ordered authority-relations. With the dead machine it works to produce the shell of a future serfdom, which may only and for all, like the fellaches in ancient Egyptian

[47] J. Habermas, *Technik und Wissenschaft als "Ideologie"* (Frankfurt: Edition Suhrkamp, 1968), p. 49.

[48] Ibid.

[49] W. Mommsen, "Max Weber's Political Sociology and His Philosophy of World History," *International Social Science Bulletin* XVII (1965), 23–45.

[50] Ibid., p. 49.

society, force man into impotent obedience. This will occur, given that the *ultimate and only value is going to become a rational administration and distribution by functionaries, who determine the shaping of human affairs.* Because this task is performed by a bureaucracy incomparably superior to any other authority structure."[51]

In this quotation the bureaucratic administration is considered in terms of formal rationality, by which it is pictured as the most efficient and, in addition, as indispensable for modern industrial society. Here Weber also hints at the possibility of a new serfdom: the bureaucracy no longer serves man and his needs, but becomes an independent body. Man, in this case, will be subordinated to a rigid bureaucratic machine which has become a goal in itself. (In connection with the debate in socialist countries concerning the question of whether or not alienation can be found in socialist societies, the problem of the role of the bureaucracy becomes predominant. We shall illuminate this in chapter 8.)

On another occasion, Weber discusses some of the ingredients constituting the "spirit of capitalism." Among other things he mentions a rational way of life, professional orientation, an ascetic attitude toward life. He also deals with the relationship between the solicitude concerning man's mundane welfare and the asceticism which, under capitalism, has been separated from its religious basis and directed toward temporal things. According to Weber this secular asceticism—he speaks of *innerweltliche Askese*—played an important role for the managerial class of the early phase of industrialization.

When discussing this problem, Weber quotes someone's statement in which the solicitude concerning man's mundane welfare had been called "a thin veil, which could be removed at any time." But things changed when the asceticism no longer concerned man's spiritual welfare, but became a part of the "spirit of capitalism." Weber continues:

Destiny transformed this veil into cast-iron shell. In that asceticism was preparing to reshape this world and to spread more and more the world's material wealth, it acquired an increasing and finally inviolable power over man as never before in history. Today the spirit of asceticism has left its shell perhaps for good, who knows? In any case victorious capitalism does not need its support, inasmuch as it is based upon a mechanical foundation. . . . As yet nobody knows who is going to live in this shell and whether at the end of this unprecedented development completely new prophets will emerge, or whether there will be a powerful renaissance of old thoughts and ideas. If none of this happens, then a mechanized fossil might develop determined to take

[51] Weber, *Gesammelte Politische Schriften*, p. 151.

itself seriously in a convulsive way. For the "last people" in this cultural development the word would instead become truth: "Specialists without spirit, pleasure-seeking beings without a heart—these no-ones make themselves believe that they have risen to heights never before reached in the development of the human species."[52]

Certainly, Weber had reservations regarding his statements, saying: All this concerns beliefs and value-judgments, which only serve to burden a historical, descriptive analysis. However, the two previous quotations (51 and 52) though taken from different contexts and written at different points in time, not only have certain phrases in common but also express serious doubts concerning the consequences of formal rational action, in fact, concerning the "final rationality" of formal rational behavior. The risk seen by Weber is that formal rationality becomes a goal in itself, efficiency for the sake of efficiency. He sees this as a threat to his value-system in which individualism and the liberalistic version of humanism play an important role.

Löwith[53] discusses the problem and asks what, in fact, is the position adopted by Weber. According to Löwith, Weber, despite his pessimism, does not consider the risks of a development toward an increasingly inhuman society to be a central problem. In order to talk about an "inhuman society," it is necessary to develop certain criteria concerning an ideal society and human happiness. These criteria then could be used as measuring rods. As opposed to Marx, who has very well elaborated conceptions in this respect and who therefore can speak of the "inhumanity of the capitalistic system," Weber does not explicitly develop such conceptions. Neither does he consider the development as positive. He tries to stand above it and to keep a neutral distance. Therefore, neither in its sociological nor psychological meaning does the notion of alienation have a place in Weber's conceptual system.

Löwith asserts that Weber's evaluation of formal rationality is ambivalent. Formal rationality appears to him as the most characteristic sign of the industrialized society. To the extent that this society is considered to represent a higher stage in a historical evolutionary process, formal rationality stands out as an advance. At the same time, Weber cannot help but question whether or not it represents an advance only. According to Löwith,[54] the key to this ambivalence can be found in Weber's conception concerning the relationship between *rationality* and *freedom*.

[52] Weber, *Gesammelte Schriften zur Religionssoziologi*, Vol. I, pp. 203–4.
[53] Löwith, *Gesammelte Abhandlungen*, p. 28.
[54] Ibid., p. 29.

RATIONALITY AND RESPONSIBILITY-ETHICS

In a discussion concerning the freedom of will, Weber raises objections to the notion of the "creative personality." In *one view* "free, creative personality" is characterized by independence, incalculability, capriciousness, by an irrationality in contrast to the deterministic notion, by which all human acts are the consequences of identifiable causes. Weber opposes a notion of freedom which presupposes an image of the impulsive, unpredictable, creative personality, independent of "a mechanical causality."

Weber points out that "an act is 'free,' the less it is affected by coercion from outside or through own uncontrolled impulses and the more it occurs as a consequence of conscious deliberations directed toward specific goals. Unpredictability, on the other hand, is the privilige of lunatics, not of creative freedom."[55]

Thus "free acting" for Weber stands out as behavior which occurs in a conscious way and which is "instrumentally rational." This means that an individual after careful deliberation chooses the most adequate means of reaching a given end. According to Weber, it is just this process of deliberation and choice that characterizes the freedom of will. Such a choice-process presupposes *knowledge* of existing means, and *expectations* concerning their consequences or effects. The temporal end-point in such a choice-process is a decision, representing a conscious choice among different, available alternatives.

On the basis of the relationship between "free action" and "instrumental rationality," then, a special type of ethics can be derived, namely, that which Weber terms *responsibility-ethics*. Assume that man investigates different alternatives for action and their consequences in relation to a certain goal. Assume, furthermore, that such deliberations lead to a certain way of acting. By so doing, man is aware of what he is doing and is ready to take responsibility for the consequences of his actions. A responsibility-ethic, therefore, means that one does not act blindly or because of social pressure, but that one is aware of possible consequences and willing to assume responsibility for one's own actions.[56]

Such a responsibility-ethic—very briefly sketched here—is by no means unproblematic. First, it requires that a clear distinction be made between means and ends because, though the responsibility-ethic (given certain goals) can advise as to choice, it need not necessarily be concerned with goals. However, certain goals may delimit the choice of means, and in addition they may themselves become means for goals placed higher

55 M. Weber, *Gesammelte Aufsätze zur Wissenschaftslehre* (Tübingen: Mohr, 1922), p. 26.
56 Weber, *Gesammelte Politische Schriften*, p. 441 ff.

in a means-goals hierarchy. Thus, the distinction between means and ends cannot be upheld in a strict sense (and therefore neither can the distinction between instrumental and value-rational behavior, which, however, does not imply that the distinction is useless for analytical purposes).

Second, means do not possess instrumental value for certain ends only. They may, furthermore, be opposed to other ends and therefore lead to acceptable consequences if one considers the first end, but completely unacceptable if one thinks in terms of the second end. Therefore, in a restricted sense at least, responsibility-ethic functions only on the assumption that the ends are not inconsistent and incompatible. In fact, the choice of ends becomes a primary problem, since there is usually mutual influence back and forth between means and ends. But taking up the problem of choice of ends means abandoning the idea of value-freedom and accepting the necessity of choosing values and making them explicit.

Finally, another important objection with regard to responsibility-ethics is the demand that the individual make decisions independent of social pressures. The objection is based not so much upon social-psychological facts concerning the existence of social pressures and the ways in which people are affected by them, but rather upon the fact that bureaucratic organizations do not demand that the individual makes the decisions for which he takes responsibility. Instead they demand that he act in accordance with the organization's rules and ends, the responsibility for his conduct being assumed by the organization. Bureaucratic organizations do not demand that the individual assume responsibility for his actions, but rather that he subordinate himself and obey the rules of the organization. The individual in turn can then defend his action with reference to orders received by him (an extreme example is the defense by the man accused of war crimes that he only carried out orders).

The ambivalence in Weber's attitude appears in the fact that the functioning of bureaucratic organizations—which he considered to be the most efficient authority-structure—delimits the functioning of responsibility-ethnics. Thus one alternative is to support the view that the individual is influenced by social pressures when acting as a member of a bureaucratic organization and therefore responsibility-ethics cannot function. The other alternative is that he is acting without consideration of social pressures. In the second case he prohibits the effective functioning of bureaucracies but fulfills the demands of responsibility-ethics.

Weber does see the contradiction and develops his analysis a step further. He distinguishes between two types of responsibility. As a member of a bureaucratic organization, the individual is responsible for his actions in his capacity of occupant of a certain role, but not in his capacity as individual. This means that he must constantly relate his actions to the goals of the organization. Eventually he can be forced to carry out acts for which he as an individual is not willing to take responsibility.

The other type of responsibility is that determined by the rules of the responsibility-ethics. Weber exemplifies the conflict by referring to a politician who acts as a bureaucrat and does not want to "take his own responsibility," implying that he does not set up goals independent of the objectives of the bureaucracy, or, given that he has such goals, that he does not try to realize them. In a criticism of the German bureaucracy, Weber lashes out against politicians who want to be bureaucrats: "The passion for bureaucratization as it is expressed here, can drive one to despair . . . as if we consciously and with will must become human beings who need 'order' [*Ordnung*] and nothing else than order, who become nervous and cowardly when this order wavers only one moment, who become helpless when we get pulled from our perfect adjustment to order. . . ."[57]

A central problem, therefore, is the counteracting of this bureaucratization of the personality: "what one can *set up against* this machinery to preserve the rest of humanity."[58] Weber poses this question, but he does not ask whether the tendencies he attacks are a part of that organizational system which he praises. Are these tendencies for compulsive order, for submission, for unwillingness "to take the responsibility" a consequence of the functioning of the bureaucratic system, or are they an expression of a special, perhaps German, version of an authoritarian bureaucracy? Can one develop a bureaucratic organization without any authoritarian elements whatsoever? Empirical evidence points to the conclusion that a bureaucracy without authoritarian elements is hardly possible, though the authoritarian components may be shaped and modified by specific traditional patterns of social relations existing in a certain culture.

There seems to me to be an inconsequent attitude in Weber's attack: On the one hand, it involves the defense of bureaucratic organizations and, on the other hand, the condemnation of unavoidable consequences (or at least consequences that are difficult to avoid) if these organizations are to function efficiently. The problem seems to become: Can one change bureaucratic organizations, e.g., by increasing members' influence over decision-making without reducing its efficiency? And if its efficiency can be saved only by keeping the bureaucratic organization intact, would it not be desirable to choose less efficiency and at the same time avoid some of the negative consequences of the bureaucratic structure? Weber

[57] Weber, *Gesammelte Aufsätze zur Soziologie und Sozialpolitik*, p. 414.
[58] Ibid.

never really poses this question, and therefore his ambivalence is understandable.

In Weber's thought the conflict between the responsibility-ethics and submission to a bureaucratic organization is never sharpened because of his image of man. He rejects the notion of man as a totality equipped with a variety of faculties, among them creative ability based upon impulsiveness and irrationality. He embraces, instead, an individualism based upon rational, conscious action and—which is most important—upon the ability to assume different roles. It is one thing to carry out one's role as an effective member of a bureaucratic organization, another thing to preserve one's individuality as a human being outside the organization. Löwith[59] uses the distinction *Mensch* and *Fachmensch*, i.e., "human being" and "expert" to characterize Weber's distinction. "To be a human-being" should then mean to preserve one's ability to take the responsibility for one's acts, to be able to act consciously and with regard to the consequences of one's action—all that even if one is forced, as an "expert" or "organizational member," to act in a different way. Intellectual honesty, as a precondition for independent choices and for the will to take responsibility for the consequences of one's action, is a central part of Weber's image of man. This person is separated from the one who plays his different role in the organizations of which he is a member. Thus—as I see it—his image of man facilitates the acceptance of contradictory tendencies. The question is whether or not the ideal human being in this context is quite the same as the schizophrenic personality.

There is another solution to the conflict. By using a certain elite-theory, for example, one based upon the notion of charismatic leadership, one could distinguish between leaders who act according to the responsibility-ethic and organizational members who subordinate themselves and carry out organizational orders.

In summary, Weber's unwillingness to deal with the negative aspects of the bureaucratized society, except for a few attacks and expressed fears, results from his emphasis on formal and instrumental rationality, his evaluation of bureaucratic organizations, his theories of charismatic leadership, and finally his image of man, which helps him to face the conflict between individual responsibility and organizational submission.

MARX AND WEBER—A COMPARISON

The difference between the theories of Marx and of Weber can be summarized in a few points.

[59] Löwith, *Gesammelte Abhandlungen*, p. 34.

There is a tendency to consider Weber and his theory of the Protestant ethic as a refutation of Marx and his "materialistic" interpretation of historical events. Sorokin,[60] to mention one name, asserts that Weber took religion as the independent variable and economic conditions as the dependent, whereas Marx tried to explain religion and other "ideological" phenomena as a function of basic economic processes. In my opinion these assertions are not correct. Neither Marx nor Weber developed theories of monocausality, ascribing to one set of factors the only determining role. Marx, by using dialectical methods, emphasized the mutual interaction of several sets of factors, where the basic process of social production becomes a determining factor in "the last instance." The meaning of this expression and the relationship between economic factors and others such as politics, science, etc., will be discussed in the last chapter.

Weber himself denied the idea that religious factors should be considered the only causal or even the most important factor in the rise of capitalism. In fact he calls this idea "lunatic-dogmatic."[61]

In an essay on the objectivity of social-scientific knowledge he makes some distinction of importance in this context: He differentiates between *economical* phenomena, economically *relevant* phenomena, and economically *conditioned* phenomena.[62] The first class of phenomena refers to economic institutions within the social structure. The second category consists of economic factors which affect noneconomic processes, e.g., religion and its value-system. The third category comprises noneconomic phenomena affected and influenced by economic processes.

Which factors are considered to be economically relevant and which will be seen as economically conditioned depends on the intricate network of causal relations put forward in a theory. By means of feedback processes their status can change so that economically relevant factors become economically conditioned ones and vice versa (see also Kozyr-Kowalski).[63]

The differences between Weber and Marx are mainly located on a metatheoretical and an extratheoretical plane. With regard to metatheoretical differences Marx never tries to exclude the basic values from which he starts. Therefore, his theories are always related to his utopian ideal of a future society. Therefore, they have political relevance.

[60] P. A. Sorokin, *Fads and Foibles in Modern Sociology and Related Sciences* (Chicago: Regnery, 1956), p. 169.

[61] Weber, *Gesammelte Aufsätze zur Religionssoziologi*, Vol. I, p. 83.

[62] M. Weber, *The Methodology of the Social Sciences* (Glencoe, Ill.: The Free Press, 1949), p. 65.

[63] S. Kozyr-Kowalski, "Weber and Marx," *The Polish Sociological Bulletin* No. 1 (17) (1968), 5-17.

Weber, on the other hand, stresses the ideal of the value-free science which *is*—and that should be emphasized—*a value*. The consequence is that, unlike Marx, Weber does not become a social reformer. However, his value-neutral position also has political consequences. The idea of formal rationality can easily be incorporated into an ideology, the aim of which is to legitimize existing economic conditions. Therefore, independent of his intentions, his theories have had a conserving effect.

For Weber socialism as a system in which "man's domination of man is abolished"[64] is utopian. The attitude toward socialism is affected in turn by Marx's and Weber's views of capitalism. According to Gerth and Mills: "For Marx, the modern economy is basically irrational; this irrationality of capitalism results from a contradiction between the rational technological advances of the productive forces and the fetters of private property, private profit, and unmanaged market competition. The system is characterized by an 'anarchy of production.' "[65] For Weber, on the other hand, modern capitalism is not "irrational"; indeed, its institutions appear to him as the very embodiment of rationality.

The difference here depends on the fact that Weber accepts as a basic goal of capitalism rentability and profits and analyzes economic behavior and institutions with reference to this goal. Marx, rejecting this goal or at least the acquisition and use of profits by private persons, puts forward other goals, e.g., the creation of a classless society. In relation to this goal, capitalism is irrational. Marx, by postulating a basic conflict between the *level* of development of *productive forces* and *relations of production*, develops a special type of "cultural-lag" hypothesis. As are all such hypotheses, the Marxian one, too, is founded on definite values. It can be shown that this hypothesis becomes meaningless if one does not take one's point of departure in a socialistic value-system[66] (see also chapter 9). From his point of view, Marx is consequent when he considers the capitalist system to be irrational.

Weber is consequent in calling it rational, as long as he considers the system in relation to profit-making as an ultimate goal. However, I doubt whether today Weber would not question the goal precisely from the premises of formal rationality. Considering that in the U.S., as well as in other societies having a capitalist system, existing production resources are often not used to their full capacity but perhaps only to 80–85 percent of this capacity and considering that a certain number of people always are unemployed and, finally, considering the devastating effects on the physical environment, the *substantial* rationality of the goal of our mode of

[64] Mommsen, "Max Weber's Political Sociology."

[65] *From Max Weber*, ed. Gerth and Mills, p. 49.

[66] J. Israel, "Problems of Marxist Class-Analysis," *Acta Sociologica* 1970, 13, 11–29.

production should be questioned. In addition it is questionable whether formal rational behavior, which does not take account of unused production resources and unemployment, really can be termed *formal* rational, especially in relation to the goal of permanent *maximized* profit-making.

At the same time one could ask whether today Marx would not question the consequences of substituting in "the name of socialism anarchy of production" by a rigid planning, leading to extreme bureaucratization and the rule of a bureaucratic-administrative class, with all its attendant negative consequences for mankind.

The metatheoretical positions adopted by Marx and Weber lead them to completely different conclusions when describing and analyzing the same phenomena. Emphasis being on the formal rational aspects of capitalism, the notion of alienation never enters into Weber's theories. Though not blind to the consequences of the development of bureaucracies, Weber never treats these aspects extensively.

This may also depend on the second type of difference between him and Marx, which I call extratheoretical. By that I refer to the differences with regard to their image of man. Marx sees man as a totality. He is not the sum of his social relations; man *is* his social relations and, as they change, man will change. (See also pages 56 and 313.) Weber, on the other hand, has the image of *homo sociologicus*. Man is the sum of the roles to which he is ascribed, and different roles demand different behavior and a different type of ethics. In fact Weber has to reject man as a totality. The "split" into different roles is a precondition for man's being able to play different roles: to function within a bureaucratic organization as *Fachmensch* (expert), to be able to make choices independently, and to assume the responsibility for his own behavior.

Both Marx and Weber accept the idea of man as a rational being in the sense of being capable of acting consciously. However, according to Marx, social conditions may prevent him from doing so, and therefore the social and economic structure of society should be changed in order to make possible man's conscious control over his physical and social environment. According to the classification used in chapter 1, Marx's theories are individual-oriented. Weber's theories, on the other hand, are mainly society-oriented. Man should act formally-rationally within a given system and in relation to the goals of the system. Even if Weber's society-oriented theories are not always explicitly formulated, this orientation can be shown to underlie some of his distinctions.

As an example, we can take the distinction between formal and substantial rationality. To the extent that he perceives the influence of standards of substantial rationality to be a "disturbance" of a consequent formal rational action, it can be interpreted as a society-oriented attitude: substantial rationality sets human needs in relation to political, hedonistic, etc., values. When substantial rationality is perceived as a "disturbing" factor in the carrying out of formal rational behavior oriented toward the functioning of the system, and when, therefore, attempts are made to overcome these disturbances, the consequences are as follows: human needs, interests, and demands are subordinated to the demands of the system.

The most decisive difference between Weber and Marx can be found in this emphasis on formal rationality. Marx also discusses the importance of formal rationality and its consequences for the process of production. But then he moves one step further and asks: What effect does it have on the producing individual? His answer, built upon the social conditions of capitalism at the beginning of the process of industrialization, is that[67] formal rationality, combined with the methods of technology, is used to increase productivity, the costs of which are paid by the workers. The means to develop the process of production are used to dominate the worker and to degrade him to a machine. This toil makes it impossible for his labor to have meaningful content.

Thus, whereas Marx is concerned with the consequences of the social and economic structure upon the life of man, Weber restricts himself to a functional analysis and describes formal rationality without going deeply into the consequences it may have for man. These differences exemplify what we mean by an individual-oriented vs. a society-oriented approach.

GEORG SIMMEL AND THE PROGRESS OF OBJECTIVATION

MAN'S TOTALITY AS OPPOSED TO DIVISION INTO ROLES

"The deepest problems of modern life derive from the claim of the individual to preserve autonomy and individuality of his existence in the face of overwhelming social forces, of historical heritage, of external culture, and of the technique of life."[68]

This quotation forms the introduction to an essay written by Georg Simmel about human psychology in the modern city. Besides dealing with the problems of the process of urbanization, he places this process into a wider framework. It exemplifies a problem of culture—to Simmel perhaps *the* problem of culture in our time—man's chances of preserving and maintaining his individuality, his personality, in the mass-society in which his social connections have become less and in which human relations involve only a part of his personality.

[67] K. Marx, *Capital*, German edition (Berlin: Dietz Verlag, 1965), Vol. I.
[68] G. Simmel, *Sociology*, trans. & ed. K. H. Wolff (Glencoe, Ill.: The Free Press, 1950), p. 409.

If one wishes to use the terminology of sociological role-theory, one could characterize the problem posed by Simmel in the following manner: How can man preserve his totality when he plays different roles, all of which constitute or involve only a part of his totality?[69] If we compare this way of framing the problem with Weber's ideas of the personality, we find quite different points of departure. As we have pointed out, Weber, denying the idea of a human totality, sees man as the sum of his roles. Simmel, starting from a totality, sees the roles as a threat to the entity. His concept of man has certain basic similarities with that of Marx—a point of view to which we shall return.

"The metropolis has always been the seat of the money-economy,"[70] says Simmel. An economic system which builds upon money, instead of on the exchange of goods, causes basic changes in the human psyche. Money economy and the dominance of the intellect—rational behavior if one wishes to use Weber's term—are closely related to each other. Man takes an objective—in the meaning of cold and uninvolved—attitude to things. In its turn, this affects the relations between people, their social interaction.

"The intellectually sophisticated person is indifferent to all genuine individuality, because relationships and reactions result from it, which cannot be exhausted with logical operations. In the same manner, the individuality of phenomena is not commensurate with the pecuniary principle. . . . All intimate emotional relations between persons are founded in their individuality, whereas in rational relations man is reckoned with like a number, like an element which is in itself indifferent. Only the objective measurable achievement is of interest."[71]

The description given here by Simmel reminds one of Weber's description of formal rationality. But Simmel puts it forward in contrast to emotional—nonrational—factors, which he considers to be the expression of man's individuality.

The objectivation of human relations is connected with the changeover from an economy based on the exchange of goods to a money economy, and with the changing role of money. From being a substance, money is transformed into a medium. It has a function, it becomes a tool in a trichotomous teleological process: the wishes or needs of the individual, which are directed to definite goals, the achieving of which is seen as a success. Simmel maintains that in our society, money has become the perfect medium, the medium per se in this teleological process. It forms a

[69] E. V. Walter, "Simmel's Sociology of Power: The Architecture of Politics," in *Georg Simmel*, ed. K. H. Wolff (Columbus: Ohio State University Press, 1959). Walter treats the problem of fragmentation in Simmel's theory.

[70] Simmel, *Sociology*, p. 411.

[71] Ibid.

joining link between the personal, demanding ego and objects outside of the ego, to which the ego's will is directed.

FROM ECONOMY BASED ON THE EXCHANGE OF GOODS TO A MONEY ECONOMY

In a heavy volume entitled *Philosophie des Geldes*,[72] Simmel not only develops his theories about money and its role but also places them in a cultural historical context. This book is full of interesting psychological and sociological observations, often interpreted in a philosophical way, where "philosophical" sometimes can be equated with "metaphysical." It is learned and full of fantasy, a remarkable product of the classical German "historically oriented speculative sociology."

"One can depict the development of every human destiny from a definite point of view, namely, that it turns out to be a continuous movement between binding and releasing, between duty and freedom,"[73] says Simmel. But one should not forget, he continues, that that which appears as freedom may in fact mean only a change in one's duties. What changes in these dialectical processes has the creation of a modern money economy accomplished for the individual?

In a social relation, every obligation or duty of one of the parties is balanced by a demand from the other party. These demands may involve both behavior and achievements; they may affect work or certain objects. The great difference lies in whether or not the demanding party in the interaction can widen his demand so that the whole of the personality of the obligated person is concerned. Otherwise it is only the products of the labor of the obligated party which are involved. The most extreme relationship between a demanding and an obligated party is slavery. In this case, the demands are not concerned with performance alone but embrace the whole person, who belongs to the demanding party. A less extreme relation occurs when the obligation is limited by time and concerns only certain work-achievements. An example of this is the crofter, who must work for the landlord without payment on three weekdays. As the demand concerns only the handing over of certain products, the freedom of the person who is obligated is increased. If, now, the crofter no longer works for the landlord but instead gives him payment in kind, the extent to which he is bound to the landlord will lessen. This is because in such a case the demanding person is not concerned with *how* the obligated person performs his duties, but only with the fact that he *does* so.

[72] G. Simmel, *Die Philosophie des Geldes* [*The Philosophy of Money*] (Leipzig: Duncker & Humblot, 1907).
[73] Ibid., p. 297.

The third stage is reached when economy based on the exchange of goods—or "payment in kind" is replaced by a money economy. In principle, this means that every *personal* obligation, i.e., a duty which involves the obligated person himself, can be replaced by a sum of money, the most neutral and uninvolved way of meeting demands and performing duties.

"The supplier, the creditor, the workers on whom one depends, do not appear as personalities, because their relations to oneself only involve one aspect, namely to deliver goods, to lend money, to work, while other aspects which could lend a personal touch to the relationship cannot be taken into consideration."[74]

MONEY ECONOMY AND HUMAN RELATIONS

According to Simmel, money economy has meant that human relations have become more neutral, less involved, which in its turn can be seen as a greater measure of freedom. To be subordinate to an impersonal collective or a rational organization feels less binding than personal dependence on another individual. One may add that in the first case it is easier for the individual to look after his own interests.

Another factor is involved here. The division of labor has meant not only that the individual comes into contact with a greater number of people than was previously the case, but also that in his work he is dependent on more people. But once again, this dependency does not involve personal relations but "objective functions."

"While in an earlier stage of development man had to pay for his few relations of dependency with the narrowness of personal relations, and often with personal irreplaceability, we are now compensated for our multiple dependency-relations by the indifference which we can show to those persons with whom we have relations, and by the freedom to replace these persons which is ours."[75]

The change in the direction of greater freedom brought about by the money economy involves the replacing of a few intimate relations with that of impersonal relations with a great number of persons, who are replaceable. Even the worker in a modern industrial enterprise is involved in this. Of course, he is chained to his machine, to his work. Seen objectively, however, it is a fact that he has increased choice: he can change his place of work, and he can change the nature of the work he does, which means greater freedom for him. But, concomitantly this may bring decreased security and less personal care on the part of his employers.

[74] Ibid., p. 313.
[75] Ibid., p. 314.

Personal relations between employers and employees are reduced to the bare minimum. Often they do not know each other—not even by sight.

"The increased self-respect of the modern worker must be connected with the fact that he no longer feels humble, but simply performs a carefully prescribed—carefully prescribed due to money-equivalence—action, which allows his personality to be free, the more objective, impersonal and technical are the task and the enterprise which provides the task."[76]

Subordination in a hierarchical system feels less oppressive, involves fewer feelings of powerlessness and valuelessness the more this hierarchical system is impersonal and serves technical ends, maintains Simmel. Literally, he says that the objective character of the goals is hardly able to create subjective experiences. From a social-psychological point of view one could object that there arises another problem. Subordination is often experienced as contrasting with ideas of equality, and that in its turn leads to conflicts and feelings of antagonism. Simmel's interpretation of the role of the worker is also interesting. He ignores one factor, namely, the role played by work in the experiencing of the self and the self-image which is formed by the individual. In his analysis he departs from Marx's ideas in which labor provides the opportunity for the individual to express his personality. He is in agreement with Marx's ideas on another point. This concerns the effect of the commodity market. Simmel maintains that the money economy has the same psychological effect on the leaders of the enterprise as it has on the workers.

In contrast to the artisans of the Middle Ages, the manager of the enterprise manufactures his products for the market. This means that he produces for indifferent customers, who are total strangers to him. His only relation with these customers is through the money—often via an intermediary—which they pay for the products. In this way the activity is objectivized and separated from the personality of the actor.

But the coin has another side. Increased personal freedom means greater isolation and rootlessness. The individual may experience freedom as a burden, when his loneliness becomes a threat. Simmel gives several reasons for these negative consequences, some of which we will take up for discussion.[77]

First, Simmel says that society is not so structured that it does not require personal involvement. An example of this is military service. Logically, it would be reasonable that a society with a money-economy

---

[76] Ibid., p. 362.

[77] Erich Fromm in his book *Escape from Freedom* (New York: Holt, Rinehart & Winston, 1941) uses the conflict between "freedom" and "loneliness" as a starting point for an analysis of psychological escape mechanism. The German Nazism he considers as a medium for such an escape. Fromm seems to draw heavily on Simmel's theories as developed in *Die Philosophie des Geldes*.

should form a professional army and pay for the activities of this army with money. Instead, military service is a step away from this neutral, activity-oriented way of thinking, as it demands personal involvement in the carrying out of the duty which has been imposed. In a democratic society, this is compensated by certain political rights, but even these presuppose a certain amount of personal engagement. Further, once a money economy has been accomplished, economic power can more easily be concentrated and the individual can more easily be controlled. When the chief relations of the individual have the character of exchange of an activity for money, control over these exchange-relations is of enormous importance: "Depending on the starting point and content, money-performance has shown itself to be the bearer of both total freedom and total repression."[78] Therefore, freedom is often seen as freedom *from* personal ties. It is a freedom *from* something without being complemented by a freedom *to* something.

Another reason put forward by Simmel is that the money economy brought with it a circulation of goods and commodities due to general buying and selling. This means that the individual develops a neutral attitude in his relationship to his possessions. Yet this can no longer help him to establish his identity in the same way that few possessions, but which were undeniably his, could. "Money not only makes it possible for us to be freed from the ties we have in relation to others, but also to those we have in relation to our own possessions."[79]

On the other hand, the individual has psychological needs, which means that he is not always satisfied with an objective payment for his performance. A businessman often wants more than money for his goods. He desires that the customer be satisfied and show this satisfaction. An artist who sells a picture wants to be appreciated for his skill. A worker who receives his wages wants to feel that his work is meaningful, that he is not merely a cog in a machine. All this suggests that the neutrality in human relations—which exchange of goods and payment of money for services brings with it—may be experienced as a lack, as the absence of something for which money cannot compensate.

THE ROLE OF KNOWLEDGE AND INTELLECT

The feeling of isolation is also brought about by another condition. Technical development constantly creates new, complex objects. It gives rise to new knowledge, and it also differentiates knowledge. Through it the collectivity as a unit is constantly widening the scope of its knowledge and achieves more and more results, while the individual is no longer

[78] Simmel, *Die Philosophie des Geldes*, p. 440.
[79] Ibid., p. 449.

able to take these in and therefore feels as if he has fallen behind. In modern industry, for instance, many workers are unable to understand how their machines work.

In fact, the problem of knowledge is one of the central problems. Money economy creates a definite style of life. As money is a medium in the most general meaning of the word—it allows itself to be used in all sorts of ways and is therefore unrestricted—a money economy means emphasizing the means at the expense of the ends. This is always presuming that the means do not themselves become ends. According to Simmel, psychologically this means a stress on the intellect at the expense of the emotions. The latter is connected with ends because ends always involve values.

The connection between money economy and the intellect builds upon an emotional neutrality and lack of involvement. This is the same as saying that emotionality—together with ends—is pushed into the background. In turn, this leads to what Simmel calls "ethical egoism" and individualism. Egoism becomes rational action, unaffected by emotions. Collective tendencies are similarly rejected as irrational.

The emphasis on the importance of the intellect for social success can be seen as the precondition for equality between people: All have the same opportunity to obtain knowledge and education. But "the superficial equality which education offers to all those who obtain it is, in reality, a grievous insult, just as are all other freedoms in liberalistic doctrines. Naturally it prevents no one from making profit in every conceivable manner, but it overlooks the fact that, due to certain circumstances, it is only those who are already privileged who have the chance of doing so."[80]

This creates social differences which are more difficult to even out than those which are not grounded in education and knowledge. To some extent, Simmel's argument anticipates our discussion of the meritocracy.

Even if workers today have a higher living standard than ever before, the gap between their way of life and that of the "upper classes" has widened. Because, says Simmel: "a general raising of the knowledge level does not mean a general levelling, but rather in fact the opposite."[81]

Apart from the money system and intellectuality, the legal system also plays a similar role. All three have one thing in common. They make equality, formally and generally, the foundation of human relations. But as this takes place only in a *formal* and *general* manner, egoism can make use of all three. The fact that they are generally accessible can serve every person, but they can also be used as a weapon against the individual.

Finally, there is a direct analogy between money and knowledge. Capital increases with the help of interest and profit. This means that when

---

[80] Ibid., p. 493.
[81] Ibid., p. 494.

the accumulation of capital has reached a certain level, capital increases of its own volition, without much effort from the owner of the capital. What Simmel means is that a similarity exists between this and the structure of our knowledge in our culture. At a certain level, the possession of knowledge requires less and less effort from the individual, as knowledge on a high level presents itself in an abstract and therefore concentrated way. This leads to the process of objectivization. It means that the results of the intellect are divorced from the actual process of gaining knowledge, so that "only the fact that one has already reached such heights makes it possible to pluck those fruits the ripening of which has occurred without our help."[82]

The final characteristic in the general cultural development is the general rationality, an ideal of knowledge which sees the world as a huge example of arithmetic. According to Simmel, this orientation to reckoning, measuring, and quantifying is intellectualism in its purest form. It stands in sharp contrast to the impulsive, emotional, more integrated personality. It purifies egoism and creates a rationality—and here Simmel is at one with Weber—whose goal is calculability: "The determining of abstract time by means of the clock, just as abstract value by means of money, makes possible a scheme of the most careful and safe divisions and measures, and endows life with an unattained transparency and calculability."[83]

OBJECTIFIED CULTURE

What Simmel once called "the tragedy of culture" lies in the whole of this development.[84] We shall begin the discussion of this problem by presenting Simmel's definition of "culture." By "culture" he means "the refined spiritual forms of life, the results of inner and outer labor."[85] But cultural phenomena embrace in fact three categories: (1) The world of objects, which Simmel refers to as "material products of culture," for example, furniture, machines, works of art, books, and tools. Even the mental products which decide men's relations to each other, namely, language, science, religion, and law, fit into this category. (2) The process through which the material and mental products are brought about. As far as the material products are concerned, the process is often a question of a change, a refinement of things within nature. (3) The process through which the individual takes onto himself the culture, obtains knowledge

82 Ibid., p. 497.
83 Ibid., p. 500.
84 G. Simmel, "Der Begriff und die Tradödie der Kultur," in *Zur Philosophie der Kunst* [*The Philosophy of Art*] (Potsdam: Kiepenheuer, 1922).
85 Simmel, *Die Philosophie des Geldes*, p. 502.

and education, "becomes cultivated." Simmel, following Hegel, calls all material and mental products "objectified spirit" and "objectified culture." The following quotation clarifies his meaning: "In language and in customs, in political texts and religious ideas, in literature and technology, is found the labor of generations, deposited in the form of spirit, or intellect, which has been transformed into objects, and from which each and every person takes as much as he wishes or is able to take, but which no individual should be able to empty."[86]

The products, both material and spiritual, which are created by means of intellectual labor therefore are called "objectified spirit" by Simmel. This involves the transformation of ideas into objects which "accommodate" these ideas. Together, these form our culture. This objectivizing, or transforming thoughts and ideas into words and "works" of various kinds, makes possible our spiritual inheritance; it "presents us with a whole world." That part of the total culture which every individual is able to make use of is interchangeably called by Simmel "subjective spirit" and "subjective culture," in contrast to the total culture, which is "objective spirit" and "objective culture" respectively.

Simmel sees as a basic problem the discrepancy between the greater scope and higher level reached by the objective culture, and the lesser scope and lower level reached by the subjective, i.e., the level which the accessible, known culture has reached for the individual.

He says that this discrepancy is constantly widening. How can that fact be explained? Generally speaking, at all times only a part of the total objectified culture can become subjective culture in every society confined by the limits of space and time. If, for instance, Newton's teaching was to be found only in a book which nobody had read, he would still be part of the objectified spirit but would belong to that part which is not accessible in our current subjective culture.

The discrepancy between subjective and objective culture depends partly on the range of the objective culture. In the Middle Ages, for example, a scientist was able to have command over all, or a great proportion of, "science." Today, a mathematician or a sociologist has command over only a fraction of his field, not to speak of other fields which are unconnected with his specialist area.

This example suggests that the discrepancy depends not only on the range of the objective culture, but also on differentiation, which in its turn is based on the process of the *division of labor*. In Simmel's view, this concerns production just as much as consumption.

First, let us take production. There are three processes involved in the division of labor: (1) differentiation of various branches of production,

---

[86] Ibid., p. 506.

(2) division of the manufacturing process, and (3) specialization, i.e., division into manual and intellectual work. These processes lead to the fact that the development of production occurs at the cost of the producer's involvement in his work. Only a part of his capacities or abilities are used, which means that relations between the producer—the worker—and his product, break down. The product becomes a lifeless object. Its meaning does not originate in the soul of the producer, but in the association between various parts produced by various persons. This, more or less, is Simmel's idea, and it shows a great similarity with the ideas held by Marx on the consequences of the division of labor. Behind such ideas lies a definite perception of man as a totality. One-sided activity means that the unified, total personality becomes stunted "because one-sided activity sucks out the energy-quantum of the personality, which is indispensable for a harmonious ego."[87]

As far as consumption is concerned, an increase is evident. But mass consumption means conformity of products, which fails to allow for the satisfaction of individual needs and tastes: in its turn, this leads to the coarsening of the individual's subjective culture.

Another factor contributing to the increasing discrepancy between subjective and objective culture is the fact that the worker is separated from his means of production. Here, too, we find that Simmel and Marx have similar ideas, though both differ from Weber. Because, in a capitalist society, the means of production are owned by a person who does not himself operate them, and those who operate them do not own them, there occurs what Simmel calls "a difference between the objective and subjective conditions of work."[88] That which the worker does—the subjective aspect—is connected neither with the tools he uses nor with the products he creates. Neither the tools, the means of production, nor the results of labor belong to the worker. They have a completely objective character. His labor power becomes a commodity: "As long as the worker creates with his own materials the work takes place within the framework of his own personality, and only departs from it as a completed object when the goods are sold."[89] When labor power is changed into a commodity, this leads to a process of differentiation within the personality, in which parts become divorced from it and become independent objects. As previously pointed out, this reasoning builds upon a concept of the unity of personality.

Here we encounter the same reasoning we found in Marx. It is founded on the concept of labor as the expression and realization of the personality.

[87] Ibid., p. 512.
[88] Ibid., p. 514.
[89] Ibid.

It involves the tarrying at the artisan form of production, and criticism of the process of industrialization.

The process of industrialization brought with it an important development, seen from the point of view of culture. Simmel says that the hierarchical structure of society is often defended by maintaining that the lowest layer of the hierarchy works for the higher layers. Their work is a necessary condition for the creation of culture—in a narrower meaning—which takes place in the higher layers of the hierarchy. But this idea receives no support from the industrial society, which is characterized by the process of the division of labor. The highly educated chemist who works to produce new textile colors, works for "the farm woman who chooses a highly coloured scarf from the travelling draper."[90] All this is possible only because of the objectivization of production, which does away with all relations between the producers of culture on the high level and the customers on the low level. Behind this observation lies Simmel's idea that the creation of culture also involves development toward "cultivation" or "refinement," which is apparent from his definition of culture as quoted earlier.

The development toward an objectified culture may be illustrated with still another example: the relation between man and the machine. The latter becomes a totality. It takes over more and more of man's work. It becomes an autonomous power in relation to man, who no longer functions as a totality, but only in certain roles: he performs certain operations which have no connection with his personality.

While man's totality becomes split, the objects receive such a totality, and this leads to the individual's feeling of estrangement with regard to the objects, i.e., he is estranged from the content of our culture. While the objectified culture develops and grows, the subjective culture of the individual is impoverished.

Another example is found in household equipment. Furniture produced by craftsmen had a certain durability, which allowed it to become integrated into the personality. Part of the individual's experience of himself, his perception of his identity, took place through those things to which he was attached. Mass production of things means that, both because of their multiplicity and their relative lack of durability, the things become objects and foreign to the individual.

A third example presented by Simmel is the rapid change in fashion which is part and parcel of the industrial society. This, too, means that an object is unable to be seen as a part of the personality, but instead is experienced as an autonomous thing.

In this way, mechanized production and mass consumption cooperate to

[90] Ibid., p. 517.

create "the atrophy of individual culture, through a hypertrophy of the objective culture."[91] Interaction between people is also affected by this development. It becomes an exchange-situation in which, during the actual exchange process itself, one tries to take just as much as one gives. To the extent that the exchange is concerned with things—this type of exchange has increased in importance—there is the risk that the interaction itself becomes objectified. This means that personal interaction is pushed to one side, man's role in the interaction becomes irrelevant, but the thing itself receives its own value: "The relation among men has become a relations among objects."[92]

SIMMEL AND MARX—A COMPARISON

Several times we have underlined the similarities between the theories of Simmel and Marx. The theory that things have been created by man for definite ends, but that they become objectified, independent of their creators and of the goals for which they were created, is very similar to the idea of *Verdinglichung*—reification.

Raymond Aron says that Simmel here returns to the Marxist theme of the magician's apprentice, with the difference that he speaks of *objectivization*, while Marx more specifically speaks of *alienation*.[93] There is no doubt that Simmel's theory can be characterized as "individual-oriented." He speaks of the personality of the individual as a totality which is split by social development. As opposed to Marx, who blames capitalism for this development, Simmel seems to see it more as an unavoidable consequence of the development of modern culture based upon money economy. He calls it "the tragedy of culture." There is another precondition for theories of alienation (see chapter 1) which we find in Simmel: the antagonism of the individual and his needs on the one hand, and society and its demands on the other. He speaks of the deep and tragic antagonism that exists in every social formation, and which means that man is subjected to two irreconcilable norms: "our movement revolving around our own centre (something totally different from egoism) claims to be as definite as the movement around the social centre."[94]

Finally, let us briefly summarize Simmel's picture of man, which forms the background to his theory of objectivization.

Simmel, like Marx, asks what is the essence of man—that which differentiates him from the animal. The answer is that man is partly a being who

[91] Simmel, *Sociology*, p. 422.

[92] Ibid., p. 388.

[93] R. Aron, "Culture and Life," in *Georg Simmel*, ed. L. A. Coser (Englewood Cliffs: Prentice-Hall, 1965).

[94] Simmel, *Sociology*, p. 248.

makes use of tools, which is connected to the fact that his behavior is always directed toward definite goals.[95] But another thing may be added here: man is an *exchanging* animal. This is only an aspect of a much more general condition. To participate in exchange presupposes a general capacity to *objectify*, i.e., "to deal with things without reference to subjective feelings or desires."[96]

But Simmel is concerned not solely with an anthropological theory, but also with a theory of psychological development and a value theory.

Mental life begins as a condition of indifference, in which the ego is not yet differentiated from other objects. The first awareness of this ego (that which G. H. Mead calls the experience of the self)[97] means that the individual begins to notice objects outside its own ego. But, asserts Simmel, self-consciousness of the personal ego is in itself an objectifying: it admits a difference between the thinking, experiencing I-subject, and the thought, experienced I-object. Here, too, the thoughts can be related to Mead's theories. The differentiation between ego and thing, between subject and object, is a precondition for the formation of the personality. Differentiation is also concerned with our needs and their satisfaction. In the beginning, the needs are not consciously experienced. Need followed by satisfaction is a single unit. It is only experienced as something divided when the individual realizes that he is asking for something he has not yet received and imagines the pleasure of it. In that way the object of our desires becomes something apart from ourselves. In the moment of consumption, in which pleasure and satisfaction are experienced, the distinction is momentarily abolished, to reappear with new needs. But the desired object is associated with a definite value. This feeling of value which is associated with things, with people and with actions, plays an important role in the formation of the personality.

According to Simmel, individuality develops partly because the individual meets a choice among those objects he desires, and partly because he limits the number of objects to which value is attached. In this way, a refining of the individual takes place. This is not just an important aspect of the personality. The very process is synonymous with cultivation. A "cultivated person" is a person who, in a double meaning, has made use of the objective culture: He has incorporated it with his personality, but as this occurs with discrimination it has occurred on a higher plane, a "cultivated level."

We see here how Simmel's concept of personality, and his ideas as to how the individual assimilates the objective culture, are permeated by

[95] Simmel, *Die Philosophie des Geldes*, p. 206.

[96] Ibid., p. 306.

[97] G. H. Mead, *The Social Psychology of George Herbert Mead*, ed. and with an introduction by A. Strauss (Chicago: University of Chicago Press, 1956).

subjective evaluations, which to a great extent seems to agree with the "German educated bourgeoisie and its ideals."

Personality is defined by Simmel as a totality of qualities, aspects of character, and powers. The personality becomes an entity when those reactions which stem from purely organismic functions are integrated with the reactions and powers that are created through the social relations of the individual, his work, and his roles. This integrated entity, which is the personality, and in which emotional and motivational factors play an important role, is integrated in the modern industrial society, with its money economy. It is this process of disintegration which stands in reciprocal relation to the process of objectivization. In a very concentrated form, these are some of the most important aspects of Simmel's view of man, his personality, and the alienating risks to which he is exposed in a society that is. characterized by industrialization. Because of the importance he ascribes to emotional factors (in relation to intellectual) in the integration of the personality, he is only partly a rationalist. Even if, like Weber, he understands the importance of rationality in modern bureaucratized industrial society, he observes this with regret. His individualism is all too deeply rooted for him to be able to take up the same position as Weber. This individualism also gives something of the background, as far as ideologies are concerned, to his version of human alienation.

DURKHEIM AND ANOMIA

THE POSITIONS OF DURKHEIM'S THEORIES WITHIN THE HISTORY OF IDEAS

In a treatise concerning the position of Durkheim's theories within the framework of the history of ideas, Nisbet[98] asserts that Durkheim was negative toward three and positive toward two of the ideological streams of his period. He was negative toward *analytical individualism*, toward the idea of *progress*, and toward *biologism*, which means the tendency to reduce social phenomena to biological phenomena, to explain social events in terms of individual, biologically founded, motivation. However, he remained positive toward, and strongly influenced by, *positivism* and *conservatism*.

In our context the latter ideology is of special relevance. Nisbet[99] mentions five conservative ideas as being important in Durkheim's theories:

[98] R. A. Nisbet, *Emile Durkheim: With Selected Essays* (Englewood Cliffs: Prentice-Hall, 1968).

[99] Ibid., p. 25.

(1) Durkheim's ideas concerning the relationship between man and society. He accepts and emphasizes the primacy of society over the individual. Seen historically, society is not a product of man's social strivings. On the contrary, man is the product of society. Marx, too, emphasized the effects of social processes, especially the basic social process, the process of production. But at the same time it is man who creates the social processes. Whereas Marx always upheld the dialectic interplay of man and society, Durkheim insists on society as the primary phenomenon. Society is a totality and is more than the sum total of its individual members.

(2) As Nisbet points out, the second idea is a logical consequence of the first: The individual cannot function autonomously, as a psychologically independent being, but is dependent on society, its traditions, moral rules, and social norms. If there are no groups able to integrate the individual and develop and stabilize his moral, then such groups must be created. This is also the solution Durkheim suggests for overcoming the state he calls "anomy," i.e., normlessness, the lack of moral rules: *corporations* should be created, organizations for men especially those with common economic and occupational or professional interests. A large part of the preface to the second edition of his book *Division of Labor* is devoted to this problem.[100]

(3) The third idea concerns the necessity of a authority able to guarantee the acceptance of moral and social group norms. To Durkheim authority is equal to discipline. Discipline is not just a means of reaching certain aims: "discipline derives its *raison d'être* from itself; it is good that man is disciplined, independent of the acts to which he thus finds himself constrained."[101] Discipline is a goal in itself, because without it society could not function. In addition, since the individual's personal interests may conflict with the interests of his group, it is only discipline that can make him voluntarily accept the aims of the group. Thus Durkheim also places importance on man as an acting being within the constraints of society. His idea concerning the primacy of society does not lead him to view man as a passive object, incapable of making his own moral decisions, mainly due to social pressures.

(4) The fourth idea concerns the role of religion within society. Since this aspect of his theory is not of importance in the context in which we wish to treat Durkheim, we will not elaborate on this idea.

[100] E. Durkheim, *The Division of Labor in Society*, trans. G. Simpson (New York: The Free Press, 1964).

[101] E. Durkheim, *Moral Education: A Study in Theory and Application of the Sociology of Education*, trans. E. K. Wilson and H. Schnurer (New York: The Free Press, 1961), p. 30.

(5) The fifth and final idea is the organic character of society. As in a human organism, each part of society—each organ—performs a certain function necessary for the proper functioning of the total system. Durkheim expresses explicitly what he means by "function." He says that the term is usually applied in two ways. It may refer to processes—Durkheim calls them "vital movements"—without reference to consequences. For example, one speaks of the function of respiration. "But we also say . . . that respiration has for its function the introduction of necessary gases into the tissues of an animal for the sustainment of life, etc. It is in the second sense we shall use the term."[102] Thus by "function" he refers to the relationship between certain processes within a given system and the effect of these processes on the total system.

To exemplify: Durkheim's organismic view influences the analysis of social problems. When, in his *Division of Labor* he discusses problems created by the economic development in industrialized society, he speaks of the necessity of social planning and of creating regulations and social bodies which like cerebral ganglions "would have the power either to stop the excitations, or to amplify them, or to moderate them according to need."[103] However, says Durkheim, such social bodies do not exist, and concludes: "What is certain is that this lack of regulation does not permit a regular harmony of functions."[104] Thus organismic thinking leads Durkheim to introduce notions of social harmony, of equilibrium disturbed by social conflicts. Therefore, conflicts are not "normal events," nor are they viewed as necessary or even desirable for social change.

This basic view of society is thus founded on certain—in this case conservative—values and naturally leads to a certain type of analysis and in the long run to certain implications with regard to social and political action.

We have previously (in chapter 1) asserted that notions concerning society as an organism and coupled with this notion of equilibrium as the "normal" state of an organism are founded, often implicitly, on conservative values. As a consequence, organismic theories of society look at alienation as a process of lack of adjustment of the individual to the demands of society. This lack of adjustment may be based on unsufficient solidarity, on lack of discipline, on the absence of moral rules or the lack of regulating bodies able to create moral constraints. Thus these theories of alienation are "society-oriented." Durkheim, much more so than Weber, represents this type of theory, and is therefore also further away from Marx. The contrast between Marx and Durkheim also illuminates the

---

[102] Durkheim, *Division of Labor*, p. 49.
[103] Ibid., p. 218.
[104] Ibid., p. 367.

importance of the underlying image of man and society for consequent sociological theorizing.

ANOMY

"We repeatedly insist in the course of this book upon the state of juridical and moral anomy in which economic life actually is found,"[105] says Durkheim in the previously quoted preface to the second edition of *Division of Labor*. According to him, there exists practically no ethical system in the economic sphere of society. There are some general and vague ideas about faithfulness and devotion which workers ought to show their employers, who in turn should not use their economic superiority against the worker but rather accept moderation. In addition employers should abstain from conduct "too openly dishonest, for all untempered exploitation of the consumer; that is about all the moral conscience of these trades contains."[106]

In addition there is another factor which weakens the already fallible moral. The few moral rules do not have strong support in any law. An ethic which is so vague and unclear and which does not constitute a coherent system cannot lead to discipline. But "human passions stop only before a moral power they respect."[107] For these reasons economic life is in a state of anomy. The fact which aggravates the situation is "the heretofore unknown development that economic functions have experienced for about two centuries. Whereas formerly they played only a secondary role, they are now of first importance. Only the scientific functions seem to dispute their place, and even science has scarcely any prestige save to the extent that it can serve practical occupations, which are largely economic."[108]

This description of the industrialized society does not differ too much from the one delivered by other critics. Durkheim—like Marx, Weber, and Simmel—uses the criticism of the process of industrialization as the foundation for his theory concerning the shape of economic functions and processes. Durkheim, too, considers the development as negative and engages in serious criticism of society. He asserts that the anomic state is the *cause*, not the result, of social conflicts, of disorders "of which the economic world exhibits so sad a spectacle."[109]

Anomy is evil not so much because the individual may suffer, but be-

---

[105] Ibid., p. 1; 2.
[106] Ibid., p. 2.
[107] Ibid., p. 3.
[108] Ibid.
[109] Ibid., p. 2.

cause this state impairs the proper functioning of society, which cannot exist without cohesiveness and orderliness. The problem of anomy, however, is treated in a more detailed way in Durkheim's book on suicide.[110] Therefore we shall discuss it briefly. The work on suicide is one of the most outstanding in classical sociology, being written with an elegance, a logical sharpness, and a convincing reasoning which make it a pleasure to read.

As in all his works, the book on suicide takes up the problem of the relation of the individual to the society. He rejects the idea of explaining suicide in terms of psychological factors. Being consequent in his rejection of reductionism and faithful to his methodological rule that social phenomena should be explained by social causes, he differentiates between suicide as an individual act and the suicide rates. It is the latter which is to be explained, since the suicide rate is a social phenomenon. Durkheim does not deny the existence of psychopathological states which may create a disposition for suicide. These states, however, do not determine suicide. First, suicides are often persons who do not have pathological dispositions; second, these dispositions do not account for variations in the rate.

The variations are correlated with a number of social conditions and social situations. Analyzing them Durkheim differentiates between three types of suicide: *egoistic, altruistic,* and *anomic* suicide. Using statistical data Durkheim points to the difference in suicide rates among Catholics, Protestants, and Jews. By showing that suicide rates are highest among Protestants, he then asserts that the Catholic Church is more integrated than Protestant churches. With regard to Jews he finds that persecution has led to a sense of solidarity. Thus, the greater independence which the Protestant churches allow to their members and the lower degree of integration is seen as one explanation for the variation of the suicide rate.

Durkheim then correlates family structure with suicide rates and finds the highest prevalence among unmarried people and married people without children. Lack of integration into the family is seen as another variable for increasing the suicide rate. Thus Durkheim concludes when people are not integrated in their religious and family groups, they become individualists; as such, they are more concerned with their own fate and their own problems and much less with the problems of the group. Durkheim in a true conservative mood and in contrast to the ideas of liberalism and individualism, which consider lack of integration into groups as freedom, equates individualism with egoism and finds this attitude as one of the causes for variation in the suicide rate. This is the *egoistic type* of suicide.

Whereas egoistic suicide is seen as a consequence of an individualization

[110] E. Durkheim, *Suicide: A Study in Sociology,* trans. J. A. Spaulding and G. Simpson (New York: The Free Press, 1951).

which has gone too far, altruistic suicide is the opposite, namely, the consequence of a lack of individualization and of a too strong integration with the individual's social group. Referring to different societies, Durkheim finds that the society may exert pressure on the individual to commit suicide, e.g., in India widows were obliged to commit suicide in order to share the fate of their husbands. Another example which he treats in detail, using statistics, is suicide among persons belonging to the military profession. They show a higher rate than civilians due to the fact that they are most highly integrated in their group and subordinated to its discipline.

In addition to lack of integration and extremely high integration, Durkheim analyzes a third type of suicide, the *anomic* one. He finds a correlation between the suicide rate and economic crisis: in periods of economic crisis suicide rates increase. However, suicide rates increase, also, when there are states of economic prosperity. In situations in which the individual becomes highly involved in his society, e.g., during war periods, there is a decrease in suicide rates.

In periods of social disintegration, when the individual's ties to his groups and to society in general are weakened, a crisis occurs. This may be the case either in periods of economic depression or when there is prosperity, the decisive factor being that in the first case the individual becomes isolated perhaps against his own wishes, whereas in times of prosperity he may desire his independence.

In cases of rapid social change—depression as well as prosperity— traditional customs are weakened, and the social control mechanisms which tend to keep society in balance are put out of order.

Anomy, in other words, is a consequence of lack of balance within the social system. Balance can be upheld only by social pressures, which in turn rest upon traditional customs and norms. Thus a central problem to Durkheim is the disturbance of the equilibrium in society. Anomy is the result. A state of normlessness, which leads to the weakening of the individual's group ties, in turn affects the group's chances of affecting the individual and his behavior.

Whereas in individual-oriented theories of alienation the societal forces become too strong and thus prevent the individual from realizing himself, in society-oriented theories the strength of societal norms prevents alienation. Its weakening leads to chaos. Durkheim maintains that in such situations there are no rules which define what is possible and what is not possible, right or wrong, which demands are normal and which are excessive; and therefore there are no limits to what a subject can demand.[111] This is the description given by Durkheim.

[111] Ibid., p. 212.

MECHANICAL AND ORGANIC SOLIDARITY

In Durkheim's writings the society-oriented approach is also revealed in its analysis of the role of the division of labor. Whereas Marx and Simmel look upon the division of labor as one of the central determining factors for alienation, in Durkheim's theory it has quite a different function. In fact, social differentiation as a consequence of the division of labor substitutes solidarity based upon mechanical social pressure by an organic solidarity.

Durkheim adds that "if this hypothesis were proved, the division of labor would play a role much more important than that which we ordinarily attribute to it. It would serve not only to raise societies to luxury, desirable perhaps, but superfluous; it would be a condition of their existence. Through it, or at least particularly through it, their cohesion would be assured; it would determine the essential traits of their constitution. Accordingly, although we may not yet be in position to resolve the question rigorously, we can, however, imply from it now that, if such is really the function of the division of labor, it must have a moral character, for the need of order, harmony, and social solidarity is generally considered moral."[112]

Though cautious in his formulations Durkheim does not hesitate to emphasize the societal role of the division of labor and especially to underline its moral aspects, i.e., its consequences for the cohesiveness and balance of society.

To study a hypothesis such as that put forward by Durkheim, one has to investigate the type of social solidarity to be found in societies in which division of labor has been effected and to compare them with other societies and the type of solidarity which is predominant there.

Durkheim distinguished between two types of solidarity: *mechanical* and *organic*. Mechanical solidarity is solidarity through similarity. In a society in which mechanical solidarity prevails, there is little or no social differentiation. Therefore, individuals are alike. Belonging to the same group they follow the same norms, have the same values, and express the same ideas. There is strong social pressure toward this type of conformity, and conformity in turn keeps society together in a mechanical way.

The other form of solidarity is based upon social differentiation. Consensus in society is not due to similarity among individuals, but to the fact that they carry out different functions which complement each other. As social differentiation increases, the need for social pressures decreases. Why does Durkheim use the term *organic* to characterize this type of solidarity? The reason is his previously mentioned organismic view which

112 Durkheim, *Division of Labor*, p. 63.

makes him use analogies: "The parts of a living organism do not resemble each other; the organs of a living creature perform a function, and it is precisely because each organ has its own function, because the heart and the lungs are altogether different from the brain, that they are equally indispensable to life."[113]

When Durkheim speaks of the division of labor, he does not refer to the technological but to the societal aspects in a sense similar to that used by Marx. The social division of labor means social differentiation, e.g., in terms of social classes. Thus, whereas Marx sees social differentiation as the basis of social conflict—such as class struggle, which he considers to be the motor for social change—social differentiation in Durkheim's view is the consequence of change and establishes the social relations necessary to keep a society in balance without too great a social pressure.

How can one study a hypothesis that division of labor produces solidarity? If one investigated a society with a high level of division of labor and found a high degree of solidarity, one would simply have accomplished circular reasoning. Neither can one look for individual factors that would be opposed to the methodological rules put forward by Durkheim. Therefore, one must look for social phenomena which are correlated with the various types of solidarity.

"But social solidarity is a completely moral phenomenon which, taken by itself, does not lend itself to exact observation nor indeed to measurement. To proceed to this classification and this comparison, we must substitute for this internal fact which escapes us an external index which symbolizes it and study the former in the light of the latter."[114]

One such external fact is law. Since the law affects social solidarity, one should differentiate different types of laws. After such a classification, one can find which type of law is correlated with which type of solidarity. Legal norms can be classified according to the type of sanctions which are connected with them. The type of laws connected with sanctions causing suffering, Durkheim calls "repressive law." Other types of sanctions do not create suffering through punishment but try to reestablish the state that has been disturbed by a criminal act. Thus the function of this type of sanctions is a restitutive one. Therefore Durkheim calls the second type of law "restitutive."

Repressive legal norms are found in a society with mechanical solidarity, whereas restitutive law is a correlate of organic solidarity. Why is this so?

In order to answer this question we must first introduce another of Durkheim's concepts, namely, "collective conscience." This is defined as

---

[113] R. Aron, *Main Currents in Sociological Thought*, trans. R. Howard and H. Weaver (London: Weidenfeld and Nicolson, 1968), Vol. II, p. 12.

[114] Durkheim, *Division of Labor*, p. 64.

"the totality of beliefs and sentiments common to an average citizen of the same society."[115] Thus collective conscience is a statistical concept. However, according to Durkheim, the collective consciousness is that which in his book on methodology he defines as a "social fact."[116] It exists independent of particular individuals. In fact, it exists before the individual is born and continues after his death. The individual's conscience is derived from the collective conscience, when the individual has learned those beliefs and sentiments which form a part of the societal frame in which he lives. The collective conscience is therefore different from the individual conscience though it can be realized only through the latter. Since it is strongly anchored in tradition, it is much more difficult to change the collective conscience than to change social and economic conditions. (This is one important fact often neglected by Marxists. They usually assume that profound changes in the economic structures will lead to changes in beliefs and sentiments, but numerous proofs that this is not the case can be given.)

The collective conscience in societies without social differentiation embraces the individual's conscience. In differentiated societies only a part of the individual's conscience overlaps with the collective conscience, since in such a society individualism grows. The individual is free to develop his own ideas and sentiments. In societies without differentiation, crimes of deviating nature threaten the society and its cohesiveness and must therefore be repressed by strong punishment. In differentiated societies deviating behavior does not threaten the organic coherence, which is built upon the division of labor. Therefore the law mainly tries to restore the situation of justice disturbed by crime.

Therefore, restitutive law is correlated with organic solidarity, which presupposes cooperation among individuals. Since social differentiation and the division of labor create cooperation, they also create organic solidarity. This is a higher form of solidarity, since it does not need to build upon conformity alone—conformity caused by fear of repressive sanctions. Though common norms and customs are also found in societies with a high level of differentiation, these norms are not as important for the coherence of society as in less differentiated societies. Cooperation and social interaction become important constitutive factors in keeping a society in balance.

Organic solidarity thus creates a state of balance in society. However, this does not exclude the existence of social problems and social tensions. But they are caused by the fact that society is still in a state of transition,

[115] Ibid., p. 79.

[116] E. Durkheim, *The Rules of Sociological Method*, trans. S. Solovay and J. H. Mueller (New York: The Free Press, 1964).

which means that all the necessary preconditions for organic solidarity have not yet been realized: "If, in certain cases, organic solidarity is not all it should be, it is certainly not because mechanical solidarity has lost ground, but because all the conditions for the existence of organic solidarity have not been realized."[117]

Therefore organic solidarity can only grow slowly in a smooth process of social change. However, when social change is rapid and not a part of an organic development, anomy results. As indicated earlier, Durkheim maintains that acute anomy is found in states of sudden economic depression as well as in states of sudden economic prosperity. These situations carry with them a high rate of social mobility. Social mobility leads to normlessness: the individual changes his social position but does not learn as quickly the norms of the class or group into which he moves. This holds for downward social mobility as well as for upward.

There develops a discrepancy between the old traditional norms and the new social situation in which the subject finds himself. Social order is upheld not only by social norms but much more by the way in which these norms become integrated into the total social situation.

What Durkheim develops here is a certain type of "cultural-lag" hypothesis, where norms do not develop as fast as other aspects of the social situation. There is one interesting point in Durkheim's analysis. By developing these ideas he presents arguments for slow social change. Thus his theories may have a conservative, political effect. For the sake of preserving a certain balance in society, one may abstain from necessary social change. One could argue, however, that such an abstention may aggravate negative social conditions and existing conflicts. This holds especially for societies with large groups of underprivileged and discriminated people. In this case slow change may prevent profound changes in the social structure necessary to accomplish the abolition of social injustices. In such a situation the price for balance in society has to be paid by those who are already the most underprivileged. The alternative is the acceptance of a certain amount of anomy as a "normal" state.

Durkheim in fact understands this point and makes it clear that "the entire morality of progress and perfection is thus inseparable from a certain amount of anomy."[118]

A central problem becomes how one evaluates the idea of progress, which social goals one strives for, and whether one considers a certain amount of anomy to be "normal." In the latter case one difficulty is to define how much anomy is "normal" and how much "disrupting."

[117] Durkheim, *Division of Labor*, pp. 364–65.
[118] Durkheim, *Suicide*, p. 364.

THE CONSEQUENCES OF THE THEORY OF DIVISION OF LABOR

Durkheim's theory can briefly be summarized as follows: social differentiation, and consequent division of labor, is the result of the process of industrialization. Thus it is a "normal" process and leads to the substitution of mechanical solidarity with organic. Social change-processes become dangerous to the balance which exists in a society only under certain conditions. One is the lack of moral norms governing economic life, a lack due to the discrepancy between the slow development of moral norms and the fast development of the production process. This "cultural lag" creates anomy.

Another negative consequence of the process of social differentiation occurs when the division of labor forces people into certain social positions, even if these positions do not correspond to their skills and gifts. Thus the process of division of labor may lead to a situation in which the individual is forced to act contrary to his wishes and abilities.

Alvin Gouldner,[119] reviewing Durkheim's theory of the division of labor, points out that after analyzing the two main problems arising in the process of the division of labor, Durkheim could have chosen either one of two positions: He could have concentrated on the anomic processes and studied the moral conditions necessary to decrease tensions arising in the process of division of labor. He could also have dealt with the problem of the forced division of labor and the consequences that it may have for the individual. "If he had pursued the latter he could, for example, have examined the reasons why hereditary transmission of wealth or position does not disappear and give way to new social arrangements more in keeping with the modern division of labor."[120]

As we know, Durkheim took the former line. Had he taken the second line, he may have perhaps approached the problem similarly to the way Marx did. The reason for his choice is probably his value-background, which made him prefer a picture of society as a balanced system built upon conformity and consensus. Thus he must disregard the role of social conflicts, which play the dominant role in Marx's picture of society as the starting point of his sociological analysis. The choice of the balance model vs. the conflict model of society emerges from different value-assumption (are these basic values selective factors in the choice of the model, or does the choice of a certain model lead to the acceptance of a certain value?) and also gives rise to different theories of society, in which certain problems are emphasized, others neglected.

In addition, not only does the model of society, but also the model or

---

[119] E. Durkheim, *Socialism*, trans. Ch. Sattler; ed. and with an introduction by A. W. Gouldner (New York: Collier Books, 1962).

[120] Durkheim, *Socialism*, p. 21.

image of man, play an important role in the theories developed, as our previous discussions have shown. Therefore we will conclude this section with an analysis of Durkheim's image of man.

DURKHEIM'S IMAGE OF MAN

As previously mentioned, society for Durkheim is more than the sum of individuals. "It is a reality *sui generis*; it has its own peculiar characteristics, which are not met again in the same form in all the rest of the universe. The representations which express it have a wholly different content from purely individual ones."[121]

If society is something *sui generis*, then sociology must be the study of that which is *sui generi*; namely, *social facts*.

What are social facts? Social facts must be different from those facts studied by other sciences, for, if not, one would not need a special science of society. "When I fulfill my obligations as brother, husband, or citizen, when I execute my contracts, I perform duties which are defined, externally to myself and my acts, in law and in custom. Even if they conform to my own sentiments and I feel their reality subjectively, such reality is still objective, for I did not create them; I merely inherited them through education. . . . Here, then are ways of acting, thinking, and feeling that present the noteworthy property of existing outside the individual consciousness."[122]

The description of social facts makes clear the relationship between collective conscience and social facts: the latter are the content of the former.

Social facts, then, are things, objects outside the individual, not created by him but transferred to him through education. In addition to their characteristics of being outside the individual and of being looked upon as things, they have another characteristic: they are endowed with coercive power, thus being a constraint to the individual's conduct.

These social facts are collective representations which refer to a vast collection of products assembled through time: "To make them a multitude of minds have associated, united, and combined their ideas and sentiments; for them long generations have accumulated their experience and their knowledge. A special intellectual activity is therefore concentrated in them which is infinitely richer and complex than that of the individual."[123]

---

[121] E. Durkheim, *The Elementary Forms of Religious Life*, trans. J. W. Swaine (New York: The Free Press, 1948).

[122] Durkheim, *Rules of Sociological Method*, pp. 1–2.

[123] Durkheim, *Elementary Forms*, p. 16.

One is struck by the similarity of the concept of collective representations and those ideas presented by Simmel and referred to as "objectified culture" (see page 129).

The description of social facts as things existing outside the individual consciousness and having a coercive, constraining power over it could be taken as an example of "reified theorizing" (a problem which will be discussed extensively in chapter 9). However, as we will show, this accusation can be rejected if one assumes that social facts, besides being represented in the individual consciousness forcing him to act in a certain way, are continuously submitted to change as well; new facts are added and old ones rejected. Thus man is not only influenced by social facts, but is also creating and re-creating them all the time (see page 57).

For Durkheim the demand that social facts be observed from the outside and considered as things is an important methodological rule. Usually we have more or less vague ideas of the state, of sovereignty, political liberty, democracy, socialism, communism, etc.[124] But we should not use concepts before we have scientifically established them: by differentiating between what we are talking about and what things really are. The same holds for economic facts. Durkheim attacks the economic theory of value, by asserting that the concept is introduced at the outset having strong ideological functions. Instead one should start by identifying the characteristics of the thing designated as value, classify its variations, and establish the causes of these variations. In this criticism we can find some similarity with the method applied by Marx, who makes corresponding demands (see page 40).

The problem as treated so far concerns Durkheim's assumption that society is *sui generis*, that is, consisting of social facts. As a next step Durkheim asserts the primacy of society over the individual. In a polemic against the ideas of utilitarianism in *Division of Labor*, Durkheim points out that the theoreticians of utilitarianism commit a common mistake by deducing society from the individual and his need for affiliation. However, Durkheim maintains that nothing in our knowledge supports the belief of a spontaneous development in which individuals living separately accepted the necessity of cooperation and united by creating a society, e.g., by agreeing on a contract.

He asserts that the contrary is true. The individual is never caught up so tightly in a social network as in the most primitive forms of society. The belief that man lived first as an individual and later has given up this individualism does not seem reasonable: "With autonomous individualities, as are imagined, nothing can emerge save what is individual, and, conse-

[124] Durkheim, *Rules of Sociological Method*, p. 22.

quently, co-operation itself, which is a social fact, submissive to social rules, cannot arise. Thus, the psychologist who starts by restricting himself to the ego cannot emerge to find the non-ego. Collective life is not born from individual life, but it is, on the contrary, the second which is born from the first."[125]

After having asserted the primacy of society over the individual, the next step is to explain what the individual is. Collective conscience must be differentiated from individual conscience in which the former is "reincarnated." Human nature consists of two parts, one individual being and one social being "which represents the highest reality in the intellectual and moral order that we can know by observation."[126] The individual being is the original and more primitive part of human nature, not affected by social norms. To a certain extent it corresponds to Freud's notion of the id. It is egoistic, directed by drives and impulses which crave satisfaction. The social being, corresponding to Freud's superego, constraints the individual being. Why does Durkheim assume that the social being represents the "highest reality in the intellectual and moral order"? The collective conscience is represented in the social being. Therefore the social being, unlike the individual being, does not strive for egoistic goals but for social goals. The society, represented through the social being, not only functions as a constraint against uninhibited instincts but is at the same time the institution "which emancipates man because it gives his life a plan, a goal and a conscious structure."[127] Thus individual goals become social goals, when the latter are internalized. However, if the latter are internalized, why then should social facts function as constraints? The way in which Durkheim uses the term *constraint* allows the interpretation that social facts function as constraints from within, i.e., when they have been internalized.

The two beings forming human nature are never united but opposed to each other. Thus, ideas concerning the creative totality—such as those found in the young Marx's and Simmel's image of man—do not occur in Durkheim's theory of man.

For Durkheim the central problem remains how society can shape its institutions, can create groups and corporations which can integrate man and have normative power over him. For him man is basically a social being able to function only as a social being within the framework of the groups into which he is integrated. The lessening of this integration leads to individualistic tendencies, resulting in anomy. Thus alienation is a state

[125] Durkheim, *Division of Labor*, p. 279.
[126] Durkheim, *Elementary Forms*, p. 11.
[127] G. Hartfiel, *Wirtschaftliche und soziala Rationalität* (Stuttgart: F. Enke Verlag, 1968), p. 233.

within society characterized by too little integration and too great a freedom threatening the acceptance of moral rules and authority which ensure discipline.

However, Durkheim does not assume an antagonism between the individual, his needs, and society; "Individual and society are certainly beings with different nature. But far from there being some inexpressible kind of antagonism between the two, far from its being the case that the individual can identify himself with society only at the risk of renouncing his own nature either wholly or in part, the fact is that he is not truly himself, he does not fully realize his own nature, except on the condition that he is involved in society."[128]

In his antiindividualistic view Durkheim represents a true conservative attitude, but in his emphasis on the social origins of man's nature and his socialized being he meets with the image of man held by Marx; thus we can find a common ground for conservation and socialist ideas. Where they differ is in their image of society, the conservatives favoring a balance model, the socialists a conflict model. Those who consider conflicts as a disturbing state will, as does Durkheim, emphasize the individual's integration into total society and advocate slow social change in order to prevent states of anomy. Socialists taking social and intergroup conflicts as the normal state will advocate the rapid change of society and emphasize the need for man's conscious mastering of social nature and nature in general. These differences are implied in our distinction of individual- vs. society-oriented theories.

[128] Durkheim, *Moral Education*, pp. 67–68.

6

ALIENATION IN CURRENT MACROSOCIOLOGICALLY AND SOCIAL-PSYCHOLOGICALLY ORIENTED ANALYSES

INTRODUCTION

The theories selected for this chapter are developed by social scientists who are Marxists or have a positive view of Marxism. Providing they move on a sociological level, it is not too difficult to analyze problems of modern highly industrialized society within a Marxist framework. The problem becomes more complicated when the analysis is performed on a social-psychological level.

For those who deal with the concept of alienation on a sociological level, the problem is to analyze social conditions and their psychological consequences in the society in which they live, i.e., the Western society and, above all, the American one. Because all the authors dealt with in this chapter live or work in the U.S. (or have done so), they have a common starting point: a critical analysis of society—an analysis which is based on observations and empirical data, but which in its conclusions goes further than these data and comprises generalizations on a macrosociological level. In their attempts to create systems, they work in a way that is similar to that of classical European sociology. The three authors with whom this chapter is concerned are Erich Fromm, Herbert Marcuse, and C. Wright Mills. The first two authors have a general background in common. They both grew up in the European sphere of culture, more precisely at the time of the Weimar Republic in Germany. Both belonged to the *Institut für Socialforschung* in Frankfurt, before Hitler's *Machtübernahme*. This was a center of sociological research which, among other things, linked together the theories of psychoanalysis and Marxism. One of the institute's largest projects was the study of authority and the family structure[1] which

[1] *Studien über Autorität und Familie*, ed. M. Horkheimer (Paris: Librairie Felic Alcan, 1936).

served as a basis for later research in that field. These investigations gradually lead to *The Authoritarian Personality*.[2]

Both Fromm and Marcuse have been and still are Marxist, neither of the two in a dogmatical way. Fromm is also a psychoanalyst, but has turned his back on orthodox psychoanalytical theory. Instead he has contributed to the formulation of a more sociologically oriented theory of psychoanalysis. An important aspect of his theory is the rejection of the Freudian instinct-theories. Because of that, neurotic conflicts are looked upon as an antagonism between the needs of the individual and the demands of the society and *not* as intrapsychological conflicts.

On the other hand, Marcuse, who is also oriented towards psychoanalysis but who never has worked as a psychoanalyist, has stuck to the original Freudian theories. In particular he has accepted the Freudian metapsychology, e.g., Freud's postulate of the pleasure principle which rules human actions until, due to societal pressure, it is replaced by the reality principle. This theory, plus Freud's theory of sublimation, has been dealt with and further developed by Marcuse.[3] In addition Marcuse was one of those who discovered Marx's so-called *Frühschriften*. His theories are characterized by a pessimistic view of man's chances of controlling the problems which have accompanied the technological development while at the same time preserving the kind of humanity which Marcuse believes desirable.

Wright Mills has a completely different intellectual background. He grew up and was educated in the U.S. and, to a greater extent than either Fromm or Marcuse, belongs to American sociology and its traditions, although he held a unique position.[4] In one respect, of special relevance in this context, his theories are in contrast to those of Marcuse and Fromm. Mills had no philosophical-anthropological theory of man and his nature. At least there is no explicit theory, though one might deduce implicit hypotheses from his theories. But what seems more probable, when reading his books, is that he has the traditional sociological image of man as a being who can be formed, who can learn his roles, who is influenced by social pressure, and so on. As a consequence of this, his theories of alienation are not based on the conviction that man has become alienated from himself or his real nature, etc. Instead alienation becomes the discrepancy between the values of the society, which are learned (and which in turn create aspirations within the individual) and the social structure of the society, which prevents the realization of these aspirations. Take, for

[2] T. W. Adorno, E. Frenkel-Brunswik, D. J. Levinson, and R. N. Sanford, *The Authoritarian Personality* (New York: Harper, 1950).

[3] For a critical analysis see J. Israel, "Sigmund Freud och psykoanalysen," in *Sociologiska teorier*, ed. J. Asplund (Stockholm: Almqvist & Wicksell, 1967).

[4] C. W. Mills, *The Sociological Imagination* (New York: Oxford University Press, 1959).

example, the concept of active participation in political processes of decision in a democratic society. Ideally the individuals should be interested in, and actively engage in, political questions. This requires a "free" shaping of public opinion, i.e., the absence of situations of monopoly by mass media. But not even a "free" forming of public opinion is sufficient if the real processes of decision have been taken over by bureaucratic institutions over which it is hard to gain democratic control.

Alienation then becomes the discrepancy in the ideals of the society—between the ways in which they are formulated and the ways in which those ideals are put into practice. The prerequisites for alienation become the basic principles of society itself, and alienation as a phenomenon can only occur within the frame of the conditions shaped by those principles. Alienation becomes "a lack of consistency between that which really prevails and that which could prevail, between present conditions which originate from the existing nature of the social system, and possible conditions."[5] The consequence of such reasoning is that alienation seen from a *formal* point of view is the same in societies with different social structures, if alienation is defined as a discrepancy between social ideals and social reality. In terms of its contents, however, alienation in a democratic society is different from alienation in a totalitarian society. It will have other means of expression in a capitalist society than in a socialist society.

Wright Mills's analysis is based upon the discrepancy between the structure of power that he finds in American society and the official ideals that it sets forth. This "American dilemma" can be derived from a sociological analysis, i.e., it can be demonstrated that alienation is a social consequence of existing discrepancies. Another problem is whether the individual is conscious of alienation—whether the discrepancy between ideal and actual conditions really penetrates his consciousness. Wright Mills gives no clear answer. The emphasis is on the level of sociological analysis.

Mills's theories are individual-oriented, as Mills places the problem of alienation in the social structure of the society. It prevents the realization of the ideals and aspirations of the individual.

Erich Fromm: Sick Individual or Sick Society?

THE INDIVIDUAL-ORIENTED STARTING POINT

In his book *Escape from Freedom*,[6] published in the nineteen forties, Fromm developed a theory which takes its point of departure in one of George Simmel's central theses: modern industrialized society has freed

---

[5] L. Sebag, *Marxisme et structuralisme* (Paris: Payot, 1964).

[6] E. Fromm, *Escape from Freedom* (New York: Holt, Rinehart & Winston, 1941).

the individual from the ties and restrictions with which the economic systems of previous ages had shackled him. But man of industrialized capitalist society has bought the new freedom at the price of increased isolation. To evade this unwelcome freedom, he has developed various defense and escape mechanisms. One of them is authoritarian submission to a charismatic leader. This presupposes a personality structure with a dominant attitude toward other people, who are perceived as weak and inferior, combined with a desire to submit oneself to a strong leader who represents a father-figure. Fromm exemplifies this escape mechanism of the authoritarian person with an analysis of German Nazism, seen from the viewpoint of social psychology. The other and less dramatic escape mechanism is submission to a coercive type of conformity, such as that which finds its expression in the American mass society. Conformity concerns behavior, goals, needs, and the ways of satisfying these needs. Conforming need-satisfaction is facilitated by a mass-producing commodity-consumption industry. According to Fromm, conformity is a superficial feeling of belongingness and therefore provides security.

In a later book, *The Sane Society*,[7] he takes up a similar problem, but now his perspective has shifted. Nazism has been defeated. The Second World War exposed what incredibly destructive powers man could create and use. This development reached its culmination when atomic energy was made available for the creation of the most extensive and dangerous means of destruction to which humanity has ever had access. Are we human beings sick, or do we live in a sick society? Fromm tries to analyze this problem, and in this connection the problem of alienation plays a central role.

From a sociological viewpoint it seems that the question which Fromm puts is a rather confusing one, at least on a first, unreflecting reading.

It does not appear to be much of a problem to decide, with the help of objective criteria, if a person is or is not sick. But a closer analysis reveals that the problem is not so simple. This is particularly—although not only —the case concerning mental health, which is hardly possible to be defined without the help of subjective value-criteria. But how is it possible to say if a society is or is not sick? In sociological theory a society is sometimes spoken of as disorganized, or disintegrated, or as functioning unsatisfactorily with regard to certain functional criteria which have been set up beforehand. But apart from this sort of problem, it is a common sociological thesis that social problems depend on the individual's inability to adapt socially. Such adaptation involves the acceptance of social norms

[7] E. Fromm, *The Sane Society* (London: Routledge & Kegan Paul Ltd., 1956; New York: Holt, Rinehart and Winston, 1955). Copyright © 1955 by Erich Fromm. Reprinted by permission of Routledge & Kegan Paul Ltd. and of Holt, Rinehart and Winston, Inc.

and values, conforming behavior in accordance with these norms, and adjustment to social institutions which are created around the norm system.

Fromm rejects this. He considers that there exist basic needs which are common to all human individuals. He is not thinking of primary, biological needs, for it is a triviality—at least from a sociological viewpoint—to state that all people require to eat and drink. The basic needs which Fromm means are basic because they are the expression of those actual conditions which decide "human existence." Man has removed himself from an animal state—a state characterized by harmony and equilibrium with nature. This human development creates a situation in which man has "self-consciousness" and in which his knowledge of himself, of nature, and of society, has become greater and greater. This increased knowledge means that man's situation appears to be more of a problem than was the case when he had less knowledge. In its turn, this creates feelings of insecurity, the need to achieve a new state of equilibrium. Such a state is interfered with by man's incompleteness. It is this, perhaps, rather remarkable description of the "conditions of human existence" which forms the basis of the various postulated basic needs. An environment which does not allow the satisfaction of these needs—we will later discuss which are these needs—prevents man from living a healthy life from a mental point of view. Instead, it creates problems and pathological symptoms. But, as it is the social organization and the structure of society which are responsible for the fact that the satisfaction of needs is prevented, it is in society that changes must be sought, especially change in the basic economic conditions, i.e., the means of producing and distributing products.

The contention is that "mental health cannot be defined in terms of the 'adjustment' of the individual to his society, but, on the contrary, *that it must be defined in terms of the adjustment of society to the needs of man*, of its role in furthering or hindering the development of mental health."[8]

According to Fromm, the development also means that new qualities appear in the human species. These qualities result in new needs, which are basic to every individual at that stage of development. A society which does not allow the satisfaction of these needs creates individuals who exhibit various disturbances in their mental life. Such a society is a sick society.

SOCIAL CHARACTER

The theory developed by Fromm is an extremely individual-oriented theory. It contains lines of thought from both psychoanalysis and Marxism

[8] Ibid., p. 72.

and is intended to integrate both these ways of thinking. However, Fromm's theory does not imply a conflict between the individual's needs and society's demands, which is unable to be solved, as does Freud, for example. Fromm's theory begins with the postulated human needs, which in an ideal social organization should form the basis for the structuring of society.

The starting point of Fromm's reasoning is a theory of *social character*. In contrast to the individual character, which embraces all characteristics and capacities specific to a given individual, the social character is made up of all that is common to members of a given social category, for example, a class, a nation, a culture. Fromm says that the social character is *"the nucleus of the character structure which is shared by most members of the same culture."*[9] However, he points out that it is not a question of the sum of all capacities which are to be found in the majority within a social category, but rather that the "structure" contains some sort of dynamic organization of capacities and characteristics. Social character is not a statistical concept. It is more nearly an ideal-typical concept. "Social character" can be easier understood if one analyzes its function. This consists of shaping "the energies of the members of society in such a way that their behavior is not a matter of conscious decision as to whether or not to follow the social pattern, but one of *wanting to act as they have to act* and at the same time finding gratification in action according to the requirements of culture. In other words, it is the social character's function *to mold and channel human energy within a given society for the purpose of the continued functioning of this society."*[10]

A possible interpretation of the concept "social character" points to the similarity between this concept and that which is called "internalized role-expectations," i.e., those role-expectations which are learned and accepted and which therefore decide the individual's actions without his ever reflecting why he behaves in a certain given manner. One could, for example, call all the role-expectations which are typical of the female sex role in our society the "social character of women." Another example concerns what Weber calls the "spirit of capitalism" which among other things is expressed by the fact that work is experienced as a need and as a self-evident duty. To the extent that the working class of the industrialized societies holds such an idea, one could say it is part of the "social character of the working class." Fromm himself says: "Capitalism functions only with men who are eager to work, who are disciplined and functual, whose main interest is monetary gain, and whose main principle in life is profit as a result of production and exchange. In the nineteenth century capitalism

[9] Ibid., p. 78.
[10] Ibid., p. 79.

needed men who liked to save; in the middle of the twentieth century it needs men who are passionately interested in spending and in consuming."[11]

The social character is formed in the process of upbringing and is maintained and strengthened by "ideological influences," transmitted via mass media, literature, religion, etc. The upbringing of children plays a very decisive part, as important aspects of the social character are grounded in childhood. Methods of upbringing are not arbitrary. They are decided by the structure of the society. In this way parents and the family play an important social role as intermediaries in this process. Fromm also points out that the theory of social character deviates most definitely from Freud's theory of libido. This theory attributes a quantity of energy to man. It also assumes that his behavior is basically governed by the pleasure principle. According to this theory, the development and change which the libido undergoes as the individual adapts to the reality principle is the basis of man's personality structure.

Fromm also considers the concept of "social character" to be important for the understanding of the Marxist theory of "material base" and "ideological superstructure." The social character is an intermediary link between the socioeconomic structure and the ruling ideas and ideals of our society. He illustrates this with the following simple diagram:

$$\text{Ideas and ideals} \quad \uparrow \quad \downarrow$$
$$\text{Social character} \quad \uparrow \quad \downarrow$$
$$\text{Economic base}$$

There is an influence which originates in the economic conditions and which reaches the superstructure through the intermediary of the social character. But as this is an important factor in the formation of the social character, there is also a sort of feedback mechanism whereby the influence takes place in the opposite direction as well.

In order to characterize the social character of the individual in advanced industrial capitalist societies, one must understand the changes which capitalism has undergone in the last century. Nineteenth-century capitalism created a social character which is distinguished by the fact that it was saturated by competition, was oriented towards ownership, was exploiting, authoritarian, aggressive, and individualistic.[12]

Drastic changes have taken place as a result of rapid technical development. In the sphere of economy this has led to the concentration of capital and also to the concentration of power. Gigantic enterprises, having many

[11] Erich Fromm, "The Application of Humanist Psychoanalysis to Marx's Theory," in *Socialist Humanism*, ed. E. Fromm (Garden City: Doubleday & Co., 1965), p. 210.
[12] Fromm, *The Sane Society*, p. 95.

employees, are characterized by the fact that there is a distinction between the leadership and the owners. This creates special problems, namely, that a group of people with jobs of a technical and leadership nature assume control over enormous enterprises, which they themselves do not own, and that these people have as their chief task the manipulation of both figures and people. The technical changes lead to mass production, which in its turn makes possible mass consumption. But production also requires this mass consumption in order to maintain a high level. With the help of advertising it seeks to stimulate the level of consumption. Hand in hand with this development goes a rise in the standard of living, particularly as far as the working class is concerned.

Two more conditions characterize capitalist, industrial society: that which Weber has called "rational calculability" and that which Fromm refers to as "quantification" or "abstraction." The latter concept refers to production which, through the process of the division of labor, becomes split and no longer has the same concrete content that it had for the craftsmen of the Middle Ages, who, moreover, produced for a circle of customers known to them. The products become commodities with a definite exchange-value. All these are familiar lines of thought which are found in Hegel, Marx, Simmel, and Weber.

SOCIAL CHARACTER AND ALIENATION

Fromm now puts the following question: What type of social character tends to develop in a society characterized by the recently mentioned social and economic conditions?

The answer is that the social character in the society which has just been outlined is characterized by alienation. Fromm uses the concept in its psychological meaning, i.e., as the condition earlier translated as "estrangement."

"By alienation is meant a mode of experience in which the person experiences himself as alien. He has become, one might say, estranged from himself, he does not experience himself as the creator of his world, as the creator of his own acts—but his acts and their consequences have become his masters, whom he obeys, or whom he may even worship. The alienated person is out of touch with himself as he is out of touch with any other person. He, like the others, is experienced as things are experienced; with the senses and with common senses, but at the same time without being related to oneself and the world outside productively."[13] Fromm's description has lost much of the complexity which the description of alienation had in Marx's writing. His analysis makes one associate it with a pathological condition, which goes under the heading "schizophrenic

[13] Ibid., pp. 120–21.

split." It is weak because it makes use of analogies and image. What does such a statement as "man does not experience himself as the creator of his world" mean, for instance? To take a further example, Fromm says that the alienated person experiences the ego as a thing. But all experience of ego presupposes that the individual experiences himself as an object for his own perception. However, it would be interesting to examine the differences between what is, from a social-psychological point of view, a "normal" condition in which the individual becomes the *object* for his own perceptions, and that condition in which Fromm says the ego is experienced as a "thing." In other words, where does the difference lie between the ego perceived as an object, and the ego perceived as a thing? Fromm gives us a hint when he says that the ego is perceived as a thing when it is not "put in relation to the self and to the outer world in a creative way." But the problem of what precisely is meant by a "creative way" still remains.

A possible interpretation is that the difference is to be found in the fact that the "normal" person's experience of himself is characterized by an active "ego," while the alienated person's self-experience is distinguished by the fact that the ego is experienced as passive, as exposed to influences from outside, without being itself able to influence the outer world. Perhaps it is this type of problem concerning the experience of the self which Fromm has in mind, although this is not clear from what he says.

Fromm tries to clarify "estrangement" by making a comparison with what in the Old Testament is called "worship of a heathen god." In this type of worship, an object is created which is given human or superhuman attributes and to the power of which the individual must submit.[14] Modern heathen-god worship expresses itself in the worship of leaders, in the cult of personality, and in all kinds of idol worship, the phenomena which Fromm believes to be the consequences of the alienated individual's feeling of weakness and nothingness.

According to Fromm, another type of worship in which the individual becomes the slave of his passions, for example, the worship of money, has a connection with human alienation. It is not quite clear if he means that such worship is a consequence of alienation or if it is an expression of it. For example, the alienated person is characterized by the fact that his basic needs are replaced by "false needs," for instance, the ownership of money.

Fromm considers that the form which consumption habits have taken is the consequence of the system of needs and experience of the alienated individual. Often we do not buy things because we need them, nor because we like them or appreciate aesthetic or other values which they may

[14] The analysis carried out by Fromm reminds one of the ideas developed by Feuerbach concerning religious alienation (see chapter 2).

possess. We purchase things in order to brag about them and for the status with which they can endow us.

Man "is consumption-hungry. The act of buying and consuming has become a compulsive, irrational aim, because it is an end in itself, with little relation to the use of, or pleasure in the things bought and consumed."[15] One may interpret these ways of thinking in such a way that the longing to possess is an alienated human need, and that the behavior which creates this craving in its turn strengthens the individual's feeling of alienation.

FROMM'S THEORY OF PERSONALITY

The social character presented by Fromm as typical of man in industrialized capitalist society is the alienated man who is a stranger to his everyday activity, i.e., to his work; who does not have a "human"relationship to the things he consumes; who is a stranger to his fellow human beings; and who is a stranger to himself. This estrangement results from those social and economic conditions which fail to permit the satisfaction of man's deepest needs. According to Fromm, alienation as a psychological state depends on the social character that develops in the capitalist society, and prevents the realization of the individual's "human nature."

Therefore, it is necessary briefly to outline the personality theory which Fromm embraces. As with other authors who adopt an anthropological theory, he starts by asking what is the difference between man and other mammals. For Fromm, the answer is that it depends on three factors: self-consciousness, reason, and fantasy. In his view these capacities are the reasons why man does not live a vegetating existence, in "harmony with nature." Instead, these three capacities insure that man perceives his life as filled with problems. "Their emergence has made man into an anomaly, into the freak of the universe. He is part of nature, subject to physical laws and unable to change them, yet he transcends the rest of nature. . . . Being aware of himself he realizes his powerlessness and the limitations of his existence. He visualizes his own end: death. Never is he free from the dichotomy of his existence: he cannot rid himself of his mind, even if he should want to; he cannot rid himself of his body as long as he is alive—and his body makes him want to be alive."[16]

This description is a considerable departure from a sociological analysis. It makes "alienation" a consequence of "human conditions." Alienation becomes an effect of certain constituent factors in human existence, and of definite social conditions.

[15] Fromm, *The Sane Society*, p. 135.
[16] Ibid., pp. 23–24.

The fact that the human being is aware of his problems prevents him from feeling pleased and fulfilled when his biological needs have been satisfied. This is because man—and according to Fromm this is generally the case—has five further needs. These have arisen as a consequence of that which is unique to human existence. These five needs are as follows:

(1) *The establishment of social relations with others.* These relations allow the individual to experience loneliness, powerlessness, and the knowledge of his own death as bearable. The need to unite with and have contact with others is so strong that man's mental health depends upon his having adequate possibilities to establish social relations. Fromm considers certain types of mental illness, e.g., schizophrenia, to be the expression of the failure to establish social relations, and this type of sickness is characterized by autistic isolation.

(2) *The need to be actively creative.* This need is closely connected to the need to belong. Human fantasy and reason make a passive, vegetating existence insufficient. Man desires to be active. He is driven by a desire to transcend the role of an organism, to rise above its accidental nature and its passivity, by becoming a creator.[17]

(3) *The need for fixed roots.* Fromm says that man's birth means the natural bond with the mother is broken. However, she continues to shelter the child. The adult person is able to stand on his own feet, but needs help and warmth and shelter, in many ways dissimilar to those needed by the child, but also in many ways similar.[18] Thus one can find in most adults a deep longing for security and fixed roots. Fromm says that one finds a mother-fixation among many neurotic people, which means that this is the pathological way of satisfying this need.

(4) *The need for one's own identity*, as a result of the individual's self-consciousness. In that man is able to experience himself, to perceive himself as an object, he has the need to give to this object a certain content. Through his activity and his social relations he feels a need to know who he is. Who exactly is this person who is an active being, who establishes social contacts? The need for identity is very closely connected to the first two needs. It is also of the greatest importance for mental health, because a person who loses his feeling of identity becomes mentally sick.

(5) *The need of orientation.* That man possesses reason and fantasy leads not only to the fact that he must have a feeling of his own identity, but also to the need to orient himself in the world intellectually.[19] He therefore has a need to analyze: in the first place to analyze the world in

[17] Ibid., p. 30.
[18] Ibid., p. 39.
[19] Ibid., p. 63.

which he lives, to make it meaningful, and to place it in its context. The need for orientation exists on two levels.

The first and fundamental level is, above all, to have a frame of reference for his orientation. It does not matter if this is true or false, as measured by objective criteria. The other level is the need really to understand, with the help of reason. Taken together, these five needs are important aspects of the conception of human nature which Fromm holds. There are various ways of satisfying these needs. Some of them Fromm considers to be "normal," others to be neurotic. The foundation of his definition of mental health is the way in which these needs are satisfied. Whether the individual establishes social relations in a spirit of love or hatred, whether his need for roots leads him to form incestuous connections or not, and so on. Fromm's definition of mental health is formulated in the following way:

"Mental health is characterized by the ability to love and to create, by the emergence from incestuous ties to clan and soil, by a sense of identity based on one's experience of self as the subject and agent of one's powers, by the grasp of reality inside and outside of ourselves, that is, by the development of objectivity and reason."[20]

This theory of personality in many ways seems problematic. Is it a social-psychological theory, i.e., are the needs which Fromm outlines general needs? Are they to be found in all people and are they able to be observed empirically? Is it instead a question of postulated needs? If so, do they form the basis of a social-psychological theory, or are they part of an ethical-normative system?

Assume that it is a question of an empirical social-psychological theory. Is it therefore the case that the needs are present with the same strength in all individuals, or is it possible that, as far as some people are concerned —perhaps even the majority—the needs are only weakly developed or found only on a latent level?

Fromm does not take up these problems. But he does discuss one problem which is connected to these questions. As the satisfaction of these needs is a precondition for mental health, one may ask: Is the man who is at a more primitive developmental stage, where he does not have these needs, mentally sick? Fromm says that the needs appear at a certain level of man's development from the animal stage to the present developmental stage, which is the "peak of this evolution."[21]

If so, the five needs would have arisen as a result of the economic, social, and cultural development. In the course of his development, man has acquired many abilities and much knowledge. This knowledge offers the

[20] Ibid., p. 69.
[21] Ibid., p. 71.

solution of many problems, but at the same time it creates many new problems, so that "human existence" becomes increasingly complicated. It is therefore difficult to see why we, in our time, should find ourselves at the "peak of development" (assuming that Fromm when using this expression is not referring merely to a triviality). If one is of the opinion that human evolution is progressing toward higher and higher levels of development, then in every epoch man will be "at the peak." This expression has another meaning if one compares a given stage of development with an ideal, some sort of "end product" for instance. Such ideas are very often found, at least implicitly, in theories of alienation. Alienation disappears when this "ideal" or "peak condition" is reached.

Let us return for a moment to our own society. Our knowledge has never increased at the rate at which it is increasing now. This means that social changes can occur more rapidly and more often than before. If it is true that the needs which Fromm postulates as common to all human nature have arisen in connection with social development, then it is possible that they are already obsolete or at least on the way to becoming outdated. Perhaps totally different new needs are in the process of development. As Fromm's postulated needs create the conditions for human alienation, this alienation may become only a superficial problem when the needs themselves change. But perhaps these are not the most important objections to Fromm's theory. Let us instead take up a further problem.

Fromm considers satisfaction of the five basic needs to be a precondition for mental health. But not satisfaction by just any method. He discusses "healthy" and "sick" means of need-satisfaction. Take, for example, the first need—the need for human contact. Such contact can be formed in relations of dominance and submission, or relations of a sado-masochistic nature. Fromm rejects such relations as unacceptable from the standpoint of mental health. They are considered to be ways in which the alienated individual satisfies his needs. Instead he outlines a relationship which is characterized by love, the content of which is such that the individual maintains his own integrity in his social relations. The individual also accepts integrity in those people with whom he interacts. In this way they meet on a level of equality and parity.

For all five of the needs, acceptable and unacceptable forms of satisfaction are developed. The unacceptable are the alienated; the acceptable, the mentally healthy. The social structure of society creates the alienated forms. It creates a discrepancy between social character and man's "real nature." But the question of whether man has certain basic needs or not is totally overshadowed by another question. Certain ways of satisfying needs are mentally healthy, because mental health is defined with the help of these ways of satisfying the needs.

It seems that Fromm moves in a circle. One way of breaking it is to develop a normative system which says how man *should* be formed, or which behavior patterns are *desirable*, with reference to ethical, political, or other goals. This seems to me to be a central and legitimate problem in all theories of alienation. I am inclined to see Fromm's definition of mental health as an element in a normative system.

HERBERT MARCUSE AND ONE-DIMENSIONAL MAN

THE CHANGED ROLE OF THE WORKING CLASS

Let us start by quoting the *Communist Manifesto*: "The history of all hitherto society is the history of class struggles."[22] Bourgeois society grew out of the struggle against the feudal society, and the destruction of the latter made the bourgeois society possible. According to Marxist theory every epoch, or type of society, comprises antagonistic powers organized in social classes. "Our epoch, the epoch of the bourgeoisie, possesses, however, this distinctive feature: it has simplified the class-antagonisms. Society as a whole is more and more splitting up in two great hostile camps, into two great classes directly facing each other—bourgeoisie and proletariat," continues the *Communist Manifesto*.[23] Just as the historical mission of the bourgeoisie was to vanquish the epoch of feudal society, so it is the mission of the working class, the proletariat, to change the bourgeois capitalist society into a socialist society.

The idea that every type of society carries within it the seeds of its own destruction is a central one in the dialectical thinking of historical materialism. It can be traced back to Hegelian dialectics, but it was Marx who formulated these ideas within a historical-sociological framework.

Marxists agree on two points but disagree on one central issue. They all accept the idea of a society as a system consisting of conflicting forces, organized as classes. They furthermore agree upon the idea of a dialectical development: one class represents and defends existing social and economic conditions, especially the basic mode of production. The other class, representing the force of progress, is in an antagonistic position to the first one. Its historical task is to negate the existing social system and to create a new society. In modern capitalist society the proletariat is the force of negation. So far all Marxists agree, and this theory clearly contains both descriptive and normative features.

The point on which they disagree is the question: How can the proletariat accomplish its historical mission? One answer is the following. If the

[22] K. Marx and F. Engels, *Manifesto of the Communist Party* (New York: New York Labor News Co., 1908), p. 8.

[23] Ibid., p. 9.

proletariat has this historical mission and has it because of its factual situation—being exploited and oppressed—then it will gain consciousness about its situation and develop its political and organizational means to accomplish its mission. This "historicist" line, counting on the revolutionary spontaneity of the proletariat, is represented by Marxist theoreticians such as the young Lukács, Rosa Luxemburg, and also by the "Frankfurt School" and its best-known representatives, namely Max Horkheimer and Herbert Marcuse. The other line is represented by Lenin[24] and has been further elaborated by the theoreticians of the Stalinist epoch. This line asserts that the proletariat is not able to acquire a revolutionary class-consciousness. This has to be brought into the proletariat by an elite organized in a revolutionary party.

The first group is accepting the Hegelian idea of the dialectical development in history toward a predetermined goal, whereas the other line rejects the idea as false and as "historicism." The first type of interpretation also builds on Marx's central sociological thesis that man's consciousness is determined by his social position. The other line emphasizes the role of scientific thinking in analyzing society and the inability to grasp the problems without being scientifically trained.

Thus the central dividing issue is whether the proletariat is able spontaneously to understand its historical mission and to develop the means of realizing the goal or whether a small elite, scientifically trained and organized in a revolutionary party, has to do the job. The answer to this question has far-reaching consequences concerning the role of the Communist party and the necessity of the dictatorship of the proletariat. Those who, like Lenin, emphasize the role of a revolutionary elite, maintain that the party never ought to lose its control since it represents the "true interests" of the masses and since its actions are built upon scientific knowledge.[25] The other line can correctly stress that the dictatorship of the proletariat turns into a dictatorship *over* the proletariat and that the revolutionary party develops, as in the Soviet Union, into a bureaucratic class. They therefore reject the elitist idea of the necessity to bring the revolutionary consciousness into the ranks of the proletariat from the outside. They assert that, for these who follow the Leninist line, the proletariat becomes instrumental for the goals of the elite; and that this instrumentality is later on justified by asserting that the revolutionary elite identifies itself with the true interests of the proletariat. These true interests are the achievement of the long-range goals of establishing a so-

[24] W. I. Lenin, *Was tun?* in *Ausgewählte Werke* (Moscow, 1946).

[25] The occupation of Czechoslovakia in 1968 becomes understandable in the light of this thesis. The Soviet leaders feared that the reforms there would result in a decrease of the control of the Communist party and, as a consequence, the risk of deviation from the Marxist-Leninist line.

cialist society, viewed as an historical necessity. In this respect the "elite" view returns to a "historicist" point of view.

There are several issues connected with these conflicting views, some of them concerning philosophical problems and especially epistemological and methodological ones, which cannot be analyzed in detail in this context. One is the problem of historical determinism. The rejection of "historicism," I think, is correct. Second, there is the problem of how consciousness develops. The Marxian hypothesis concerning the relationship between social position and consciousness is only partly correct: there are workers who lack a "proletarian" consciousness and there are intellectuals, often without contact with the working class, who are revolutionaries. The Marxian hypothesis leaves out the whole process of indoctrination by means of primary socialization, i.e., upbringing and through education and the role of modern mass media in this process. In a society in which education and mass media play a dominant role, their effect on consciousness cannot be neglected. So far, there seems to be support for Lenin's reasoning. On the other hand, the opponents are correct when they point to the consequences of an elitist theory. They also are correct when they assert that the working class often becomes a means in the hands of an uncontrolled bureaucratic elite. They also are correct in denying that daily political action could be based on a scientific theory only, without introducing value assumptions and goals. This is exactly what the proponents of the Leninist line assert. Marxism to them is not only a scientific theory; it is sometimes considered to be a verified scientific theory as well. They deny that values are a part of Marxist theory. In this view regarding social science they share opinions with logical empiricism and other positivistic approaches. Those who oppose the Leninist line accept the idea of values as an integrated part of a social science, but conclude sometimes, like Lukács, that there are two social sciences: a bourgeois built upon bourgeois values, and a proletarian social science built upon socialist values.

In this short resumé some of the conflicting views and their consequences are presented. Marcuse clearly opposes the Leninist line. He represents the Hegelian, "historicist," and anti-elitistic interpretation of Marxism. His central problem is which role "the forces of negation" play in the highly industrialized society of today.[26] He says that Marx thought that industrialism had created the preconditions for the realization of "reason and freedom," provided the capitalist structure could be replaced by a socialist structure. The change, however, must take place by means of a revolution and a revolutionary class. Socialization of the means of production is not sufficient; neither is the rational use of these means.

[26] H. Marcuse, *Reason and Revolution* (Boston: Beacon Press, 1960). The remarks are to be found in the epilogue to the 2nd edition (London: 1955), which is omitted in this edition.

These thoughts were written under the impression of the developments during the period of Stalinism in the Soviet Union. Means of production had been socialized, but a society freed from pressure of the state apparatus had not been accomplished. The association of free producers which was Marx's vision had not come about.

Marcuse reasoned as follows: A negation of the capitalist society presupposes the liberation of man. New principles and values can be realized only by a class that is free from the old, repressive principles and values, because, as Marcuse asserts, in its strict sense liberation presupposes freedom. The former can be reached only if it is brought about and maintained by free individuals—free from the need to dominate and to oppress and free from the interests in doing so.[27] Thus Marcuse found a central dilemma: liberation presupposes freedom from repression, but freedom from repression can be achieved only in a society in which man has become liberated. Liberation from capitalistic exploitation through socialization of means of production did not lead to freedom from repression, as the example of the Soviet Union showed. In the other highly industrialized society, the U.S., capitalistic exploitation and the institutions built upon it prevented man from developing the needs for freeing themselves. In any case the working class did not develop its own political organizations necessary for the struggle against capitalism. Thus the question became: Is the working class still the "force of negation"?

Marcuse continued to concern himself with the problem of the historical role of the proletariat and the ways in which the social conditions in highly industrialized countries change that role. The analysis is now concentrated on tendencies in the most highly developed contemporary societies.[28]

CONSEQUENCES OF TECHNICAL DEVELOPMENT FOR THE WORKING CLASS

According to Marcuse, the situation of the working class in the technically most highly developed societies has undergone decisive change on four counts:

(1) Mechanization of work means that both the amount and intensity of the physical energy needed for work have been considerably reduced. For Marx, the worker was a person who toiled and slaved, who was totally exhausted at the end of the working day. He was a man who lived in poverty and misery while producing the necessities of life. He was shut out from society and felt himself to be an outcast. Exploitation of the worker was clearly a physical phenomenon; his impoverishment was both

---

[27] Marcuse, *Reason and Revolution*, 2nd ed.

[28] Herbert Marcuse, *One-Dimensional Man* (Boston: Beacon Press, 1964; and London: Routledge & Kegan Paul Ltd.). Reprinted by permission of the Beacon Press and of Routledge & Kegan Paul Ltd., copyright © 1964 by Herbert Marcuse.

economic and cultural. The long working day of the early period of industrialism, the limited degree of mechanization of labor, the lack of such means as could make easier the physically most demanding tasks— for example, transportation of heavy objects—meant that in part alienation had a biographical anchoring. Marcuse quotes a French author who says: "During the past centuries, one important reason for alienation was that the human being lent his biological individuality to the technical apparatus."[29]

Even in mechanized and automated production there still exists a strong inhuman aspect, namely, psychological stress. But it is no longer of the same proportions as that of physical fatigue. There are other difficulties instead: the monotony of the work, the tempo of the conveyer belt which controls the activity of the worker rather than vice versa, the barriers against communication between the workers during the actual process of production, the utilizing of only a small part of the worker's physical and mental capacities, because only certain hand movements are required of him, etc.

Mechanized and automated production has largely replaced muscular strain with mental strain and stress. The skill of the hand has been replaced by the skill of the head. Marcuse points out that this, what he calls "masterly enslavement,"[30] is typical not only for the worker in the technically most highly developed societies, but also for white-collar workers, the major portion of whom carry out monotonous routine work. Whereas the worker in a previous epoch was "the living denial of his society," the worker "in the advanced areas of the technological society lives this denial less conspicuously and, like other human objects of the social division of labor, he is being incorporated into the technological community of the administered population."[31]

(2) Technical development means a new stratification in society. There occurs a certain degree of equalization between white-collar workers and workers within the industrial enterprise. The group of lower officials increases, while the number of workers directly engaged in production decreases. This is a consequence of the changed technology and, above all, of automatization. Mechanization meant that machines were used by the workers as "individual" means of production in the actual process of production. Automation creates a *machine system*. Manufacturing becomes an automated process, in which the task of the worker is to look after control panels, or to supervise the machine system and repair faults when

29 Ibid., p. 24.
30 Ibid., p. 25.
31 Ibid., p. 26.

they occur. Automation seems in a qualitative way to change relations between living and dead labor: it has developed to the point where productivity is decided by the rational functioning of the machines and not by individual production.[32] As a consequence, the measuring of "human output" is replaced by measuring of the effective use of the machines and the equipment. For the worker all this involves a change in his relations to other social classes, a change in the wage system, and a change in the organization of the work process.

(3) Changes in the type of labor and in the production process affect the attitude and consciousness of the worker. He develops new needs and aspirations; his standards, consumption habits, and leisure activities are adapted to those of other classes, in particular the middle class. Marcuse asks if such changes in "consciousness" are possible without changes in the "social situation." As a Marxist, he denies this. In fact, changes in conscious attitudes and evaluations are based upon the position of the worker in the production process. Above all, his integration within the factory itself is important. Mechanization and automation, it is true, bring with them negative consequences: unemployment caused by technological change and rationalization of the work process; decreased chances for advancement, since as a precondition more and more technical knowledge is required; increased power and control for the management of the industrial enterprise, but decreased power for the employees, etc.

However, against these tendencies, which from the point of view of the worker are negative, one might show others: technical development creates greater mutual dependence, and therfore leads to greater integration. In its turn, this leads to increased interest in active participation in the running of the enterprise and an increase of participation in the decision-making processes.

(4) Management and ownership of means of production have become separated. The industrial enterprise is run by management. It is true that they are placed there by the owners and are responsible to them. But the managing group does not coincide with the owners. Their methods of managing the enterprise have changed. Dominance and authoritarian leadership has been turned into administration, Marcuse asserts. The language of power is replaced by a flexible and manipulating leadership style; authoritarian force, by the principle of "human relations." "The tangible source of exploitation disappears behind the façade of objective rationality. Hatred and frustration are deprived of their specific target, and the technological veil conceals the reproduction of inequality and enslavement. With technical progress as its instrument, unfreedom—in

---

[32] Ibid., p. 28.

the sense of man's subjection to his productive apparatus—is perpetuated and intensified in the form of many liberties and comforts. . . . The slaves of developed industrial civilization are sublimated slaves, but they are slaves, for slavery is determined, neither by obedience nor by hardness of labor but by the status of being a mere instrument and the reduction of man to the state of a thing."[33]

The latter point is central for Marcuse's thinking: the shorter working day, greater opportunities for recreation, higher standards of living, and more convenience mean that man forgets he is powerless and that decisions, even those concerning his life and death, may be taken over his head, with his having almost no influence over them.

THE ROLE OF TECHNOLOGY

The development of technology has a central role in Marcuse's analysis. When discussing Max Weber's concept of formal rationality, Marcuse asserts, as pointed out in chapter 5, that this type of rational acting, from being *instrumental* for the production process, has become *a goal* in itself. But not only that. It has spread to all areas of societies and has permeated them deeply. Based upon scientific principles, the efficient apparatus of production and administration has become the dominating feature in the highly industrialized societies. In earlier phases of the process of industrialization, those in charge of the production and administration apparatus—technocrats and bureaucrats—were in the service of a ruling class. Now they themselves have developed into a ruling class using formal rational behavior not only for efficient production but also for dominating and ruling society, by setting efficiency as an ultimate goal. Thus the question "Efficiency: for what and at what costs?" is subordinated to the goal of achieving efficiency and is seldom asked, if asked at all.

Marcuse points out that, in addition to technology, natural science upon which technology is based introduces the concept of formal rationality. Since "formal rationality" is a value, he denies that the natural sciences are value-free, as they assert.

Marcuse thus seems to concentrate on the criticism of science and technology as such, not on its use, e.g., in a society with a capitalistic structure. In fact, he postulates a convergence between societies with different social structures—capitalist and socialist—when they are subjected to the same type of formal rational behavior as a consequence of the level of development of technology. The risk, in Marcuse's thinking, is that technology develops its own laws to which man is subjugated but which he cannot control. Thus technology is perceived as the force of total reification.

[33] Ibid., p. 32.

Consequently, Marcuse also points out that revolutionary thinking must create a new technology, a technology of and for emancipation. However, it never becomes clear what such a technology should look like.[34]

DOES TECHNICAL DEVELOPMENT REFUTE CENTRAL MARXIST THESES?

Reifying technology makes man in the highly developed industrial civilization into slaves, who, however, are compensated for their serfdom by high standards of living. Therefore they do not see any reason to protest against existing conditions. Marcuse's view is pessimistic, and it is so for two reasons: (1) The working class has lost its possibilities of playing the role of "the negating force," and (2) the technological development prevents any greater social change in the direction of socialism, because at present there exist mechanisms that maintain or create a certain stability. Each condition will be discussed briefly.

As we saw, Marcuse gave four reasons for the change in the situation of the working class, which therefore no longer constitutes a living opposition to the established society. *Physical exploitation* has for great parts of this class largely ceased. *Economic impoverishment* has been stopped and to a certain extent changed into increasingly higher standards of living. Marcuse points out the connection in Marx's theory between physical exploitation and economic impoverishment. Even if this impoverishment is now of a cultural and psychological nature, there is a basic difference between men who live in poverty and misery and those who are "culturally impoverished," but who own their own houses and have cars and television sets.

One important argument can be brought forward against this description. Whereas Marx saw the increasing polarization within a certain national economy, the polarization today occurs between the "rich" and the "poor" countries, between the highly industrialized nations and the nations of "the third world." There the impoverishment is increasing, whereas high standards of living in the industrialized world are, to a large extent, built upon the exploitation of the poor nations. Thus the conflict between classes within one society seems to have moved into a conflict between technically developed and underdeveloped parts of the world. Thus the traditional role of the proletariat could be ascribed to the people of the Third World. This point is taken up briefly in Marcuse's latest writings.[35]

[34] J. Habermas in his book *Technik und Wissenschaft als "Ideologie"* (Frankfurt: Edition Suhrkamp, 1968), and C. Offe, "Teknik und Eindimensionalität," in *Antworten auf Herbert Marcuse*, ed. J. Habermas (Frankfurt: Edition Suhrkamp, 1968) develop the criticism of this point.

[35] See H. Marcuse, *An Essay on Liberation*, quoted after the Swedish translation (Stockholm: Aldus/Bonniers, 1969).

Yet another circumstance seems to oppose a central Marxist thesis. The increase of the machine's importance and the decrease of the role of human labor in the production process seems to affect the theory of surplus-value. According to Marx, new values are created by human labor only. The machine is able to transfer only its own value on the products produced. Surplus-value is the result of the exploitation of living labor.[36] Automation seems to alter this fact until a point is reached at which it is the machine and not man who determines productivity.

But the most important argument against the chance that the working class will play the role Marx thought it would, is that workers no longer experience life in capitalist society as intolerable. But, says Marcuse, they do not find it so because social developments compensate the individual

[36] Marx differentiates between constant capital, i.e., capital invested in means of production (as raw material and machines) and variable capital, i.e., capital invested in labor power. The first-mentioned type of capital is called "constant" because, according to Marx, it cannot create profits. It transfers only its own value onto the products. Labor power, however, creates surplus-value, which is the price received for a commodity and which transgresses the total cost for means of production as well as for the labor power (*Capital*, Part I).

The central point is that only work creates new values, namely, the exchange-value of a commodity. Marx calls the relation between surplus-value and the sum of the total capital the "profit-rate." The relationship between the surplus-value and the variable capital is called "surplus-value-rate" (*Capital*, Part III, f).

Through the development of technology the share of the constant capital in the total capital is increased, whereas the part of the variable capital is decreased. Expressed in another way: The value of the machines per worker increases. The process of production becomes more capital-intensive. One consequence of the technological development and the increase of the share of constant capital is that the profit-rate decreases if the surplus-value-rate is kept constant. But on the other hand the profit-rate increases also with increased share of the constant capital if the surplus-value-rate increases. That occurs, e.g., if productivity per worker increases and if increased wage costs are compensated by still larger increases in prices of the produced commodity. Even with higher wages and increased capital costs the surplus-value-rate can increase if productivity is increased.

Marx assumed that if the profit-rate in highly mechanized enterprises decreases (e.g., when the surplus-value-rate remains constant), capital is transferred to less mechanized and therefore more profitable enterprises (more profitable because the variable capital there is greater in relation to the constant capital). The development, however, has shown that wages can increase to such a degree that profitability can be increased only by increased mechanization and thereby by increased productivity per worker. Marx's central thesis that only work creates new value has been severely criticized (see, e.g., E. Heiman, *History of Economic Doctrines*, New York: Oxford University Press, 1964). One important problem is how "value" is defined when one discusses the hypothesis that only work creates value. Another argument is that the work-value theory should be considered mainly as a normative theory, not as price-theory (J. O. Andersson "Om arbetsvärdelärans giltighet" ["On the validity of the work-value theory"], *Häften för kritiska Studier* nr. 4, 1968, 55–57).

Marx himself has treated this problem in a detailed way in Vol. III of *Capital*, where he shows that the theories concerning surplus-value-rate and profit-rate do not hold for the explanation of commodity prices in *one* company, but that rates be considered as "average rates" for prices within a total social system. For a detailed analysis of this problem, see chapter 3 in Vol. III of *Capital*.

for his frustration by giving him a high level of consumption. This brings us to the second point: that the social structure prevents great social changes.

The technically highly developed society has created a situation in which freedom from want among the members of society is, if not achieved, at least within the bounds of possibility. Technological development should make it possible to further man's autonomy through shortened working hours and increased leisure. But with mass media and the commercialization of possibilities for leisure, Marcuse maintains that the development is actually going in the opposite direction. The domination of society over the individual is beginning to adopt totalitarian forms. However, this is not the traditional exercise of power, using terror and oppression. Society's totalitarian influence over the individual occurs through the use of the possibilities of technology's manipulative control over man, thereby creating a social control which is as subtle as it is effective. Marcuse maintains furthermore that the goals of the social system are irrational. A completely rationalized technology is used for irrational goals. Take, for instance, the amount of productive resources used for producing weapons and war materials. This is explained by the threat created by atomic weapons. This threat of an atomic catastrophe is used in order to get support for those forces which serve to maintain the threat. The society—Marcuse refers both to U.S. and the Soviet Union—attempts to create a defense against an atomic war by arming for such a war. In this way a large percentage of social resources are used for building a defense which in itself creates forces that constitute a threat to peace.

Another way of misusing existing resources is to build a demand for high consumption among the members of society. Consumption fails to satisfy existing needs; moreover, new—and Marcuse calls them artificial —needs are created by means of advertisement, propaganda, and other ways of influence. These needs are created because consumption in the highly industrialized countries becomes a necessary prerequisite for production and not the other way around. Mass consumption makes possible mass production, which in turn is a prerequisite for high standards of living based upon mass consumption. This paradoxical situation is restricted to a small part of the world, whereas in a large part of the world the basic needs of the population cannot be satisfied. This emphasis on consumption also leads to waste, since products often have low quality and therefore a short life-span.

The question is why individuals accept such irrational goals. Marcuse gives two answers. One is that there exist the means to dominate and to manipulate the individual; this makes opposition either meaningless or extremely difficult. The other answer is that man has become so alienated he no longer has correct ideas concerning his "real" needs, which are replaced by "artificial" needs. The first answer presupposes an image of society in a condition of equilibrium, despite rapid changes which take place. The second answer builds on Marcuse's ideas regarding human nature and "real" needs as a part of it. We will discuss both problems, but let us first describe some of the social control mechanism postulated by Marcuse.

SOCIAL CONTROL AND ONE-DIMENSIONALITY

In a society characterized by "a rising standard of living, non-conformity with the system itself appears to be socially useless, and the more so when it entails tangible economic and political disadvantages and threatens the smooth operation of the whole."[37] Only a minority who have not shared in the rising standards have reason to be in opposition, but they lack the means of power and political influence. Political power is in the hands of those who control the technological apparatus. With the help of the bureaucratic apparatus, the government can maintain its power if its succeeds in mobilizing, organizing, and making use of all technical and scientific resources. But, in doing so, society in its totality is involved, without regard to individuals or groups and their special interests. This creates common values which override existing differences of a political or economic nature.

Freedom of speech exists, but how can it be free and critical when the individuals are constantly subject to indoctrination by mass media, says Marcuse? Thought processes become one-dimensional. In fact, mass consumption presupposes conformity of values, of habits of emotional and intellectual reactions. These are created, among other things, by means of mass communication. The satisfaction of needs through mass-produced goods in turn confirms the correctness of the attitude and values, and makes it possible for the mass-communication media to be effective in their indoctrination, which, according to Marcuse, they are. The result is a "false consciousness" immune to critical analysis. Specific to this one-dimensional thought is that it prevents the individual from noticing other dimensions and therefore imprisons him within one dimension. The one-dimensional man lives in a society that uses many opportunities to satisfy needs, that instead of using force has learned to manipulate man so cleverly that, by means of mass-communication, it has created such an intellectual conformity that man can neither form new ideas nor develop any new desires, nor break out of this situation. The one-dimensional man is the perfectly alienated man.

[37] Marcuse, *One-Dimensional Man*, p. 2.

Marcuse also introduces what he calls the alienation of the artist. The concept of alienation, as it has been used up to now, has always had a negative meaning. But Marcuse also uses the concept in a positive sense when he speaks of art and literature. Their traditional task was to create works which "expressed a conscious, methodical alienation from the entire sphere of business and industry, and from its calculable and profitable order."[38]

Marcuse is putting forward the common hypothesis that artistic and literary creation often presupposes separation from society's values and the relinquishing of conformity in both thought and deed. He means, further, that artistic alienation involves a conscious attempt to transcend the barriers within which the majority of society is enclosed. This results in the artist's experiencing himself as alien not only to the "normal" existence but also to the "alienated existence" ("alienated" used here in the negative sense), which depends on man's relation to his work and the products of his work.

But, according to Marcuse, in the technically highly developed society, the artist no longer has the chance to express his "positive alienation," i.e., to be a subversive force. Society now accepts even subversive truths, yes, even meets them with indifference, because the influence of the artist is seen as so meager that he is not perceived as a threat. Even if the artist and the author do not find themselves on the one-dimensional plane, the results of their work are incorporated with the society or treated as harmless curiosities.

SOME CRITICAL REMARKS

Marcuse's analysis presents several interesting observations on a generalized level, which makes it difficult to give a detailed criticism. Such a criticism can be made on both an empirical and a theoretical level. Some of the critical arguments on the empirical level can be summarized in the following way: Marcuse "over-estimates the effectiveness and the inner purposiveness of the technology for accomplishing integration and economic stabilization, whereas diverging tendencies and interests are under-evaluated to the same degree."[39] There the conflicts and lacks existing within such a "closed" system are disregarded or not sufficiently emphasized. Another argument can be directed against the notion of the total manipulation of the individual's needs and the consequences of this manipulation, namely, the smoothing out of existing class-differences.

[38] Ibid., p. 58.
[39] W. F. Haug, "Das Ganze und das Andere," in Habermas, *Antworten auf Herbert Marcuse*, p. 53.

Another criticism could be directed against Marcuse's assumptions that the development of technology has come to a point where the basic problems facing the world as a totality could be solved if existing resources were distributed in a rational way.[40] Is it not possible to visualize the simultaneous further development of technology and a redistribution of existing resources, etc?

The main criticism, however, must be launched on a theoretical basis since Marcuse's theory is not consciously presented as an empirical theory but as a critical one, placing itself in opposition to existing positivistic theories by questioning their value-basis and—again consciously—by taking a starting point in a different value-system and therefore developing alternative solutions. As are all sociological theories, Marcuse's is built upon a model of society of a postulative kind. Marxist-oriented sociological theories view society as a system of opposing forces. An alternative model sees society as a system striving for balance, restricting conflicts to the role of disturbing forces, whereas conflicts in the first type of model are the central driving forces in a steadily ongoing process of change.

Marcuse himself says that he vacillates between two contradictory hypotheses: (1) "that advanced industrial society is capable of containing qualitative change for the foreseeable future; (2) that forces and tendencies exist which may break this containment and explode the society."[41]

Now in my opinion the emphasis is on the first hypothesis, though it shifts to the second one in a book published after the May, 1968, revolt in Paris.[42] The hypothesis of a closed social system's being able to keep itself in a continuous state of balance, by minimizing antagonistic conflicts, by manipulation of the individual through high consumption, is entirely in agreement with conservative social theories. For example, in a very critical review MacIntyre[43] pointed out the similarity between Marcuse's description of the modern technological society and Parsons's ideas concerning the tendency of a social system to maintain itself in a state of balance. Also the idea of one-dimensionality of values resembles the hypothesis of the "death of ideology" as advocated, e.g., by Tingsten in Sweden and referred to by Lipset.[44] They, too, emphasize the lack of ideological conflicts existing in modern society and assert the existence of a common "super-ideology." These theories not only neglect existing conflicts on an ideolog-

---

[40] Offe, "Teknik und Eindimensionalität," p. 85.

[41] Marcuse, *One-Dimensional Man*, p. xv.

[42] Marcuse, *Essay on Liberation*.

[43] A. MacIntyre, "Herbert Marcuse," *Survey* 62, (1967), 38–44.

[44] S. Lipset, *Political Man: The Social Basis of Politics* (Garden City: Doubleday and Co., 1960).

ical level, but can themselves be viewed as an "ideology" in the sense in which the term is used by Marx and Mannheim (see page 93): it presents the theoretical defense of existing conditions and tries to legitimize the behavior of elites in dominating positions.

Another criticism of the theories of Marcuse concerns the question of the effects of technology as a consequence of its use in a (late-) capitalistic society or whether the consequences are the same in all highly industrialized societies independent of their social structure. Thus the problem can be boiled down to the question of late-capitalism or highly industrialized society.[45] Marxist critics have pointed out that Marcuse places the emphasis on technology and not its use within a capitalist society.[46] However, if in accordance with the Marxian model, one considers technology to be a main productive force, then its development should affect the other principal Marxian factor, namely, the relations of production. On one point Marcuse's analysis seems to be correct: the development of technology has given rise to a technocratic and bureaucratic elite. This elite has established itself as a class in the Marxian sense, having the means of production and the use of the social product at its disposal without necessarily owning these means of production. Furthermore, this technocratic-bureaucratic class shows great similarities though functioning in two such different societies as the U.S. and the Soviet Union (see also chapter 9). Thus one can advance a theory that the level of development of technology leads to the creation of new class divisions in societies with a capitalist as well as a socialist structure of the Soviet type. The differences, then, between these two societies can be ascribed to political and ideological factors, being in the final analysis dependent upon the mode of production, but having a certain autonomy in influencing social events.

Let us summarize: Marcuse's pessimism depends on two main factors. In the first place, the development he sketches seems to refute the Marxist theory concerning the capitalist society's carrying within itself the seeds of its own destruction. Instead of a "revolutionary" or socialist working class, he finds a class which enjoys the affluent society and therefore replaces class struggle with common interests.

To that could be added empirical evidence showing that socialist revolutions have not been carried out in industrialized societies, but in countries with a relative degree of underdevelopment with regard to economy and industrialization. To a much larger extent, revolutionary movements have been supported by peasants and landless agricultural workers than by a working class in an advanced industrialized society. This phenomenon in

---

[45] For a discussion of this problem, see T. W. Adorno (ed.), *Spätkapitalismus oder Industriegesellschaft* (Stuttgart: F. Enke Verlag, 1969).

[46] Haug, "Das Ganze und das Andere."

itself should motivate a revision of those assumptions which predict that the technically most highly developed capitalist societies will have as their distinctive marks greater and more intensive antagonistic conflicts than will agrarian societies with, e.g., a feudal structure, and therefore that within themselves they should shelter the forces of negation to a greater extent than underdeveloped societies. Neither need one accept without qualification the hypothesis that the working class, more than peasants, should form the basis for radical social change. In fact, it seems reasonable to predict that future large social changes of a revolutionary kind, if they occur at all, will emanate from the technically underdeveloped areas of the Third World.

The second reason for Marcuse's pessimism is based upon what has been termed his "conservative romanticism." This again is related to his image of man, a mixture of psychoanalytical ideas and humanistic ethics. It leads him, e.g., to advance ideas about human self-realization based upon a society which maximizes the possibilities for such a self-realization. In Marcuse's analysis it seems that the development goes in a direction which removes the goal of human self-realization. We will briefly discuss these aspects of Marcuse's theories and try to analyze them critically.

PLEASURE PRINCIPLE AND REALITY PRINCIPLE IN INDUSTRIALIZED SOCIETY

Marcuse accepts the instinct theory developed by Sigmund Freud in its final version, implying the existence of two basic instincts, a life and a death instinct, Eros and Thanatos. He also accepts the Freudian meta-psychology: in the beginning human behavior is directed by the *pleasure principle*. Later on in the process of socialization it is replaced by the *reality principle*. That occurs when the individual has learned to substitute immediate satisfaction by delayed need-satisfaction, among other things to achieve long-term goals. It also means restrictions placed upon the experience of pleasure and the substitution for joy and play by work and toil.[47]

Freud asserts that all culture—using the concept in its widest sense—presupposes the repression of original drives and the sublimation of instinctual energy. In Freud's view the basis for the reality principle is the fundamental fact that "the struggle for existence takes place in a world too poor for the satisfaction of human needs without constant restraint, renunciation, delay. In other words, whatever satisfaction is possible necessitates *work*, more or less painful arrangements and under-takings for the procurement of the means of satisfying needs. For the dura-

---

[47] Marcuse develops these ideas for the first time in *Eros and Civilization* (New York: Vintage Books, 1955), p. 11 ff.

tion of work, which occupies practically the entire existence of the mature individual, pleasure is 'suspended' and pain prevails."[48]

The ideas expressed here are in psychoanalytic terminology similar to the ideas presented by Max Weber concerning the relationship between puritanism and "the spirit of capitalism."

For Marcuse the central problem becomes the following: Is it possible to create a culture not without sublimation, but without repression? To use his own words: Can a "non-repressive culture" be created? The Freudian theory means that the repression of instinctual energy and its transformation into social or socially acceptable energy is a condition sine qua non for society to accomplish the work necessary for the existence of a culture. Marcuse asks whether the liberation of the instincts and the erotization of the whole life is possible, if work can be retransformed into pleasurable and joyful behavior.

One possible development—which, however, is not advocated by Marcuse—could be sketched in the following way: The technical development and the change in the character of work from physical toil to mentally demanding activity could lead to the fact that the reality principle is increasingly weakened since it no longer fulfills any social purposes, as it does in societies finding themselves in the first stages of the process of industrialization. These stages are characterized by a necessity to accumulate capital to a large extent and to do this rather rapidly. Capital accumulation generally can be accomplished in two ways: by contribution of capital from outside the society, being in the first stages of industrialization, and by the exploitation of human labor as a source of the creation of new values, an exploitation to the utmost degree. That would be true for all societies independent of the social structure within which this early and "primitive" accumulation of capital occurs. Thus, the same conditions occurred in England during the eighteenth century as in the Soviet Union during the thirties and in China today. Hard work and toil can be achieved in two ways: by force, either physical or social, e.g., low standards of living and poverty and/or by making labor an inner necessity. This is accomplished by creating a moral in which labor is conceived of as a duty and not only that, but as man's foremost duty. Therefore, early accumulation of capital seems always to be accompanied by a puritan moral. In England and on the Continent, puritanism was expressed in the guise of the "Protestant ethic." In the Soviet Union in the twenties and thirties and in China of today a work-moral is founded and perpetuated by emphasizing the importance of unselfish work associated with ideas of "revolutionary purity."[49]

[48] Ibid., pp. 32–33.
[49] Jan Myrdal, "Puritanism och revolution" ["Puritanism and Revolution"], *Ord & Bild* 55 (1966), 467–70.

However, when a society reaches a certain degree of industrialization and a high standard of living, when working hours become restricted and when work is no longer physical toil, when human labor becomes expensive and technical rationalization and further economic growth is based upon the increasing use of machines in a automated technology, then a traditional puritan moral loses its function. In fact, the consumption society cannot reward traits such as orderliness, thrift, and the abstinence from need-satisfaction as does the puritan moral. Instead it must develop a moral which emphasizes the right for need-satisfaction, the right to create new needs, the importance of spending money.

The change in attitudes toward sex and the decrease or dissolution of existing sexual taboos in a society such as the Swedish and other highly industrialized societies might then, among other things, be explained as a consequence of the changed way by which capital is accumulated. "Sublimation" of energy is no longer as necessary as in the past, since economic growth can be accomplished by other means and since the satisfaction of, e.g., sexual needs no longer affects production in the same way as in a society with a low degree of industrialized technology.

However, the new situation need not necessarily lead to greater sexual "freedom." The emphasis, as in the consumption society, may be shifted from sexuality to "artificial" needs to buy and own things. These needs are "artificial" from a normative point of view if they strive for the acquisition of things not mainly for consumption but for the fact of owning them. A "weakened" reality principle then could lead to alternative action: to decreased puritanism and greater sexual freedom or to an orientation toward material consumption with the need to own things as a central motive. However, it is clear that these two alternatives theoretically do not exclude each other. In practice they may do so, if increased consumption is possible only by increased income and this income only can be acquired by accepting of a second job during what ought to be leisure time, which in this case is again filled by work.

Other factors may play a dominant role. The decrease of a puritan ethic is also related to traditional values. In Swedish society, for example, there exist traditionally strong inhibitions against aggressiveness and violence, whereas the inhibitions against sexual activity are weaker in proportion to aggressiveness. In the American society the opposite is true. There exists a traditional value-system dating back to the frontier period which allows aggression and violence and which makes it socially more acceptable than the expression of sexual needs. Thus the American culture is to a much higher degree than the Swedish one a "violent culture."

Such an explanation, as roughly outlined here, presupposes quite a different metapsychological theory. It must reject the idea of the necessity of instinctual repression and sublimation and replace it by another theoretical starting point. Since Marcuse, however (as stated above), is dedicated to traditional Freudian concepts, he suggests a different explanation.

SURPLUS REPRESSION AND THE PERFORMANCE PRINCIPLE

Marcuse differentiates between repression primarily of instinctual satisfaction and a *secondary* repression, also called "surplus repression."[50] The primary repression is a consequence of the idea that instincts are basically asocial in their orientation, an idea which will be critically viewed later. However, if this view is to hold, one consequence is that all societies must protect themselves against the basically asocial tendencies that are inherent in human nature. This is Freud's postulate accepted by Marcuse, who develops psychoanalytic theory even further the addition of the secondary repression to the primary one is not necessary for the development of self-control of biological-instinctual energy. It is forced upon the individual by social instances representing society and its power structure. Thus the secondary or surplus repression is dependent upon existent relations of dominance and authority. The controlling social instances include parents, since the family structure and the system of upbringing are closely related to the total societal system.

The type of repression of instinctual needs employed depends on the existing social and economic system with its specific power structure. The way the reality principle is formed varies from society to society. It undergoes changes in the historical process. Marcuse asserts that repression in a market economy is different from the one employed in a planned economy.

The specific form which the reality principle assumes in a capitalistic market economy is called by Marcuse the "performance principle." A performance is an activity which is important not only for what is involved—e.g., which capabilities are used—but also for the result obtained. Performances can be measured and individuals rewarded and differentiated according to their performance, which in turn presupposes continuous competition among individuals. In addition performance is an activity, the result of which can be appropriated either by the performing subject or by others.

The performance principle is an. expression of existing social class-differentiation and is forced upon those who are subjugated to the power of a dominating class. The performance principle leads to coercion and subdues the individual. In the highly industrialized society this pressure toward performance is compensated to a certain degree by allowing some

[50] Marcuse, *Eros and Civilization*, p. 34.

of the instinctual energy to become free. Thus in order to uphold surplus repression, some of the primary repression is abolished. The individual is allowed to express some of its instinctual needs: aggression, related to the death instinct, and sexual activity. Therefore the apparent liberalization of sexuality and the weakening of sexual taboos is not real liberty but just a "desublimation." This is shown by the fact that sexual behavior often becomes exploitive and mechanized and that it lacks erotic qualities.

"Compare," says Marcuse, "love-making in a meadow and in an automobile, on a lovers' walk outside the town walls and on a Manhattan street. In the former cases, the environment partakes of and invites libidinal cathexis and tends to be eroticized. Libido transcends beyond the immediate erotogenic zones—a process of nonrepressive sublimation. In contrast, a mechanized environment seems to block such self-transcendence of libido."[51] What occurs is "repressive desublimation."

Marcuse thus differentiates between three types of sublimating situations: (1) repressive sublimation, (2) repressive desublimation, and (3) nonrepressive sublimation.

The first type, repressive sublimation, is the traditional way of sublimation: the repression of primary instinctual energy and its transformation and orientation toward socially acceptable goals. In highly industrialized societies repressive sublimation leads to the development of the performance principle by additional surplus repression. The repressive desublimation, however, permits increased satisfaction of instinctual needs. This in turn leads to greater dependence, to lesser freedom. The individual is permitted greater possibilities for superficial pleasure experiences in order to counteract opposition and revolt against the mechanized and bureaucratized life, built upon a technology which has been developed to be the most perfect instrument for human domination.

According to Marcuse, the increased sexual freedom is one way to repress or prevent active opposition to the existent social system. Alienation becomes more acceptable through desublimation. It is perceived as a normal state by the one-dimensional man, since he is alien to his "real needs." Marcuse assumes that repression of instinctual needs and repressive sublimation creates a need for opposition and for liberation. Desublimation pacifies and allows substitute satisfaction. Therefore the individual becomes satisfied and adjusted to existing social conditions and no longer develops the desire to emancipate himself.[52]

[51] Marcuse, *One-Dimensional Man*, p. 73.

[52] An alternative hypothesis concerning the relationship between sexual activity and active opposition to existing society is developed by Wilhelm Reich, who, like Marcuse, combines psychoanalysis and Marxism. He, however, sees the freeing of sexual impulse as an activity which creates a critical and active oppositional attitude toward the existing social system. See, e.g., his *Massenpsychologie des Faschismus* (Copenhagen: Verlag für Sexualpolitik, 1933).

SOME ADDITIONAL CRITICAL REMARKS ON MARCUSE'S THEORY

A criticism of Marcuse's theory can be based upon the model of man he uses. Since this model is the Freudian one, criticism has, first, to be directed to this model.

Freud's model or image of man is heavily influenced by mechanistic ideas. Man is viewed as a physiological machine driven by instinctual energies. These energies, bound to two main instincts, initiate action. If for a certain reason action is inhibited, energy will be transformed. This means that it can be used for a secondary type of action substituting a primary one directly related to the satisfaction of basic instincts.

Second, in Freud's view man is basically asocial in two respects: (1) he is inherently asocial, aggressive, and brutal,[53] (2) he is guided by the pleasure principle, which is in conflict with demands society may direct toward its members. Thus the negative picture of man basic to Freud's model is a mixture of Hobbes's misanthropic view on man and hedonism considered to be asocial.

Third, Freud conceives of culture as the result of the sublimation of the energy of the "lower" instincts for "higher" goals. In this respect Freud's concept of culture clearly has a value bias related to the ideas of romanticism.

Marcuse takes over this metapsychology, which is somewhat surprising since it contradicts the image of man developed by Marx. Marx (see chapters 3 and 9) does not have a mechanistic model of man, but views man as a historical product of those social conditions he has created himself. In addition to this dialectical interplay between man as a species and his social environment, a *specific* human being *is* what his social relations are. Again these social relations are determined by the basic mode of production.

Thus Marx uses a "process model"[54] of man (and of society) and not a mechanistic one. Neither is there any assumption about man's nature being basically good or bad. Nor is "culture" viewed as a product of instinctual sublimation, but is closely related to the basic process of production. It is viewed as the superstructure of the material basis.

Thus human behavior in the Marxian model is a consequence of social conditions, in the Freudian model a consequence of basic instincts and the transformation of instinctual energy. Marx uses a sociological model; Freud, a biological-psychological one. To the extent that Marcuse accepts

[53] See, e.g., S. Freud, *Civilization and Its Discontents* (London: Hogarth Press, 1949).
[54] On the distinction between mechanistic models and process models in the social sciences, see W. Buckley, *Sociology and Modern Systems Theory* (Englewood Cliffs: Prentice-Hall, 1967).

this later model, he places himself outside and in opposition to the Marxian modes of explanation.

There is another important difference. The acceptance of basic instincts and of the pleasure principle, according to which man strives for satisfaction independently of what society demands of him, presupposes a basic conflict between man and society. However, in Marxian thinking (see chapters 1 and 9) there exists no conflict between man and society, but the conflicts which exist concern a struggle between man and nature which he transforms in the process of production. In turn, this struggle leads to conflicts *within* society, namely, between existing classes. Thus in this respect, too, Marcuse places himself in opposition to Marxian thinking.

I have underlined the points on which Marcuse differs from, or is opposed to, Marxian thinking since he considers his theories to be Marxist.

In addition to the criticism raised against the model of man and metapsychological assumptions, one can also go into more detail.

Marcuse's acceptance of the Freudian instinct theory, and especially of the idea that these instincts are basically asocial, is strange. If one considers man as a historical product, then a specific type of man found at a specific historical epoch is the product of the social environment he has created. Thus a reasonable assumption is that man's "natural history"[55] leads to adaptation to social conditions created by himself and thus to a continuous change in human nature. It is therefore difficult to understand why, after such a long development, man should remain basically asocial, i.e., in contradiction to his own creations. The social environment created one has to view as a function of human nature. Thus the idea of the basic asociality of man contradicts the notion of the dialectic relationship between man and his environment.

Moreover, the theory of sublimation implicitly makes value-assumptions. It differentiates between "lower" animal instincts—and the behavior they give rise to—and "higher" cultural activities. Thus not only are there introduced value-judgments concerning *different human activities* (some of which are devalued, whereas others are highly estimated), in addition, *specific values* concerning so-called "cultural" activities are assumed. The values according to which certain cultural products are evaluated are not only based upon a romanticist ideology but also correspond to a large degree to those in which bourgeois upper-class aesthetics of the nineteenth and the beginning of the twentieth century are anchored.[56]

Instead of accepting the idea of sublimation as a necessary precondition for "cultural" activities, one could as an alternative look at man as a totality. Sexual activities and creative activities occurring in the same

---

[55] S. Moscovici, *Essai sur l'histoire humaine de la nature* (Paris: Flammarion, 1968).
[56] See, e.g., chapter 9 in Marcuse, *Eros and Civilization.*

person influence each other as a feedback mechanism: sexual activities may stimulate creative ones, and these in turn may stimulate interaction leading to sexual activity. Such an alternative model would add a fourth cell to Marcuse's typology. As seen previously (see page 180), he uses two variables: repression and sublimation. For each variable he uses two values; namely, repressive and nonrepressive, as well as sublimation and desublimation.

	Sublimation	Desublimation
Repressive	1) Traditional society	2) Current society
Nonrepressive	3) Marcuse's ideal	4)

Cell 4 must be an empty one in Marcuse's model. However, if one replaces "desublimation" with the more adequate "nonsublimation," then the fourth cell is no longer an empty one but represents a society in which no repression of sexual needs is necessary, as well as sublimation not occurring. Such a combination, however, presupposes an alternative hypothesis concerning the relationship between sexual and creative activities. One such alternative hypothesis is that formulated above concerning a feedback relationship in man, viewed as a totality. In addition "culture" must be viewed not as an individual but as a social product. A society characterized by nonrepression and nonsublimation would be one in which work is reduced to a minimum and leisure time gives rise to a variety of activities. A rational use of the existing productive forces, i.e., for nondestructive purposes and the just distribution of the social product, would be the preconditions for such a utopian society.

As a final point of criticism, Marcuse's comparison of love-making in a meadow and in a car may be quoted. In this example his romantic ideology is revealed. One aspect of such an ideology is the Rousseauean idea of man's natural environment. I have difficulties in understanding why, for a person living in a society with a highly developed technology, it should be more eroticizing to make love in an environment which was "natural" for man in the preindustrialized society than in an environment which *is* the "natural" one for him: the one created by modern technology.[57] What we want to question is the idea that certain environments, certain ways of living should be more "*natural*" than others. This idea

[57] See, for an excellent discussion of the problem, Moscovici, *Essai sur l'histoire.*

coupled with the idea "back to nature" is in my opinion not only romantic metaphysics but in contradiction to the idea of the dialectic relationship between man and his environment.

HUMANISTIC IDEAS IN MARCUSE'S THEORIES

The solution which Marcuse favors, i.e., nonrepressive desublimation, makes necessary a distinction between "genuine" and "artificial" needs. If sublimation ought not to be experienced as repressive, it should lead to the satisfaction of "genuine" needs. Thus the idea of nonrepressive sublimation also makes it necessary to develop criteria according to which needs can be classified. In my opinion this is possible by introducing explicit value-criteria. Those criteria, however, have to be formulated in a way which makes them independent of the definition of repression and/or sublimation. If not, one arrives at a circular reasoning.

Marcuse's definition of "artificial" and "genuine" needs does not avoid this risk. Concerning artificial needs he says: " 'False' are those which are superimposed upon the individual by particular social interests in his repression: the needs which perpetuate toil, aggressiveness, misery, and injustice. Their satisfaction might be most gratifying to the individual, but this happiness is not a condition which has to be maintained and protected if it serves to arrest the development of the ability (his own and others) to recognize the disease of the whole and grasp the chances of curing the disease."[58]

In addition he mentions the needs for relaxation which have been taken care of by commercialized interests, the need for a high standard of living as a goal in itself. Instead such a standard of living, in Marcuse's view, ought to be a means for the satisfaction of genuine and basic human needs and result in a state in which man would be free from anxiety and guilt. That would form the basis for a *pacified existence*. Marcuse sketches an utopian society built upon humanistic ideas of human self-realization borrowed from the German romantic thought, psychoanalysis, and Marxism—developed, however, in an original way.

Marcuse points out that his ideal deviates from the humanism of the nineteenth century, which also influenced Marx's thinking. Traditional socialist humanism is no longer considered adequate by Marcuse.[59] This is due to technological development. Marx's ideas of the creative human being and of work as the expression of human self-realization, found in his early writings, have been made obsolete by the development of technology, which Marx could not foresee. Such a technological society im-

[58] Marcuse, *One-Dimensional Man*, pp. 4–5.
[59] H. Marcuse, "Socialist Humanism?" in *Socialist Humanism*, ed. E. Fromm (Garden City: Doubleday and Co., 1965), p. 99 ff.

plies "the assimilation of freedom and necessity, of satisfaction and repression, of the aspirations of politics, business and the individual."[60]

In his latest writings Marx revised his ideas and thought that perhaps labor could not be transformed into creative activity. But the abolishment of a market economy making possible a shorter working day would provide possibilities for the individual for self-realization during leisure time. Leisure time would *transform* man. Marcuse says that though leisure time has increased it has not led to the transformation of man: "in the capitalist and the communist systems, the subject of free time is subordinated to the same norms and powers that rule the realm of necessity. The mature Marxian conception, too, appears idealistic and optimistic."[61]

As long as want and poverty exist in a large part of the world, traditional humanism must remain a dominant ideology. But in the highly industrialized societies the technological apparatus has become totalitarian and dominates man's total life. The solution can no longer be found in the humanization of work and its conditions but in the humanization of our life conditions: the planning of other types of cities, the prevention of destruction of our environment, social planning in general on a broad basis, and last, but not least, the creation of secure measures against atomic warfare threatening the existence of man.

Among theories of alienation the one developed by Marcuse is one of the most stimulating—also stimulating criticism. In it technology—and the social system created on modern technology—becomes the alienated system per se, since it deviates from traditional values and seems effectively to prevent their realization. However, the pessimistic outlook has been changed in Marcuse's latest work. In this he lets the words spoken by a black girl constitute a guideline. Responding to the question, What would people in a free society do, she responded that in such a society for the first time people would be free to think about what to do.[62]

C. WRIGHT MILLS AND MASS SOCIETY

CRITICAL ANALYSIS OF MARX

C. Wright Mills treats the problem of alienation both in his own theories[63] and in a critical analysis of Marx and his theories.[64]

---

[60] Ibid., p. 101.

[61] Ibid.

[62] Marcuse, *Essay on Liberation.*

[63] C. W. Mills, *White Collar* (New York: Oxford University Press, 1956) and *The Power Elite* (New York: Oxford University Press, 1959).

[64] C. W. Mills, *The Marxists* (New York: Dell Publishing Co., 1962).

Mills treats Marxism as a *political philosophy* and presents four criteria according to which one can evaluate such a philosophy.[65] *First*, a political philosophy is an *ideology*; *second*, it is an *ethical system* with given ideals and goals for action; *third*, it mentions the *means* for realizing these goals.

The *fourth* and last criterion for a political philosophy is its *theoretical content*. The theories concern man, society, and history; they formulate hypotheses concerning the development of society and the driving forces behind this development. They concern the functioning of society and the role of the individual and classes of individuals within the social structure.

In a critical analysis of a political philosophy, it is necessary to distinguish the above-mentioned four constituent elements. In addition, when analyzing Marx in his theories, one must maintain the distinction between a model and a theory. A model is a more or less systematic review of those elements which it is necessary to take into account if one wishes to understand reality. A model is neither true nor false. A model may be more or less useful and applicable.[66]

Such a definition of a model permits a distinction between Marx's attempts to present the economic and sociological categories necessary and/or sufficient to analyze a society in general and the capitalist society in particular and the theories developed on the basis of such a model. In fact Marx's model consists of two elements. One is the basic categories for sociological analysis. The other category consists of methodological rules concerning the way such an analysis should be carried out. The first element has a descriptive function; the second, a normative function. I wish briefly to exemplify the two elements. Among the basic concepts involved in the model one finds *productive forces* comprising man, machines, raw materials, science and technology, and *relations of production*, comprising power and ownership relations, which in turn point to class division. Productive forces, relations of production, and the products produced together form the *mode of production*.

Methodological rules make assumptions concerning basic processes in society as well as about rules of analysis. The rule that one should base analysis on the basic social process of production is an example of the first. The rule that, when analyzing society, one should concentrate on conflicts and study society as a totality belongs to the second type.

Failing to distinguish between a model with its descriptive and normative function, and theories based upon this model and having an explanatory function, has led to many misunderstandings. The Marxian model has been rejected by adversaries together with the theories he pre-

[65] Ibid.
[66] Ibid., p. 36.

sented. On the other hand, the supporters of Marxism have, besides treating the model as a theory, sometimes pretended that everything Marx wrote are *verified* theories.[67]

The consequence of differentiating between a model and a theory is that a model can still be useful even if theories based upon it are not verified, or are no longer verified, because in social science verified theories may affect and change the conditions upon which the theory was based.

In the case of Marx's theories we now know that some of his predictions were not verified by the social and economic development in highly industrialized societies. Mills also underlines that the Marxian model is the great contribution to sociology. According to him, it is still vivid and provides a classical instrument for the analysis of man, society, and history.[68]

Mill's criticism of the Marxian theories also concerns the problem of alienation. Mills first makes clear that a high material standard of living and alienation are not mutually exclusive. Alienation in the Marxian sense concerns the individual's relation to his labor and the products of his labor. Individuals can experience themselves as alienated even if they have a high material standard of living and if physical want is absent. Therefore Mills asserts that the existence of alienation is theoretically possible even if the theory of impoverishment has not been verified.[69]

In addition, Mills emphasizes the distinction between alienation and "lack of satisfaction in work" as the concept is usually treated in traditional industrial sociology. In Marx's theories the concept of alienation presupposes normative assumptions concerning the ideal of labor and the meaning labor *ought* to have for man. Perhaps the type of estrangement experienced by man in society today and in his work-situation does not contradict Marx's theories, but he does not analyze this type of alienation or estrangement. In particular the relation between the individual and the product of his labor is not at all discussed in theories concerning "satisfaction in work." Later we will discuss the distinction between alienation and satisfaction by referring to a concrete situation (see chapter 8).

One of Mills's criticisms of Marx is the romantic ideal of labor found in the theories of the young Marx. Mills tries to show that the ideal work situation for Marx was the one represented by the small artisan. The ideal of craftsmanship comprises six features: (1) the driving motive behind labor is the product and the process in which it is created; (2) the daily work is meaningful because it is not separated from the final product;

[67] Concerning the scientific status of Marxism, see J. Witt-Hansen, *Historical Materialism*, Book 1 (Copenhagen: Munksgaard, 1960), and J. Israel, "Problems of Marxist Class Analysis," *Acta Sociologica* 1970, 13, 11–29.

[68] Mills, *The Marxists*, p. 36.

[69] Ibid., p. 86.

(3) the artisan himself has control over the labor-situation; (4) he is, in addition, able to learn from his labor and to improve it; (5) no distinction exists between work and play, and finally (6) the craftsman's labor completely determines his style of life.[70]

These ideals cannot be applied to the labor of a modern industrial worker. The question concerning the attitude man has to his labor is, in both capitalist and noncapitalist societies, an empirical question, and Mills asserts that it is a question for which we do not have an adequate answer. In any case, he adds, the state in which Marx left the concept of alienation is insufficient, and in addition the concept is vague.[71]

Thus Mills's criticism is directed, first, against the normative anchoring of the concept in romantic ideals of craftmanship; second, against the lack of empirical data. The first critical argument is correct; however, it applies only to the young Marx. The second argument can be refuted by referring to empirical studies of alienation, which, however, mainly concentrate on the psychological aspects of alienation and therefore miss the sociological aspect (see chapter 7).

Mills underlines that the type of activity which characterized the craftsman's work has today, in technically highly developed societies, been restricted to leisure time and trivial hobby activities. Only a few workers with training within specialized occupations and some intellectuals belonging to a privileged group, able to determine its own working hours and for which labor is a "creative activity," may have ideal labor conditions.

Mills definitely states—and I think this is a central argument—that few workers, if any, compare their own labor with the ideal represented by the craftsman's activity. Most often they do not know anything about these activities. It is senseless to compare a craftsman and an auto worker, a traditional merchant with a sales-clerk, a book-keeper with an computer attendant: "For the historical destruction of craftmanship and of the old office does not enter the consciousness of the modern wage-worker or white-collar employee; much less is their absence felt by him as crisis, as it may have been if, in the course of the last generation, his father or mother had been in the craft condition—but, statistically speaking, they have not been. . . . Only the psychological imagination of the historian makes it possible to write of such comparisons as if they were of psychological import."[72]

Since most workers and white-collar workers active today have not experienced the transition from the artisan mode of production to modern,

---

[70] Mills, *White Collar*, p. 220.
[71] Mills, *The Marxists*, p. 112.
[72] Mills, *White Collar*, p. 228.

technically highly developed production, the ideal of labor as a creative activity is irrelevant and does not enter their minds. For the most part labor is unpleasant, a coercion one has learnt to accept. However, the question which Mills touched briefly is the relationship between the goals of society, its social structure, and the individual's labor. Labor might be instrumental for individual goals, outside the work situation, which is the predominant type today. Or it might also be instrumental for the achievement of important social goals with which the individual identifies. Ideally such a situation exists in societies like the *kibbutz* in Israel and in underdeveloped nations struggling for their development, such as the Cuban society.

Mills thus does not neglect existing social conditions. He maintains that one can understand the meaning of alienation without being forced to accept the metaphysical idea that man realizes himself in his labor. "The objective alienation of man from the product and the process of work is entailed by the legal framework of modern capitalism and modern division of labor."[73]

One can analyze the factual conditions under which the individual is forced to work. In particular he studies white-collar workers and their situation. White-collar workers constitute the American middle class, having replaced the traditional entrepreneurial middle class and its value system. One question in his analysis is whether the conditions of labor among special white-collar groups are such that they lead to the development of alienation. One condition he studies is the development of a "personality market."

THE PERSONALITY MARKET AND MARKETING

The main trend in modern capitalist society is the transformation of everything into a commodity, thus making it available for the market and for exchange. Mills uses this central Marxian idea in his analysis of white-collar workers.

The basic change within the middle class is the transition from being small, independent entrepreneurs to being white-collar workers and functionaries in the same position of dependence as the manual worker. They have as little personal relation as the worker to the work they carry out or to the products of their labor. They also are influenced by the division of labor; consequently, in many cases they cannot use the skills and abilities which they have acquired. Office work has become mechanized. The working conditions for manual workers and white-collar workers have largely been equalized.

---

[73] Ibid., p. 225.

Most important, however, is that the white-collar worker, like the manual worker, is placed in a bureaucratic organizational structure, the goal of which is the continuous rationalization of the production process in order to increase output, productivity, and profits. The white-collar workers are as dependent and powerless as are the workers, both in an objective sense and subjectively in the experience of their own situation. They have very little influence in planning their work or in modifying the plans to which they have to subordinate themselves. The dependent position is extended far up in the bureaucratic hierarchy and also affects those white-collar workers who are professionals.

In the preindustrialized society the individual sold commodities to each other. In the industrialized society employees sell their labor and services. However, there are some basic differences between workers and white-collar workers, especially those among white-collar workers who are engaged in sales activities. White-collar people learn to sell their "social personality." This occurs in a society dominated not only by the market but by a marketing ideology as well. It is expressed by the idea that everything can be sold with the right methods and with effective methods of influence, e.g., advertisement. Marketing can be used for the sale of ideas, political programs, and even religious salvation. More and more, activities are considered as sales activities.

There are two opposing tendencies. Relations on the market become anonymous and impersonal. However, people engaged in sales activities are requested to behave as if they were personally involved and interested in the customer. Personal traits, even intimate ones, become arguments for sale and therefore themselves commodities on the labor market. The salesperson is required to develop a stereotyped mask of personal interest in the customer: "Kindness and friendliness become aspects of personalized services or of public relations of big firms, rationalized to further the sale of something. With anonymous insincerity the Successful Person thus makes an instrument of his own appearance and personality."[74]

Thus, the personality is transformed into a commodity of great commercial relevance. According to Mills there are three conditions under which a "personality market" can function effectively: (1) the employee is part of a large bureaucratic system, selected, trained, and supervised by his foreman higher up in the hierarchy, (2) his role within the bureaucratic organization is to be in touch with clients and to represent the firm through his own personal appearance and behavior, (3) most of the customers have to be anonymous because the "personal" relation to the client is only a mask, trained behavior without emotional involvement.

[74] Ibid., p. 182.

Mills exemplifies his thesis with a description of the behavior of sales personnel. At the beginning of their career salesmen are often unaware of the discrepancy between what they think of the customer and the way they conduct themselves in relation to him. However, mass-produced commodities cannot attract the customer sufficiently. Therefore the "pleasant" personality of the salesperson gains importance. The friendly smile becomes a commercial necessity. The knowledge that it is often his own personality rather than the commodity that is important for the sale influences the salesman. Since it is impossible for him to involve himself personally with every, anonymous customer, he experiences the transformation of his personality into an instrument for a certain purpose: sale. Thus, the consequence becomes self-alienation. However, the customer also knows and reveals the commercialized personality traits of the salesperson. Therefore there develops a social relationship in which one person tries to make the other believe, whereas the other in response makes the first believe that he does not understand the true attitude. The result becomes that "men are enstranged from one other as each secretly tries to make an instrument of the other, and in time a full circle is made: one makes an instrument of himself, and is estranged from It also."[75]

Thus, in a market economy, man becomes a commodity as labor power. His activity becomes instrumental for purposes outside the labor situation. In addition, his personality becomes a commodity, and his social relations are built on a secret understanding of each other's motive that nobody, however, recognizes publicly. Thus total alienation is created in the labor situation as well as in daily social relations.

One problem is: To what extent do the roles the individual has been trained to play on the "personality market" influence his life, especially his private life outside the commercial sales relationship? Mills develops a hypothesis that the quasi-personal relationship between salesman and customers creates a general suspicion in interpersonal relations. Knowing how he can make-believe interest and emotional engagement, he may fear that another person's real interest and engagement in a strictly private situation is only a way to hide the fact that the other wishes to exploit him. A very interesting empirical problem, rarely studied by sociologists or social psychologists, is the extent to which "sales relations" are carried over into interpersonal relations in general.

In one sphere, not dealt with by Mills, the "personality market" probably plays an important role which may have important consequences for the functioning of a democracy. I refer to the effect which the personality has on the marketing of political programs and ideologies by mass media

[75] Ibid., p. 188.

such as television. To the extent that people in a democratic society are unable to differentiate between a person and the ideas he represents, the personality and appearance of a politician may play a dominant role, especially in elections. Ideal politicians then became second-rate actors, sufficiently insincere to become first-rate actors, and for precisely that reason appearing as the "ideal" politician. Since, in addition, they have a certain routine regarding how to act publicly and how to use the medium by which they transmit their message, they gain advantage over their more sincere and often more intelligent competitors. The less the differences between competing political leader or parties, the more probable it is that the displayed personality of the politician has an important effect. In this field, too, sociologists could further develop Mills's hypothesis concerning the function of the personality market.

THE CHANGED ROLE OF INTELLECTUALS

Mills dedicates quite a detailed analysis to the "intellectuals." First, he makes clear that intellectuals are not a homogeneous social group, but that the analysis must take into consideration the different social functions which intellectuals may perform. In addition, subjectively different abilities and skills may be of importance.

Intellectuals are specialists on symbols. They produce, distribute, and maintain distinct types of consciousness. How does this group of people function in the society to which Mills refers?

As a sideline Mills discusses the positive type of alienation: intellectuals and especially artists being alienated from the bourgeois society. In that case, alienation is a source of strength. But, as does Marcuse, Mills thinks that this positive type of alienation presupposes freedom and independence which to a large degree no longer exist. The intellectuals themselves have been integrated into the bureaucratic apparatus and therefore no longer possess the necessary freedom for positive alienation.

In particular the development after the Second World War has marked the intellectuals and their activities. "Bureaucracy increasingly sets the conditions of intellectual life and controls the major market for its products. The new bureaucracies of state and business, of party and voluntary association, become the major employers of intellectuals and the main customers for their work."[76] In this quotation is expressed Mills's central hypothesis concerning the changed role of the intellectuals.

The integration of intellectuals into powerful bureaucratic organizations influences them in different aspects. For example, it becomes difficult to maintain diverging opinions if the individual is economically dependent on

[76] Ibid., p. 149.

the organization. Those intellectuals, however, who try to stay outside bureaucratic organizations experience that technical, economic, and social organizations separate them from their potential public and that these organizations are owned and managed by those who effectively can hinder or prevent the necessary contacts with the public. Mills attributes great importance to this problem of decreasing possibilities of directly reaching those to whom the intellectuals address themselves. Intellectuals live through and with communication. Knowledge and opinions that cannot be communicated have no social effect. In addition, lack of communication has a direct effect on the process of acquiring knowledge. The type of knowledge possessed by intellectuals is often of such a kind that its true relevance can be established only through others competent to make adequate judgments. The integrity of intellectuals, therefore, is to a large degree based on chances of free and adequate communication.

Mills maintains that the development of large bureaucracies created "ideological demands." Bureaucracies build up "symbolic fortresses" in order to create an ideological defense of their own activities. One such defense strategy is to hire scientists to investigate problems and to use their results for decision-making processes. However, the question is whether research findings are used for the very decision-making process, or whether they are used only for prestige purposes. Reference is made to scientific studies, the results of which, however, have never been considered by those holding power positions. For them it is sufficient to say that they have cooperated with scientific experts, in order to give their actions the prestige accorded to science in our society. Thus, to a large degree scientists have a legitimizing function.

Intellectuals often face a dilemma. Shall they be employed in bureaucratic power structures—governmental or private—and be forced to relinquish their independence, or shall they doom themselves to powerlessness, especially with regard to political influence? The consequence is lack of involvement or, if involvement occurs, it leads to frustration because it cannot be connected with real influence and the opportunities to influence events. In both cases there are a series of escape mechanisms. Mills calls one of them "the fetish of objectivity," a special variant of the "alienation cult."

"Objectivity or Scientism is often an academic cult of the narrowed attention, the pose of the technician, or the aspiring technician, who assumes as given the big framework and the political meaning of his operation within it."[77] The technically oriented scientists—not a unusual phenomenon in the social sciences—is aloof or stands beside controversial problems. Instead, if at all, he complains about powerlessness and alienation.

[77] Ibid., p. 160.

Thus the alienation cult is a way to complain without wanting to do anything about the situation. It is, in Mills's words, the fashionable way to be overwhelmed.

The background to the situation of intellectuals are changes in the social structure in the U.S. which have lead to the development of powerful elites on the one hand and the mass society on the other, both being opposed to each other and at the same time dependent on each other.

POWER ELITES

Power has to do with the decisions man make concerning the conditions shaping their lives, and concerning those events that form their history. The explication is taken from one of Mills's essays on the American power structure.[78] One of his basic theses is that, in the type of overdeveloped social system exemplified by the American society, there has occurred a concentration of decision-making, i.e., power in political, economic, and military institutions. These institutions are dominated and ruled by groups of people, who form different power elites, closely connected with each other and to a certain degree interdependent.

Mills sketches the development of the power structure in the U.S. He distinguishes five periods in this evolution. The first period starts at the period of the American Revolution. Political, economic, and military institutions, though separated, were united to high degree, since people in leading positions could easily shift from one institution to another. The second period, embracing the early nineteenth century, showed a plurality of decision-making groups in top positions forming loose coalitions. The third period, characterized by the beginning of corporate economic power, is dated to the late 1860s, whereas the fourth period is the period of the New Deal. The fifth period, the beginning of which Mills dates to the end of the Second World War, is characterized by a series of structural changes. In the political field there is a concentration of power in the political elite and simultaneous decline of popular influence and debate of political alternatives. "America is now in considerable part more a formal political democracy than a democratic social structure, and even the formal political mechanics are weak."[79] Economy and governmental institutions become more and more interrelated to the point where they can no longer be distinguished as two separate structures: partly the administration, especially its executive branch, has been enlarged and has assumed economic planning and controlling functions; partly the elite

[78] C. W. Mills, *Power, Politics and People* (New York: Ballantine Books, undated), p. 23.

[79] Mills, *The Power Elite*, p. 274.

from the economic world, e.g., from the large corporations, have obtained influence and important positions within the government and the administration.

Another important structural change occurs within the military structure. Not only has the military apparatus increased in number, but its tremendous influence on American politics and economic life is undeniable. "The seemingly permanent military threat places a premium on the military and upon their control of men, material, money and power; virtually all political and economic actions are now judged in terms of military definitions of reality."[80]

This is partly connected with the changed role of the U.S. in world politics, which among other things has replaced isolationism with doctrines that make possible U.S. interference at any spot where a threat against American interests is felt. Since the American economy is built upon the necessity of importing raw materials from all over the world, military strength is necessary to control and to protect the sources for the functioning of the American economy. The large corporation, on the other hand, is dependent on the military establishment, since the military can give large orders to industry, and this makes corporations partly independent of the fluctuations and uncertainties of the market.[81] Thus the structure of the American economy necessitates a large military establishment, the effectiveness of which in turn depends on the economic structure.

The economic structure is a mixture of permanent war economy and private corporation economy, capitalism dominated by the multinational large corporation. "American capitalism is now in considerable part a military capitalism, and the important relation of the big corporation to the state rests on the coincidence of interests between military and corporate needs, as defined by warlords and corporate rich."[82]

The power elites are composed of politicians in top administrative positions, the leading people in business and industry, and the top echelon in the military structure. The power relationship and the distribution of actual power varies; but, asserts Mills, in the period starting at the end of the Second World War, the economic and military elite have closely cooperated and therefore have been able to increase their power. In any event all three power elites participate in the most important decision-making processes.

[80] Ibid., p. 275.

[81] These ideas have been further developed by J. K. Galbraith, *The New Industrial State* (London: Hamish Hamilton, 1967) and are well documented by C. Julien, *L'empire américaine* (Paris: Editions Bernard Grasset, 1968).

[82] Mills, *The Power Elite*, p. 276.

Members of these elites are characterized by their conviction that they are doing their duty. They themselves define what their duties are. In other words, they define the goals for their actions. They do not only follow given orders; they also give orders. They are not only members of a bureaucracy; they also command bureaucracies. They possess top positions in the total social structure of the U.S. According to Mills, the question concerning the groups and strata from which the elites are recruited is not so important. Which function they perform is more important. Neither is it so important whom and whose interests they represent. More important are the consequences of their power positions for the American social structure and the democratic system. One of the consequences is the development of what Mills terms the "mass society." Before discussing this problem, we will treat some of the arguments criticizing the theory of the power elites.

In an interesting analysis of Mills's theory, Bottomore[83] asks why one should speak of *three* different *power elites* and not *one ruling class* in the Marxist sense. Mills rejects the idea of a ruling class. He stresses the meaning of "class" as an economic category, whereas "ruling" refers to political categories. Thus the notion of a "ruling class" implies a theory that an economic class can rule by making political decisions. This is exactly what the Marxian theory assumes. The *owners* of the means of production form a ruling class because ownership of means of production provides the means not only for economic decisions but, indirectly, for political and military decisions as well. Thus economic power is considered as the more basic. Those in charge of political and military decision processes are viewed as being dependent on the ruling class and often are also seen as those who carry out decisions made by the ruling class. According to this view, therefore, the ruling class "controls the means of political domination-legislation, the courts, the administration, military force and the agencies of intellectual persuasion."[84]

The relationship between economic, political, military, and ideological sources of power has become more complex. In the Soviet Union, for example, the different means of power are concentrated in one bureaucratic stratum, which can be seen as forming a class, depending on which criteria are used for class differentiation. In certain countries, e.g., in Latin America, there still exists a ruling class in the sense in which Marx describes it. In a Scandinavian country like Sweden the situation is somewhat different. A strong labor movement has been in control of the political decision-making process for nearly forty years. Thus there exist possi-

[83] T. B. Bottomore, *Elites and Society* (London: George Allen & Unwin, 1964).
[84] T. B. Bottomore, *Classes in Modern Society* (London: George Allen & Unwin, 1965).

bilities of restricting and controlling economic power by means of political decision-making processes. However, in spite of the long period during which political power has been possessed by the labor movement, no *basic* changes in the economic system have been carried out. The system is still predominantly based on private ownership of means of production with a strong concentration in a few hands.[85] In addition, there are still large differences in income and wealth, though a redistribution has occurred to a certain limited degree. Furthermore, since economic processes are central in any society, the economic system and the social structure erected upon it have a decisive influence on all types of decision-making. Therefore the political control of economic processes reaches its limits at the point where the laws of the economic system cannot be changed without basic alterations in the total structure. This becomes clear especially in cases in which the dependence of Swedish economy on the international economic system prevents or restricts decision-making, e.g., with regard to foreign policy.

In an interesting analysis Wesolowski[86] tries to unify the theory of the ruling class with the theory of the power elite. The ruling class is defined in the Marxian sense, as the owners of the means of production. The power elite, on the other hand, "is a product of the political structure of society. It consists of individuals who take part in the process of shaping and making State decisions or who exert a direct influence on those who do."[87] Thus the power elites both possess influence and are themselves the decision-makers. The relationship between the ruling class and the power elite can be threefold: (1) they are completely separated groups, (2) there is a certain degree of overlapping, (3) the power elite belongs to the ruling class, though not all members of the ruling class belong to the power elite. Also the influence of the ruling class can be of three different kinds: (1) political decision-making is completely dominated by the ruling class, (2) the power elite supports and strengthens the dominance of the ruling class by its political decisions, (3) the political elite delimits the dominance of the ruling class.

The ruling class can strengthen its power through the wealth it possesses, through control over mass media, through informal contacts with the power elite. Its power is decreased by factors outside its own country (such as resistance in other countries), by the increase of that part of economy which is owned and controlled publicly, and by the existence of political organizations, trade unions, and other interest groups.

[85] S.O.U., *Ägande och inflytande inom det privata näringslivet* (Stockholm: Public Investigations, 1968), 7.

[86] W. Wesolowski, "Ruling Class and Power Elite," *The Polish Sociological Bulletin* No. 1. (11) (1965), 22–37.

[87] Ibid., p. 23.

Thus in this theory the existence of a ruling class is not denied, but a variety of relations with a power elite is postulated, along with a variety of restrictions on its decision-making power.

Can this model also be applied to the social structure analyzed by Mills, i.e., the American structure? Let us examine Mills's arguments. As mentioned above, his first argument for rejecting the idea of a "ruling class" is that it is a mixture of political and economic criteria. According to Mills, "class" is an economic category. However, one may object that different types of criteria can be used for the differentiation of people into classes. In addition to economic criteria, one can use, for example, political and ideological criteria. Marx, too, used political and ideological criteria in addition to economic, since he made use of several class definitions.[88] Thus the rejection of the idea of a "ruling class" must be based on other arguments.

Another of Mills's arguments is that the notion of the "ruling class" does not allow for sufficient autonomy in decision-making in political questions, as well as the decision made by the military elite. Again one could object by referring to Wesolowski's analysis of the relationship between a ruling class and a power elite. This relationship allows different degrees of autonomy.

The most important argument, however, concerns the question of whether ownership of means of production is the most important means of power. In a society where technology contributes to the creation of large monopolylike corporations, *control* over the means of production is important, rather than ownership. Control and ownership can be united; however, control can also be exerted without ownership rights: through possession of technical knowledge, through controlling the recruitment to the top stratum, through defining the goals without interference from owners or controlling processes.

If "ruling class" is defined with the help of ownership of means of production, then the power elites which Mills describes do not form a "ruling class." If, however, one defines "ruling class" with the help of criteria, e.g., common interests, meaning common aspirations based upon common values and directed toward common goals, then there seem to be clear tendencies that the different elites together form a "ruling class."[89]

Mills maintains that the three power elites base their power on different means, namely, economic, political, and military. However, there is an intimate interaction between the elites and they often display common

[88] See, for a discussion of Marx's definitions of class, Israel, *Problems of Marxist Class Analysis*.

[89] J. K. Galbraith stresses, in his aforementioned book on *The New Industrial State*, the common goals of the technostructure and the military and administrative bureaucracy.

interests, though there may also be conflicting views and aspirations. In general, Mills is not pursuing a class analysis, but differentiates between the powerful elites which are supplemented by the powerless people forming the mass society.

Now this kind of analysis has been disputed by such people as David Riesman, who carries out an analysis of a different kind though on the same macrosociological level.[90] The differences between Mills's and Riesman's views have been summarized in a systematic way by Kornhauser.[91] We will use his comparison as a starting point. Mills's power structure consists of three levels: (1) a limited power elite at the top, (2) a middle level consisting of different interest groups and their representatives trying to influence the power elite, (3) the mass society consisting of the unorganized and powerless majority. For his part Riesman does not recognize the existence of a power elite. Therefore, his model consists of only two levels corresponding to Mills's second and third. Instead of a power elite, he maintains, there exist veto groups. These veto groups are organized interest groups, which try to advance their own interests and block the actions of other groups. There is no special power group. Rather, the different groups opposing each other form a system of countervailing powers, i.e., the power of a certain groups is counteracted by the power of other groups, and in this way a state of balance is achieved. Veto groups, in addition, direct great efforts toward the unorganized masses in order to get their support or to win them over for their goals.

The use of these two diverging power models leads to different consequences with regard to the analysis of the American social structure. Whereas Mills asserts that a concentration of power has occurred, Riesman maintains that power has been spread. Whereas Mills consequently asserts that a majority of decisions is taken by the same limited group, Riesman thinks that the content of the decisions to be made influences the choice of those who participate in decision-making processes. Riesman sees a danger in the possibility that power may be split among a multitude of groups, whereas Mills emphasizes the risk of centralization of power in a bureaucratic apparatus.

The differences between the analysis of Mills and Riesman depend to a large degree on the models of society which form the basis of their analyses. Riesman postulates a model of society which, according to traditional liberal values, assumes a balance created by countervailing powers constituted by opposed but not necessarily conflicting and antagonistic groups of classes. Mills's model does not view the social system as striving for balance. Instead he uses a polarization model where power is a zero-

[90] D. Riesman, *The Lonely Crowd* (Garden City: Doubleday Anchor Books, 1955).
[91] W. Kornhauser, " 'Power Elite' or 'Veto-Groups,' " in *Class, Status and Power*, ed. R. Bendix and S. Lipset (New York: The Free Press, 1966).

sum phenomenon, i.e., where the concentration of power in one group leads to the corresponding amount of powerlessness among the rest. The brief comparison between Mills's and Riesman's analyses emphasizes the role of postulative models of society for the development of a theory.

However, the problem of power and power distribution can and should be viewed from two angles: (1) *Who* has the positions and the means to make and to execute decisions? (2) *Which* inhibitions and restrictions are met by those who possess power positions and own the means of power? To what degree are those who make decisions subject to rules which delimit their power? To what degree are they forced to seek support for their decisions? To what extent do they need to cooperate with and need to compromise with certain groups?

Mills analyzes the power conditions existing in a centralized and bureaucratized political, economic, and military apparatus. Riesman directs his attention to the problems of control of those in power positions and the ways in which this control functions in a given social structure. In one respect, however, Riesman and Mills agree. The development of power conditions has favored a social structure in which the interest of large majorities in political problems has decreased, just as has their chances of exerting influence. It is this aspect—the developing of a mass society—which is of importance for the analysis of the problem of alienation.

THE MASS SOCIETY

Notions of the mass society presuppose a definition of "democracy" which emphasizes participation in political decision-making processes on a broad basis. The mass society means a deviation from a democratic ideal state in which popular participation is maximized. Mills defines democracy at one time in about the following way: Democracy implies that all those persons who in a direct way are affected by a certain decision have an effective chance of making their voices heard and are able to influence the decisions. This in turn means that all power is based on legal grounds and all who make decisions have to take public responsibility for them.[92]

Mills's explication is based upon the classical notion that all power in a democracy is vested in the people. For his analysis he distinguishes between the "public" and the "masses." According to his view· the transformation of the "public" into a "mass" is one of the most important changes which have occurred.

To understand the meaning of this process of transformation, one has to proceed from traditional liberal notions concerning democracy. Mills

[92] Mills, *The Sociological Imagination*, p. 188.

mentions four: First, individualism, which in the mass society has been substituted by collective economic and political forms. Second, the notion of peaceful and natural harmony of diverging interests, which create a state of balance. This has been substituted by class conflicts leading to organized pressure groups. The third notion concerns a rational human attitude, implying that all social action is based upon lengthy deliberations between individuals. In the mass society decisions are based upon the advice of experts, who in turn serve certain interests. *Rationality* as a consequence has become *rationalization* in the psychoanalytic sense of the term, i.e., explanations trying to legitimize actions. Fourth, there are notions that public opinion should form the basis of decisions and that those who make decisions should follow expressed public opinion. Such a public opinion does not exist in the mass society, and that which now is labeled as "public opinion" is created and directed by mass media.

One could argue against the ideal picture of a democracy in which the "public" has a ruling power. It is difficult to find a society in any period in which this ideal had been realized. But Mills does not make any such assumptions. Instead he speaks of tendencies in different directions. Instead of tendencies toward the realization of ideal democracy, the development now tends to go in the direction of these conditions which characterize the mass society. In the consequent argumentation Mills mentions four criteria or dimensions for judging the degree to which the mass society has already been established.

The first dimension concerns the relationship between opinion makers and opinion receivers. In the society analyzed by Mills the opinions of a speaker who in an impersonal way directs himself toward millions of listeners are often transmitted by mass media. Thus, opinion formation is a one-sided process.

The second dimension concerns the extent to which the opinions presented can be criticized or questioned. The structure of opinion leadership in modern society determines who can speak, when, and how much. In extreme cases, Mills says, mass media are monopolized and opinion receivers become completely passive.

The third dimension refers to the extent to which public opinion can influence decision-making processes and, in particular, such decisions as are of importance for a majority. The degree of influence of an individual depends on his placement in the power structure. Often influence is restricted to decisions concerning local issues.

Finally, the fourth problem concerns the degree to which institutionalized authority can exert control over the individual and carry out sanctions against him. At the one end of the dimensions there is individual autonomy and freedom of control. At the other end there is continuous supervision by a network of controllers and informers enforcing uniformity of behavior.

By analyzing society and by determining the values which a given society has on these four dimensions, one can find the degree to which a society has developed toward a totalitarian structure. Mills emphasizes that the American society had quite a long way to go in the direction of the totalitarian structure, the analysis being carried out in the beginnings of the fifties. However, the development of powerful, centralized bureaucracies weakens the influence of small groups, local organizations, and politicians in the middle range of the structure.

In addition, interest organizations such as trade unions have a tendency to develop more and more in the direction of bureaucratization. As a consequence social distance between the members of the organization and the leadership is created and increased. The members' influence is decreased, and their chances of influencing decision-making or of active participation of other kind are weakened.

More and more people become passive, and fewer and fewer obtain greater and greater power by occupying positions at the top of bureaucracies. In addition there is the effect of mass media. The mass media do more than transmit information for independent opinion formation. Through the media's mixing of information and values, a risk for manipulation of the individual is created—a manipulation which is subtle and of which people may not be aware. One important argument against the risk of manipulation is the longer school training and education which more and more people receive, and which ought to make them more critical and stimulate independent thinking. But, Mills maintains, schools are increasingly oriented toward that type of education which is important for the occupational life and which therefore in the first place satisfies the demands of those having leading positions in the power hierarchy. A more general training in liberal arts and an education for a general and critical political attitude has been subordinated to training in those fields which are "useful."

The tendencies toward the mass society are increased by the process of urbanization. People live in metropolitan areas without social contact with each other, anonymous and isolated. They meet each other in predetermined role-situations. Therefore, their interaction follows definite norms and to a large degree lacks the intimacy of personal contact. Man becomes a part of a large structure which does not provide for personal environment. The isolation and lack of personal contacts increases the individual's dependence on mass communication media. "But the man in the mass does not gain a transcending view from these media; instead he gets his experience stereotyped, and then he gets sunk further by that experience. He cannot detach himself in order to observe, much less to evaluate, what he is experiencing, much less what he is not experiencing."[93]

Everything becomes self-evident. The individual questions neither what he desires nor what he can achieve. He has lost his independence and, in addition, his desire for independence. His life is turned into conformity and is dominated by routine activities. He is not interested in rational analysis upon which action could be based, and he lacks the necessary preconditions for such action. The individual loses his interests in politics because he experiences his lack of influence.

This is the gloomy picture which Mills paints. The mass society and the power elites supplement each other.

The state of alienation which Mills describes and analyzes concerns the discrepancy between certain democratic ideals and the possibilities which society offers for their realization. It is the discrepancy between the potentialities a society has or the potentialities it should have if certain normative standards are applied and the factual way in which it develops. Thus Mills develops clearly a discrepancy-theory of alienation, in which the social structure is seen as an alienated structure—alienation from ideal states—and in which social processes are viewed as alienating processes. Thus, in this part of the theory, alienation—as differentiated from the theory of alienation developed in connection with the personality market —is a sociological and not a psychological theory. Clearly this variant of alienation theory presupposes a value system according to which actual social conditions can be judged. There is one important objection to this type of discrepancy theory. Since ideals per definition are such that they cannot be realized, there will always exist a discrepancy between ideals and reality. At the moment at which ideals would approach realization, new, more distant ideals would be created. Why then use discrepancy as a measure of alienation? Although Mills does not do this explicitly, the problem persists. Either there will always be alienation, because there will be no society free from social problems, nor one realizing an ideal state of affairs. Or, if one accepts this thesis, then alienation could be defined as a discrepancy which is "greater than the normal." However, defining a "normal" discrepancy is very difficult.

Like Marcuse, Mills keeps his analysis on a macrosociological level, analyzing society as a totality, but, contrary to Marcuse, his analysis is within a sociological frame of reference. Partly this is a consequence of the fact that he does not start from a normative theory of man. In the theories which were referred to, Mills is rarely interested in "human nature," though implicitly he has a theory of man, e.g., as an active, inde-

[93] Mills, *The Power Elite*, p. 322.

pendent, critical, participating being. But, in turn, this depends on the societal ideals on which he builds and which contain elements from the theoreticians of liberalism and democracy, but also certain Marxian elements. With this ideal as a basis he critically attacks the American society. In doing so, he follows the tradition of classical sociologists and their critical analysis of society. For him social criticism becomes a central sociological task. In this respect he differs in a positive way from that which has become so dominant in current sociology: the interest in details, in small problems, in technical aspects, etc., which leads to an abundance of trivial research and to a neglect of society as a totality. The sociological imagination does not see the whole for all the details it deals with and because of its determined attempt to be a positivistic science.

7
ALIENATION IN EMPIRICALLY ORIENTED SOCIOLOGY

INTRODUCTION

In current empirical sociology, e.g., American, the concept of alienation plays an important role. According to Nisbet,[1] the thesis concerning the alienation of the individual in the mass society has become nearly as prevalent as the doctrine concerning enlightened self-interest was generations ago.

In theoretically oriented writings concerning the problems of alienation in this empirically oriented sociology, one often finds reference to Marx and a theoretical affinity to his ideas.[2] There are, however, important differences between Marx and those who have today taken up the discussion regarding alienation.[3] In his theories Marx in a general way paints

[1] R. Nisbet, *The Quest for Community* (New York: Oxford University Press, 1953), p. 15.

[2] See, e.g., R. Blauner, *Alienation and Freedom* (Chicago: University of Chicago Press, 1964); *Man Alone*, ed. with an introduction by Eric and Mary Josephson (New York: Dell Publishing Co., 1962); E. Mizruchi, *Success and Opportunity* (New York: The Free Press, 1961).

[3] There is one analysis of the concept of alienation, as used by Marx, which deviates from the usual one. I am referring to L. Feuer, "What Is Alienation? The Career of a Concept," in *Sociology on Trial*, ed. M. Stein and A. Vidich (Englewood Cliffs: Prentice-Hall, 1963). Feuer asserts that the concept of alienation and theories of alienation in the writings of Feuerbach concerned the resistance of romanticist philosophy against sexual puritanism and the artificial life that was a consequence of these repressive attitudes. Feuer maintains that alienated man in this context means man's being alienated from his own body, i.e., from his nature, as a consequence of asceticism. He also asserts that the concept of alienation had the same meaning for Marx and that in his early writings he considered love and sexual activity as the source of man's experience of reality. Marx in Feuer's interpretation becomes a forerunner of psychoanalysis. Thus the socioeconomic theories of the young Marx are transformed into

his gloomy picture of capitalist society. His economic theory very often deals with detailed problems, whereas his sociological analysis often is carried out on a more general and abstract plane. The historical analysis again is performed in an "ideal-typical" way. Sociological problems are not always taken up in detail. For example, a very important question like the one concerning classes and the definition of the class concept is not found in one context but appears in different parts of his work. The third unfinished volume of *Capital* ends just as the analysis of the class concept begins.

In fact, an interesting contextual analysis shows that Marx did not use *one* class-concept, but at least six different ones, depending on the type of analysis he carried out and the type of problem he was interested in.[4] In his sociological theories Marx finds time both for polemics and for moral indignation. The latter is directed against the inhuman social system and is always implicit in all his sociological analyses.

Positivistic and empirically oriented sociology is at the outset much more careful. It tries anxiously to avoid large, sweeping generalizations and tries instead to anchor its theses in empirical data. This sociology is microsociology; it deals with definite, well-delimited problems but not with society at large. Sometimes research based upon this orientation has a tendency to exclusiveness. *One deals* with minor problems often in an intriguing way, but sometimes it may be difficult to discover the relevance of the problems for sociology as a social science. The German philosopher and sociologist Adorno once characterized this type of sociology as "sociology minus society."[5] An empirically oriented sociology can also mean that questions of methodology are considered more important than the problems to be studied. The consequence, then, will be that methods are allowed to determine the problems which are to be studied and not—as it ought to be—the other way round.

It would, however, be unjust to equate empirically oriented sociology— and this type of sociology I call "microsociology," lacking a better expres-

psychosexual ones. Feuer mobilizes some few quotations where Marx speaks about love in relation to alienation, but disregards the continuous reference to *work as central human activity* and a special ideal of work from which man is alienated. In addition to the numerous quotations presented before, let me just add a final one: "In the real world of practice, this self-alienation can only be expressed in the *real, practical relation of man to his fellow man*. The medium through which alienation occurs is itself a practical one. Through *alienated labor*, therefore, man . . . produces the relation between himself and other men (*Mega I.3*, p. 91; *my italics*).

[4] See B. Lindensjö, "Marx's klassbegrepp," *Häften för Kritiska Studier* I, No. 4 (1964), 20–27; and J. Israel, "Problems of Marxist Class Analysis," *Acta Sociologica* 1970, 13, 11–29.

[5] T. Adorno, "Sociology and Psychology," *New Left Review* No. 46 (1967), p. 78.

sion—although within empirical sociology one can find interesting theoretical approaches. These theories can often be characterized as "theories of the middle range."[6] Often they have a high grade of precision which is preceded by attempts to clarify and analyze the concepts. In this way one can avoid dealing with pseudo-problems. The analysis of empirical data certainly does not become less complicated, but more unambiguous.

We have previously shown that the concept of alienation is not unambiguous. In fact, usually it covers two completely different categories of phenomena. One comprises social processes, the other psychological states which need not necessarily be consequences of these social processes.

The psychological conditions or states play a relatively unimportant role in the theories of Marx. The emphasis in his theories is on social processes and their effect. In empirically oriented sociology, however, a central role is played by the psychological state of alienation, the individual's estrangement. The individual's experience of his own situation is the object of investigation against the background of sociological phenomena. In addition, more or less clearly expressed values and other types of presuppositions constitute the foundation for the description and analysis of the psychological as well as the sociological conditions. The social criticism, which is of so much importance to Marx, disappears almost completely in these studies. The social structure of society is often accepted in its current shape. The possibilities of the individual for social adjustment are the starting point of the theories concerning alienation, where alienation meaning "the experience of estrangement" often is perceived as being equal to lack of social adjustment. This, however, does not necessarily mean that social adjustment is valued as something positive and lack of adjustment as something negative, even if such evaluations often can be found implicitly.

If we wish to apply our scheme of categorization mentioned in chapter 1, we could say that in empirically oriented sociology, theories that deal with the problem of alienation are usually society-oriented. This is because, among other factors, they do not contain so many points of views which are critical to existing society and its social structure.

In the next section we will start with a discussion of Seeman's theoretical approach which plays an important role in the analysis of the concept of alienation. We will also discuss the application of this concept to problems of modern industry referring to several studies, among them the one by Blauner and by the Swedish sociologist Dahlström. The next aspect that we will discuss is the theoretical development of the concept of alienation carried out by the Finnish sociologist Allardt. Finally we will show how

[6] R. Merton, *Social Theory and Social Structure* (Glencoe, Ill.: The Free Press, 1967).

his points of view are applied in a study by Mizruchi, which leads to the conclusion of this chapter.[7]

FIVE PSYCHOLOGICAL DIMENSIONS OF ALIENATION (SEEMAN'S THEORY)

In Seeman's opinion, the subjective experience of alienation which usually has been discussed in current theories is not a uniform experience but can be analyzed along five dimensions. Seeman calls these dimensions experiences of powerlessness, of meaninglessness, of isolation, of normlessness, and of self-estrangement.

In analyzing these five dimensions, I shall attempt to find how they can be connected to Marx's theories to which Seeman refers. The analysis will also consider other sociological theories and the connection with them. Finally, I will try to show how these dimensions can be applied to the "industrial worker" and his social position.[8]

POWERLESSNESS

Powerlessness refers to "the notion of alienation as it originated in the Marxian view of the worker's condition in capitalist society," says Seeman.[9] He defines powerlessness as an *expectancy* held by an individual that he cannot determine the outcome of his behavior or reinforcements he seeks. Seeman remarks that he does not think "that the expectancy usage is as radical a departure from Marxian legacy as it may appear."[10] However, according to my previous interpretation, Marx did not deal with psychological states, but social processes. Seeman, however, transfers the analysis from a sociological to a social-psychological level.

A person feels powerless in the "modern industrial society" when he realizes that he is unable to influence his own destiny in the social system to which he belongs. Here "social system" may refer to the society as a whole or to certain limited social organizations, for example, a company in which the person is employed. Seeman's definition describes powerlessness as a feeling within a person that the probability that he can influence

---

[7] M. Seeman, "On the Meaning of Alienation," *American Sociological Review* XXVI (1961), 753–58; Blauner, *Alienation and Freedom*; E. Dahlström et al., "Arbetsanpassning," in *Teknisk förändring och arbetsanpassning* (Stockholm: Bokförlaget Prisma, 1966); E. Allardt, *Samhällstruktur och sociala spänningar* (Tammerfors: Söderström & Co., 1965); Mizruchi, *Success and Opportunity*.

[8] Blauner, *Alienation and Freedom*.

[9] M. Seeman, "On the Meaning of Alienation," 784.

[10] Ibid., 785.

the satisfaction of his needs by his own acts is very low. Seeman's definition is rather vague, but it can be given a more concrete form by taking, as an example, a worker in an industrial enterprise. He may feel powerless when he feels that he is controlled by others, without being able himself to influence them. But powerlessness can be experienced in other relations besides relations with other people. It can also occur if the technological system, for example, work at a conveyor belt, makes it impossible for him to exert any influence over the speed of the work and the operations or motions which he must carry out. The individual fails to see himself as an active being, experiencing himself as a passive object, lacking a will of its own. This aspect of powerlessness is closely connected to Marx's analysis of the process of the division of labor and its consequences. Seeman points out that this powerless-dimension approaches Marx's concept of man as alienated because he and his labor have been transformed into commodities, others having at their disposal the means of production used by him in his work. We can summarize the aspect of powerlessness as it may be applied to the industrial worker, as follows: [11] The worker is a highly mechanized industrial enterprise first feels himself to be powerless when he sees that others have the power of decision over him, especially as far as his work is concerned. Second, the feeling of powerlessness occurs when the worker is unable to *influence* the decision-making processes of the leadership of the enterprise. Third, it occurs when the individual has no influence over his employment and the terms of his employment. Finally, the feeling of powerlessness may occur when the worker is unable to influence or control the work process, for instance, the speed of the conveyor belt.

Powerlessness among the employees holding a subordinate position is counterbalanced by a concentration of power among the leaders. A special problem, which I shall not take up here, is the situation existing between actual, i.e., objective powerlessness, and the subjective experience of this. Another interesting question is to what extent does active participation in a trade union reduce this feeling of powerlessness?

There is one problem which is really not touched in this description. Why do workers experience powerlessness? One could think of a person being completely satisfied by having no power and no influence on his conditions of work. As Dahlström[12] et al. point out, the hypothesis concerning the powerlessness of the industrial worker presupposes certain assumptions concerning his motivational structure. One has to assume certain needs, e.g., one of self-determination and self-control. If these needs are frustrated, then powerlessness will be experienced. Thus assump-

---

[11] Blauner, *Alienation and Freedom*, p. 2.
[12] Dahlström, *Teknisk förändring och arbetsanpassning*, p. 127.

tions concerning experiences of powerlessness and the other dimensions to be discussed presuppose a certain image of man, especially of his motivational structure. These needs are usually learned and lead to certain expectancies.[13] The discrepancy between expectancies and the objective situation then creates the postulated experiences of powerlessness.

MEANINGLESSNESS

Seeman calls the second dimension meaninglessness. This is experienced when the individual no longer understands the functioning of the social organization of which he is a part. As a result, the individual can no longer predict the consequences of his own actions, or he fails to understand the meaning of his actions.

Once again, there is a connection with Marx's ideas regarding the consequences of the process of division of labor, when one tries to apply this experience-dimension.[14] The more differentiated the division of labor becomes within an enterprise, the fewer the operations carried out by a single worker. The more complicated the whole labor-process becomes, the less the worker has a conception of the whole. Therefore, he loses insight and understanding, and experiences his labor as something meaningless. Only those people who hold more elevated positions in the hierarchy of the enterprise are able to have a conception of the labor-process as a whole, and see its complexity. According to this concept, work becomes meaningless when: (1) the individual has to repeat the same hand movements day after day, when he becomes "drowned in his daily routine"; (2) when the worker is not allowed to work with the whole product, but only with parts of it, so that often he never actually sees the finished products, and understands neither their construction nor their function; (3) when the responsibility of the worker for the work he undertakes is either limited or nonexistent.

Again the hypothesis concerning the experience of meaninglessness presupposes certain needs or certain ideals concerning work. Dahlström et al. talk of a need for meaningful work. Meaningfulness must be established by different factors, one of these being the type of product produced: "A unique (individual) product as a ship or a house demands work being inherently meaningful," the authors assert[15] without really arguing for such a surprising statement. The other two factors postulated to influence meaninglessness are the organization of the working process and demands for occupational skills.

---

[13] Seeman, "On the Meaning of Alienation."
[14] Blauner, *Alienation and Freedom*, p. 3.
[15] Dahlström, *Teknisk förändring*, p. 130.

NORMLESSNESS

The third aspect Seeman calls *normlessness.* The concept is connected to the theories developed by Emile Durkheim. As mentioned in chapter 5, Durkheim analyzed social situations in which the social norms that regulate the moral behavior of the individual broke down. However, "moral" is seen as a very wide concept. In a work situation, normlessness (according to this definition of the concept) may lead to the breaking down of the "natural solidarity" which exists between workers.

Seeman undoubtedly has some connection to Durkheim, but he gives a somewhat different content to the concept of "normlessness." In doing so, he connects himself to Robert Merton,[16] who has analyzed various types of social deviance. Assume that a person has definite social values and goals, for example to succeed, to climb the social ladder, to make a career for himself. Consider, also, that he is unable to reach these goals in a legal way. This may be due to certain lacks in his own personality, or to a social structure which allows only those persons who belong to certain social classes to succeed, while those who belong to other given classes are not given access to those means which are necessary to achieve success. If such a person identifies with the social values and goals, he may try to reach generally accepted goals, using illegal means. For Merton a great deal of criminal behavior, organized crime in particular, is the expression of a situation in which man has accepted social goals, but lacks legitimate means to reach them. Therefore, according to Seeman, normlessness is the experiencing of the inability to reach socially acceptable and desirable goals through those channels which are accepted by society, or by the social organizations to which the individual belongs.

There is another aspect of normlessness. The industrial society cannot function if the worker has not learned a work-moral, i.e., learned that he should "work in the sweat of his brow." For the individual, labor must be seen as something self-evident and not simply as a means of satisfying other needs. Such a conception is weakened through monotonous, routine labor, which makes the working hours a necessary evil, leisure becoming the only part of man's life in which he can experience satisfaction. Thus, the experience of normlessness can also reveal itself in the feeling that work is no longer a goal in itself.

Finally, the concept of normlessness has a third and more specific aspect.[17] Assume that in a modern industrial concern the main goal of the leadership is that the employees work as effectively as possible, in order to create maximum profit for the enterprise. The goals of the

[16] Merton, *Social Theory and Social Structure.*
[17] Blauner, *Alienation and Freedom.*

employees do not necessarily tally with those of the company. They require good working conditions, high wages, and satisfying social conditions. If the goals of the employees and the leaders do not agree with each other, or are in opposition, conflict will result, especially as far as the social norms regarding the carrying out of the job, speed, etc., are concerned. Seen from the frame of reference of the leadership, the employee's behavior may be considered as the expression of normlessness. Therefore, the concept of normlessness presupposes, first, the acceptance of certain goals and, second, the acceptance of certain norms or types of behavior to reach these goals.

ISOLATION

Seeman calls the fourth aspect of his theory of alienation isolation. This is an extremely vague concept, used to denote many different phenomena. Seeman tries to make it more precise by connecting it to the distinction between goals and means, which has already been referred to. An alienated person who experiences normlessness accepts the goals, but it not concerned about using legal or legitimate means to reach these goals. A person who experiences isolation has gone a step further. He does not accept the goals, whether they are societal or limited to the social organizations to which he belongs.

According to Merton, when a person no longer accepts the goals of the social system, there are two alternative reactions. One concentrates on means, and in a very restricted way tries to cling fast to these, the result being a sort of rigid ritualism. An example would be an official in a bureaucratic organization who rigidly adheres to the letter of the rules and regulations, even if by so doing he hinders the organization from achieving its goals. Such a rigid, ritualistic state may be seen as a reaction to the psychological discomfort which results from the inability to identify oneself with socially accepted goals. The other alternative is that the individual experiences his negative attitude to the socially accepted goals so strongly that he retreats from his social roles and isolates himself.

In this way, certain conditions of mental illness may be seen as a consequence of the alienation of the individual. Isolation thus obviously presupposes a need for affiliation or belongingness.[18]

SELF-ESTRANGEMENT

The fifth and final aspect which Seeman takes up is called self-estrangement. To say that a person has become self-estranged presupposes some

18 Dahlström, *Teknisk förändring*, p. 19.

conception of what constitutes self. If, as does Marx in his early works, one considers that activity is a central aspect of human nature, and that the individual realizes himself through creative work, then the person who no longer experiences his work as something satisfying is alienated, in the meaning of self-estranged. This also applies to other activities which are important for the individual. They are undertaken only under duress, or, if other ways of satisfying needs can be achieved, as a means of reaching them. Seeman defines self-estrangement as a condition in which the various activities of the individual are no longer a goal in themselves, but are carried out with a view to economic or other rewards, which are achieved by means of these activities.

In a modern industrial concern, this form of alienation would mean that the individual is not interested in his work, and is in no way involved in it. The lack of involvement would be noticable by the fact, among others, that interest is concentrated on the time factor, rather than on the work itself. The individual is not interested in what he does, or how he does it, but only in the amount of time it takes and the speed with which he is able to pass the time. Involvement in work is also dependent on the opportunities the individual has of experiencing his activity as meaningful and of exercising control over it. Therefore, this aspect of the experience of alienation is closely joined to meaninglessness and powerlessness.

Dahlström et al. make this a basic point. Referring to Etzioni[19] they speak of involvement in work vs. work seen as instrumental for other purposes, e.g., acquiring the money necessary for leisure. Consequently they define alienation as the "absence of involvement in work."[20] This raises an important question. Is involvement in work dependent on psychological factors, e.g. a certain need-structure, or is it in the first case dependent on the existent social structure with certain conditions of ownership and especially with the distribution of power? We will return to this question later on in this chapter and in the following chapters.

SOME THEORETICAL PROBLEMS

Seeman's theory is social-psychological, not sociological. It is concerned with the experience, not with social processes. The problem is, how did Seeman choose these five dimensions, is there a relation between them, and if so, what is the relation?

We do not receive a direct answer to our questions from Seeman's presentation. He simply points out that "the concept of alienation has been

---

[19] A. Etzioni, *A Comparative Analysis of Complex Organizations* (New York: The Free Press, 1961).

[20] Dahlström, *Teknisk förändring*, p. 130.

used in five different basic ways,"[21] and that he has tried to define these. Up to now, our analysis suggests that Seeman's statement is not entirely correct. Even if one disregards the fact that he does not deal with sociological processes, the five psychological dimensions represent a selection. Seeman presents a preliminary classification, but not a systematic typology, as the logical relations between the various dimensions are not stated.[22] He does not account for the way in which these dimensions have been chosen. One possibility is that he has searched the relevant literature and made semantic analyses of the various ways of using the terms which he found. Another possibility is that Seeman took as his starting point a psychological theory, and then tried to clarify the various meanings which the concept of alienation can have when it is put in relationship to this theory. I suggest that Seeman chose the latter method.

He starts from two concepts used in the psychology of learning: "expectancy" and "reward."[23] His idea seems to be that the individual has definite expectations that his behavior will yield a certain reward or satisfaction of needs. When these expectations are constantly frustrated, Seeman says that the individual feels himself to be powerless. In that case an important problem is, Why does the individual fail to change his expectations or to find new goals which give reward, or both? In other words, under what conditions does the individual continue to retain the same expectations and goals, despite the fact that he experiences powerlessness, and under what conditions does he change his expectations and goals and avoid the feeling of powerlessness?

Seeman does not take up these problems, though in my opinion they are important. A worker at a conveyer belt, for instance, may have the expectation that he will be able to influence his working situation, perhaps by exerting influence over the speed of the belt. When he becomes convinced that this is impossible, he is faced with two alternatives: he may look for new work, or he may relinquish his aspirations and try to explain away his changed attitude by saying, for example, that the wages are so high that it is worthwhile continuing the job, despite the disadvantages, or by saying that it is difficult to find another job.

But there is a third alternative: he may remain where he is without relinquishing his expectations of influencing his working situation. In this he may receive support from a political conviction, or he may participate in trade union activity or in social interaction with his workmates. Perhaps only if he chooses the third alternative one really can talk about alienation. In the other cases it may be just lack of satisfaction in work (see page

[21] Seeman, "On the Meaning of Alienation," 783.

[22] Allardt, *Samhällsstruktur*, p. 81.

[23] Seeman, "On the Meaning of Alienation," 783.

187). Alienation, as defined here, presupposes a discrepancy between the expectations of the individual and the way in which the social system functions, which prevents him from attaining the goals of his expectations.

This analysis is supported by the results of a study of a mental hospital undertaken by Israel and Johansson.[24] The attitudes of the personnel to the goals of the wards were studied. Goals were divided into custodial and therapeutic, and the actual goals of the various wards were then judged, using objective criteria. The results showed that people with a therapeutic goal who worked in a ward with custodial goals, and vice versa, were those who felt themselves to be powerless. Those persons whose personal attitudes were congruent with the goals of the wards did not feel this powerlessness.

The second problem concerns the question of whether or not there is an association among the five dimensions which allows them to be fitted into a structure. One might investigate which of the five dimensions show higher correlations with each other, than with the rest. Another possibility is that the dimensions might be ordered in the form of a cumulative scale. A third possibility is that their psychological structure be studied. One might, for instance, assume that the experience of meaninglessness causes the experience of powerlessness, and that this in its turn leads to normlessness, i.e., that the individual feels that by using legitimate means he is unable to reach the goals of his expectations. In its turn, this may mean that the individual relinquishes his goals and so experiences self-estrangement. All these are only ideas as to how one might further develop Seeman's theory.

One of Seeman's explicit aims is to render the concept of alienation more useable for empirical research.

An empirical theory that wishes to describe or explain social conditions must formulate its propositions in such a way that it is possible to specify these conditions under which the theory holds. In addition, in order to be able to put forward testable hypotheses, one must limit the theory. Later we shall discuss Seeman's theory as applied to the area of work in a society with a highly developed technology.

ALIENATION IN MODERN INDUSTRY (BLAUNER'S AND GOLDTHORPE'S RESEARCH)

Blauner[25] has employed Seeman's scheme in an analysis of the situation of American industrial workers. His contention is that even if few American

---

[24] J. Israel & S. Johansson, "Kustodialism och alienation bland vårdsavdelningspersonalen på ett mentalsjukhus," *Sociologisk Forskning* II (1965), 63–77.

[25] Blauner, *Alienation and Freedom.*

sociologists today consider that the working class in the U.S. is a potentially revolutionary force, in accordance with Marxist ideas, theories of the alienation of workers in the work process are nonetheless valid. In his view, this is due to the effect of modern technology on the worker. This particularly concerns the increasing division of labor within the enterprise. Blauner says: "Today, most social scientists would say that alienation is not a consequence of capitalism per se but of employment in the large-scale organizations and impersonal bureaucracies that pervade all industrial societies."[26]

If, like Blauner, one rejects the idea that alienation is a consequence of the capitalist mode of production, it is possible to put forward at least two hypotheses: (1) It is wrong to assume that the worker must be either alienated or nonalienated. Instead one should state the conditions under which a worker can be alienated. (2) There exists a structural differentiation within modern industry, which means that certain conditions can be assumed to be more alienating than others. These are the factors which must be specified.

TECHNOLOGY, THE DIVISION OF LABOR, SOCIAL ORGANIZATION,
AND ECONOMIC STRUCTURE

Blauner indicates four factors which are of great importance in the shaping of the work process. The first is technology, which varies in different branches of industry. Technology refers to the machine system, the degree and extent of mechanization, and the technical knowledge and ability which is demanded. Three factors decide the type of technology used: (1) the extent to which technical and scientific knowledge has been able to be exploited, in the manufacturing processes, (2) the economic and technical resources which a given enterprise has at its disposal, (3) the products being manufactured.

In his analysis Blauner compares four industries using different forms of technology. The first was a printing firm, with a great variety of products and where, in addition, there still remained some work requiring craftsmen. This meant that the work process had not entirely become a standardized, routine activity. For handsetters, for instance, the work was quite varied.

The second enterprise belonged to the textile industry, with spinning and weaving as its chief work processes. The main task of the workers was to look after the machines.

The third enterprise belonged to the motor industry; it was characterized by large conveyer belts and a highly advanced division of the work

[26] Ibid., p. 3.

process into simple operations, most of which could be carried out by an unskilled worker.

The fourth enterprise, finally, was a chemical industry, more specifically an oil refinery, and this employed the most advanced technology. To a very great extent, automation had been introduced into the work process. With the exception of those employees concerned with repair, the main task of the workers was supervision of the control panels, an easy but not very varied job. However, it was a job which involved a good deal of responsibility.

These four enterprises used by Blauner in his research, represent four branches of industry utilizing different kinds of technology. Variation in the degree of mechanization is particularly noticeable. The printing trade had the lowest degree of mechanization. The oil refinery, on the other hand, had already replaced a mechanized production process with automation.

Technology affects the workers' opportunities of controlling the work processes. It affects the structure of the work groups. Finally, it affects leadership and the formation of leadership.

The second factor indicated by Blauner is the process of the division of labor, i.e., the ways in which one work process is divided up into sub-operations, and how these, in their turn, are carried out by the workers. Technology sets certain limits to the division of labor, but, at a given technological level, the process may assume a variety of shapes.

The four enterprises studied by Blauner illustrate different forms of the division of labor. While technology affects the aspect of powerlessness, Blauner asserts that the process of the division of labor affects the experience of meaninglessness.

The third factor he takes in consideration is the social organization of the enterprise. This can be analyzed with regard to the degree of bureaucratization which has been reached by an enterprise. In bureaucratic organizations, formal rules and methods tend to replace informal and personal social relations. According to Blauner, the printing works and the textile industry are less bureaucratized than the motor industry and oil refinery. He does not say to what extent this may depend on the size of the enterprise in question. Therefore, he says traditional relations are more strongly anchored in the first two industries than in the latter two.

Finally, the fourth factor is the economic structure, which expresses itself in such factors as market competition, concentration within industry, the profit margin, rate of growth, etc. In his view, these factors affect workers' alienation, so that when an enterprise gains high profits and has good opportunities for development, the employees are "less subjected to intensive pressure, more likely to be free from fears of unemployment and to have opportunities to advance."[27] It is not quite clear if Blauner intends this as a postulate or as a hypothesis. We shall return to that later. The fact that these four factors vary in different branches of industry, and within different enterprises in the same branch, means that every industry, so to speak, creates its own special type of worker. Therefore, according to Blauner, it is impossible to study alienation as a general phenomenon. In addition, he makes another limitation by saying that conscious actions on the part of the leadership of the enterprise, and personality factors among the workers, affect alienation.

SOME RESULTS

The main empirical data for Blauner's research was mostly from interview data collected by Elmo Roper in 1947 for the magazine *Fortune*. He complemented his figures with some case studies. Thus, Blauner's data are relatively old. In addition, the data were not collected with a view to undertaking studies of alienation, but in order to study attitudes to work. But is lack of satisfaction at work the same as alienation? (Mills, for instance, maintains that the attempt to reduce alienation to the degree of satisfaction at work misses the main point; the fact that the individual becomes a commodity, an object, i.e., that which has here been termed *reification*, instead is important, see p. 187).

Blauner largely finds what he expects to find. Degree of dissatisfaction and lack of morale in work is found to vary within different branches of industry. The printing workers, both printers and typesetters, had the most secure position, partly because of the position of the trade unions. The level of technology, which allowed some work of a craftsmanlike nature to remain, gave them relative freedom and control over the work process. There the workers did not complain much about the pressures of the work process. Many of them thought that they were able to try out their own ideas, and only a very small percent complained of tiredness. In the work itself, the experience of meaninglessness was reduced because the work was more varied. Nevertheless, 36 percent were prepared to change their job, given the opportunity to do so. The textile workers had much less control over their work and were subject to considerable pressure. They complained that they had to work too quickly, and a third of them thought that their work was tiring, etc.

In the motor industry, Blauner found an even higher degree of alienation. In fact the car worker is, according to his view, the prototype of the alienated worker. Such workers have very little control over the techno-

[27] Ibid., p. 10.

logical environment. They are ruled by the conveyor belt, over which they can exert no influence. Division of labor is so advanced that most of the jobs are of the same character, a few of them demanding absolutely identical operations. In addition, the motor industry is organized into large units, which results in the bureaucratization of the social structure.

Those who were most satisfied were the employees of the oil refinery. They experienced a high degree of security. The work itself demands more mental than physical exertion, and the workers, who were highly trained, had quite a large degree of freedom. The work is not pressing and has no monotonous rhythm. The worker himself is able to decide how often, or at what intervals, he will control the production processes, although he has no influence over it, this being automatic.

Blauner's data consist mainly of informal descriptions of the work process, of the conditions of work and employment, and of the economic position of the enterprises, etc. These data are complemented by questions regarding attitude to the work, formulated in a research tradition oriented to problems of work satisfaction. He undertakes no real tests of hypotheses concerning the connection between the four sociological factors—namely, technology, division of labor, social structure, and economic structure— and the various psychological dimensions of alienation. This is largely because the interview questions do not measure the various dimensions of alienation, though Blauner tries to use questions concerning satisfaction in work for this. The most interesting aspect of his study is the detailed description of the work processes in various industries. It presents a vital picture of the extreme variation which lies behind the expression "work conditions in modern industry."

A COMPARISON WITH EARLIER DISCUSSIONS OF ALIENATION

A central thesis in this book is that theories of alienation presuppose theories, or at least conceptions, about man and his nature, his expectations, needs, and values.

Blauner adopts a traditional notion of the meaning of work, in particular that work offers the chance for self-realization. On this point he is fairly explicit: "I assume that work which permits autonomy, responsibility, social connection, and self-actualization furthers the dignity of the human individual, whereas work without these characteristics limits the development of personal potential and is therefore negatively valued."[28]

Even if the factors which he mentions are vague, and therefore problematic, it is nevertheless correct to say that Blauner takes his starting

[28] Ibid., footnote p. 15.

point in values. Indirectly, these values involve a critical, negative attitude to the technological development of industrialized society, and to the social and economic conditions existing in such a society.

Our statement that Blauner takes his starting point in values can be interpreted in at least three ways, each having different consequences. One interpretation is that Blauner personally accepts as positive the evaluation of work as something which allows autonomy, responsibility, etc., and feels that men should strive after such work. This interpretation is not very likely. The second interpretation is that Blauner's theory recognizes as an integral part of human nature the striving after work which fulfills the conditions mentioned above. However, I doubt that a sociologist with an empirical, positivist orientation would make such assumptions about human nature, at least not in an explicit way. The third and most likely interpretation—most likely because it is in accord with the "sociological picture" of man—is that Blauner means that man in our culture learns to place a high value on work which allows him to realize himself in a special meaning. In consequence, then, it is the impossibility of satisfying those expectations resulting from learned values which leads to the experience of alienation.

However, Blauner seems also to assume that not all people have learned these values to the same extent. He points out that all people do not demand work which can lead to self-realization, in the meaning which has been given to this term. In his analysis of the experience of powerlessness among workers in the textile industry, he points out that, from an "objective" point of view, the technological conditions and the division of labor should cause intense feelings of powerlessness. In spite of this, he says that this rarely happens, maintaining that this depends on the following fact: "Textile workers have been drawn largely from traditional elements of society—the foreign-born, rural southerners, women, and the uneducated. . . . Workers with traditional orientation do not value control and self-expression as much as do modern industrial workers; the absence of these factors therefore does not result in felt self-estrangement."[29]

For that reason, he introduces the individual's level of aspiration with regard to those factors which give a positive value to the work as an "intervening variable."

This is interesting. He has had to choose between two alternative explanations when there was no association between his postulated social conditions and subjective experience of alienation. (1) He could have questioned whether the social factors (technology, division of labor, etc.) are sufficient or relevant variables. He fails to do this, and we shall return

[29] Ibid., p. 80.

to this problem later. (2) He chooses the explanation which is presented here, i.e., to introduce further psychological variables.

This brings with it several assumptions of which some, to say the least, are dubious. The introduction of a variable "level of aspiration with regard to opportunities for self-realization" excludes the interpretation that the need for self-realization through work is part of "human nature." Instead, it gives some support to our third interpretation, that these values regarding self-realization are learned. Blauner seems to be of the opinion that such learning occurs in special environments: in highly developed urban societies, though not, for instance, in the southern states, i.e., in the "underdeveloped" countryside environment. Does this mean, for example, that small-holders or independent farmers outside the industrial tradition would not award high value to "work which allows autonomy, responsibility," etc.—that they would not appreciate the value of being able themselves to decide their speed of working?

Further, it appears that he does not think that high aspirations with regard to the character of the work are to be found among people with a traditional attitude. What is meant by "traditional"? One meaning glimpsed in earlier alienation theories is in contrast to that which Blauner appears to employ. In these theories, the "traditional" attitude of the craftsman to work is seen as nonalienated, in contrast to the attitude of "modern man."

Why is it that industrial workers, who have accustomed themselves to working under monotonous and routine conditions in bureaucratic organizations, should have developed these aspirations?

It is, perhaps, that man who has not lived in an industrialized environment possesses the same aspirations, but either is unable to verbalize them or is resigned and therefore lowers his aspirations?

Quite clearly it is not sufficient merely to introduce psychological variables such as level of aspirations, if at the same time one is not able to say how these variables are related to the basic assumption regarding learned needs and values. With the help of a diagram, Figure 6, we will now summarize Blauner's theory of alienation.

SF refers to sociological factors of which Blauner, as previously indicated, mentions four: technology, division of labor, social organization, and economic structure. These are affected by an "intervening variable," Pl, which means the policy of the leadership of the enterprise, i.e., its conscious attempts to affect the social variables. SV refers to social values which are learned and which in their turn have a nonspecified relation to LA, i.e., the level of aspirations of the individual. These are looked on as intervening variables which affect PS, i.e., the psychological states. (We have taken only four, as Blauner excludes "normlessness.") SF is seen as independent and PS as the dependent variable. There are no feedback

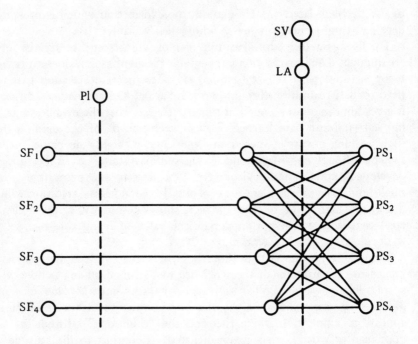

Figure 6. Diagrammatic representation of Blauner's conceptual frame of alienation.

mechanisms. Nor are there the social processes, as in Figure 3 (see page 54). This model is much simpler than that presented in Figure 3.

ARE THE CONDITIONS OF OWNERSHIP OF NO IMPORTANCE?

We shall take up yet another point in Blauner's theory. He introduces "economic structure" as the independent variable. But this variable does not include those factors which Marx saw as the most important in the "economic structure" and as a central factor in the growth of alienation: the conditions of ownership. This is not because Blauner is unfamiliar with Marxist theories. On the contrary, he discusses the association between alienation and the private ownership of the means of production.

His reasoning can be summarized as follows: Industrial workers are most interested in concrete questions involving employment and control over the work processes, but they are less concerned with what Blauner considers to be the more abstract aspects of powerlessness, i.e., who owns the means of production and therefore has power over the workers. He puts forward two arguments for this: (1) While the possibilities of controlling the work processes vary from industry to industry, the conditions of ownership remain constant. Normally, therefore, the employees do not develop expectations for gaining influence in this area, Blauner asserts.[30]

The first argument means that expectations are affected only, or mainly, by those actual conditions which vary, but not by those which are constant, because comparisons can be made only under variable conditions. But he misses one important point. Constant conditions can be compared with conditions in a hypothetical future. The individual's expectations may be affected by his political ideology and his view of what a future society should be like by his utopian ideals.

(2) "Orthodox marxism," Blauner says, "saw the separation from the means of production as the central fact of capitalism, the inevitable consequence of which would be the worker's general alienation from society. This has not happened: manual workers have required only steady jobs, reasonable wages, and employee benefits to put down at least moderate stakes in society and industry."[31]

Of course, Blauner adds that the fact that the means of production are not owned by workers perhaps unconsciously affects the worker's alienation, in the form of feelings of powerlessness; but he then goes on to discuss other aspects of powerlessness.

Blauner may be right, but he can never know this if he does not investigate the attitudes of the workers to the conditions of ownership. The interesting aspect of this argument is that it is presented in a rather categorical form, almost as a postulate. The consequence is that, in a possible empirical investigation, the question of whether or not the conditions of ownership affect the experience of alienation is neglected. In an interview study, the answers received depend on the questions asked. In addition, there is no chance of studying one's predictions if those predictions are not formulated as testable hypotheses. The example can perhaps be taken as an indication of how even empirically oriented science depends on values and above all on those values that are dominant in the society in which the scientist lives. The next example indicates that this may have severe consequences for sociologists in particular.

A STUDY IN AN ENGLISH MOTOR INDUSTRY

One of Goldthorpe's studies,[32] which took place at Vauxhall car factory in Luton, England, illuminates some of the problems which are discussed here.

---

[30] Ibid., p. 17.

[31] Ibid.

[32] J. H. Goldthorpe, "Attitudes and Behavior of Car Assembly Workers: A Deviant Case and a Theoretical Critique," *The British Journal of Sociology* XVII (1966), 227–44.

Goldthorpe investigated a random sample of a hundred workers. These formed 79 percent of the whole random sample, so that dropout is rather large. All worked on a conveyer belt.

Goldthorpe maintains that car workers are one of the work groups most often the subject of research, and he presents an impressive list of such investigations. This is because in car factories the workers are employed at a conveyer belt, which is conceived of as the classic symbol of oppression by the machine in our industrialized age.[33] Therefore, the car worker has become the prototype for the worker who is estranged from himself. It is precisely this that Goldthorpe questions. He believes that too much emphasis has been placed on the effects that technology has on the attitudes and feelings of the workers. He maintains that too little emphasis has been placed on the worker's adjustment to his job, asking why it is that many workers prefer to work at a conveyor belt, even if other possibilities are offered.

The workers studied by Goldthorpe were not at all satisfied with the work itself. They complained of the monotony and had a purely instrumental attitude to their work: for them, it was, above all, a means of achieving certain outside goals. Goldthorpe says that in this respect the results support Marx's thesis: that work is in itself no longer capable of satisfying a need, and can mainly serve as means for satisfying needs outside the working situation. It may be added that Blauner agrees with this thesis. For him, however, the instrumental attitude to work is the expression of self-estrangement.[34] Goldthorpe, in turn, has a central hypothesis that deviates from Blauner's theory. He maintains that the instrumental orientation is not a *consequence* of the technological shape of the work, but rather that the workers sought the job because they had a strongly instrumental orientation. In other words: the instrumental orientation, to the degree that it is the expression of self-estrangement, is seen as an independent not a dependent variable. The workers did not become alienated due to the conditions of work, but were already alienated when they sought these jobs: "If, therefore, these workers are to be considered as 'alienated,' the roots of their alienation must be sought not merely in the technological character of the plants in which they are now employed, but more fundamentally, in those aspects of the wider society which generate their tremendous drive for economic advancement and their disregard for the costs of this through the impoverishment of their working lives."[35]

Goldthorpe does not look upon the workers' alienation as the consequence of purely technological conditions, but as the consequence of

[33] C. R. Walker and R. H. Guest, *The Man on the Assembly Line* (Cambridge: Harvard University Press, 1952).

[34] Blauner, *Alienation and Freedom*, p. 119.

[35] Goldthorpe, "Attitudes and Behavior."

social conditions. Without being a Marxist, he stands very much closer to Marx's ideas than does Blauner, for example. To use one of Marx's ideas, the workers' alienation lies in the fact that they have accepted themselves as a commodity. Their psychological experience of alienation is a consequence of the process of reification. Thus Goldthorpe's theory of alienation is sociological, not psychological.

One of the problems he studied is the effect of the instrumental orientation on the workers' relations to the factory and its leadership. It has generally been said that, because of their alienation, workers in the motor industry have hostile attitudes toward the firm. Among other things, this has expressed itself in the many strikes which have taken place in the American automobile industry. But Goldthorpe is opposed to this, too, and says that in using the Vauxhall factories as the object of his study he would find different results, because there had rarely been a strike in that enterprise. In addition, the frequency of absence from work was very low, and the turnover of the labor force was on average 9.7 percent per annum, a figure which is by no means high. The interviews revealed fairly positive attitudes to the enterprises. On the question as to whether Vauxhall, as compared to other enterprises known to the respondent, was better or worse than most, 74 percent replied that it was better than most. (We must remember that the dropout was 21 percent and that many who were negative toward the firm, and therefore did not wish to be interviewed, may be found in this group.)

The results suggest, Goldthorpe feels, that dissatisfaction with the work itself can exist side by side with a positive attitude toward the enterprise, if the economic needs of the workers are met. This is especially so where the workers have an instrumental orientation. "Thus, in spite of the deprivation which their jobs on the line may entail, these men will be disposed to maintain their relationship with the firm, and to define this more as one of reciprocity and interdependence rather than, say, as one of coercion and exploitation," Goldthorpe concludes.[36]

EPILOGUE TO THE VAUXHALL STUDY

"Rarely can a sociological study such as this have been so cruelly been put to the test. Scarcely one month after the publication of Goldthorpe's findings, on 17 and 18 October 1966, the Luton car workers broke into open rebellion," the English sociologist Blackburn writes.[37]

An incident took place at the factory which the newspaper *The Times* described as a "near riot conditions." The workers went on strike and at

[36] Ibid.
[37] R. Blackburn, "The Unequal Society," in *The Incompatibles: Trade Union Militancy and the Consensus*, ed. R. Blackburn and A. Cockburn (London: Penguin Books in association with *New Left Review*, 1967).

the same time tried to storm the administration building, while the police had the greatest difficulty in preventing them from assaulting a representative of management.

What lay behind this? According to the *Daily Mail* newspaper, quoted by Blackburn, a trade union leader explained that an investigation showed that Vauxhall's profit per annum per employee was 900 pounds, while figures for Ford and BMC were 600 and 300 pounds respectively. In addition, the workers were disturbed because more than half of the company's profits of 13 million pounds had been sent to the mother company, General Motors, U.S.A. It also appeared that the company had decided to shorten working hours to four days per week, which reduced wages by 20 percent. This was a result of the economic policy of the British government.

It is very likely that the reasons mentioned here are all connected with each other. The profits of the enterprise became of importance in shedding light on the workers' situation, when the profit was placed in relation to the wage reductions which threatened the workers. Blackburn maintains that Goldthorpe's analysis is invalidated because of these incidents. But it is not so certain that he is correct. One way of analyzing the incident is to start from the instrumental orientation of the employees toward their work. This affects their relations to the company. As long as the enterprise satisfies the needs which the instrumental orientation brings with it, the workers are presumably not concerned with the amount of the company's profits. It is only when they feel that the company has let them down by drastic wage reductions that profit and the conditions of ownership are actualized. A sociologist oriented toward Marxism could quite likely explain it as follows: The workers are already alienated when they join the company. Their attitude is a consequence of reification. In turn, this means that they lack class-consciousness. They are interested only in making money. It is first when their opportunity for moneymaking is threatened that they notice the existence of class conflicts. It is only then that they begin to say of the company that "instead of sending profits to General Motors they could maintain the wage level."

This suggests that Blauner's thesis—that the conditions of ownership are not important for the workers—is, to say the least, much too simplified.

ALIENATION AS POWERLESSNESS AND UNCERTAINTY (ALLARDT'S THEORY)

Seeman's theory does not satisfy the Finnish sociologist Erik Allardt.[38] He considers it to be too vague and, as an example, takes the dimension called *isolation*. First, Allardt says that isolation is not simply an emotional state,

[38] Allardt, *Samhällsstruktur*.

but a form of behavior. But Seeman speaks of experiences and feelings. In this case, isolation can either be equated with meaninglessness (if the individual is no longer concerned with goals) or is the same as normlessness (if he is unaware of the norms). One can object to Allardt's reasoning by presenting an interpretation other than that given by him. It is possible that Seeman means that a person can be concerned about the goals, but nevertheless feel that he is unable to reach them. In this case meaninglessness is not the same as isolation. It is also possible that a person has knowledge of the norms, but feels that he will not reach his goals if he behaves in accordance with accepted norms. Here, normlessness is not the same as isolation. However, this distinction is a matter of secondary importance. Several other problems remain.

A more important criticism which Allardt makes of Seeman is that his typology is only a preliminary classification. No logical, psychological, or sociological connection between the various dimensions has been constructed by Seeman, so Allardt tries to do this.

POWERLESSNESS AS A BLOCK TO PARTICIPATION IN SOCIAL EXCHANGE

Allardt proceeds from the fact that alienation is a psychological condition, an emotional experience. To begin with, he differentiates between powerlessness and the other aspects, dealing with powerlessness first. The starting point of his analysis is theories which regard social interaction as a process of exchange.[39] This means that if two persons interact with each other of their own free will, (i.e., the interaction can be discontinued if one or both wish it), the interaction takes place only if they can offer each other rewards or utilities.

The rewards and utilities may be either of a material or psychological nature, for example, appreciation or praise. Thus power can be defined as the ability to influence the utilities and rewards received by others.[40] Allardt uses this definition of power in his reasoning regarding alienation, but first he makes a distinction. He maintains that a person can be alienated in his relations to other people, i.e., a kind of individual alienation. But, within a society, people belong to groups, or subcultures, in which they are well integrated, although these groups or subcultures are themselves alienated in relation to the rest of society.

If a person or group feel that they have the necessary preconditions for social exchange, for example, adequate resources, but that because of the structure of society they are prevented from using these resources, they

[39] P. E. Blau, *Exchange and Power in Social Life* (New York: John Wiley & Sons, 1964); G. Homans, *Social Behavior: Its Elementary Forms* (New York: Harcourt, Brace & World, 1961); J. W. Thibaut & H. H. Kelley, *The Social Psychology of Groups* (New York: John Wiley & Sons, 1959).

[40] Homans, *Social Behavior.*

feel powerless.[41] Therefore, powerlessness becomes a consequence of the *discrepancy* between the evaluation of one's own resources and the chances of using these to influence the results of social interaction.

However, if this hypothesis is correct, there is an implicit assumption which Allardt does not mention. The discrepancy is experienced only if individuals hold values which say that they are entitled to use their resources on terms which are equal for all, or at least on terms which can be specified. At the same time there may be individuals and groups who have insight into their own resources but who, for various reasons, are willing to refrain from using them. In other words, they have accepted a subordinate position in society, and accept the fact that they are prevented from using their resources in the social exchange-process. Thus, these individuals and groups ought to be unable to experience powerlessness.

Values regarding equality, or regarding the same chances as far as use of resources in social interaction is concerned, are often part of the ideologies of those social and religious movements which are opposed to capitalistic society. To illustrate his argument, Allardt takes an example from the history of the labor movements.

In many European countries, the labor movement was most radical when the workers were not allowed to take part in political and social life: "Europe's history over the last century shows quite clearly that the most radical workers' movements occur in those countries in which a politically conscious and organized working class had to wait a long time before general and equal suffrage became a reality."[42] The workers felt powerless because they felt that they had resources to influence social exchange but were prevented from using them. Therefore, they were alienated from the society, at the same time that cohesion among them was strong and "class consciousness" lively. It might be added that the political successes of the labor movement—for example, the holding of political power for a long period as in Sweden—brought with them opportunities to influence social exchange, for instance, by means of the social reforms which were initiated. This has meant that workers are now very unlikely to be alienated from society to a large degree. At the same time, cohesion and solidarity have probably diminished in trade unions and within the political branch of the labor movement in Sweden.

ALIENATION AND SOCIAL PRESSURE

The second type of alienation to which Allardt refers occurs in situations in which the individual experiences indifference and uncertainty. Allardt builds his analysis on Durkheim's distinction between mechanical and

[41] Allardt, *Samhällsstruktur*, p. 83.
[42] Ibid., p. 82.

organic solidarity (see chapter 5). Mechanical solidarity is a consequence of strong social pressure in a society which has little social differentiation in the form of division of labor. Organic solidarity is a consequence of weak social pressure combined with a high level of division of labor. With organic solidarity, social pressure is replaced by agreements regarding social exchange.

Alienation in the form of a state of indifference and uncertainty presupposes *little* division of labor and *weak* pressure to conforming behavior as well. The reason is "that if pressure toward conformity is considerably reduced, without division of labor being differentiated, the chances of predicting human behavior are also reduced. In a society characterized by mechanical solidarity the predictability of norms is guaranteed, while in a society characterized by organic solidarity, agreement regarding exchange makes prediction possible."[43]

Thus lack of differentiation and relatively weak social pressures in combination create uncertainty. Social pressure toward conformity can be directed toward various social phenomena. The pressure may be directed toward acceptance of social values, which in turn indicate desirable and undesirable social goals. The social pressures may also manifest themselves as directed toward social norms and role-expectations, i.e., expectations as to how the individual, as the occupant of a certain position, ought to behave. Finally, conforming behavior can be related to the definition of a situation. These four categories, then, can be arranged in a hierarchy of importance.

Allardt defines the second type of alienation as uncertainty with regard to one or several of the four social phenomena. If one assumes that there exists a hierarchical relationship between values, norms, role-expectations, and definitions of the situation, then these four phenomena can be ordered according to a cumulative model. This model may be presented in the following way.[44]

	Uncertainty with regard to			
Type of alienation	values	norms	role-expectations	definition of the situation
Meaninglessness	+	+	+	+
Normlessness	−	+	+	+
Role- or self-estrangement	−	−	+	+
Accidental alienation	−	−	−	+
No alienation	−	−	−	−

[43] Ibid., pp. 83–84.
[44] Ibid., p. 86.

Thus Allardt is able to elaborate a structure regarding the different dimensions of alienation. Compared to Seeman's analysis he employs three of Seeman's dimensions and adds a fourth one. "Isolation," on the other hand, as a special dimension is abandoned. It remains to relate "powerlessness" to this structure. We will return to that. Let us first discuss the cumulative model.

Meaninglessness is the most serious form of alienation. It involves uncertainty both with regard to values, norms, role-expectations, and definition of the situation. Next follows normlessness, and so on. As the model is cumulative, a person can be uncertain regarding the definition of the situation, but secure as far as the other three factors are concerned. But a person could not be uncertain regarding role-expectations and certain regarding the three other factors. If he is uncertain as far as role-expectations are concerned, he must be uncertain at least regarding the definition of the situation.

If the model here were to be used in empirical research, it would probably be quickly evident that it does not function as a perfect cumulative scale. Experience of the so-called Guttman scales supports this, but it is interesting as a theoretical model because it indicates relations between various dimensions of alienation. Allardt points out that the division into types of alienation is incomplete, as it pays no regard to the extent of alienation. A person can be uncertain as far as one area of his life is concerned, for example, work, but secure with regard to another area. In connection with this, uncertainty should be seen as a continuous variable. This means that a person can experience various degrees of uncertainty, or, in other words, that uncertainty can vary in intensity.

There is an important difference between the two types of alienation with which Allardt experiments. The first concerns the experience of powerlessness caused by the discrepancy between social resources and the inability to use them in social interaction. The second type of alienation, uncertainty, occurs when there is a lack of balance between the existing social pressure in the society and the extent of the division of labor. As indicated earlier, the first type presupposes social values which the individual has made his own.

The second type of alienation, on the other hand, does not presuppose the acceptance of values, as it is a consequence of the relations between various factors in a social structure. It presupposes only that the postulated connection between social pressure and the division of labor really does create the expected reactions.

THE RELATIONSHIP BETWEEN POWERLESSNESS AND UNCERTAINTY

If powerlessness occurs as a consequence of the individual's experience that he possesses social resources, but is prevented from using them, the experience may be justified if it is in accordance with actual conditions. If, however, the feeling does not agree with actual conditions, it may be due to an erroneous perception or definition of the situation. In that case, the experience of powerlessness would be a consequence of uncertainty.

There is another relation. As previously stated, powerlessness presupposes the acceptance of certain social values, for instance, that all members of a society shall have the right to make use of their resources in social interaction. If a person believes that these values are valid, but if in practice this is not so, then he must feel uncertain about existing social values. Once again, powerlessness presupposes insecurity. If, in this case, the individual had possessed the "correct" social values or had had a correct perception of these values, he would not have experienced powerlessness.

By the example we have given we tried to create relationship between uncertainty and powerlessness on a social-psychological level. Allardt chooses a different level—a sociological level. He believes that a certain type of social structure facilitates the growth of alienation. He proceeds from individuals in a society, the extent of their social resources, and the degree of social pressure. In both cases he simplifies his analysis by assuming two values for both variables: small and great resources, and strong and weak social pressure. The model can be presented as a fourfold table.[45]

Allardt offers some explanation for cells 1 and 4. In a society with strong social pressures and, as a consequence, uniformity in the social system, those who limit their social exchange are often those who hold traditional attitudes. An example would be religious individuals who associate only with people belonging to their own groups. Other similar people are scientists, technicians, and other specialists who live in a ivory tower or in some other way isolate themselves. According to Allardt, they are more self-satisfied than alienated. These two groups are to be found in the first cell.

In the fourth cell we find those who possess many resources. Their world is differentiated and, because they have many roles, they do not feel alienation—they are socially active.

Allardt tries to place the experience of alienation in relation to the social structure of society. He earlier maintained that alienation defined as uncertainty, i.e., as found in cell 2, occurs in societies with a low degree of division of labor and weak social pressure to conformity. That would mean that this type of alienation is not found in highly developed industrial societies, because, to the extent that division of labor has been accomplished, organic solidarity results. This means that social pressure is not of the same importance for the individual's changes of orienting himself. If this type of alienation occurs in a society with a high degree of division of labor, it is necessary to presume that only persons with great

[45] Ibid., p. 88.

	Resources for social exchange	
	Small	Great

Values, norms, role-expectations, and the situation form a uniform system	1. No alienation
	   Traditionalists
	   Specialists
		3. Lack of power, which expresses itself in aggression and desire to change the distribution of power. Alienation from the subculture; dogmatists and aggressive innovators

Pressure toward conformity is weak concerning definition of situation role-expectations	2. Alienation
	
	a. occasional
	   alienation
	b. role-alienation
		4. No alienation:
		   socially active
		   citizen

norms	c. anomic alienation	
values	d. meaninglessness	

resources can orient themselves and benefit from the social situation when social pressure is weak. But in this case it is not the intensity of the social pressure which is decisive, as far as alienation is concerned, but rather the access to resources for social exchange.

Similar objections can be raised against alienation defined as powerlessness. Strong social pressure occurs in societies with low division of labor, bringing with it mechanical solidarity. As a result, great resources are not necessary in social exchange. This, too, should be a form of alienation which does not occur in highly developed industrial societies. If this type of alienation is to occur in such societies, then a social pressure stronger than "that demanded by necessity" (i.e., that demanded by a differentiated division of labor) is presupposed. Individuals who oppose this pressure would then be alienated, while conformists would not experience powerlessness.

Our interpretation of Allardt's theory means that if alienation is put in relation to the social conditions which exist in a highly industrialized society, the powerless are alienated because they do not accept existing social conditions preventing them from participating in the social exchange process. The uncertain are alienated because their resources are insufficient, whereas their attitude to society is hardly relevant for alienation.[46]

Powerlessness becomes a sort of "positive" alienation, corresponding to the artistic alienation referred to by Marcuse (see page 173). Uncertainty is a "negative" type of alienation.

Furthermore, people who feel powerless because of the discrepancy between their values concerning participation in the social exchange process and their factual chances may be those politically active, e.g., in the labor movement. They often are social reformers or revolutionaries, those who have "class-consciousness." Thus experience of alienation may be an important motive for political activity. This hypothesis is contrary to a common one, that alienated people are passive and politically disinterested (see also chapter 8).

ANOMIE AND CLASS STRUCTURE (MIZRUCHI'S RESEARCH)

Mizruchi[47] deals with some of the problems which can be derived from Allardt's theory, particularly the question of whether the type of alienation which is defined as uncertainty, occurs in a highly industrialized society among people who possess few resources for social exchange. Mizruchi's research, however, has no connection with Allardt's theory and takes an entirely different point of departure.

THEORETICAL POINT OF DEPARTURE

In Durkheim's theory (see chapter 5) anomie was a condition in a social structure, in which the norms and goals of the social systems no longer influenced individual behavior. This is a state of "normlessness." Robert Merton takes up Durkheim's ideas and develops them.[48] Merton, following Durkheim, calls the discrepancy between social goals and the lack of means to reach these accepted goals "anomie." There are various ways of adapting to this condition. One is that the individual continues to strive

---

[46] Bo Andersson has, in a discussion of Allardt's theories ("Erik Allardt's makrosociologi," *Sociologisk Forskning*, III, (1966), 22–31), pointed out that the degree of division of labor probably affects the individual's notions concerning the exchange possibilities he has. Alienation then would occur, if members in a social system become conscious of the possibilities of exchange, which members belonging to other systems have. The individual's reference group, i.e., the group or the system which he uses for comparison purposes will in this case become an important source for the development of alienation.

[47] Mizruchi, *Success and Opportunity*.

[48] Merton, *Social Theory and Social Structure*.

after the accepted goals, but does this by using illegal means. Merton calls this adaption mechanism "innovation."[49] Another mechanism—rebellion— means that the individual rejects both the accepted goals and the norms, and tries to replace them with new ones. Both innovation and rebellion theoretically are easily linked to Allardt's concept of powerlessness.

Those people who belong to lower social groups and classes have fewer resources and are less able to take part in social exchange. Therefore, individuals are affected differentially by the tension between accepted goals and lack of resources to reach them, depending on where they are situated in the class structure.

The anomic social circumstances, as described by Durkheim and Merton, are accompanied by psychological states in which anomie is experienced. Various ways of measuring these states have been developed. One method is the use of an attitude scale, developed by Srole,[50] which procedure is used by Mizruchi. The scale measures five aspects of feelings: (1) A feeling that those with power, and the leaders in society, are not concerned about the individual and his needs. (2) A feeling that it is impossible to understand the society and its social systems. Because of this it is impossible to predict the consequences of one's own actions and the actions of others. (3) A feeling that the individual is incapable of reaching the goals he has set up for himself and that the chances of his doing this are all the time diminishing. (4) A feeling of meaninglessness because both norms and goals no longer function. (5) A feeling that one's social relations are in the process of disintegration and that one receives no support from other people.

These five dimensions are closely connected both to Seeman's and to Allardt's analyses. However, Srole, like Seeman, does not arrive at a logical connection between the various aspects. His third dimension corresponds to some extent to Allardt's normlessness, his fourth, to meaninglessness, and his fifth, to role-alienation. In general, one can say that the five aspects measure insecurity, rejection, and isolation. The theoretical difference between the subjective experience of anomie and the subjective experience of alienation is minimal.

CLASS BELONGINGNESS AND SUCCESS

Certain preconditions are necessary if a person is to experience anomie: he must accept social goals regarding success. Further, he must feel that the means which are at his disposal to reach these goals are insufficient.

[49] Ibid.
[50] L. Srole, "Social Integration and Certain Corollaries," *American Sociological Review* XXI (1956), 709–16.

The consequence is that the individual feels powerless, in Allardt's meaning of the term, or anomie in Srole's presentation.

First Mizruchi asked his respondents how important it was to get on in life. Not surprisingly, the majority accepted and placed great importance upon success values. However, the tendency was somewhat more pronounced among working-class people than among middle-class people. As the members of the former class have fewer resources at their disposal than the middle class, anomie should be more prevalent in what Mizruchi refers to as the lower classes.

Another problem is whether class differences affect definitions of "success." Mizruchi finds that the definition depends very largely on class belongingness. Material and economic success are valued most highly by the lower classes. The middle class speaks of prestige and status as far as success is concerned. Education does not have the same meaning for the lower class that it does for the middle class. For the latter, education is often seen as a goal in itself, and a symbol of personal ability. As, in reality, education is an important factor for success, the evaluations regarding education which are made by members of the lower classes prevent them from achieving the same degree of success as that achieved by people in the middle classes, who realize how important it is to gain a good education. The lower classes not only possess fewer resources, but in addition have a poorer knowledge of which resources are relevant than does the middle class.

A recurrent idea is encountered: that "getting on" depends on the individual and his ability. The evaluation of the importance of social factors for success are not as emphasized. Mizruchi feels that this individualism is an important "ideological" factor, which partly explains why the working class in the U.S. has not had a revolutionary or socialist orientation. The cause of what is called "the apathy of the working class" is not so much lack of class-identification in itself, but the particular formulation that has been given to "the American dream," writes Mizruchi.[51] The negative content of this evaluation is that if an individual is not successful, he has only himself to blame.

From the sociological point of view we are faced with a situation of strong social pressure, at least as far as evaluations regarding success are concerned. At the same time, the situation of "the lower classes" is characterized by a lack of sufficient resources to participate in a social exchange which can lead to success. Above all, they lack education and also those evaluations which are of help to the individual in obtaining an education.

In Allardt's scheme this situation would be placed in the first cell, i.e.,

[51] Mizruchi, *Success and Opportunity*, p. 89.

that which is characterized by few resources and uniformity of value (see page 232). According to Allardt, alienation does not occur in this sort of situation. But Mizruchi hypothesizes that this situation creates anomie. Assuming that *anomie* has the same, or similar, meaning as Allardt's alienation, in the form of *uncertainty*, we have two contrasting hypotheses. Therefore, we will take a closer look at the relationship between class structure and anomie.

CLASS BELONGINGNESS AND ANOMIE

Mizruchi uses work and education as criteria for class belongingness. He combines them into an index in which the two factors have different weights, in accordance with Hollingshead's procedure.[52] Mizruchi finds a clear relationship between social class belongingness and anomie: anomie is stronger in the lower classes than in the middle classes.

In order to analyze his data more closely, Mizruchi uses another index of class belongingness i.e., income. When he holds education constant, his results do not completely support his first findings. As his data are complicated, we reproduce his table below:[53]

Income and anomie controlled for education (in %)

	Primary school		High school		College	
Income	Above 5000	Below Dollars	Above 5000	Below Dollars	Above 5000	Below Dollars
Anomie						
Low	11	8	27	24	51	34
Medium	42	31	54	44	41	34
High	47	61	19	32	8	32

Anomie, expressed as a percentage, is highest among those with least education. In all education categories it is shown that those with lower incomes have a higher degree of anomie than those with higher incomes. In the group who have only primary school education, however, there is no statistically significant relationship between income and anomie. It seems that higher income does not entirely compensate for the feeling of insufficiency in the social exchange which apparently comes with low education. Considering those who only have primary education, one finds the highest average anomie-level in this category. This goes against Allardt's hypothesis, on condition that we assume that for these groups, too, uniform values exists.

[52] Ibid., p. 163.
[53] Ibid., p. 93.

In the two categories in which the individuals have higher education, the relationship between income and anomie is statistically significant. Here we have an example of status-incongruency,[54] i.e., lack of agreement between two variables which affect the status of the individual. The individuals with high education often expect high incomes. When the results of social interaction—here measured by income—do not correspond to the individual's resources, anomie is experienced. Presuming once again that these persons are influenced to accept uniform values, Allardt's hypothesis receives some support: people with relatively large resources—in the form of education—feel alienated when they experience themselves as not receiving enough in exchange for their resources. According to Allardt, they should experience "powerlessness." Unfortunately, the measure of anomie used by Mizruchi is not a good indicator of powerlessness.

We can summarize Mizruchi's results so that, presuming that the individuals accept positive values regarding success, they feel themselves to be alienated when they do not have those resources for social interaction which lead to success. This is so even if, relatively speaking, they are successful measured by income. To some extent these results oppose Mizruchi's contention that the lower classes use economic indicators as success symbols.

On the other hand, among those having greater resources, alienation occurs when their relatively greater resources fail to result in economic success i.e., when they experience a condition of "status-incongruency." Mizruchi's interpretation is not quite the same as that which I have suggested. In his view, anomie in the middle classes occurs when the individual perceives that his opportunities for success are limited, while in the lower classes expectations of achieving success are low, and this in its turn creates anomie. In Mizruchi's opinion, the experience of anomie is tied up with class belongingness insomuch as different social factors affecting the occurrence of anomie are of varying importance in different classes.

[54] See, e.g., G. E. Lenski, "Social Participation and Status Crystallization," *American Sociological Review* XXI (1956), 458–64; and A. Malewski, "The Degree of Status Incongruency and Its Effects," *The Polish Sociological Bulletin* No. 1 (1963).

8

ALIENATION IN SOCIALIST SOCIETIES

INTRODUCTION

With de-Stalinization came a considerably freer Marxist debate in the socialist countries of Eastern Europe.[1] A central theme in this debate was the institutionalization of Marxism and the lack of intellectual content which was connected to this. The Polish philosopher Leszek Kolakowski formulated the problem in these words:

"The word 'Marxism' has not meant a doctrine with a certain content, but a doctrine which has exclusively been formally defined, more specifically, through the decrees of certain infallible institutions (valid at the time) which in one epoch have been embodied in 'the world's greatest researcher into language,' 'greatest historian,' 'greatest philosopher,' 'greatest national economist.' "[2]

During the process of de-Stalinization, science was freed from ideological control; therefore, such problems as the goals of socialist humanism and the closely related problem of alienation could be discussed. Those who experienced Stalinism were in great need of an explanation of what had taken place, of how it was that it had happened, and of why there had been no opposition. The personality cult—which is often given enormous importance—is not in itself a sufficient explanation. The question then arises: Under what social conditions could the personality cult emerge and develop?

[1] This chapter was written before the events in Czechoslovakia. The trend of a freer discussion seems to have been arrested, if not reversed, since this new development.

[2] L. Kolakowski, *Der Mensch ohne Alternative* (Munich: R. Piper & Co., 1960). Quoted after the Swedish edition.

It is in this context that alienation once again became a current problem and many people began to ask if alienation could be found in socialist states as well as in capitalist society. A comprehensive literature already exists in this field, written by philosophers and social scientists who live and work in the socialist countries of Eastern Europe. We shall here refer to some of the lines of these debates.

Does Alienation Exist in a Socialist Country?

In 1965 the Polish philosopher Adam Schaff, at that time a member of the Central Committee of the Polish Communist Party, published a book entitled *Marxism and the Human Individual*, in which he wrote: "For Marx it was an axiom that economic alienation is the basis of all forms of alienation. This means that putting an end to economic alienation, by abolishing the privately owned means of production, automatically ends all alienation. Is this really true? Is alienation an impossibility in a socialist society, i.e., is it unable to proceed from a source other than private ownership? It is this question which makes of alienation a problem that is both current and important from socialism's as well as capitalism's point of view."[3]

Schaff's book awoke a lively discussion in Poland, but he is neither the first nor the only one to have asked if alienation is a historically necessary phenomenon, bound up with the conditions of production of capitalist society, or if it can make its appearance in socialist societies, too, though in a new guise. In recent years the question has been widely discussed in the socialist countries of Europe. Besides the Polish philosophers and sociologists, Yugoslavian scientists have in particular taken part in discussions, and in Hungary and Czechoslovakia the theme has been taken up and dealt with.

In the Soviet Union it seems that the question put by Schaff has largely received an unequivocal "No" in reply. Alienation does not appear in a socialist society. In an article on alienation in the *Soviet Encyclopaedia*, Ogurzov maintains that the Marxist concept of alienation refers to important, but historically passing, social conditions, based on the division of labor and private ownership. Therefore, the problem of the alienation of labor becomes a theoretical and logical question: Are the three conditions that Marx said were the cause of economic alienation *necessary* or *sufficient* conditions? If private ownership of the means of production, division of labor, and the fact that labor is a *commodity* together are *necessary* conditions for alienation, then this does not exist in socialist

---

[3] A. Schaff, *Marxismus und das menschliche Individuum* (Vienna-Frankfurt-Zürich: Europa Verlag, 1965), p. 142.

countries because there the means of production are socialized. This is the case even if the other two factors remain. If on the other hand the three factors are *sufficient* conditions for the occurrence of alienation, then alienation also exists in socialist countries, because both the division of labor and the fact that labor has the character of a commodity are also found in socialist lands.

If the problem is formulated in this way, then the answer is given, in that one has decided to consider Marx's three factors as either necessary or sufficient conditions for alienation. But Schaff has another answer. Assume, he says, that the basis of all forms of alienation is economic alienation. From this it does not logically follow that the abolishing of private ownership of the means of production must lead to the end of all alienation, whatever the form it takes in social life. In fact, whether or not alienation occurs in a socialist society is not a logical but an empirical problem. What do the empirical facts tell us? Let us once again quote Schaff: "The situation is clear: in all forms of socialist society known to us at present, different types of alienation occur. This means that it is not automatically true that the abolition of private ownership of the means of production leads to the disappearance of alienation."[4]

This is an unambiguous answer. Schaff maintains that, from the Marxist viewpoint, his thesis is not unreasonable. Socialism is a transitional stage on the way to communism. During this transitional period it is necessary to change the class consciousness of the people, which is still influenced by traditional ways of thinking. In addition, the state remains as a controlling power, and must do so as long as socialist countries exist in the world encircled by hostile capitalist regimes. Schaff continues by alleging that four forms of alienation, or alienation-creating conditions, exist in a socialist society: (1) The state and its bureaucratically organized power of control. (2) Alienation of labor, due to the fact that it still retains its character of commodity. (3) The alienating effect of the division of labor. (4) The institution of the family as a factor in alienation.

THE FAMILY AS AN ALIENATED INSTITUTION

For Schaff, economic alienation is the central problem, and the family is given only as yet another example of how social institutions can become reified. But first we will take up his discussion of the family.

In Marxist literature the family has been dealt with, among other people, by Engels, although mainly from a cultural-historical standpoint.

---

[4] Ibid., p. 168.

In Engels's work on the family and the origins of private property, he does not predict how the family will develop in the socialist society. Schaff takes as his starting point the fact that the type of family with which we are familiar from the capitalist society and its class system should alter, as a consequence of the changes in the social and economic conditions that take place in a socialist society. It is true, he says, that some of the functions which earlier belonged to the family will be transferred to social institutions such as schools and enterprises of various kinds. (But the same thing occurs even in nonsocialist countries: In Sweden, for instance, there is a strong tendency to remove the upbringing and educational functions from the family and transfer them to the school.) The economic situation of women changes, and also her social position and sex-role, which in turn has important consequences for relations between married couples. (But similar changes both in attitudes and actual circumstances are also taking place in the Swedish society, without any revolutionary changes in the economic structure; it seems to be sufficient that women are more and more in demand on the labor market.) Authority relations between parents and their children also change. (But the same thing also occurs in nonsocialist countries.) But despite these changes, Schaff maintains, the traditional form of the family remains, without anyone's being in a position today to say anything reasonable about its continued evolution. One may add in parentheses, Engels's remarks from *The Origins of the Family, Private Property and the State.* Writing about the future of the family he says: "That will be settled after a new generation has grown up: a generation of men who never in all their lives have had occasion to purchase a woman's surrender either with money or with any other means of social power, and of women who have never been obliged to surrender to any man out of any consideration other than that of real love, or to refrain from giving up themselves to their beloved for fear of economic consequences. Once such people appear, they will not care a rap about what we today think they should do. They will establish their own practice and their own public opinion. . . ."[5]

This statement is remarkable in that it stands in sharp contrast to the predictions, made with a Utopian strength, as to what the economic and social structure of society will be when capitalist society is dead and buried.

Schaff rounds off his critique of the institution of the family by pointing out that it looks as if socialist society would have accepted the bourgeois family, with its Protestant puritanism and its hypocrisy. The example

[5] K. Marx and F. Engels, *Selected Works* (Moscow: Foreign Language Publishing House, 1949), Vol. II, p. 219.

which Schaff gives here could be looked upon as the reification of a social institution. Starting from a sociological point of view, one could analyze the conditions in the following way: If, in a socialist society, the family still retains its traditional form, with traditional values and attitudes, then it is difficult for it to fulfill one of its functions, namely, the socialization of the children. This means that it would be unable to mould the type of person who accepts the values of the socialist society as self-evident and who learns to behave in a way that is in agreement with those expectations which society has of the individual in his various roles. In such a case, the goals of the family as an institution deviate from society's goals. To avoid conflicts it must be, as it were, screened off from the rest of society. In this way there is the risk that it will become an isolated institution, which is not influenced by society's values and goals, having its own existence, divorced from the other social institutions, and becoming, in Lukács's terminology, *reified*.

THE ALIENATION OF LABOR IN SOCIALIST SOCIETIES

According to Schaff, the other big problem of alienation in the socialist society is the alienation of labor. It is true that, as far as the means of production are concerned, private ownership has been abolished, and the alienation-creating phenomenon which is a consequence of class conflicts in the capitalist society is also abolished (if one uses the conditions of ownership as the main criteria for the concept of class, as does Marx). But despite the socialization of the means of production, human labor is still a commodity, which the individual exchanges for another commodity, represented by money. As a result, the products of human labor are also commodities. This means that even in a socialist society there is a commodity market—of a different type than that found in capitalist societies, certainly, but nevertheless a commodity market, with its own intrinsic laws.

Almasi, professor in Budapest and pupil of Georg Lukács, illustrated this thesis with the following example.[6] Taking Marx's thesis that the existence of a commodity structure brings with it the risk of "commodity fetishism" as his starting point, he maintains that this can also be observed in a socialist society. It is expressed, for instance, in the values of the individuals, which he compares to the values of shares on the stock exchange: A person is valued according to a measure which says how

[6] M. Almasi, "Alienation and Socialism," in *Marxism and Alienation*, ed. H. Aptheker (New York: Humanities Press, 1965), p. 139.

much his ability or his skills are worth, whether they are an asset to him or not, whether he can expect to advance in the hierarchy or not. The concrete person almost disappears or is comprehended only to the extent that he is the agent of political, economic, and other values and interests.

A common argument is that the commodity form of labor, and the structure of the market, appear only in the socialist stage of development. When a socialist society changes over to the communist stage, these phenomena should disappear. But even on this point Schaff is doubtful. Against the background of the experience, which has been gained in socialist countries, he says that it is highly doubtful if labor as a commodity can be abolished.

It was Marx's dream that at some point, labor could be replaced by "free activity," but later (in *Capital*, for example) he rejected this and accepted the idea that labor is "necessary."

But Schaff wonders whether the ideas of the young Marx regarding labor build in any case on the evaluation of labor as a means of self-realization. If one does not accept these evaluations, one may instead study those conditions under which the individual can come to enjoy his work, independent of whether it is "necessary" or whether it is "free activity."

In a critical analysis of Stalinism, the Yugoslavian sociologist Vranicki[7] put forward yet another argument: that even in the Soviet states man remained a labor force. He means that this is so because the individual is prevented from taking part in the leadership of production and in the distribution of the products which result from it. Total and centralized planning is combined with the sole right of the state to decide over surplus value or profit. Such planning brought with it the creation of a strong, central bureaucracy where the omnipotence of the political state-apparatus is "necessarily accompanied by the universal powerlessness of the individual."[8]

THE PROCESS OF THE DIVISION OF LABOR

The third problem concerning alienation depends on the process of the division of labor. It occurs in a socialist country, and is strengthened there to the extent that the society is industrialized and modern technology utilized. Marx's idea of a human being who is able to do every-

[7] P. Vranicki, "Socialism and the Problem of Alienation," in *Socialist Humanism*, ed. E. Fromm (Garden City: Doubleday & Co., 1965), p. 281.
[8] Ibid.

thing and therefore is able constantly to change his occupation is an impossibility in today's society.[9]

In the article in the *Soviet Encyclopaedia* previously referred to, Ogurzov makes a distinction between *specialization* and *professionalization*. What Ogurzov means is that through the process of the division of labor, the worker is allowed to undertake certain operations only. During his lifetime he may only use a fraction of his total knowledge and ability. Ogurzov calls this type of division of labor "professionalization." Automatized production, which forms the technical base of the communist society, makes possible the abolition of the process of division of labor and professionalization. However, specialization remains, i.e., different individuals have different types of activity, aimed at specific goals. It is not quite clear just where the difference lies between professionalization (which is the consequence of the alienated division of labor) and specialization.

One possible interpretation is that Ogurzov is thinking of the difference between labor that takes place at a conveyer belt, at which every worker carries out one operation, and the supervisory task a worker fulfills when he sits in front of a control panel in a completely automated manufacturing process. It is true that such automation does away with the type of division of labor that occurs at a conveyer belt, but it depends in its turn on the technological level, a level which is found in both capitalist and socialist societies.

It was Schaff's meaning that the process of the division of labor is a technical problem which has very little to do with the form of society: "Work at a conveyer belt, for example, *is* work at a conveyer belt, irrespective of the type of society, although conditions of work in general may not be the same."[10]

Almasi[11] agrees with this way of thinking. He also sees the process of the division of labor as a consequence of technical development, which,

---

[9] It is not probable that in a future society there will occur a development in a direction which Marx predicted. Automation and short working hours, as well as long school and professional training, can give the individual in highly industrialized societies new possibilities. Work will cover only a short period of life or a short working day, and the broad knowledge which man will acquire will make it possible for man to have at least two different jobs, for example, one intellectual and one manual (see H. Zetterberg, "Framtidens klassamhälle" ["The Class-Society of the Future"], in *Det svenska klassamhälle* [*The Swedish Class-Society*] ed. A. Murray, Stockholm: Verdandi Debatt, 1967). However, this must remain speculation, at least as long as a major part of the population of the earth lives in poverty and misery. To increase the standards of living of those people will be a more important problem than the individual's life in industrially highly developed societies either with a capitalist or socialist social order.

[10] Schaff, *Marxismus*, p. 178.

[11] Almasi, "Alienation and Socialism."

therefore, is unable to be abolished within a foreseeable time-span. But monotonous, routine-type work need not necessarily lead to alienation if the individual is given the opportunity to make use of his other abilities and knowledge by active participation in social processes. These processes are partly concerned with co-influence and co-decision making in the enterprises in which the individual works, and partly with the active participation in all activities having as their aim changes in the social structure of society.

A Yugoslavian statement stresses the same idea: the process of the division of labor which creates alienation can be counteracted by seeing to it that the workers themselves administer the enterprises in which they are employed. Vranicki, for example,[12] maintains that the participation of the workers in those decision-processes concerned with the organization of work, the planning of production, and the distribution and use of surplus value are necessary, but not sufficient, conditions for the transforming of the worker from being a cog in a machine to being an active factor in society.

The State and the Bureaucracy

What is it that has prevented the workers in the socialist countries from becoming active? According to Almasi, one of the reasons is the all-embracing bureaucratization. He mentions as an example how "socialist competition" at places of work (a competition which initially was intended to stimulate the workers to increase production) began spontaneously. Very soon it was changed to an official, bureaucratically directed activity, with production figures which were settled in advance and in which exhorting promises were made to the workers, etc. In that way an initially spontaneous activity became transformed into a bureaucratically directed action. Superfluous bureaucratization consequently did not facilitate a greater realization of man's personality and its potentialities, but locked him up in his work and private life.[13]

Here Almasi touches on a central theme in all discussion about alienation in socialist society. This is the question of the controlling power of the state in general, and the very marked bureaucratization which was brought about by this: "One cannot deny," says Schaff, "that the state exists in the socialist society—we praise its power daily."[14] The controlling power of the state has two functions; one is an external function,

[12] Vranicki, "Socialism and the Problem."
[13] Almasi, "Alienation and Socialism," p. 133.
[14] Schaff, *Marxismus*, p. 170.

the other an internal function. Toward other countries, the state must ensure that a strong fighting force is able to defend the socialist system in a situation in which war is never very remote. In this respect, the controlling power of the state must be seen in a wider context: the capitalist states exist side by side with the socialist states, and it is this which prevents the reduction of the state's controlling power as far as defense is concerned.

To that must be added (in Schaff's opinion) the alienating conditions created by atomic energy. In a world where man's power over nature is greater than ever before, the risk of total extermination becomes for the first time a very real one. It would therefore be entirely unreasonable to suppose that people will not feel themselves threatened, even if they live in a socialist society. Marx's idea of *Verdinglichung*—reification—is illustrated by the fact that we live in a world in which the powers that man has created may exist independent of him and out of his control.

But even if the coercive power of the state is necessary to ensure the security of a country, the defense function is not a sufficient explanation as to why the power of the state is so strong inside:

"The state as an apparatus of coercive power does not appear only as an outer-directed, but also as an inner-directed force. The answer to the question of how it is possible that alienation of such strength could occur is found in that period which was characterized by the cult of the personality—and this was so in all socialist countries. This is the story of an incredible alienation, when those forces created by man in the best faith and for the most honorable ends, were torn from his hands and, as a hostile force, began to destroy and tear apart their creator."[15]

Marx dreamed that the state would wither away, as classes disappeared. Suppose now that the defense function of the state—i.e., the outward directed function—could be discontinued. Could one then expect, as Marx thought, that the state as an organ of power on the inside would fade away and be replaced by only the state functions of administration? The apparatus of the state has shown no signs of decaying. Rather it has developed into a gigantic machine. Schaff believes that the founder of Marxism could never have realized which, or how many, functions the state would one day assume: planning of the entire economic and social life; leadership of the state-run industries; leadership of the scientific, cultural, and artistic institutions. In addition, the state administers health services, social insurance, communications, etc. The more technology develops, the more the state apparatus comes to embrace all areas of life. Because of the amount of technological knowledge which is required (and the specialization which goes with it), the

[15] Ibid., p. 171.

state bureaucracy becomes an apparatus which is staffed by specialists, technologists, and professional administrators. Even if the maximum of democratic control was achieved, it would still come nowhere near to the ideal type of society which Marx had in mind when he said that society would be transformed into an association of free producers.

According to Schaff, this is because centralization of leadership and administration has become a technical necessity.

The result of this development is an all-powerful bureaucracy, bound by its own laws, which sets itself free from the very goals for which it was created and turns against the very people it was intended to serve.

In discussions in socialist countries it is constantly being pointed out that the existence of a bureaucratic apparatus, which functions independently of democratic control and without influence from outside, is an inheritance received from Stalinism. The first socialist revolution took place in a backward country. There was, to use Perry Anderson's characterization, a shortage of *commodities* due to an underdeveloped industry, a shortage of *people*, because many were illiterate, a shortage of *values*, manifested in the lack of traditional democratic institutions, and a shortage of *time* in which to create industrialization while under threat from outside.[16] In turn this brought with it a stress on the importance of the process of industrialization, and the emphasis was on the technological level, while the problems affecting human relations receded into the background.

It may be added that psychological and social-psychological problems were, as usual in Marxist theorizing, neglected. Thus, as Marcović points out: "Problems of coal and steel pushed back problems of man. Communism was conceived more as a wealthy society, and less as a humane and democratic one in which 'free development of each individual is the condition of the free development of all' (*Communist Manifesto*)."[17]

As Schaff has pointed out, bureaucratization has meant that a new layer, a new class, has arisen in the socialist countries. The power which is in the hands of this layer depends, among other things, on the hierarchical and authoritarian structure of the bureaucratic apparatus. How this bureaucracy functions and what social consequences it brings with it, have been analyzed by Marković.[18] First he attempts to delimit bureaucracy. The political bureaucracy is a homogeneous social group, which is professionally engaged in politics, and which has succeeded in

[16] P. Anderson, "Problems of Socialist Strategy," in *Towards Socialism*, ed. for *New Left Review* by P. Anderson and R. Blackburn (London: The Fontana Library, 1965). See also I. Deutscher's analysis in *The Unfinished Revolution: Russia 1917–1967* (London: Oxford University, 1967).

[17] M. Marcović, "Humanism and Dialectic," in Fromm, *Socialist Humanism*, p. 81.

[18] M. Marcović, *Dialektik der Praxis* (Frankfurt Editions Suhrkamp, 1968).

avoiding democratic control. Because this group commands such power, it is able to award to itself special material privileges. These three conditions—to be professionally engaged with politics, to be outside control, and to have privileges—are all three *necessary* conditions and together *sufficient* conditions for the existence of a political bureaucracy.

The first condition, that of being professionally engaged in politics, means that a group becomes closed and isolated in relation to other groups in society. The bureaucracy is isolated from the masses in whose name it governs. As far as the economic and political decision processes are concerned, the majority of the people become powerless objects, manipulated by the bureaucracy.

Election exists in name only, and the masses have no chance whatsoever of exercising control. The bureaucracy transfers the influence of the voters to the party and party organizations. The chance of getting rid of, or replacing, the members of the bureaucracy by means of vote becomes quite illusory, because the masses are unorganized, isolated individuals, incapable of political action.

Finally, the third condition means that the bureaucracy has the monopoly on decision-making processes regarding distribution and use of the social products. This monopoly is used by the bureaucracy to their own advantage. Marković says that this does not occur at random, because the bureaucracy is a social stratum which recruits its members from among people who no longer have any revolutionary humanistic ideals, and whose human needs are underdeveloped. The need to possess social power is basic to the life of a bureaucrat. But among other things power demands an unlimited supply of goods.[19]

The social consequences are as follows: man loses control over the political institutions which he himself has created, and which function in his name. He is powerless, and political activity becomes meaningless. Therefore, political activity ceases to be creative activity. Instead, a person who participates in politics becomes alienated from himself and from his most basic needs. Man becomes divided into a "political man" and a "private man." It was just such a division which was scorned by Marx as typical of bourgeois society.

In a bureaucratic social structure, man becomes alienated from his fellowmen whether or not he belongs to the ruling or the ruled groups. If he is a member of the ruling group, then his role leads him to concentrate on his social status within the authoritarian hierarchy. His relations with others are decided by the positions held by these others.

If he belongs to the ruled group, then he often becomes politically apathetic. Due to the strict supervision of the ruled by the bureaucracy,

[19] Ibid., p. 103.

an atmosphere of suspicion, dishonesty, and pretense developed. Under the drastic conditions of a bureaucratic society (during Stalin's period), an individual had periodically to hide his political opinions, even from the members of his own family. The conclusion is that a socialist society must be constantly on its guard against a bureaucratic development.

But what are the consequences of such a development? Vranicki, the Yugoslavian sociologist quoted earlier, maintains that as long as man creates forces that can turn against him—and this will happen in all societies—alienation will be a central problem in a socialist society: "Therefore, contrary to the thesis of the superfluity of the problem of alienation under socialism, we must advance the thesis in the most decisive manner possible that the problem of alienation is the central problem of socialism. . . . If the problem of socialism is not comprehended in these terms, the end result may be the evolution of political forms into paroxysm of dehumanization."[20]

The solution to the problem sought in Yugoslavia is the dividing up of the economic decision-making processes. To a great extent, planning takes place centrally, but workers' councils within the various concerns have the right of decision over production, and over the use of the profit made by the concern. The intention is that by means of this type of self-administration, the influence of the individual will be increased, which will hinder the growth of an all-powerful centralized bureacracy: "Self-administration is the dialectical negation of the so-called state-socialism, with its inherent tendencies toward bureaucratization."[21]

Alienation in Cuba

The problem of alienation has also been studied, using traditional empirical methods, in a socialist country. In 1962 the American sociologist Maurice Zeitlin[22] went to Cuba to investigate the attitudes of the workers toward the Cuban revolution. This investigation is unique in its kind. Zeitlin received permission from the (then) Minister of Industry, Ché Guevara, to undertake an interview-study of a representative sample of Cuban workers. Zeitlin had certain relevant qualifications of his research. He had been in Cuba after the revolution and, with another American sociologist, had published a book on the development of Cuba

[20] Vranicki, "Socialism and the Problem," p. 280.

[21] Marcović, *Dialektik der Praxis*, p. 104.

[22] Maurice M. Zeitlin, *Revolutionary Politics and the Cuban Working Class* (Princeton: Princeton University Press, 1967). Copyright © 1967 by Princeton University Press.

after 1959, i.e., after Fidel Castro came to power. In addition he was well known to the authorities, and he could speak Spanish.

The investigation took place in the summer of 1962, i.e., before the so-called missile crisis. Zeitlin and his wife did all the interviewing themselves. The method of sampling was such that Zeitlin chose at random twenty-one enterprises from a list which had been placed at his disposal by the Minister of Industry. These enterprises were spread over the whole country. As the sampling was so arranged (that the probability a given enterprise would come into the sample was proportionate to the total of employees of the enterprise), it was mainly the larger industries, which came into the sample. Then, in every enterprise a new random sample was drawn of ten employees. Only eight of those who were chosen refused to be interviewed.

Zeitlin takes up a critical stand. He wonders: Is it possible to use methods and data from an opinion-investigation in a country where opinion is not free?[23]

The fact that the interviewers were American must have awakened certain suspicions on the part of the respondents, who perhaps took greater care in the way they worded their answers, etc. On the other hand, the fact that they had received permission to undertake the study must have appeared as a sign that they were not hostile to the Cuban revolution.

Zeitlin takes the very low percentage of refusers as a sign that he succeeded in overcoming suspicion which may have existed. He also says that many who were interviewed showed a negative or even critical attitude toward the regime, and he interprets this as a sign of freedom of speech. Although the country felt itself threatened (the abortive Bay of Pigs invasion had taken place only about a year before) and although there had been much sabotage, there was a large measure of freedom of speech. Zeitlin asserts that organized deviance was not possible in the country at that point in time. Nevertheless it could be observed throughout the country that Cubans could speak freely about anything they wished without fear of reprisals from the government, and they did so.[24]

An interview took between one and three hours, and in Zeitlin's view it was quite impossible for a respondent systematically to try to fool the interviewer. Contradictions would have been discovered, which is indeed what happened. Finally, Zeitlin wanted to test hypotheses and undertake a theoretical study. Descriptive data were of minor importance. Neither did he estimate any population parameters. All this can be seen as an indication partly that the data he obtained were relatively

[23] In Poland opinion surveys have been undertaken regularly during a long period. In the Soviet Union they have been carried out in a more continuous way since 1965.
[24] Zeitlin, *Revolutionary Politics*, p. 17–18.

reliable, and partly that, even if they were not reliable, this could not influence the results to the same extent that would have been the case had he undertaken a descriptive study.[25]

At the time of the revolution Cuba was to some extent industrialized. A working class had existed for many years in the towns and was organized into unions. Even if Cuba was, and still is, mainly an agricultural society, there is also an industrial tradition. One of the problems studied by Zeitlin was the occurrence of alienation among the workers. First, he gives a background description of the postrevolution development.

"The Cuban revolution gave new public esteem and respect to manual labor, nationalized industry, and abolished the private appropriation of the workers' products. Social relations in the plant were also altered radically in an egalitarian direction by the revolution. Here, then, was an exceptional opportunity to study the political meaning to the workers of fundamental changes in their work situation—in their role in the organization and control of production and of the products of their work."[26]

Of the twenty-one heads of enterprises, ten had been workers prior to the revolution and two had been members of the guerilla army. Their salary was no higher than that received by the professionally trained workers, and there was a relatively small salary-spread.

The workers were given the opportunity to take an active part in the running of the enterprise through special advisory council meetings, but many workers seemed to have been ignorant of the existence of these councils.

The answers given to the questionnaire indicate that many workers were of the opinion that the revolution and nationalization of industries had affected their attitudes toward their work in a deep-rooted manner. But more important was to see what type of changes had taken place, and how change affected, or was affected by, other attitudes. Among those who had been workers before the revolution, Zeitlin found that the following reported changes:[27]

---

[25] Zeitlin gives a striking example concerning the troubles which the wording of questions may carry with it when asked in another culture. In a pilot study in which he tried out his questionnaire, the following question used in an American study was included: "Aside from personal friends or relatives—of all the people you hear or read about—could you name three individuals whom you admire very much?"

None of the ten persons interviewed mentioned Fidel Castro, in spite of the fact that their answers to other questions indicated that they were positive toward the Cuban revolution. When Zeitlin asked directly why they had not mentioned Fidel, the answer was that the persons interviewed considered him to be a "personal friend" and that this category was excluded in the question.

[26] Zeitlin, *Revolutionary Politics*, pp. 190–91.

[27] Ibid., p. 199.

Attitude toward work

Before nationalization	After nationalization	N	%
Negative	Positive	64	43
Negative	Negative	25	17
Positive	Positive	53	36
Positive	Negative	5	3
	Total	147	99

For about three-quarters of those who had been negative toward their work before the revolution, the socialization of means of production by the state had meant a positive change in their attitudes toward their work; "For them, apparently, socialization of means of production was not a romantic myth or an empty political slogan; for with it came a fundamental change in their work and their commitment to it. Socialism provided them with a desire to work which they had not experienced before. This transformation in their work commitment, in turn, has been basic to their support of the revolution."[28]

Zeitlin says that two hypotheses could explain the results: (1) A change in attitude to work (in a positive direction) affects the attitudes toward society and the social structure. This means that the attitude to work is taken as the independent variable, the dependent variable being attitude to society. (2) The contrary may also be true. Political attitudes are the origin of attitudes to work.

Referring to research by the French sociologist George Friedman, Zeitlin maintains that the workers who feel themselves exploited in a capitalist society find their work debasing. For those who supported the revolution, political attitude is the independent variable and the attitude to work the dependent variable.

Therefore, Zeitlin divided up his respondents according to their attitudes toward the revolution (measured by an index based on several questions) and compared "attitude toward revolution" with "attitude toward work":

Attitude toward the revolution	Attitude toward work				
	Negative-Positive	Negative-Negative	Positive-Positive	Positive-Negative	N
Favorable	51%	17%	31%	1%	106
Indecisive	37%	13%	50%	0%	16
Hostile	16%	20%	48%	16%	25

[28] Ibid.

Those workers who support the revolution showed a stronger tendency to report a change in attitude toward work in a positive direction than those who are undecided or hostile to the revolution.

Up to now, the results which have been presented have little to do with alienation. Rather, they are concerned with the question of work-satisfaction. Earlier we asserted that lack of satisfaction and alienation cannot be considered to be equal phenomena (see chapter 7). Zeitlin is also of this opinion. He feels that one must draw a distinction between those who are dissatisfied with their work because they have no control over the means of production, i.e., because they do not have power, and those who are simply dissatisfied with the type of work they have. Only the first group can reasonably be considered to be alienated. The second is just dissatisfied.

Therefore Zeitlin made a special study of workers whose attitude toward work had altered from negative to positive (i.e., sixty-four workers) and asked them why this change had taken place. He divided them into two groups: (1) those who gave as a reason for change the fact that an end had been put to alienation or, more precisely, to alienating circumstances within the social structure; (2) those who gave as a reason for change an improvement in work conditions. In the first group were categorized answers which had, for instance, the following content:[29] "We worked for the boss before. We work for ourselves now." Or: "The difference is the following: Before I worked for another individual or for a company. Now I work for the people, that is to provide new hospitals, houses, etc., and whatever else the country needs most." In the second category were placed replies such as: "Now I have secure work. I don't worry about getting sacked or laid off," or "Now if I want to talk to a fellow I don't have to look over my shoulder." Zeitlin compared reasons for dissatisfaction with work before the revolution with attitudes toward the revolution.

Reason for dissatisfaction before the revolution	Attitude toward the revolution			
	Favorable	Indecisive	Hostile	N
Alienating conditions	100%	0%	0%	25
Other reason	74%	15%	10%	39

Of the first group 84 percent had a *very* favorable attitude to the revolution, against 61 percent of the second group who stated this. Those workers who gave as a reason for a change in their attitude to work the fact that alienating conditions had been done away with, showed a more positive attitude to the revolution than those who stated the other reason.

[29] Ibid., pp. 206–9.

Zeitlin says that one can argue that this is self-evident. Those who had experienced a feeling of alienation to work before the revolution, would naturally support the revolution because it abolished private ownership. On the other hand, the results can be interpreted as supporting Marx's thesis that private ownership of the means of production leads to alienation. But to me Zeitlin's results seem to be more complex than this. As I see it, they can be summarized in the following hypothesis. In a capitalist society, workers who experience themselves as exploited feel alienated because the means of production are in private hands, and because as employees they have no influence over the process of production. For them, the *conditions of power* are of decisive importance. Those workers however, who are not happy with the work processes, and other conditions at their place of work, are *not alienated* but only dissatisfied, or fail to experience "enjoyment at work." Thus, there should be a clear difference between alienation and dissatisfaction. The consequence is that only the politically conscious workers are able to experience alienation; or, to express it in Marxist terminology, the experience of alienation presupposes class consciousness. Such a hypothesis is meaningful in many respects, among others in connection with the idea which in recent years has been put forward by socialist theoreticians in Western Europe. They have discussed the question of how workers can be made interested in socialism, after want and poverty—the main driving forces toward socialism—are no longer factors of importance. One of the answers has been that the work itself is alienating and that this alienation should be an important driving force in the adopting of a socialist position.[30] If Zeitlin's analysis and my hypothesis, which builds upon it, are realistic, then this should be incorrect. It is not alienation which makes the workers "class-conscious" (and therefore socialist) but rather it is, above all, "class-conscious" workers who experience alienation. For the others, the problem of work is a question of lack of satisfaction or enjoyment in their work.

But this hypothesis also has repercussions for the discussion of alienation in socialist societies. Perhaps workers there do not feel alienated, as Schaff assumes, because of the technology of the work process. Perhaps working at an assembly line *is different* if one experiences that the result of one's own work is taken care of by a powerful bureaucracy, or if— through elected workers' council as in Yugoslavia—one has influence on the work process as well as on the ways in which the result of the work is to be used. Thus alienation in work in socialist societies may be the consequence of existing power conditions as well as it may be in capitalist societies.

[30] A. Gorz, *Stratégie ouvrière et néocapitalisme* (Paris: Editions du Seuil, 1964).

9

THE PROBLEM OF REIFICATION

INTRODUCTION

All empirical theories in the social sciences are preceded by models of man, of society, and of the interaction of man and society. These models are of a normative kind and delimit the way empirical theories can be formulated. Their true nature is concealed, since they usually are not formulated explicitly but have to be deduced from statements forming parts of empirical theories. In addition, the statements of these models often are formulated as descriptive statements, which is a second reason for concealing their true nature. The more that theories concern macro-problems, the more clearly does their normative basis stand out. The more that theories are concerned with "positive facts" and nothing more, the less are the normative foundations made clear. In fact, if one accepts a positivistic position of studying only what can be empirically observed, the more one will tend to reject the idea of the normative foundations of empirical theories. Still one can find it. Thus traditional behaviorism has the normative notion "that all organisms, including man, are essentially passive automata controlled by the environment, whose sole purpose in life is the reduction of tensions by adaptive responses."[1] Whether this is the case or not cannot be decided by reference to empirical data, since these data in fact are a consequence of looking at the world through the glasses of these normative notions. Take another example: Homans's[2] theory of social behavior is partly built upon the mechanistic model of man prevalent in Skinnerian behaviorism, partly on elementary notions

[1] A. Koestler, *The Ghost in the Machine* (London: Pan Books, Ltd., 1970), p. 17.
[2] G. C. Homans, *Social Behavior: Its Elementary Forms* (Harcourt, Brace & World, 1961).

of utility to be found in neoclassical economics. Thus Homans has assured himself a double and therefore really secure normative basis.[3]

Marx's original theory of alienation is build upon ideas that man realizes himself by work, that ideal work is creative work, and that values are created by human work only. It can be shown, as Myrdal has done,[4] that such notions are founded in natural law: property has its natural justification in the labor bestowed upon an object. However, if man is not allowed to appropriate the products of his work, he will feel alienated. Thus alienation has a double root. (1) Man cannot realize himself through creative work, since division of labor transforms work into routinized activity. (2) The institution of private property of means of production prevents man from appropriating the product of his work. The first notion, concerning creative work as the central aspect of man's nature, Marx had taken over from German romanticist philosophy, and he abandoned it quite early. The second idea, however, he never abandoned.

The basic notion of man's nature which was substituted for the first one can be summarized as the notion of man's self-generation. Marx postulates that man is the creator of his own world, of which at the same time he is a product. This dialectical notion of man's basic nature and activity can be understood only if it is placed in a historical context. Man creates his own world in a dual way. First, he creates in the process of production objects for the satisfaction of his needs. Second, he also creates the social institutions within which the process of production, distribution, and consumption is organized. These social institutions function as social facts in the sense that Durkheim uses the term. They exist before and independently of the individual and constrain his actions. However, this does not mean that they are not created by man. It means only that they are created in earlier phases of the historical development. Man then is born into existing institutions and is affected by them. In this sense he creates his social world and is created by it.

The process of social production as mentioned satisfies his needs. There is a tendency for continuous development of the tools of the production process, e.g., in developing technology. The advancing technology, however, does not only create products that satisfy needs, but also creates new needs, which in turn are incentives for the development of new technological means. Thus, the central idea in Marx's image of man

---

[3] See, for detailed treatment, J. Israel, "Postulates and Construction in the Social Sciences." in *The Context of Social Psychology*, ed. J. Israel and H. Tajfel (forthcoming).

[4] G. Myrdal, *The Political Element in the Development of Economic Theory* (London: Routledge & Kegan Paul, 1965).

is that of unlimited potentials which man has as a species. The question becomes, then, whether man uses his potentials in a "rational way". Now "rational way" cannot be defined without reference to certain value standards. For Marx "rational" means planning the process of production in such a way that man governs the social forces he has created and is not governed by them as by blind forces. Furthermore it means the just distribution of the social product, leading to the abolishment of want and poverty. The question then became for the Marx: Why does man not act in a "rational way"? One of his answers was that the functioning of the capitalistic economic system makes this impossible. The goal of this system is to produce for profit, and this can be done by producing commodities which can be sold on a market. To produce for profit is not considered as a psychological motive, but as a sociological characteristic inherent in the economic system. Capitalists would not survive if they did not follow the rules of the system. Now the system also has a tendency to transform man into an object—a commodity—both as labor power and as consuming power. In the first case he sells his work; in the second he buys commodities whether he "needs" them or not. This process of transformation of man into objects or things can be called "reification." A sociological analysis shows that the abolishment of private property of means of production does not, as Marx thought, solve the problem. Instead a state capitalism may arise, as in the Soviet Union, in which man still is labor power though not consuming power and in which, moreover, he becomes an object for a large bureaucratic apparatus. The tendency for bureaucratization, however, also is found in societies with a capitalistic system and is due to the development of technology.

The reification of man is, in addition, maintained by the development of psychological and sociological theories which postulate man as a passive mechanism and which assume that modern technology has its own inner logic that cannot be changed and to which man has to subordinate himself whether he wishes or not. Thus the central problem becomes: How is it possible to stop and change the reification of man, and how is it possible to reveal these theories which are reified and therefore strengthen man's factual reification? One solution is the acceptance of the basic principle of methodological individualism as an alternative: that there does not exist any social tendency which "could not be altered *if* the individuals concerned both wanted to alter it and possessed the appropriate information."[5] The problem then becomes, as Schopenhauer

[5] J. W. N. Watkins, "Methodological Individualism and Social Tendencies," in *Readings in the Philosophy of Social Science*, ed. M. Brodbeck (New York: The Macmillan Co., 1968), p. 271.

once stated: "Man can will what he wants, he can, however, not will what he wills." Perhaps, therefore, the task of the social sciences ought to be to search for the "unintended social repercussions of intentional human actions"[6] in order to increase the chances for man to will what he wills.

Is "Alienation" a Theoretically Fruitful Concept?

AMBIGUITY AND VAGUENESS

The discussion of theories of alienation, starting with the formulations they originally received in Marx's theorizing, and of the ways in which the theories have been developed in current empirical–positivistic sociology, has, if nothing else, shown the *ambiguity* of the term "alienation" and the *vagueness* with which the concept has been used.

Following the usual procedure we will make a distinction here between *ambiguity* and *vagueness*.[7]

Vagueness is a characteristic pertaining to a *concept* and its meaning. "I shall say that a concept is vague when there easily occurs uncertainty, whether a thing should be classified as falling under the concept or not, and when this uncertainty cannot be removed by appealing either to (further) *facts* about the case or to existing *criteria* for the application of the concept."[8]

In this sense it is easy to show—and in fact this book should be a proof of it—that the concept of alienation is vague.

Ambiguity, on the other hand, refers to the characteristics of a certain *word*. "Ambiguity may be defined as a (logically) accidental identity of words standing for different ideas."[9]

Now again, this book should have proved that there is a great variety of ideas for which the word *alienation* is used. This is probably not purely accidental because some of the ideas are related to each other. However, it has been pointed out that the word is used to denote many and completely different phenomena. It may refer to sociological processes, as well as to psychological states. In addition, identical or similar phenomena have been denoted by different terms. Thus, in some cases the same phenomenon has interchangeably been labeled *alienation or anomie*.

---

[6] K. Popper, *Conjectures and Refutations*, 3rd ed. (London: Routledge & Kegan Paul, 1969), p. 342.

[7] G. H. von Wright, *The Varieties of Goodness* (London: Routledge & Kegan Paul, 1963).

[8] Ibid., p. 14.

[9] Ibid.

In this book I have tried to treat theories of alienation which concern certain and, in my own opinion, central sociological factors: the social conditions under which individuals produce the material and mental conditions for their own life. It is these conditions which have been called by Marx "mode of production" and which in modern sociological theory, in a rather more limited sense, are usually called "conditions of work." Therefore the theories of alienation which have been taken up deal, to a large extent, with the individual's relation to his work, with the social relations between individuals during the process of production, with power conditions and social stratification, and also (as, for example, in the theories developed by Allardt, see chapter 7) with the conditions of social interaction and social exchange in general.

A systematic attempt to describe and analyze current sociological and psychological literature (which I have not tried to achieve) would have resulted in the unearthing of a large number of books and articles that use the term *alienation*, dealing with everything from low participation in elections, race discrimination and other social conflicts, to individual neurotic behavior.

A term which has been used to denote such a wide variety of phenomena may possibly be valuable in political communication—though I doubt it—but certainly not in a more scientific context. There is the risk of its losing its value as a term that can be used in a theoretically fruitful way.

I do not think it would be impossible to carry out a semantic analysis which would make possible the delimiting of the phenomena denoted by the term. Having arrived at such a definition one could go on to analyze the concept to which the term refers, and determine its meaning. In fact, part of my endeavor has been devoted to the attempt to analyze and give an explication of the concept as it has been used by Marx and others. However, I prefer to use terms within sociological and social-psychological theories which do not carry with them the burden of ambiguous usage to such an extent. For that reason I would suggest that the term *alienation* be discarded from sociological and social-psychological theorizing and that other, more clearly delimited, terms be used in its place. For example, I find it difficult to understand why one defines alienation as powerlessness, normlessness, meaninglessness, etc. Would it not be just as easy to use terms such as *powerlessness, normlessness*, etc.? This should be particularly true since in this case one attempts only a preliminary classification of some dimensions without trying to construct a theoretical structure of their relations.

However, let me stress that the first reason given for rejecting the term *alienation* is not the most important. The other, which I will now mention, seems to me to be of much greater importance.

VALUE PREMISES

There are further objections to the use of the term *alienation*. Assuming that it is possible to make the concept precise, the next problem is the following. An analysis of theories of alienation presupposes the analysis of the implicit or explicit assumptions of such theories. I have tried to show in my analysis that the term *alienation* as used by Marx presupposes certain theories concerning man and his nature and certain theories concerning society and its structure, and finally certain assumptions concerning the relationship between man and society. I have also tried to show that all these theories concerning human nature, the nature of society, and the relationship between individuals and society contain normative elements which are a part of those theories. These concern, among others things, the evaluation of work as human activity and as activity which makes possible self-realization. I have also tried to show that value-premises, often implicit, are to be found in more limited empirical theories (see, for example, the discussion concerning the assumptions made by Blauner, page 220).

Sociological theories often build upon definite value premises even if the creators of the theories are not necessarily conscious of this or are often unwilling to admit it. I do not consider that it is wrong to create a theory having its starting point in certain value premises, but certain demands should first be met. First, all the value premises should be stated in a clear and explicit manner.[10] Second, certain demands should be made regarding the value premises. They must be realistic in a certain sense, where "realistic" can be defined as, e.g., in the way the Yugoslavian philosopher and sociologist Marković" does it. He analyzes theories of human nature as preconditions for theories of society and says that, in order to be realistic and useful, each idea about how man *ought* to be should be based on an objective evaluation of the actual possibilities for his development. Such an objective evaluation is possible only on the basis of reliable knowledge about how man actually *is*. This is especially true if one assumes that "human nature" is not something definite, but rather that it develops in the course of the historical development of man and society. This is one of the central points in the second theory of man developed by Marx (see page 56). However, Marx's first anthropological theories of man, as developed in *Economic and Philosophical Manu-*

---

[10] See Gunnar Myrdal's treatment of the value problem in *Value in Social Theory* (London: Routledge & Kegan Paul, 1958), or in the prologue to the first volume of *Asian Drama* (London: Penguin Books, 1969). See also the treatment of the problem in T. S. Simey, *Social Science and Social Purpose* (London: Constable and Co., 1968).

[11] M. Marković, "Marxist Humanism and Ethics," *Inquiry* VI (1963), 18–34.

scripts, were of such a nature that one may question whether they were "realistic" in the sense in which the term is used by Marković.

When Marković develops his theory concerning a "realistic" approach to human nature, he suggests five characteristics typical of man. We will present them in addition to those which have been asserted by others and which we have presented previously. In Marković's view man is an *active, social*, and *rational* being. He continuously *creates* new knowledge and in a certain sense is *free*—he can choose between various alternatives which exist for him or to which he has access.

So far the description of man presented by Marković does not create problems. Its emphasis on *rational* aspects rather than on emotional and unconscious motivation is in the tradition of Western philosophy and corresponds with Marx's own view. The same holds true for the emphasis on activity and creativeness and on man's basic social character. The problems first arise when one tries to apply this *description* of human nature and to make it the basis for a theory of human behavior within a *social context*. Then it is no longer possible to talk about man as an "active being." One must also specify the *type of activity* instrumental for certain social goals.

Marković himself points out that man's activity can be both constructive and destructive. Thus, we have to introduce normative or ethical standards as to which activity is desirable in a certain social context and which is not. In other words, one must develop a theory regarding how man *ought* to be active in relation to certain goals.

Being active in a constructive and in a destructive way are examples of desirable and nondesirable characteristics. Therefore, when developing a theory of man in which "being active" is a central characteristic, one first must establish criteria in order to be able to decide whether or not something represents this characteristic of "being active." However, in addition to these criteria one must also have criteria which makes it possible to evaluate whether different activities are desirable or nondesirable. These criteria should (if one does not accept what we usually call "destructive activities" as desirable) form the basis for the evaluation and recommendation of *specific* activities, in order to avoid speaking about "activity" in a very general way.

There are still more problems. Usually it is possible to determine whether or not an action can be characterized as "constructive" or "destructive" only by taking into account the consequences of the action. For example, is the research work which led to the construction of an atom bomb a constructive or destructive activity? Was the work of German physicists in the U.S. who were refugees from Hitler's Germany more constructive than the work of the German physicists who remained in Hitler's Germany? We shall not attempt to initiate a discussion concerning these complicated problems, which are usually dealt with within the framework of utilitarian ethics. Let us return to the young Marx and his normative theory of human nature.

One of the central theses in Marx's writing is that man's activity, including his work activity, must be considered and judged in relation to the social context in which he lives. Man's activity occurs within a definite social system and is determined by the existing conditions of the basic process of material production, as are his social relations with other men. However, the question is whether the first theory of alienation, as developed in the *Manuscripts*, takes given conditions or a normative theory as its point of departure. If the latter is the case, then the question becomes whether these normative conditions appear today as *realistic* ones.

My hypothesis is that young Marx's theory concerning man's nature contained value premises which were anchored in a specific historical period characterized by specific conditions: it was a situation marked by the transition from the artisan to the industrial level of production. The rapid development of productive forces places new demands on man and his social relations in the process of production. Marx's theory of man as developed in the *Manuscripts* was characterized by romantic ideas and notions concerning the nature of work, which, in my opinion, were influenced by the historical situation preceding the process of industrialization.

However, this theory of man is a necessary—though sometimes implicit—condition for the formulation of his first theory of alienation. But already in *The German Ideology* Marx abandoned his anthropological theory (see page 56) and changed his ideas concerning alienation. Thus, there is an interaction between his new theory of man and his changed view regarding alienation. The latter demands new premises, contained in the new theory of man, and this theory shifts the emphasis in his new theory of alienation to what we will discuss as "reification."

In the *Manuscripts* Marx developed a theory concerning the relationship between man's nature and the type of work he was forced to carry out under the social conditions of early capitalist society. He considered this type of labor to be *external* to the worker "that is it not a part of his *nature*"[12] (my italics). Why was it not a part of his nature? First, because the worker was unable to "fulfill himself in his work,"[13] second, because he could not freely develop his "physical and mental energy,"[14]

---

[12] *Mega I.3*, p. 85.
[13] Ibid.
[14] Ibid.

and third, because work was no longer a need in itself, but only "a means for satisfying other needs."

As pointed out earlier (see chapter 4), Marx has a notion partly concerning "ideal man" and partly concerning "ideal labor." These two notions are the basis of this theory of alienation: He relates *factual* labor determined by historical conditions to *his notion of ideal labor* and finds a discrepancy: therefore labor is alienated labor—alienated from the ideal of labor. The worker himself has an emotionally influenced perception of his work and experiences a discrepancy. Since his labor does not fulfill basic needs in his "ideal" personality, he *feels* alienated.

Thus "the approach to this problem had the consequence that the young Marx did not consider that which later was at the center of his interest, namely, the analysis of how a special social form of activity grows out of the relations between *one* concrete individual to another (or many others), how this activity becomes an isolated one in the continued development of the real relations between individuals, and how finally this activity becomes an alien force," says the Soviet Russian philosopher Dawydow[15] in an intriguing analysis of the problem. He adds that Marx's conclusions depend on the normative ideals which precede and form the point of departure of his analysis. Marx's ideal of labor contains notions concerning individual self-realization through work, notions which also are found in later sociological theories.

The ideas concerning self-realization appear now to have been influenced by the existing conditions in preindustrialized, precapitalist society, being a part of the romanticist criticism of industrialized society. Among other things this criticism contained nostalgic, though probably not very realistic, views as to the work situation of the artisan, whose situation probably influenced Marx's ideal. The artisan could perhaps be seen as able to realize himself in his work activity. In a society marked by a highly developed level of productive forces—to use a Marxian term—labor assumes quite a different character for the majority of people than it had for the artisan of an earlier historical level of development. Today it is probable that only a minority of people carry out work activity that creates a feeling of self-realization, an activity in which they can express their creative abilities as could the artisan. For many people work is a tedious, monotonous, and routine activity. This seems to be true whether the social system in which they work can be characterized as capitalist or socialist. As has been indicated, it is no less monotonous to work at an assembly line in a factory in the U.S. than to do so in the Soviet Union. In both countries work is a commodity and is

15 J. N. Dawydow, *Freiheit und Entfremung* (Berlin: VEB Deutscher Verlag der Wissenschaften, 1964), p. 49.

paid for as such. Therefore it has an instrumental value: it is the method of obtaining means to satisfy needs and desires. (However, reports, e.g., from Cuba,[16] show that involvement in work changes when the work is perceived as a means of reaching social goals in a society undergoing radical social change, and when the individual identifies himself with these social goals.)

The question is whether the interpretation of self-realization presented here is correct. "Individual self-realization" can be conceived of as the individual's realization of his own abilities, talents, strivings, goals, etc., without taking into consideration the social context within which such a realization can take place. Is it this type of "individualistic" and "egoistic" self-realization that the young Marx is thinking of when he discusses the problem?

Another interpretation is possible. As early as in the essay "The Jewish Question,"[17] he analyzes the distinction between man as an individual and man as a social being, stressing the fact that human emancipation means the socialization of man, i.e., the transformation of his "individual, egoistic being" into a "social, cooperative" one.

Thus, one may suggest another interpretation of self-realization: "Since the individuals mutually define each other through their social relations, occurring in a historically determined social context, 'individual self-realization' is possible only as one aspect of a collective realization."[18] Marx was probably concerned not so much with individual self-realization as with humanity.

Therefore the main argument against Marx's first theory of alienation is not the objection that self-realization through labor is a non-realistic normative precondition for this theory. The main argument must be directed against his conception regarding the ideal of labor and the ideal relation man ought to have to his work activity.

Another argument against the theory of alienation is of a more empirical nature. Marx states three social conditions for the development of alienation: private property, labor power as a commodity, and division of labor. The question is to what degree these three conditions are dependent on the organization of society, i.e., its social system and/or its level of technology. Only one condition, that concerning private ownership of means of production, can be shown to be dependent on the structure of the social system. The process of the division of labor—both

---

[16] M. Zeitlin, *Revolutionary Politics and the Cuban Working Class* (Princeton: Princeton University Press, 1967).

[17] *Mega I.1*, p. 599.

[18] G. Fredriksson, "Alienation eller reifikation," *Socialistisk Debatt* No. 3 (1968), 34.

with regard to that occurring within the process of production and that which occurs within society, e.g., between manual and intellectual work— is also concerned with the level of technological development. The third factor, labor power as a commodity, is also found, e.g., in the Soviet Union. It is thus necessary to supplement the Marxian dichotomy, *capitalist* vs. *socialist* type of social system, with another variable, namely, *high* vs. *low* level of technological development.

The three causal factors, then, seem to be the consequence of a complicated societal structure in which ownership conditions and technological factors interact.[19]

A final argument against the first theory of alienation lies in a distinction between "concrete" and "abstract" labor made by Marx and further developed by Sebag.[20] "Concrete" labor is activity which is understood and experienced as such, and cannot be traced back to other kinds of activity. "Abstract labor" is general consumption of energy regardless of the purpose for which the energy is used.

Sebag maintains that in his sociological analyses Marx compared concrete with abstract labor. This comparison made it possible to explain the functioning of the capitalist society. *Concrete* labor is the activity carried out by such artisans as the blacksmith, the carpenter, and the tailor, resulting in products, which were created by a man's activity. Concrete labor meant (1) the use of certain manual abilities, (2) the use of a certain material, (3) the production of a product with a definite relation to the need of the buyers, for whom it was often produced.

Abstract labor is the labor that characterizes industrialized society, which produces for a market. Through the division of labor, man is a part of a system in which—within certain limits—he can be exchanged for and substituted by other subject, such a substitution having no effect on the production process. To use prevalent sociological terminology— the individuals have certain roles associated with certain positions and characterized by the fact that role-behavior is largely independent of individual characteristics. As far as the functioning and goal-achievement of the system is concerned, it is not important who is the incumbent of a position.

Men are no longer individuals in the production process, and their varying characteristics do not influence this process to any marked extent. The concrete relations between producers and consumers have been broken down, and in its place impersonal relations have been

---

[19] One could also assert that the occurrence of, e.g., labor power as a commodity in the Soviet Union indicates that there does not exist a socialist but a state capitalist system.

[20] L. Sebag, *Marxisme et structuralisme* (Paris: Payot, 1964).

established, through a market in which the value of commodities is determined by price-mechanism and exchange-conditions. The result is that the individuals, as well as the products, have been transformed into commodities, impersonal things which can easily be substituted by other commodities.

If this description of social conditions influencing labor activity is correct, the normative basis of a theory of alienation must be changed. The problem is no longer the individual's relation to his work, but his position within the basic process of production and exchange. The fact that man is transformed from an active, working subject into labor power, from an individual having various talents and abilities to an exchangable commodity, from an active subject into a passive object, into a thing, should have a deep influence on the normative premises for a theory of alienation.

The acceptance of this reasoning leads to several consequences. First, there is a change of emphasis from labor and working conditions to the analysis of the structure of the basic process of social production and the ways in which the social product is distributed, i.e., to commodity relations and market conditions. Second, it presupposes a change in the theory concerning human nature from a philosophical-anthropological to a sociological-normative theory. Third, there is a shift from problems of self-realization—individual and collective—to problems of the rational and conscious organization of social processes and social development: How can man direct and regulate the social forces he himself has created rather than being blindly subjugated to their influence and dominance?—this becomes the central problem. How, in the light of the development of technology and bureaucratization, can social conditions be created which guarantee an existence worthy of human beings? What are man's chances of using social and material resources in a planned and systematic way and in cooperation with other men in order to realize certain basic ideals as are referred to by such terms as *democracy, equality, liberty,* and so on.

The threefold change, i.e., other normative preconditions and goals, as well as a change of emphasis in the sociological analysis, can be summarized as the transition from a theory of *alienation* to a theory of *reification,* a change which is implied in the theoretical development in Marx's thinking. This change is understood when one compares his *Manuscripts* with *German Ideology* and the writings which followed, culminating in *Capital.*

The first argument against the use of the term *alienation* in theories concerning basic societal processes was of a logical-semantic kind. The second is of a theoretical kind: Theories of alienation are often anchored in normative theories that can be seen as unrealistic in the sense that they do not sufficiently take into account existing social conditions, which have altered not only the conditions of living but also man's "nature," as this term refers to a structure which has been molded and changed in a historical process.

Our third argument against the use of *alienation* is also of a theoretical nature.

THE CONTRADICTION BETWEEN INDIVIDUAL AND SOCIETY

In the first chapter we maintained that theories concerning man's alienation usually presuppose assumptions or theories concerning conflicts, or contradictions, between the individual and society. These contradictions are usually considered to be antagonistic. Either the individual has to renounce some of his basic strivings in order to subordinate himself to society, or society's demands have to be changed in order to allow individual self-realization. Implicit in these theories, usually, are notions concerning balance or equilibrium, either being strived for by the individual or being a precondition of the "normal functioning" of a society. The states of balance within society are disturbed by individual strivings, whereas states of balance within the individual are disturbed by societal demands.

If such assumptions underlie theories of alienation, and can perhaps even be considered as necessary conditions for such theories, an important question is how reasonable such assumptions really are.

One might assert that both individual-oriented and society-oriented theories of alienation are reified theories (for the definition of "reified theories" see page 326). Both types of theories look at the "individual" and/or "society" in an abstract way, without taking into account the fact that an individual and his wishes are influenced and shaped by other individuals to whom he relates. At the same time "society" is, as Marx repeatedly points out, the sum total of all social relations. In addition "society" is those organizations in which these relations occur and those institutions which regulate their interaction in a normative way. "Society" is nothing but individuals interacting with each other, individually and in groups. "Society" has a certain structure related to the basic process of social production, created by man and his goals and divided into substructures. In turn these substructures (political, economic, etc.) influence the behavior of their members who are influenced by the social structure. Thus, from a sociological point of view, it is irrelevant to construct an antagonism between "the individual" and "the society." Antagonism and conflicts occur *between* groups within the total system of a society; and these conflicts are, according to Marx, related to the mode of production which is dominant within a society: the conflict is a consequence of the level of development of the productive forces and the ways in which the social relations are organized in the process of social production.

In Marx's own words, "all production is acquisition of nature through the individual within and by means of a certain social structure."[21] Thus another—though perhaps less important—interpretation is that in Marx's theories man does not stand in opposition to society, but in opposition to "nature," in the struggle for his livelihood.

Either one tries to interpret Marx's conflict theory as conflicts occuring *within* society, or as the "conflict between man and nature" (the two interpretations are not mutually exclusive); implicitly or explicitly there cannot be found any antagonism between *man and society* in the theoretical development of Marx's thoughts after the writings of *Manuscripts*. Thus, if we assert that notions concerning the existence of antagonistic states between the individual and society are necessary conditions for a theory of alienation, then either this assumption is false, or the absence of such assumptions suggests that theories of alienation are unfounded. However, the problem is eliminated when one makes the transition from a theory of alienation to a theory of reification. In this case we can abandon all notions which regard man as alien either to his nature or to society because of the basic contradiction between men and society. "Reification" denotes a social process concerning men's relation to each other and to the objects of their activity. Consequently, the problems are located *within* society, and in addition there occurs a shift from a psychological to a sociological level of analysis: If "reification" refers to a process in which social relations gain the character of "relations between things," i.e., lose their social meaning, then it is sufficient to describe the conditions under which such social processes occur and to analyze their social consequences.

So transition from a theory of alienation to a theory of reification is not only in accordance with the theoretical development of Marx's thinking, but also, and much more important, it disentangles this theory from erroneous and even metaphysical preconditions. Therefore our third reason for casting aside theories of alienation is distinct from our second reason, as it renders unnecessary the making of certain assumptions about society, whereas our second argument tried to dissociate itself from certain notions concerning human nature.

ALIENATION AND REIFICATION

It is desirable to return for a moment to the relationship between the terms *alienation* and *reification*. In Figure 2 (chapter 3) I attempted an

[21] K. Marx, *Grundrisse der Kritik der Politischen Ökonomie* (*Rohentwurf*), (Berlin: Dietz Verlag, 1953), p. 9.

explication of the various terms and concepts. *Alienation* was there defined as a social process with a broad meaning. *Reification* was considered as one type of social process, which could be subsumed under *alienation*. Reification, therefore, seems to be a more specific social process, occurring under certain social conditions and leading to certain social consequences. As indicated above, an analysis of reification can be carried out on a sociological and not a psychological level. One psychological problem can, however, be studied, namely, the ways in which reifying social processes are perceived and experienced.

Though the concept of *reification* is more limited than the concept of *alienation*, it is still sufficiently general to allow one to study social processes occurring in societies having varying social structures, e.g., capitalist as well as socialist societies. Reifying processes in societies with different social structures will probably have different characteristics, and the emphasis may be changed. But, in general, a theory of reification has a wide range of application. Its political importance has been characterized in the following way: "Our current historical situation thus makes it clear again and again that social institutions—social-economic conditions, which produced man's social process of production, political organizations (e.g., the state) and legal norms, but also political theorems—raise themselves as independent powers above those human beings, who have created them. . . . As long as this situation exists, it will also be a continuous task to make man master of his own history. . . ."[22]

THE BACKGROUND TO THE THEORY OF REIFICATION

THE FETISHISM OF COMMODITIES

Berger and Luckman[23] point out that it is a paradoxical situation, that man is capable of creating a complicated world and at the same time can experience his own creation as something impersonal, existing independently of human beings and their activity. Man can experience the fact that social organizations have their own laws outside human control and influence.

Marx dealt with the same problem. How is it, he asks, that the social system, which man has created, appears as something "given by nature"? Society—its institutions and organizations as well as the forms they have taken—is a product of historical development: "The universally developed individuals, whose social conditions are regulated by their own

---

[22] W. Abendroth, *Antagonistische Gesellschaft und politische Demokratie* (Neuwied: Luchterhand, 1967).

[23] P. Berger and T. Luckman, *The Social Construction of Reality* (Garden City: Doubleday & Co., 1966), p. 57.

common social relations as well as by their own common social control, are not products of nature but products of history."[24] The fact that these conditions appear as alien, objective, and independent, Marx continues, proves only that men have not tried to plan and create them in a systematic and conscious goal-directed way. They are created by men without long-term planning and without an understanding of the long-term consequences of their own actions.

This is especially marked in a society dominated by a market structure and an economic system in which the products of human labor are commodities and in which man himself is transformed into a commodity.

Marx makes a distinction between "factual conditions" and the "shape" in which these condition "appear." Marx maintains that a commodity, for example, is on a superficial level, something self-evident, even something trivial. As long as it has a *use-value*, it means only that it has certain characteristics which can satisfy human needs. It is when objects become exchange-products and receive an exchange-value that their character is no longer self-evident, but becomes mystified.

Men produce with each other and for each other. In the basic process of production they establish certain social relations with each other. That was also true between producer and consumer, and seller and buyer, as long as the products were not produced for an impersonal market. However, when things are produced for a market, their value is no longer determined by their ability to satisfy needs, but by laws, e.g., those of demand and supply, which give these products an exchange-value and transform them into commodities.

The social character of the process of production is no longer clear to the individual, and labor tends to become something objective, something which appears as a thing, rather than as social relations. The fact, for instance, that men carry out the *same type of work* in a process of interaction appears to those people who see only the end products, as the *equal value* of these products. The fact that man must use a certain *amount of working time* stands out "objectively" as the *size of the value* of the products. *Social relations* between producers are hidden by the conditions of the market, by the ways with which the products are bought and sold. To quote Marx: "Whence, then, arises the enigmatical character of the product of labor, as soon as it assumes the form of commodities? Clearly from this form itself. The equality of all sorts of human labor is expressed objectively by their products all being equally valued; the measure of expenditure of labor power by the duration of that expenditure takes the form of the quantity of value of the products of

[24] Marx, *Grundrisse*, p. 79.

labor; and finally, the mutual relations of the producers, within which the social character of their labor affirms itself, takes the form of a social relation between the products."[25]

Thus the fact the we buy and sell objects or things impersonally, i.e., where objects sold are not produced for certain, known consumers, makes us forget that the production, as well as the distribution of products, is a social process. It also leads to the decreasing importance of human beings as producers although the value of objects is increased. Thus, men become unimportant and things important. In the production process machines are often considered more valuable than human beings. Effectiveness and profits are preferred to human values. All these social phenomena are referred to by Marx as the role of commodities within capitalist society.

"A commodity," says Marx "is therefore a mysterious thing, simply because in it the social character of men's labor appears to them as an objective character stamped upon the product of that labor; because the relation of the producers to the sum total of their own labor is presented to them as a social relation, existing not between themselves, but between the products of their labor."[26]

Commodities gain a life of their own, which appears as independent of human action. Goldmann asserts[27] that this notion has become a fundamental psychological reality, which among other things is reflected in our language habits. We say, for example, that "a certain enterprise yields profits" or "the stock market shows a rising tendency" or "the price of raw material is falling." This is not simply a reflection of our need to shorten our communication, i.e., to make it less redundant, as it is faster to say "an enterprise gives profit" than "the workers and engineers working in this enterprise are producing profits." Goldmann maintains that our language is reflecting a general ideology or a certain value-system, in which notions of the independence of economic factors are predominant and in which the role of human beings in the production process is reduced.

Marx suggests that in order to find an analogy to the commodity phenomenon, one "must have recourse to the mist-enveloped regions of the religious world. In that world the productions of the human brain appear as independent beings endowed with life, and entering into relations both with one another and the human race. So it is in the world of commodities with the products of men's hands. I call this the fetishism which

[25] K. Marx, *Capital*, German edition (Berlin: Dietz Verlag, 1965), Vol. I, p. 7.

[26] Ibid., p. 72.

[27] L. Goldmann, *Recherches dialectiques* (Paris: Librairie Gallimard, 1959).

attaches itself to the products of labor as soon as they are produced as commodities, and which is therefore inseparable from the production of commodities."

This fetishism of commodities has its origin, as the foregoing analysis has already shown, in the peculiar social character of the labor that produces them.

> As a general rule, articles of utility become commodities only because they are products of the labor of private individuals, or groups of individuals, who carry out their work independently of each other. The sum total of the labor of all these private individuals forms the aggregate labor of society. Since the producers do not come into contact with each other until they exchange their products, the specified social character of the labor of each producer reveal itself only in the act of exchange. In other words, the labor of the individual reveals itself as a part of the labor of society, only by means of the relations which the act of exchange establishes directly between the products, and, through them, indirectly between the producers. To the latter, therefore, the relations connecting the labor of one individual with that of the rest appear not as direct social relations between individuals at work, but, as they really are, material relations between persons and social relations between things.[28]

The fetish character of commodities depends on the social organization of the process of production. Marx also calls this "total labor process." All individuals participate in this "total labor process" and are dependent on each other. The dependence is often mutual dependence. However, no common goals for production and the use of the products exist because production takes place for a market and the use of the products is determined by their exchange-value. The social and cooperative character of the total labor process is also veiled by the fact that the interacting individuals have little or no influence over this process. Since no common goals exist and since the individuals have little or no influence, they become indifferent to each other and to each other's needs. They exchange their labor or labor-power for money, and use this money to buy objects. Social relations between individuals are transformed into exchange relations of a nonsocial kind, in which the individual perceives himself as an object, as a commodity, and in which he perceives others as objects. Thus the total process of social interaction appears as an exchange of objects in the form of commodities, i.e., of certain exchange-values.

Because commodities are things, and as things play such a dominant

28 Marx, *Capital*, Vol. I, p. 73.

role in the interaction process, individuals perceive that they are dominated and ruled by things. In turn, this strengthens their experience of powerlessness based on a real lack of influence.

In the capitalist mode of production it is necessary to transform products of labor into commodities, since the production process is directed by the market, i.e., by the exchange of commodities. This analysis, which make capitalist modes of production responsible for the commodity relations, can, however, be questioned in the light of the economic development of the socialist countries in the Soviet sphere.

Marx continues his analysis by saying that one should not, as economists usually do, accept the commodity as something self-evident, as a starting point for an analysis. Rather, he says, one should question the starting point and study the ways in which products of labor are transformed into commodities. One will find that the capitalist mode of production with private ownership of means of production is a necessary condition for the circulation of commodities which in turn influence the process of production. Interestingly enough, such analysts of modern corporations as Galbraith[28] stress the fact that these corporations have a strong tendency to control the laws of the market or to abolish "free market conditions." This is accomplished by means of control over the material necessary for production, control over labor, and control over the process of consumption through the influencing and controlling of consumers and their behavior. Thus the development of the productive forces has led to the creation of large corporations, which in turn can function only through long-term planning and control of the conditions of production and the sales of the products. Thus the fetishism of commodities seems to be substituted, or at least supplemented, by the actions of large, impersonal bureaucratic organizations.

Marx had another vision. He says that by developing other models of production all the mystery surrounding commodities and their world disappears. We need only think of a community of free producers, who jointly own the means of production and who experience their individual labor power in a self-conscious way as a part of the total societal labor power. Their production will be social; their product jointly owned. A part of this social product will be reinvested and therefore used to create new jointly owned means of production. Another part is distributed among the members of the society according to the amount of time they have placed at the disposal of society. Working time in such a social system has a dual function. Its planned use determines what can be produced. At the same time it is a measure of the individual's part in the total social product. In Marx's own words:

[29] J. K. Galbraith, *The New Industrial State* (London: Hamish Hamilton, 1967).

This vision of the future society is as follows: Let us now picture to ourselves, by way of change, a community of free individuals, carrying on their work with the means of production in common, in which the labor power of all the different individuals is consciously applied as the combined labor power of the community. . . . The total product of our community is a social product. One portion serves as fresh means of production and remains social. But another portion is consumed by the members as means of subsistence. A distribution of this portion among them is consequently necessary. The mode of distribution will vary with the productive organization of the community, and the degree of historical development attained by the producers. . . .

The social relations of the individual producers, with regard both to their labor and to its products, are in this case perfectly simple and intelligible, and that with regard not only to production but also to distribution.[30]

This simple and ingenious solution, which Marx sketches, has rarely been achieved not even where an application of his theories has been attempted. In the Soviet Union, too, commodities, and therefore commodity relations, exist. Labor power is still a commodity. The producers are not free and organized in their own associations, but are ruled by powerful bureaucracies which plan and direct the total process of production and which have control over the ways in which the social product is distributed. This also refers to that part which goes to the producers, i.e., workers, for their own private consumption. It is evident that the distribution occurs according to principles which are different from the one Marx mentions: the amount of time made available by the subject to society and his participation in the total process of social production. Inequalities with regard to the distribution of the social product for private consumption has led to the development of new privileged strata (see chapter 8).

The change in the conditions of the basic process of social production, e.g., the abolishment of the private ownership of means of production, is perhaps a *necessary* condition for a planned economy. It is at any rate not a *sufficient* condition for the achievement of the basic changes in society in general, which was Marx's dream.

The question is whether commodities and commodity relations are a consequence of the *capitalist* mode of production or a consequence of the *industrialized* process of production. The question receives even greater justification when one discusses the development of the theory regarding fetishism of commodities.

In fact, the question concerning a market economy, including the commodity and exchange relations vs. planned economy, and the ques-

[30] Marx, *Capital*, Vol. I, pp. 78–79.

tion concerning the ownership of means of production, are two different, though related, problems. This is emphasized in the following quotation from an essay by a Swedish economist: "It cannot be emphasized strongly enough that adopting a position with regard to the principles of the market-economy has to be differentiated from the question concerning the choice of the structure of ownership."[31] The same author also points out that it is historical conditions which have created this mixing of the problem of ownership with that of the market economy. In other words, it is due to historically determined conditions that private ownership of the means of production and a market economy developed simultaneously. However, according to the previously quoted author, it is neither an economic nor a social necessity that they are interwoven with each other. As the development in the Soviet Union has shown, it is possible to combine socialized means of production, i.e., public ownership, with either a planned economy or an economy ruled by market mechanisms. At the same time, private ownership can be combined with a market economy and with governmental control and planning. Thus we can conceive of two continuous variables. One of these is laissez-faire market economy vs. planned and centrally controlled economy; the other is privately owned vs. publicly owned means of production.

The interesting problem here is that the analysis using continuous variables[32] is not in accordance with the common interpretation of Marxian theories, in which one uses dichotomic variables and conceives of capitalist and socialist social systems as completely opposed to each other and having no possibilities of transitions. The political consequence of such a view is the recommendation of a revolutionary social change as opposed to gradual reformist change. Again, the acceptance of continuous variables in the description and analysis of social system does not necessarily imply a recommendation of gradual social change, though empirically both these attitudes may go hand in hand. However, it is possible to describe society in terms of continuous variables and still recommend revolutionary social change.

Another problem should here be mentioned briefly. Marx conceives of capitalism as a necessary historical stage in a process characterized by a continuous development of the productive forces. In Marx's analysis capitalism develops when the process of industrialization starts and the development of productive forces, e.g., of a new technology, demands the accumulation of capital to a degree previously unknown. The ques-

---

[31] A. Lindbeck, "Fördelningspolitik i blandekonomin," in *Välståndsklyftor och standardhöjning* (Stockholm: Bokförlaget Prisma, 1967).

[32] G. Adler-Karlsson, *Functional Socialism* (Stockholm: Bokförlaget Prisma, 1969); and J. Israel, "Zwei Probleme des Sozialismus," in *Club Voltaire Jahrbuch für kritische Aufklärung* III, ed. G. Szczesny (München: Szczesny Verlag, 1967).

tion is: Would industrialization have been possible without capitalism? In other words, are private ownership and market-economy necessary conditions for the development of industrialized society, or is the relationship between these two structural variables only accidental? I do not wish to discuss here complex problems involving expressions such as "historical necessity," etc., because that would lead us into complicated problems of the theory of science and of the methodology of history. Instead, we can look at the actual development.

The thesis developed by Marx is also supported by other, non-Marxist, economists. Thus Keynes[33] asserts that economic development was built upon a social system which made possible large capital accumulation and that this accumulation was the precondition for industrialization. Keynes thinks that the fantastic accumulation of capital could not have occurred in a society in which wealth had been equally distributed. Instead two conditions were necessary for industrialization: on the one hand the accumulation of wealth in the hands of capitalists, who used it for new investments; and, on the other hand, a working class who, through ignorance, powerlessness, existing social values, and attitudes, etc., was forced, or was willing to accept, a situation in which they were exploited. So it seems that Keynes, too, accepts capitalism as a necessary stage in the historical process. However, the process of industrialization during the twenties and thirties in the Soviet Union, and the same process today in China, shows that the capital accumulation necessary for industrial development can be achieved without a capitalist social structure. The central problem seems to be how one can motivate people to work and at the same time abstain from a high level of consumption in order to make possible capital accumulation and new investments. In other words, how can one make man abstain from the fruits of his own work in order that future generations might enjoy the results of his tremendous efforts? Capitalist economy was one way, in the process of European industrialization. Between 1920 and 1940 the Soviet Union chose quite a different way. The way chosen by China differs from the Soviet pattern. Today, however, one factor seems to stand out. People living in the highly developed industrialized nations pursue as a main social goal immediate and high-level consumption—consumption which should be steadily increasing. The majority does not wish to abstain, even to limited degree, from the pursuit of these goals, in order to make it possible for the people of the underdeveloped areas of the world to achieve the same goals within a period which is at least in the distantly foreseeable future. Whereas earlier the process of industrialization forced certain generations to abstain from enjoying the pleasure of con-

[33] J. M. Keynes, *Economic Consequences of Peace*, quoted after J. Robinson, *Economic Philosophy* (London: Penguin Books, 1968).

sumption for the good of future generations, these generations have themselves little understanding of the fact that they can enjoy their lives because of previous sacrifices. Were it so, they may perhaps show greater consideration for the problems of the Third World. In my opinion this is one of the greatest moral problems of our time. The functioning of our economy so that a high level of consumption *among those living in the industrialized world is* a precondition for increasing productivity, i.e., for economic growth (this growth is often defined as increasing consumption, see page 301), makes a manifest and acute problem of this moral dilemma.

Before I start discussing Lukács's theories, I wish briefly to comment upon the method Marx used in his analysis. It is characterized by an attempt to differentiate between the *forms* under which social conditions *appear* and what they *really are*, i.e., what kinds of social mechanisms and relations a sociological analysis can reveal. What Marx does is to carry out an analysis of concepts and theories of classical economy and attempt to *relate* and to *reduce* them to sociological categories. That would seem to be a fruitful method if one considers the fact that economic theories build upon assumptions of a sociological and social-psychological nature. Economic theories usually build upon certain ideas concerning "man and society" or "man in society." Thus, as our analysis of theories of alienation (see chapter 1) shows, there seem to be implicit in these theories assumptions about the "nature of man" and of "the structure of society." The same holds for macroeconomic theories. As Hofmann[34] points out, three problems are usually taken up: (1) conditions of human action, i.e., assumptions concerning driving forces which make man interested in economic behavior and interaction with other men with regard to economic goals, (2) the problem of the social stratification of a society, especially with regard to income and wealth, and (3) the problem concerning the development of society. As Hofmann indicates, these three problems are intimately related to each other. The ways in which they are answered affects the economic theories developed (or the ways in which economic theories are developed demands certain implicit or explicit assumptions of the above-mentioned kind). There is no doubt that assumptions made by economists, e.g., concerning "economic man" as a rationally choosing individual with a clear and well-known hierarchy of preferences and acting to increase utility in a maximal way, are erroneous from a sociological point of view. What Marx attempted was, to quote a Czechoslovakian philosopher, to dissolve a world of pseudo-concreteness, a world characterized by a complexity of conceptions in man's daily world. These conceptions ob-

[34] W. Hofmann, *Universität, Ideologie, Gesellschaft* (Frankfurt: Edition Suhrkamp, 1968).

tain (since they seem to refer to and explain a social world marked by regularity and order) a status of lawfulness which makes them natural and self-evident.[35]

Marx saw as one of his tasks to reveal this world of pseudo-concreteness and in particular the premises and values upon which the conceptions are built.

It is clear that even Marx's scientific method rests on certain value premises, although these are not the same as those used, for example, by the economists of his period. The question is whether or not all social scientific research which attempts to follow new paths must question that which Galbraith[36] calls "conventional wisdom." One task is to show that that which appears to be empirical fact can so appear only because certain values affect the total social system, creating conditions which then become empirical facts. These values then function as the accidental conditions for certain empirical phenomena. For those observing these empirical conditions, it is not this accidental nature which stands out. Instead the empirical facts are looked upon as inevitable, as something "bestowed by nature." Conceptions which refer to such empirical conditions without questioning them constitute "conventional wisdom."

I will try to illustrate that. In our society it is an empirical fact that within an enterprise the right to decide was located in the owner of capital and in those persons appointed by him as the administrators of the enterprise. This empirical fact rests upon notions of a normative nature which prescribe that the right to make decisions is a part of the function of ownership.[37] Those who own capital ought to determine how it is used.

Assume that one substituted this normative principle with another, for example, that those who work in an enterprise *ought* to have the right to make decisions, whereas the owners of capital are only guaranteed reasonable gain. A social system which is built upon such normative principles will naturally give rise to different empirical facts as far as the conditions of power within an enterprise and probably also within society in general are concerned. Many value premises could be quoted which form the basis of social facts. For example, the existing sex-role divisions and the behavior of men and women in our society builds upon these values. Or take the existing system of social stratification, which is assumed to rest upon the value of an individual's work for the functioning of the society. In this case one must ask what is meant by the value of an individual's work, and what is meant by the functioning of society?

---

[35] K. Kosik, *Die Dialektik des Konkreten* (Frankfurt: Suhrkamp Verlag, 1967), p. 9.
[36] Galbraith, *The Affluent Society* (London: Hamish Hamilton, 1958).
[37] Adler-Karlsson, *Functional Socialism*.

Marx attempts to reveal that that which stands out as empirical fact (or as "natural law") can, in fact, be referred to certain categories and social relations which are intimately connected to certain values. The distinction between that which "stands out as real" and that "which is real" has no metaphysical meaning. Marx defines the difference between these two types of phenomena in the following way. "The former [i.e., the phenomena as they appear] are reproduced directly and spontaneously as current modes of thought; the latter [the hidden conditions] must first be discovered by science. Classical political economy nearly touches the true nature of things without, however, consciously formulating it."[38]

Current notions and ways of reasoning are usually put in opposition to scientific knowledge. According to Marx, the task of science consists of showing that that which man considers to be necessary depends on accidental, i.e., historically accidental, values which are to be found within the social system. Because that which man considers to be necessary affects his behavior, a discrepancy arises between the explanation man gives for his behavior, and the reasons for that behavior which scientific analysis can present. One of Marx's explanations is that the conceptions of reality which are held by an individual are dependent on his class belongingness, e.g., that the values held by an individual depend on his social position. This holds both on a theoretical and nontheoretical level. Systems of explanation which are tied to certain class positions Marx calls "ideologies." The task of science, then, is to reveal that which is "ideology" and that which is scientific explanation.

FROM FETISHISM OF COMMODITIES TO REIFICATION

In Marx's theories the market system, in particular the form it assumes in capitalist society—especially during the period when it was still characterized by Manchester liberalism—is the social origin of the fetishism of commodities. This system is characterized by the fact that use-value is substituted by exchange-value, that human relations between individuals are substituted by object relations between buyer and seller. This is true both with regard to commodities and with regard to labor power. Labor power is transformed into a commodity and therefore into an object. The producers become differentiated from their products, which do not belong to them and which emerge as impersonal things. Lukács[39] goes a step further. He relates the fetishism of commodities to other social conditions, particularly to the development of bureaucracy and its functioning. As mentioned earlier, he had been a

[38] Marx, *Capital*, Vol. I, p. 564.
[39] G. Lukács, *Geschichte und Klassenbewusstsein* (Berlin: Karl Dietz Verlag, 1923).

student of Max Weber's and now used Weber's theories about bureaucracy and rationality to supplement Marx's theory of the fetishism of commodities. Therefore the theory of reification can be said to be built upon a synthesis of some of Marx's and some of Weber's thoughts. Max Weber points out how modern capitalism cannot function without formal rationality and calculation, how bureaucracy is the power system which, from the point of view of formal rationality, is the most effective one, and how other institutions are affected by this development. In particular, he mentions the legal system and how it becomes rationalized and bureaucratized. This leads to the fact that it loses any arbitrariness it may possess, and makes possible accurate predictions concerning its method of functioning. (See chapter 5.)

Lukács's reasoning goes something like this. A market system leads to the fact that the commodity form gains a universal function. This means that *qualitatively* different things are considered as being in principle *similar* with regard to *quantity*. (Half a bottle of whisky is the same as half an hour's work or the pay received for this work.) To achieve such a similarity function, one must measure work performance very exactly. This is accomplished by time studies. (Lukács says that by means of these studies "the rational mechanization penetrates deeply into the worker's soul."[40]) In its turn, that is one of the preconditions for the division of labor, which, as a consequence, transforms labor into abstract, though rational, partial operations. Central to this development is the possibility of calculating and accounting for all work behavior. The consequence is that from the point of view of the producer the labor process is no longer a unified, continuous process, but a repetition of partial operations. The worker's own individual characteristics soon become seen as sources of error in a production which otherwise functions in a rational and accountable way.

Man becomes a mechanical part of a mechanical system. One of the consequences is that social contacts in the labor process diminish, as the individual is transformed into an isolated atom.[41]

[40] Ibid., p. 99.

[41] In this connection it is interesting to point out how our language habits have been adjusted to existing values. When we talk about "the human factor" and its influence, we often imply that man introduces an irrational element into a perfect and mechanically well performing system. Take, as example, the notion that an airplane accident was due to the "human factor." Human behavior thus is identified as *irrational*, whereas robotlike functioning is conceived of as *rational*, as predictable behavior. The notion of the irrationality of the "human factor" is an example of the fact that the reification of man is not yet complete. At the same time it is interesting to note that this expression is used when one tries to explain lack of functioning. The concept "human" has in this connection a negative connotation: the goal is the elimination of the disturbing "human factor" or to prevent its influence, so that a mechanical system can function in a perfect way.

However, atomization and isolation is only one side of the problem. They correspond to a regularity in the social structure, a regularity which, in Lukács's view, is for the first time in history extended over all types of life manifestations. Thus, we have two tendencies: on the one hand, the individual's isolation and atomization; on the other hand, his total dependence on society and its mechanisms. Atomization results in the individual's being more easily ruled and manipulated.

Lukács asserts that the phenomenon of reification is often recognized, but that it is not placed in relation to existing economic conditions. It is from these economic conditions, namely, the capitalist mode of production, that they originate. Among other things, this is because the capitalist mode of production affects all social phenomena. "Thus the capitalist development has created a legal system which corresponds to its needs and which is fitted to its structure." The same is true of the structure of the state, and, as a main witness for this, Lukács refers again to Weber's comparison between state bureaucracy and the bureaucracy existing in private enterprise.

It is notable that in this description Lukács himself used a "reified" language, when maintaining that "the capitalist development" has created its own institutions and organizations. One might get the impression that not man but an impersonal power had created certain human institutions.

This depends on the fact that Marxist theory denied that "capitalists" are the cause of certain social conditions, for example, exploitation. It is "a capitalist system" which gives rise to these conditions, the capitalists themselves being the prisoners of the system, since seen from this point of view the system possesses its own laws, independent of the desires of individuals.

Bureaucracy is part of the institutions and organizations created by the capitalist development. It is related to the process of division of labor in industry. Within bureaucracy there occur formal rationalization and systematic division of function, which leads to the fact that all questions are considered in the light of strict, formal, and rational principles. This leads to the formalizing of human relations. In fact, Lukács asserts that total submission to the "system of object-relations" is a precondition for bureaucracy's functioning. Bureaucrats themselves feel that it is not only their duty to submit themselves to the rule of the bureaucratic organization, but also a matter of honor, i.e., a moral duty.

"The transformation of the commodity-relation into a ghostlike reification is not, therefore, complete when all objects of need-satisfaction become commodities. It influences the total structure of the human consciousness: the abilities and capabilities of man are no longer closely knit into a organic unit in the individual, but appear as 'objects' which man 'owns' and 'sells' in the same way as the things in the world around him."[42]

In Lukács's analysis, much more strongly than in the theories of Marx, the point is made that the theory of reification means criticism not only of the capitalist mode of production but also of industrialization, rationalization, and bureaucratization, even though Lukács considers the latter phenomena to be a consequence of capitalism.[43] How much more realistic, and even to a certain extent more visionary, Weber's assumption emerges today, i.e., that no socialist society which wishes to have an effectively functioning apparatus of production can do so without formal rationality and bureaucracy.

The central problem, therefore, is not, for instance, how one is able to avoid the development of a bureaucracy, but how one is able to control this bureaucracy in such a way that it does not become dictatorical or despotic and that, in exerting its power, it does not become independent of those in whose service it was originally created. The concept of reification is useful and therefore important in such an analysis.

THE PROCESS OF REIFICATION

WHAT IS REIFICATION?

In an essay on reification Lucien Goldmann[44] *exemplifies* the process of reification following the Marxian analysis of commodity and commodity relations. Take the owner of a factory, Goldmann proposes. In order to produce, he has to buy machinery and raw material and hire labor. He then starts the production process, and finally he tries to sell his products. At two points of the production process he is confronted with a market: (1) before he can produce, i.e., when he has to buy the material and the machinery necessary for the production as well as when he has to hire his workers; (2) when he wants to sell the finished products.

The traditional producer and capitalist (not the "mature corporation" described by Galbraith[45]) is confronted with the market "on which events appear as the result of blind laws, being independent of his personal will. These events are ruled by the price, i.e., by objective characteristics of things. Thus the market economy obscures one of life's most essential areas—the economy—the historical and human character of

[42] Lukács, *Geschichte*, p. 106.
[43] Ibid., p. 112.
[44] Goldmann, *Recherches dialectiques*.
[45] Galbraith, *The New Industrial State*.

social life. Man is transformed into a passive element. He is ascribed to the role of an on-looker in a drama, which is continuously renewed before his eyes and in which *dead things are the only really active elements.*"[46] (My italics.)

Probably an economist would argue that today the notion of a market's functioning in a completely blind manner, i.e., regulated only by supply and demand without social planning or governmental or private interference, is a myth. It is a notion which does not correspond to reality. In a mixed economy of the Swedish type, price mechanisms are controlled in different ways. In a society in which large corporations dominate, these corporations actively try to regulate and control market mechanisms. In societies with a planned economy, on the other hand, there is a tendency to introduce price mechanisms into the economy.

At present I do not wish to discuss the relevance of objections which can be raised against Goldmann's description, important as such objections may be. Instead I wish to analyze his exemplification of the process of reification.

In the first place there exist certain *social processes*, which are anchored in definite social conditions. The processes concern the "behavior" of objects—dead things—in a market situation. As commodities their exchange-value, being perceived as an objective characteristic of these things, determines their "movements."

Second, there are *cognitive processes*, an experience of the social processes leading to a notion that man has surrendered to blind powers beyond his control.

Third, there exists a certain relation between the *social processes* and the *cognitive* ones. The cognitive processes are assumed to occur under conditions whereby it is impossible for an individual to reveal and to understand the "true" nature of the social processes, namely, that commodity relations veil relations between human beings.

There are two problems: (1) Is the description of market conditions correct in the sense that man is exposed to powers beyond his control? (2) Independent of the correctness of the actual social conditions, is man able to experience the fact that he is exposed to blind powers?

Let us start with the second question, to which the answer is apparently in the affirmative. Certain types of magical thinking can be used as an example. There is sufficient material from folklore to show that man is perceived as being exposed to powerful nonhuman entities, which direct him and force him to act independent of his own will.

However, magical thinking can also be characterized by anthropomorphism, i.e., a tendency to ascribe human characteristics to dead things

[46] Goldmann, *Recherches dialectiques*, p. 88.

such as plants and other objects found in nature, as well as to living objects, e.g., certain animals, which then rule man.[47] Therefore, if reification is a tendency to ascribe to nonhuman objects the ability to rule man, then there seems to be some similarity to magical thinking (or to religious, as Marx also points out in his analysis of commodity relations). Thus reified thinking is correspondent to anthropomorphism. This may give us a hint as to how we can delimit reification as a cognitive process.

So far we have discussed the problem on a "pretheoretical level," a level on which knowledge is arranged and ordered in a way which differs from the systematic classifications and the specific modes of thinking which characterize the "theoretical" or "scientific" level. Thus "pretheoretical" knowledge partly builds upon preconditions which differ from scientific ones and therefore may lead to other explanations.[48] Also, in our society knowledge can be divided into "prescientific" and "scientific." The "prescientific" level comprises the ways in which people construct their social reality,[49] which then influences their behavior, as well as these commonsense explanations of facts and events, which are used when scientific explanations are unavailable or unknown. Prescientific thinking can be characterized in different ways. For example, there may be attempts to establish causal relations between two or more factors, which in fact relate in a statistical covariation only. It may concern the establishment of causal relations when such relations do not or cannot occur. A third example of such thinking is the drawing of wrong conclusions from facts or erroneous generalizations either from correct or incorrect relationships.[50]

[47] C. Lévi-Strauss, *The Savage Mind* (London: Weidenfeld & Nicolson, 1966). In his analysis of totemistic systems of classification Lévi-Strauss discusses identification between man and animals. He quotes a zoologist, who says that contacts with a dolphin made it difficult for him to consider it as an animal. Comments like these, Lévi-Strauss adds, corroborate the fact that theoretical knowledge may be inconsistent with emotional experiences and that knowledge can be objective as well as subjective at the same time.

[48] Ibid., chapter 1.

[49] See Berger and Luckman, *Social Construction of Reality*.

[50] An example using my own experience may illustrate that. Some years ago on a holiday in Germany we spent the night in a small country-inn. My youngest son wanted a Coca-Cola for supper. However, the wife of the owner refused to serve the soft drink and suggested that he should drink milk. Somewhat surprised, I asked her for the reason of her refusal. She answered that if children drink Coca-Cola before going to bed, they wet the bed, adding that 90 percent of all American children had enuresis. This is a good example of how two events are brought together in a cause-effect relationship, which is difficult to verify. By using a correct syllogism (soft drinks leads to enuresis; American children drink soft drinks; American children have enuresis) with *wrong* premises, an unwarranted generalization is achieved.

The example also may point to the fact that increased knowledge and higher education may make it more difficult for a person to develop prejudices.

It is apparent that on the prescientific level many notions exist which can be classified as "reified." Take, for example, notions that the individual is powerless, that he totally lacks the possibility of influencing society and consequently his own fate, but that instead he is exposed to uncontrollable, impersonal forces. Notions of powerlessness can be classified as reified notions to the extent that the forces to which an individual perceives himself as subordinate are not really human powers or are not perceived as such.

However, on a scientific level of explanation, too, there may be theories which can be characterized as reified. We shall return to a discussion of this problem on page 326, where we will attempt to present metatheoretical characteristics of reified theories.

So far, we have dealt with reification as a cognitive process on a prescientific commonsense level as well as a phenomenon on a scientific, theoretical level.

The cognitive processes must be related to factual *social processes* which can be characterized as "reification processes." We will try to describe this in the next section and also make an attempt to give a first definition of reification.

Social processes can be studied on different levels of abstraction. One very abstract level is when the social system is considered as a totality. When Marx, for example, speaks of the "capitalistic market-system" or of the "mode of production," he discusses phenomena on a general and abstract level. Thus, reification can be discussed and analyzed on a general level where social processes are considered in their totality.

However, a social system is made up of subsystems, which in turn consist of different social organizations. One such organization is a bureaucracy. Since *bureaucratic organizations* play an important role in the discussion of reification, we will consider them in a special section.

Reifying social processes may affect the *social interaction of individuals*. This social interaction, which can be described as being a consequence of reifying social processes, is another problem which will be taken up. Finally, we shall briefly discuss an additional problem to be considered—a consequence of reifying social processes, namely, relations between an *individual and objects*. At first glance this may appear surprising. Objects are things, and how can a person's relation to things be something other than a "thinglike" relation, i.e., a reified one? The answer depends on the definition of reification.

We can now summarize. In the next section we will discuss reifying social processes and attempt a definition. Then the following phenomena will be touched upon: (1) theories which can be characterized as reified (which means that we do not discuss *theories* of reification, but metatheoretical characteristics of theories concerning society, which according to these characteristics can be classified as "reified theories"); (2)

bureaucratic organizations and their place in a theory of reification; (3) relations between individuals, which can be characterized as being a consequence of reifying social processes; (4) relations between individuals and objects, also being the effect of reifying processes.

AN ATTEMPT TO ANALYZE REIFICATION

In order to analyze the process of reification, we will begin on an elementary level, using Marx's analysis. The basic social process is the process of material production. In the manner of traditional economics, Marx, in the *Grundrisse*,[51] analyzes four processes and discusses their relationship to each other: production, distribution, exchange, and consumption. Together these four processes form the economic system of a society. Each process can be seen as occurring within a subsystem. Each subsystem influences the others. When changes occur in one subsystem, they will lead to changes in another subsystem. Thus Marx develops a system approach in which he speaks of the reciprocal interdependence of the different processes.[52]

Production is the process by which nature is transformed into objects for human need-satisfaction. *Distribution* concerns the ways the total social product is divided and which part is attributed to a special person or group. Distribution is dependent on social laws, which in turn reflect the power structure, i.e., the distribution of power within a given society.

Exchange is a mediating activity in which production and distribution are related to each other. An exchange of abilities and capacities, however, also occurs within the process of production. Such an exchange presupposes a division of labor. The intensity, the extent, and the mode of exchange is determined by the mode of production.[53]

Consumption as the final goal is the process by which objects become the means of enjoyment and need-satisfaction. Consumption creates needs for new products and thus becomes the driving force for production.[54] Production as such is a means for consumption, which in turn is a means for production. Marx maintains that in addition production is also a process of consumption, e.g., of raw material and machinery. Similarly consumption has producing effect, e.g., man's ability to work.

So far, our discussion has concerned only the most elementary economic processes (though they are often neglected in sociological theories). The specific problem which man encounters in the capitalistic, or

[51] Marx, *Grundrisse*, p. 11.
[52] Ibid., p. 20.
[53] Ibid., p. 47.
[54] Ibid., p. 13.

(as Marx also calls it) the bourgeois, society, is the "dissolution of all products and activities into exchange-values."[55]

In previous historical periods having other modes of production (e.g., in a feudal system), individuals were placed in a relationship of *personal dependence* on each other. The new mode of production makes people independent of each other in their *personal* relations and therefore also *indifferent* to each other. However, in the process of production, distribution, exchange, and consumption (though least in consumption), they are mutually dependent on each other because their activities supplement each other as a consequence of the division of labor and are necessary for the functioning of the social system. Thus the "mutual and comprehensive dependence of individuals, who are indifferent to each other, forms their social context. This social context is expressed in the *exchange-value*, through which for each individual his own activity or his product first is transformed into an activity or product; the individual must produce a general product—the exchange-value."[56]

Thus Marx asserts here that an activity as such or an object as such is, within the social context of the society he criticizes, of no value for an individual if he cannot use it to exchange it for another activity or product. In addition, the power which a person has over others or over social assets is anchored in the ownership of exchange-values, which can be measured by the amount of money one owns or has available, because money is the generalized exchange-value.

Marx maintains that the transformation of all activities and products into exchange-values leads to the neglect of all that is individual, personal, and specific. Relations determined by exchange-values are impersonal relations. They are objective relations, in the sense of relations between objects. They are reified relations. "In the exchange value the social relations of persons are transformed into the social conduct of objects."[57] Thus individuals feel that they are no longer affected by or subjugated to personal, human influences but to impersonal, objective, thinglike conditions, which they cannot change. Thus the transformation of interpersonal processes into "objective" processes carries with it a feeling of being a powerless object directed by forces outside human control. The transformation of all activities and products into commodities, i.e., exchange-values, therefore, is the basis for the process of reification. The experience of being dominated by reified powers is the cognitive counterpart of these social processes. It is the perception and experience of reification.

[55] Ibid., p. 73.
[56] Ibid., p. 74.
[57] Ibid., p. 75.

However, one central problem is whether this process of transformation is both a necessary *and* sufficient condition for the process of reification to occur. I do not think so, but to make that clear we must make a further analysis.

Let us start with the process of exchange. We can distinguish among *subjects*, who relate themselves to each other in a certain way, *objects*, of their exchange, and the very *act* of exchange and the conditions under which it occurs.

We shall begin with the subjects and, for our purposes, call them *seller* and *buyer*. The seller owns certain objects that he wants to transfer to the buyer. For the seller the object has a certain exchange-value, and one may assert that objects have exchange-value for the seller only. For the buyer an object has exchange-value only if he, in turn, does not desire to consume it but to exchange it.

We must then ask why the buyer enters into an exchange-relation with the seller—assuming he is not forced into it. The specific *characteristics* possessed by the *objects* offered by the seller, and the *need structure* of the buyer, which in turn is perceived as being related to specific characteristics of a given object, endow it with a special value: its *use-value*. Thus an object has *use-value* to a buyer—and only to a buyer. The use-value of an object (and an activity) is determined by its instrumental capacity, i.e., by its ability to serve as means for need-satisfaction or being instrumental for the achievement of a certain goal. Thus the distinction between the use-value and the exchange-value refers to the distinction between the relationship of a subject to an object's having instrumental value, and a value which, though it may be affected by the instrumental value, is determined by other factors. These other factors are a part of the social situation. Thus the scarcity of a certain object plays an important role, and scarcity can be measured by the relationship between supply and demand. Another important factor in the social situation—and in my opinion a decisive factor—is the power relation between seller and buyer. A third factor is the labor necessary to produce an exchange-value. Thus the use-value of an object is determined by such "subjective" conditions as individual or social needs. Exchange-value is apparently determined by "objective" conditions inherent in the acts of production, distribution, and exchange.

The use-value of an object varies with the capacity of a given object to satisfy certain needs and the intensity of a given need. To say that the use-value of an object varies with the intensity of a need also implies that if one reaches the point of saturation, the use-value of an object becomes constant or decreases. According to the so-called marginalist-theory, the utility of an object—and utility can be defined as use-value —increases the more one receives of a certain unit of an object. However, the increase in use-value (utility) becomes less for each additional unit of the object until saturation is reached.[58] This means that the amount one is willing to pay for an additional unit of an object decreases. However, the amount one is willing to pay is the cost, and the cost of an object is its exchange-value. Thus, if an object cannot be obtained without cost, exchange-value and use-value are related to each other according to certain regularities, i.e., laws.

Let us take an example. Since the use-value of an object depends on the intensity of a need, the use-value of water is the same for a thirsty "buyer" sitting in a kitchen, where he can turn on the faucet, and for an equally thirsty man in a desert. The exchange-value of the same unit of water may, however, differ depending on its supply. Assume that in the desert there is only one well with a limited supply. Assume, also, that there are many buyers in the desert and that they agree to divide the supply equally. In such a case the exchange-value of the supply will be the same for all. But assume now that one and only one of the buyers possesses a gun. He is now able to control the well and will become a seller. An exchange-relationship is established which previously did not exist. This is important because exchange-relations evidently can be established only as one or several subjects own objects (or activities) which others do not. Therefore exchange-relations presuppose the existence of scarcity and ownership of property and (in the case of abilities) division of labor.

The seller possessing a gun can now determine the exchange-value of the water for each buyer separately or for all of them together. Thus, below a given level of need-intensity, the exchange-value depends on the amount of supply and on the power relations existing between seller and buyer. There are additional factors which enter into the picture. Assume that the buyers in the desert are all friends and attached to each other and furthermore that they have a common goal—e.g., the wish to survive—and that they know that they can do this only by supporting each other. Assume, finally, that a few of them are experts in finding their way in a desert.

We have now defined three types of social relations existing between the subjects: (1) personal relations based upon mutual liking, i.e., emotions; (2) relations based upon the existence of a common goal; (3) relations based upon division of labor or of role-differentiation. A fourth relation based upon power has been mentioned previously.

Assume that the individual possessing the gun watches the well because one person has become wild due to thirst and uses too much of the supply. If the seller still distributes the water equally, he facilitates

[58] L. Söderström, *Människa eller konsument* (Stockholm: Gebers, 1968).

the achievement of the common goal. His behavior is thus cooperative. If, however, he takes possession of the well in order to prevent certain of the buyers from acquiring the water, he excludes them from the common goal. In relation to them he becomes competitive. If he sells the water cheaper to those he likes, he still has a personal relation to the buyers. If he does not care who buys the water, but only cares that the buyer can pay the demanded price, i.e., the exchange-value, then he has based the exchange on completely impersonal criteria. (This is probably what Marx aims at when he says that the transition of all objects into exchange-values leads to the dissolution of all personal relations: He expresses an hypothesis concerning the exchange-process under certain conditions, namely, a market in which the seller does not know the buyer and therefore does not become related to him on a personal-emotional basis.) The impersonal basis is the buyer's ability to produce the price, i.e., the exchange-value (usually money).

The analysis just carried out concerned exchange processes with regard to the *distribution* of the social product. With regard to the process of production, the exchange relationship between the seller and the buyer is another. Let us return to Marx in order to get some hints from his analysis. When discussing the meaning of "productive work," Marx makes reference to different economic theories and the ways in which they have dealt with the problem. In opposition to these theories he presents his own analysis. He relates "labor" to "capital" and states that in a social system in which production is based upon capital, labor is productive only if it *increases* capital. If the function of capital is to reproduce itself and to increase its value, labor has a *use-value* for capital: "As a *use-value* labor exists only *for* the capital and is *the* use-value of the capital itself, i.e., the mediating activity by which it increases its value."[59]

Now for the worker labor or labor power has no use-value, since he must sell his labor power. For him labor has only an exchange-value. The new values created by labor—and according to Marx's theory of value, labor alone creates new values, i.e., exchange values—are taken care of by persons other than the workers. Labor could be of use-value to the worker under two conditions. First, if the result of his labor could be his own, i.e., if the increase in capital could be used by the worker. Thus labor would indirectly become a use-value for him. Second, if labor were a creative activity, which it is not. The worker instead becomes impoverished since "the productivity of his work becomes an *alien* power"[60]

[59] Marx, *Grundrisse*, p. 213.
[60] Ibid., p. 214.

by increasing the power of the capital which takes care of the result of his labor.

Thus Marx developed this second theory of alienation thirteen years after he wrote his first. Three elements are of importance here. (1) In the relationship between the seller and the buyer, the *buyer* has power over the seller (whereas in the previous analysis the power relationship was reversed). (2) Labor has exchange-value for the seller and use-value for the buyer. (3) However, use-value here does not satisfy a need of the buyer but is a *function* of something the buyer owns (capital). Therefore the instrumental relationship is also different. Instrumental here means "functional to certain goals."

AN EXPLICATION OF CONCEPTS TO BE USED

At this stage it may be worthwhile to attempt a definition of our concepts. The explication will concern concepts considered to be necessary, though not sufficient for the development of a theory of reification.

We will start with the subjects of the process of exchange.

A *seller* is a person possessing objects or activities which other individuals need and which he is willing to exchange either voluntarily or by means of force.

A *buyer* is a person, who needs, desires, or strives for certain objects or activities, which other persons are willing to exchange.

Scarcity is the difference between the amount of an object or activity which is demanded and the amount which is supplied. If the difference between demand and supply is negative, we will speak of scarcity.

A remark should be made here. There is a difference between need and demand. A buyer may demand something which he needs. He may also abstain from demanding something he needs because he has not the resources for exchange. Finally he may demand something which he does not need, because he has resources for exchange.

Demand, then, is a function of an individual's buying resources and his needs. If needs and resources have an appropriate relation, i.e., if resources under given conditions make it possible to acquire the quantity of something necessary to satisfy existing basic needs, then need and demand will be equal. If resources are too few in relation to needs, then need will be greater than demand. If resources are too many in relation to need, then demand will be higher than need.

Use-value is the value of an object or activity related to a buyer, either to satisfy his own needs or as instrumental for the functioning of something he possesses. Use-value as a relational concept thus is the function of *intrinsic characteristics* in the object or activity and of the *need-structure* of the buyer.

Exchange-value is the value of an object or activity demanded by a seller in the process of exchange. Exchange-value is a function of the cost of necessary *work* to produce the object or activity and of *demand* and *supply*.

Objects or activities having an exchange-value will be called *commodities*.

Power will be defined in the *process of production* as the buyer's ability to determine the exchange-value, i.e., the costs of an object or activity for the seller in an exchange-relation.

For the *process of distribution, power* will be defined as the seller's ability to determine the exchange-value, i.e., the costs of an object or activity for the buyer in an exchange-relation.

Let us here make another distinction. Using a different definition of power Stinchcombe[61] differentiates between "control over resources" and "control over people." The same distinction can be also expressed as "rights regarding things" and "rights regarding persons" or as "property" vs. "authority."

Resources will here be called objects or activities which are *necessary* for the production or acquisition of exchange-value, e.g., capital, knowledge, abilities, information.

Resources can be *controlled* by ownership or by the power to dispose of them. *Controlling* resources means being able to *make decisions* concerning the use of resources.

In a society characterized as "capitalist," and in those "socialist" societies where exchange mainly concerns commodities (both with regard to objects and to working power, as in the Soviet Union), the ownership or disposition of objects and activities as necessary for the production of exchange-values is a *precondition* for *power* (power, as in our definition, always refers to power over persons). This hypothesis, though almost trivial, is nevertheless central to our theorizing. However, it must be supplemented by another hypothesis that power over persons in turn tends to increase control over resources. This will lead to a polarization of power and subsequently to asymmetric relations between those controlling resources and those not doing so, parallelled by being powerful and powerless respectively.

In our definition power is a relation between *groups* or *classes* of people. In general this type of definition can refer to either *subjective* or *objective* power. "Subjective power" definitions are those which make

---

[61] A. L. Stinchcombe, *Constructing Social Theories* (New York: Harcourt, Brace & World, 1968).

assumptions concerning the will of individuals being involved in a power relation. Thus a definition in terms of influence is an example of subjective power: x's ability to influence y means that x *wants* y to behave in a certain way and y either can *accept* or does not *wish* to follow x's wishes.

Our definition is an objective one in the sense that power relations are defined independently of the will and intentions of the people involved. A certain position in a social structure for a person or class of persons thus may determine their power independently of their intentions and wishes. Only a change in the existing social structure will lead to a change in power relations.

Sometimes power is conceptualized as being "intrinsically" asymmetric. This is not so in our definition. In an exchange relation buyers and sellers could be considered as equal under certain social conditions. Also asymmetric power relations are the consequences of certain—in our case social—conditions, e.g., the ownership or power of disposal of resources.

Power as a relation can be also conceptualized with regard to its *scope*, i.e., the number of areas in which a person has power, and its *extent*, i.e., the number of persons over which one person, group, or class can exert power.[62]

Finally we have to define *location of control*. The control over resources may be located in persons, groups, or special decision-making centers within an organization. Location of control will now be defined in terms of three dimensions: (1) *visibility* of decision-making persons, groups, or centers for those over whom power is exerted; (2) the *distance* in terms of hierarchical levels between decision-making persons, groups, or centers and those over whom power is exerted; and (3) the *accessibility* of decision-making persons, groups, or centers for those over whom power is exerted. As we shall see, the three dimensions are interrelated. Whereas so far our definitions have concerned subjects and objects in the exchange process and their properties, we have not yet defined relations between subjects. These relations will be defined in terms of *three dimensions*: (1) *kind* of relations, (2) *differentiation* of relations, (3) *interdependence* of relations. We will attempt to define these three dimensions.

Kind of relations is a combination of three subdimensions: (1) The degree to which one knows a person, i.e., the degree of directness of a relation. This subdimension has the polar points personal-impersonal relation. (2) The emotional value of this relation, which will range

---

[62] E. Dahlström has, in an interesting article ("Exchange Influence and Power," *Acta Sociologica* No. 9 (1966), 273–84) made an attempt to conceptualize power and power-relations and to integrate "power" defined in terms of influence with "power" defined in terms of exchange.

positive-neutral-negative. (3) The intensity of the emotional involvment, ranging high-low involvement. If we arbitrarily divide the first and the last subdimensions into two values and the second one into three values, we will get twelve cells referring to different *kinds* of relations.

1. Degree of directness of knowledge

		Personal		Impersonal	
	2. Involvement	High	Low	High	Low
3. Emotional value	Positive	1. $+++$	2. $+-+$	3. $-++$	4. $--+$
	Negative	5. $++-$	6. $+--$	7. $-+-$	8. $---$
	Neutral	9. $++0$	10. $+-0$	11. $-+0$	12. $--0$

We have assigned combinations of values to each cell by using + or— or the 0 sign (the first sign always refers to degree of knowledge, the second to involvement, the third to value). Later these combinations will be of importance for our theoretical reasoning. However, even now we can try to reduce the matrix and to arrange the remaining combinations in a special rank-order. At first glance it seems unreasonable from a psychological point of view, to combine the value neutrality with any degree of involvement. Thus it may be sufficient to reduce the four cells 9—12 to two, namely + 0 0 and — 0 0. This means that we have one category of personal relations with no involvement and one of impersonal relations with no involvement.

Let us now discuss cells 3 and 4. There we have a relation which is impersonal but positive and either high or low in degree of involvement. Here the degree of involvement seems to be less important than the fact of positive emotional involvement in an impersonal relation, and we propose to reduce these two cells to one — + +. Finally we have cell 8, where there exists a low negative involvement in an impersonal relation. We propose to reduce this cell by referring it to category — 0 0. Thus eight categories remain which we will order and try to describe.

1. $+++$
2. $+-+$
3. $+--$
4. $++-$
5. $+\ 0\ 0$
6. $-++$
7. $-+-$
8. $-\ 0\ 0$

The scale starts with a relationship of intensive positive involvement of a personal kind, e.g., a relationship characterized by love. The second rank refers to relations of the friendship kind; the third to a personal relation of unfriendliness, which is increased to hate in the fourth category.

The fifth category is of a somewhat different quality. There is a personal relation of indifference, a relation which characterizes most interpersonal relations on the job, etc. Probably indifference is a way of making a relationship less personal. Then we come to impersonal relations of an intense, positive nature. This will be found, e.g., in the relation of people to their idols. This category may give us an idea of the relationship between reifying processes and the cult of idols. In the seventh category we have an impersonal relation characterized by hate. This is what may be experienced by people who, for example, have strong race prejudices. Finally we have the eighth category, in which there is an impersonal relation of indifference. This relation may occur either if one is uninterested in persons, or when one perceives them as objects. However, before we can clarify the difference, we must define the next dimension.

Differentiation is defined in terms of symmetry and asymmetry of relation. Symmetrical relations are relations in which the other is experienced and treated as one's equal. Asymmetrical relations are relations in which the other is experienced and treated as either superior or inferior. Relations of dominance and submission are one example of asymmetric relations. For our continued analysis of reifying processes, this dimension will be of special importance. Specifically we will have to deal with asymmetric relations. The dimension of symmetric–asymmetric relations can be thought of as referring to the "generalized other." In this case a person or group of persons are defined in their totality as, e.g., inferior (to use an asymmetric relation). The relationship may also apply to specific characteristics used to categorize people. There may occur different combinations. For example, a person is considered to be symmetric in one respect and asymmetric in another. Attempts to generalize relations (as, for example, may occur when people are prejudiced) will be of special interest.

We can now combine this dimension with our scale. We will concentrate on asymmetric relations where the other is experienced as *inferior* in a total way. Category 1: $+ + +$ may characterize an authoritarian father loving his son, or a man in love with a woman whom he categorizes according to extreme traditional sex-role characterizations. Thus we may find different examples for the different categories. Most interesting for our purposes is the part of the scale beginning at category 5. This categorizes a personal relationship of complete indifference where the other is considered as an inferior subject. This relation may exist, for instance, in authoritarian organizations, as in a military outfit between a sergeant and a private. The important factor is that the relationship is still personal. In the next scale the impersonal relation is combined with a liking of that other being considered inferior. Idols may look at their fans in this way. In the next category, an intense dislike of the inferior person e.g. as is the case in relations between a white and persons of another color, whom he hates. Finally the eighth category is one of impersonal relations and total indifference with regard to involvement, but where the other is experienced as inferior. This may lead to the perception of the being as an object, a thing. Thus the second part of our scale seems to constitute a scale of dehumanization when the relationship becomes asymmetric and has a specific content, e.g., if it is characterized by inferiority.

We may also, for a moment, look at category $-++$ under symmetric conditions. This may be the case when a person identifies himself with a group which he considers as his equals. For example, engaging oneself in actions for discriminated groups may depend on the definition of the relationship in the mentioned way. Later we may have to say something concerning the social conditions under which relations are likely to become symmetric or asymmetric.

We will now define the last relation *interdependence*, which will be defined in a traditional way:[63] Two subjects, x and y, are related to each other in a *cooperative way*, when they have a common goal and x's actions to reach the goal facilitates or makes it possible for y to reach the common goal, where x and y are individuals or groups. Two subjects, x and y, are related to each other in a *competitive* way if they have a common goal and x's action to reach the goal prevents y from reaching the common goal, where x and y are persons or groups.

Goals are usually arranged in hierarchies in such a way that lower order goals become means for higher order goals. Thus it may occur that in such a goal hierarchy there exist competitive as well as cooperative goals. Thus workers and management may have a cooperative goal for production. However, with regard to the share of the results of production their relation is competitive. Since production as goal is a means of attaining profits, this second goal is placed higher in the hierarchy. The distribution of the profits is an even higher goal. Thus cooperative subgoals may be means to competitive "final" goals. I think this is what Marx refers to when he emphasizes that production is a social process which nevertheless leads to the private appropriation of the results of the productive process.

If a hierarchy with several subgoals exists, then the relationship concerning interdependence will be determined by the structure of the goal located highest in the hierarchy.

---

[63] M. Deutsch, "An Experimental Study of the Effect of Cooperation and Competition upon Group Process," *Human Relations* II (1949), 199–231.

In addition to power relations there may be interdependence between buyers taken alone and between sellers taken alone. There may also be interdependence between these two categories.

Finally interdependence can also be related to our scale of "dehumanization."

REIFYING PROCESSES

As previously mentioned, one of Marx's central themes holds that the transformation of use-values into exchange-values is a central determining factor for the process of reification. Our analysis now aims at an attempt to place this hypothesis within a wider sociological content.

Let us start with power relations in the exchange process associated with the social process of production and of distribution of the social product. We defined the exchange relations as being reversed. In the process of production the buyer has power over the seller, whereas in the process of distribution the relationship is reversed: the seller has power over the buyer to the extent that he can determine his costs.

The next step is to develop a hypothesis concerning the interrelationship of exchange-relations within production and in distribution. Assume the same agent—being a person, group, or an organization—has the control over resources necessary for exerting power in both basic processes. Let us call this agent C which can stand for *"capitalist," "corporation,"* or *"central* planning and administration agency." These alternatives are chosen in order to underline that the theory can be applied to traditional capitalist enterprises, to multinational "mature" corporations, and to the centralized bureaucracies e.g. to be found in the Soviet Union.

Further, let us call the other agent in the process of production W, referring to "worker," blue-collar as well as white-collar. Finally, let us call the last agent in the process of distribution R, referring to receiver or consumer. We can depict the social situation in which C controls resources, both for the production and distribution processes, in the following way:

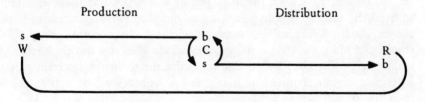

Figure 7. Power in production and distribution process.

The arrows indicate the direction of power. Thus the same agent C has power over W in the production process and power over R in the distribution process. In order to do this, he has to assume the role of the buyer (b) as well as the role of the seller (s). Being the buyer affects the resources he uses for being the seller, and being the seller affects the resources he can control for being the buyer. This is indicated by the arrows going from b to s, in C. Finally the seller W is, at the same time, also the buyer R, i.e., the consumer. This is indicated by the line drawn from W to R. Thus our first central hypothesis is: The more C owns or has at its disposal—the resources necessary or sufficient for exerting power in the production process as well as in the distribution process—the greater becomes the asymmetry of the power relations between C and W and C and R. Since W and R in general are the same agents, the hypothesis implies that their degree of power concerns exchange in both the production and distribution processes.

In this hypothesis as in our definition, we differentiate between ownership and disposal as means of control over resources. The two relations may be correlated, although this is not necessary. In Marx's theory ownership of resources, e.g., means of production, is a decisive factor.

In contrast to Marx's assertion, power can be exerted without ownership by disposing of the basic means of production. In fact, if one combines ownership and disposal, four combinations may be arrived at:

Ownership

		Yes	No
Disposal	Yes	1. Traditional capitalists	2. (a) Technostructure of large corporations (b) Planning bureaucracy
	No	3. Small stockholders	4. The majority of people

In cell 1 we have the traditional capitalist as depicted by Marx. In the second cell we have both the managers of private corporations, as found in the U.S., and the people belonging to the planning bureaucracy in the Soviet Union. Whereas the members of the technostructure may own stocks and often do, the planning bureaucracy does not usually have any economic profits but may be able to secure for themselves certain privileges as a higher standard of living and a higher level of consumption than the population in general.

In cell 3 we have the small stockholders, who have ownership rights but usually no control over the enterprise.

To give another example of the distinction between ownership and disposal of means of production, we can refer to the Yugoslavian system, where the workers employed in a factory by means of their workers' council have the right of disposal of the means of production, though these are owned by the state. Moreover, in this type of social organization, control, or at least a decisive part of it, may be vested in the technical experts who direct a company and are responsible to the workers' council.

Thus ownership may or may not be associated with control and power. Dahrendorf,[64] who has made a detailed analysis of this problem, asserts that the relationship between property and power is such that property is always associated with power, but that this relation cannot be reversed. Our attempt at an analysis, however, indicates that not even the first part of the hypothesis is necessarily correct. There is property without power, represented, as previously mentioned, by small stockholders.[65]

Marx foresaw this development. In the third volume of *Capital* he discusses joint-stock companies and analyzes the separation of ownership and control. He speaks of the transformation of capitalists into directors and of capitalists being merely stockholders having no function in the process of production. Marx characterizes these companies by saying that they present "the abolition of the capitalist mode of production within the capitalist mode of production."[66] He also has an hypothesis that since the managers, as opposed to stockholders, participate in the production process, there should be complete alienation of capital owners and a bringing together of workers and managers. However, in the theory of reification here presented, we will develop the reverse hypothesis. Those people being in control of the means of production—whether they own stocks, like the mangerial group in the U.S., or

[64] R. Dahrendorf, *Class and Class Conflict in an Industrial Society* (London: Routledge and Kegan Paul, 1959).

[65] The notion of separating ownership and control has given rise to a controversy dealing with two problems: (1) whether individuals being in control of large corporations also are stock-owners or not, (2) whether the goal of large corporations—as distinct from the goals of capitalistic entrepreneurs—no longer is profit maximization. Galbraith has argued along the line that the technostructure has goals different from those of the capitalist owners and that these goals, instead of profit-maximization, are economic growth and financial independence. P. A. Baran and P. M. Sweezy (*Monopoly Capital*, London: Penguin Books, 1968) point out that the members of the technostructure usually also are large stock-owners. Furthermore, they state that the goal of large corporations is the aquiring of profits, though it may not necessarily be profit maximation. See also J. S. Early, "Marginal Policies of 'Excellently Managed' Companies," *The American Economic Review*, March, 1956; R. Scheehan, "Proprietors in the World of Big Business," *Fortune*, June 15, 1967; and G. Kolko, *Wealth and Power in America* (New York: F. A. Praeger, 1962).

[66] Marx, *Capital*, Vol. III, p. 454.

whether they have no property rights, as in the Soviet Union—will more and more increase the distance between themselves and the workers (and consumers). This will be a consequence of asymmetric power relations.

We assume here that the base of power is not necessarily the ownership of means of production, but that being in position to dispose of these means is the base of power. However, this answer is not satisfying because one could insist on asking how a certain group or class can have at its disposal the means of production. The *first* answer is that usually they have the necessary skill and knowledge to make decisions for the process of production. Thus the first factor contributing to their power is their expertness. This expertness often makes them unsubstitutable. *Second*, they control the recruitment to empty positions within the top hierarchy. This increases existing power since people selected are dependent on those selecting them. *Third*, they can use the resources to control or influence channels of informations. This implies that they are able to legitimize their power position and to spread the content of this information. In other words they have the means to develop and spread ideologies which legitimize existing power conditions. *Fourth*, these power-elites—to use C. W. Mills's concept—are intimately associated with those elites having at their disposal the monopolized means of force, i.e., the military elite. "Intimate association" here means, first, common goals and, second, interdependence in achievement of these goals. Thus, Galbraith indicates how the military elite can give huge contracts to the large corporations, thus ensuring their effective functioning and decreasing their economic risks. The military elite, on the other hand, needs the managerial and technological elite in order to be able to acquire the material means for their power: effective and technically highly developed weaponry. *Finally* there are close associations between the political elite, which makes decisions concerning, among other things, the use of the means of force. Here again the close association is based upon common goals and cooperative interdependence in the achievement of these goals: to keep themselves in power. In societies lacking parliamentary forms of governing, the political elite can base its power on the monopolization of force and on the means of indoctrination. But they may also do so by satisfying the basic needs of the ruled and by making available large amounts of consumer goods not needed for basic need-satisfaction. In societies with a parliamentary system a high standard of living has become the way of getting the acceptance of the ruled. Thus attempt at abolition of unemployment, of need and want, of poverty and the establishment of affluence is the way to stay in power. Now the technological elite is capable of creating the conditions for these goals. Therefore, their own goal is high productivity by effective use of capital resources and working power and by exploitation of technological advances and scientific findings. Thus their subgoals are high productivity and a continuous attempt to achieve more perfect technological processes. Since these subgoals are necessary for the achievement of the goals of the political elite, this elite will do everything to facilitate the achievement of the goals of the technological elite. Finally the question is no longer whether high productivity is a means for a higher goal in the goal-hierarchy, e.g., the establishment of high standards of living. Instead high productivity and a continuous and steady economic growth are perceived as ultimate goals having as one consequence a rising standard of living.[67]

We will now try to present this analysis in a diagrammatic form, Figure 8.

The diagram needs little explanation. The power invested in ownership of means of production is delegated by giving the disposal of these means to a certain elite. Their bases of power are partly this disposal, partly the factors mentioned at the right. This elite is closely connected to and interdependent with the military and political elite. In a society like the Soviet Union with public ownership of means of production, the disposal of these means is also a base of power for the political elite. This is indicated by dotted lines.

We will now return to the economic processes of production and distribution.

In our previously mentioned hypothesis, concentration of power in the agent is facilitated by alternating between the role of the buyer of commodities and the role of the seller of other commodities. To the degree that W, by selling his activities to C, contributes to the creation of new resources necessary for C to control the exchange process occurring in production and in distribution, he increases C's power and decreases his own. Furthermore, to the degree to which R, by buying commodities, contributes to the creation of new resources for C to increase his control, he also decreases his own power. Thus since W and R are the same persons, their activities contribute to increase their powerlessness and to increase the power of C. Using systems theory we thus have two feedback processes: one within the subsystem made up by C and his

[67] J. K. Galbraith has an interesting comment on the tendency to consider economic growth and high productivity as a major goal. In his book *The Affluent Society* (London: Hamish Hamilton, 1958) he mentions that the Republican administration in the U.S. used a dominant argument in the election campaign of 1954. It maintained that the year had been the second best in American history. Nobody, Galbraith says, was in doubt what "second best" referred to. It did not refer to "health standards" or to "number of individuals in institutions of higher learning" or to "number of religious conversions," but to the size of the gross national product. The importance of production was a value shared by Democrats as well as by Republicans, communists as well as reactionaries.

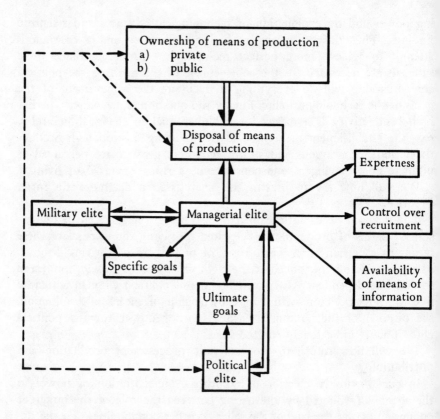

Figure 8. Diagrammatic representation of economic processes and the ways they are controlled.

two roles and one in the total system, where W and R affect the function of C in the exchange-process and C affects the function of W and R.

This is what Marx probably refers to when he speaks of the worker's becoming more and more powerless, the more he works. Let us draw a new diagram, Figure 9.

C exerts power over W, which through his activities increases the production resources of C. Since increased production resources also increase C's distribution resources, W indirectly contributes to increasing C's power over R, which as a consumer increases the production as well as the distribution resources of C.

A few objections could be raised. In modern industrialized societies certain controlling factors exist in order to give support to W and R and to increase their power in the exchange process. One regulatory force is the state, which tries to strengthen W's position by means of laws con-

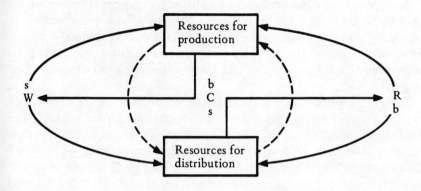

Figure 9. Feedback mechanism indicating how production resources increase distribution resources and vice versa.

cerning working time, holidays, and other regulations concerning the role of W in the production process, e.g., establishment of minimum wage level. Secondly we have trade-union organizations which function as W's representative in relation to C. With regard to R's power there is a liberal dogma asserting that it is R who has power over C: through his choice the consumer determines what he wants and, through mediating market mechanisms, exerts power over C. However, such analysts of modern, highly industrialized societies as Galbraith[68] and Baran and Sweezy[69] assert that in societies in which the economic processes are dominated by large corporations, the functioning of a free market is a myth. Instead, they maintain that devices have been developed to bring the market under the control of C.

Let us for a moment follow the argument advanced by Galbraith. The significant mark of our age is the rapid development of technology. The new productive forces continuously being developed and applied demand large capital investment and a great amount of time in which to plan new products. Thus, producing a new car model presupposes a large time-span between its design and the moment when it can be sold. This in turn creates the necessity to anticipate the consumers' behavior. In order to avoid a situation in which products that have cost a large amount of capital will not be sold, the large corporation "must take every feasible step to see that what it decides to produce is wanted by the consumer at a renumerative price."[70]

[68] Galbraith, *The New Industrial State.*
[69] Baran and Sweezy, *Monopoly Capital.*
[70] Galbraith, *The New Industrial State*, p. 24.

But it is not only the processes of distribution and consumption which have to be controlled (as by means of advertising and propaganda dispersed by powerful mass media and other information devices); control must also be extended over the supplies necessary for production. Supplies means both raw material and other necessary products and labor power.

Galbraith suggests three ways in which the market can be controlled: (1) by *superseding* it. This means that supplies which are strategic for production are taken over by the corporation and access to supplies thus becomes a matter of internal decision and independent of external "disturbances." (2) The market can be *controlled* by C as a buyer as well as a seller, and (3) it can be *suspended*. This can be done through monopoly or by contracts which ensure supply at a certain cost level.

Thus it seems that market mechanisms are neutralized, but market relations may still signify the social relations existing between men: they are still buyers and sellers.

By using means of influencing buyers, C can exert power over R by creating demands for commodities, which have little or no connection to R's need-structure as well as by creating value-systems concerning the desirability of a high consumption. According to Galbraith, they also try to exert control over the raw material necessary for production and decrease the proper functioning of trade unions. At the same time Ws being Rs with a high standard of living (usually equated with high level of consumption) get less and less interested in participating in trade-union affairs or in other spheres in which they could gain influence, since they are pacified by the increasing rewards that they receive in the exchange process of distribution.

Furthermore, many large corporations are multinational and therefore able to exert influence over governments, especially in smaller countries. In a review concerning multinational coporations Adler-Karlsson[71] speaks of three categories of action leading to conflict with national government: political action, profit maximizing, and profit distribution. With regard to the first problem he gives example of large oil companies utilizing the power of the U.S.A. to exert influence in smaller countries on governments who resist their demands. He exemplifies the second type of problem by referring to the utilization of those labor markets which are cheapest (e.g., gas tubes for gas sold by a large corporation in Sweden are produced in Singapore, since a worker there makes in a week what a Swedish worker makes in a day). Furthermore, profit can

[71] G. Adler-Karlsson, in a newspaper article in *Dagens Nyheter*, Stockholm, 30th of March, 1969.

be increased by using the cheapest capital market. By redistributing profits between different national companies, legalized tax evasion is possible. Also, monopolies can be created and in such a way market mechanism put out of function. Finally with regard to profit distribution a highly centralized control can make plans for differential investments in various countries both affecting its own profit and, which is more important, the economic development of small countries.

These descriptions and analyses refer to highly industrialized societies with large corporations. In societies having a system in which means of production are nationalized, the role of corporations may be taken over by centralized bureaucratic planning and steering agencies and organizations.

In the previous analysis we have tried to show how C's power in the processes of production and distribution is anchored in the social structure of a society and its prevailing power relations, which in turn are based upon the existence of a certain class structure within society.

We will now discuss the consequences of being in control of resources necessary for the process of production and the process of distribution. Control, i.e., decision-making is carried out through special decision-making bodies. These bodies are guided by goals defined by those possessing power. We have mentioned these goals, and we will have more to say about them later. At this point we will discuss the location of decision-making: we will present the following hypothesis. The larger the organization controlled by C, the more distant are the bodies making the decisions from those being affected by them, namely W and R. The more distant the decision-making body the more invisible its functioning.

Distance between decision-makers and those affected by them, between people with power and those without, between rulers and ruled has several consequences. If the goals of those making decisions are different from, or even antagonistic to, the goals preferred by those being ruled, distance between these groups will lead to lack of knowledge concerning divergent or antagonistic goals. Thus the powerful group can pursue their goals and disregard the wishes of other groups. Distance will protect them from knowledge of these goals. In certain cases this lack of knowledge will be used to assert that there is unanimity in goals between rulers and ruled, e.g., when the ruling group or class speaks in the name of the "people" or "the masses" or "the proletariat."

As hypothesized, distance is also correlated with degree of visibility. Lack of visibility with regard to the process of decision-making and the bodies of decision-making creates the impression among the ruled that power is exerted by unknown agents, which in turn leads to the fact that they experience themselves as unable to explain the intentions, goals, and functioning of the invisible powers. Those making decisions, on the other hand, gain protection from interference by invisibility, so invisibility strengthens their chances of exerting power without themselves being controlled and without being held responsible for decisions made. Thus invisibility makes difficult or prevents democratic control.

Distance and invisibility have a certain relation to our third variable, defining "location of power." We present the following hypothesis: The more distant and the more invisible are decision-making bodies from those being influenced by their decisions, the less there will exist *access* to these bodies and to the resources they control. As a consequence of this hypothesis, changes in existing power relations are made difficult. Distance and invisibility function as perpetuating forces, making decision-making bodies and their agents inaccessible and therefore difficult to control.

Distance and invisibility have a further effect. Not only are holders of powers invisible, due to distance, to those being ruled, but in addition those being ruled are invisible to those in power. As a consequence, relations between those who make decisions, i.e., have power, and those who are ruled and without power become impersonal in the sense in which we previously defined impersonal relations, namely, a relationship characterized by lack of personal knowledge and emotional neutrality (see page 294). Through the polarization of power these personal relations also become asymmetric. Those in power consider themselves as superior, and the ruled as inferior. Probably identical perceptions develop among those who are ruled. The consequences of impersonal and asymmetric relations are that human beings are transformed into objects. In the process of production man is transferred into labor power, into a "production factor," as modern economic theories so adequately call it. As a production factor, men lose their human identity. They are employed as long as their labor power is necessary but are dismissed when machines can take over or when restrictions in the process of production have to be made.

Workers are labor power, i.e., objects or things seen from the point of view of their utility to create the profits necessary for new investments, which in turn are necessary in order to keep the system going. The goals of those who possess control over the means of production control the functioning of the system. Therefore those who are in possession of the control become the prisoner of the system as well as those who function as labor power.

In societies which are economically underdeveloped, as the countries in Latin America, this transformation of man into a means of creating surplus value is not concealed as it is concealed in the highly industrialized countries. In the underdeveloped countries—"economic satellites to metropoles," as Frank[72] calls them—exploitation is not concealed. To a large degree this has to do with the fact that the low standard of living in these countries does not make the inhabitants potential buyers of commodities, i.e., R in our model. Their situation is similar to that of European workers at the beginning of the era of industrialization.

In highly industrialized countries the situation is different. Man does not represent labor power only. He is not merely a *production-factor*, but also a potential buyer of the goods produced—of commodities. He becomes another object, a *distribution factor*, meaning the receiver and purchaser of commodities, i.e., exchange-values.

If one defines consumption as a function of the exchange-value *and* the use-value of given objects, then the problem becomes: how is use-value eliminated in the process of consumption?

Previously we defined use-value as a function of the interrelationship between the individual's need-structure and "intrinsic" characteristics of the object. Exchange-value, on the other hand, is a function of three factors: (1) the labor necessary to produce an object, (2) the supply, and (3) the demand.

However, demand was defined as a function of the need-structure of an individual and his available buying resources. Thus if the consumption society is characterized by a tendency to acquire things, not according to the need-structure of the individual but according to his buying resources, then it can be shown that the use-value of an object no longer plays a role in the process of consumption.

If, in the consuming object, demands are created which are independent of his need-structure (and that can occur if his basic needs are satisfied and available buying resources are high), then objects are not bought because of their "intrinsic" ability to mediate need-satisfaction. Rather they are bought by relating the existing buying resources to the exchange-value of objects. This presupposes that a demand is created by mass media and other means of social influence. In this way the exchange-value, but not the use-value, of an object becomes the important characteristic of objects being consumed. Later we will return to the problem of the relationship between use-value and exchange-value in consumption. However, in the distribution process, control over exchange-values increases the power of C over R. For C, R becomes *consuming objects*: in the process of distribution, commodities are put on the market not in order to satisfy needs, i.e., for their use-value, but in order to meet a demand which is related in the first place to exchange-value, and only in the second place to use-value satisfying needs. In fact,

---

[72] G. A. Frank, *Capitalism and Underdevelopment in Latin America* (New York: Monthly Review Press, 1967).

sometimes things are produced in such a way that they become detrimental to basic human needs. Cars with built-in deficiencies, making a potential risk of driving, are examples of objects' being detrimental to satisfaction of such basic needs as security and survival. Other examples are objects the use of which destroys or poisons or pollutes our natural environment, thereby creating tremendous problems, if not for us then for future generations.

The analysis concerning the transformation of R into consuming objects is illustrated in the following diagram. There the exchange-value of objects and their use-value is depicted as a function of several factors. In addition the relationship between exchange-value and use-value is indicated. Furthermore, the individual's need-structure is related to use-value. If consumption is the result of all the factors included, then no reifying processes are hypothesized. When consumption is a consequence of the factors related only by dotted lines, then reifying processes occur.

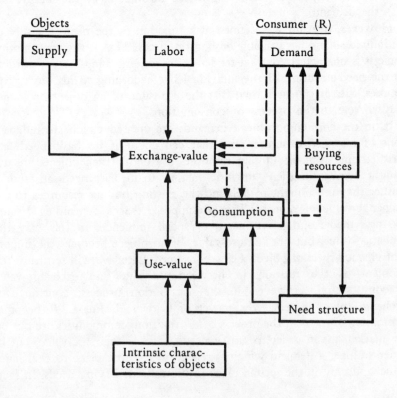

Figure 10.   Process of reification in consumption.

It can also be formalized in the following way:

1. $C = f (Ev + Uv)$
2. $Uv = f (ns \times ic)$
3. $Ev = f (l + s + d)$
4. $d = f (ns + br)$

C stands for consumption
Ev for exchange-value
Uv for use-value
ns for need-structure
ic for intrinsic characteristics of objects
l refers to labor necessary to produce an object
s stands for supply
d stands for demand
br stands for buying resources.

If ns $= 0$, then equation 2 is eliminated and C becomes a function of Ev. ns $= 0$ when d becomes a function of br.

Reifying processes in the field of consumption are a matter of degree. It seems difficult to assert that commodites bought should have only exchange-value and *no* use-value for the buyer. It seems, however, to be an outstanding feature in the consumption society that the use-value of a commodity is not determined *directly* by the existing need-structure but very often *indirectly* mediated by the exchange-value of a commodity. Take, for example, commodities bought for the status they may give to the buyer. Take a high-priced car's being a status symbol. It is the exchange-value of this car which mediates the use-value, i.e., its value to satisfy the status-need of the buyer.

We thus make a distinction between *direct* and *indirect* use-value. An object has *direct* use-value when it satisfies *basic* needs. *Indirect* use-value has an object when its use-value is mediated by its exchange-value and when it is instrumental for the satisfaction of *secondary*, socially determined *aspirations*. Thus we reserve the term "need" for "basic physiological and psychological needs." (See also the discussion in this chapter under the heading "The Psychological Process of Reification.")

We can now summarize. In the process of production man is turned into an object, i.e., labor power, and the result of his labor is used partly to make possible new investment in the productive apparatus, partly— in the highly industrialized societies—to increase his private consumption and to make it independent of his need-structure to a high degree. As labor power, labor has an exchange-value for W who sells it and little use-value for him, since it is seldom satisfying and since its results cannot be appropriated by those producing them. This depends on the fact that chances of influencing decision-making in the sphere of production exists neither in capitalist countries nor in the Soviet Union for W. As R, W becomes a buyer of exchange-values. He is perceived by the seller, i.e., by C, as a means in the distribution process: A high acquisition rate for consumption thus becomes necessary for the production process. Consumption becomes a prerequisite for production. For C both W and R are objects in these processes. Men perceive themselves as objects, as things in their roles of both Ws and Rs. This is the psychological aspect of reification.

A final central question becomes the following. Is this process of reification an *unavoidable* consequence of the development of technology? Is man forced to become the slave of machines—compelled by the very forces he has created and from which he cannot escape? If such is the case, then the analysis must end with a statement to the effect that man's fate is irrevocably determined by technology. In our opinion, such a conclusion represents a case of reified thinking.

A SUMMARY AND AN OUTLOOK

The basic feature of our epoch is the continuous and rapid development of science and technology, i.e., the productive forces available to mankind. "Technology means the systematic application of scientific or other organized knowledge to practical task," says Galbraith.[73] Systematic application of science and other knowledge means acting in what Max Weber called "an instrumental rational way." Instrumental rationality implies that, given *certain goals*, expectations concerning the most economic and efficient ways of reaching the goal dictate action. As Habermas points out,[74] rational behavior in this context concerns (1) selection of means and (2) the choice of strategies when alternative means are available. Rational instrumental action is usually based upon formal rules derived from empirical knowledge. The choice of strategies is usually based upon analytical knowledge such as mathematics and logic.

Thus, instrumental rational thinking emphasizes the means of action and does not discuss the goals, which are considered as given and unchangeable. This partly depends on the fact that instrumental rational action can refer to empirical knowledge for its legitimation. However, as has previously been pointed out, empirical knowledge, at least in the

[73] Galbraith, *The New Industrial State*, p. 12.
[74] J. Habermas, *Technik und Wissenschaft als "Ideologie"* (Frankfurt: Edition Suhrkamp, 1968).

field of social science, is a consequence of historically determined conditions which are often based upon social values and goals.

There is a second reason why so little attention is given to goals. Instrumental rational action has become an ideology in the sense that it is used for legitimizing existing social conditions, for example, the power structure responsible for goal-setting. Actions are defended on the grounds that they are carried out in a "scientific way" or that they are "efficient from a technological point of view" or, finally, that they are "rational from an economic point of view." Scientists and technicians thus defend their actions against criticism and try to legitimize them by the very criteria with which they have been planned and executed. By referring to their own expertise and to the lack of technical knowledge among their critics, the tautological circle of defending actions—by using exactly the same criteria upon which they are based—is fulfilled.

So science and technology serve not only as productive forces but also as means of social domination. Whereas science had an emancipating effect during, for example, the period of the Renaissance—when it freed man from the power of dogmatic social forces—this is not so today when science and technology are tending to become means of social dominance.

A final reason for the dominance of instrumental rational action is the role of social planning. Many observers agree that a market economy cannot function because of the technical development and its needs, and therefore social planning becomes a necessity. But planning may also be conceived of as instrumental rational action. Habermas[75] speaks of planning as instrumental rational action of a second order and another observer calls it "the economic technique of intervention."[76] Thus planning, as a *technique*, represents instrumental rational action and is considered to be indifferent to goals imbedded in a social philosophy.

In this way the impression is created that social action more and more becomes a consequence of the way in which technology functions. Economic processes are pictured as necessary consequences of the development of technology. To use Marx's terminology: the productive forces determine the mode of production. The level of development of the productive forces demands the production of long series in order to make possible the use of machinery which rationalizes the process of production. In turn, the use of machinery demands large capital investments. These are possible only through increased sales, which mean control over the market and increased consumption. Thus consumption becomes a necessary condition for rational production, which in turn makes

[75] Ibid.
[76] J. Ellul, *The Technological Society* (New York: Alfred A. Knopf, 1964).

possible those investments necessary for still more rational production. Every new technological development leads to new demands for rational behavior and for diminishing economic risks and also to new demands for long-term planning.

The goal of the technocratic elite becomes continuous economic growth, which is defended by stressing that it is this growth which makes possible higher standards of living. Not only are these goals seldom discussed, but also the way in which economic growth is usually measured is not neutral but implies certain values. The usual measure is the gross national product per capita and its increase over time. However, by this measure, production for space travel and military equipment counts as much as health services, schooling, and the creation of parks. In addition, the measure does not take into account the existing distribution of income among the inhabitants of a certain country, and so on. Economic growth is measured by the total amount of products produced and services rendered without taking into account either the type of production and the ways in which resources are used, or considering the possible lack of equality in the process of distribution.

Thus, the main problem becomes: Can a change in emphasis from instrumental-rational thinking to value-rational thinking be achieved? In other words, is it possible to shift the emphasis from the instrumental aspects to the goal aspects, thus questioning the purposes of economic growth especially in a world in which a polarization has occurred? One-third of humanity controls up to 90 percent of all available resources, largely making use of them for the benefit of this one-third, while the rest of the world lives in poverty and want.

The second problem becomes: How can goal-setting and decision-making processes be democratized in such a way that limited power-elites, using an immense bureaucratic apparatus, are not able to make their decisions without being exposed to effective control by the vast masses of people?

"The direction of technical progress is today still determined by societal interests, which grow naturally from the compulsion to reproduce social life, without being understood as such and being confronted with the declared political goals of social groups," Habermas[77] says. For that reason the discrepancy between technological development and the goals of society becomes more and more marked. Instrumental rationality serves goals which seem irrational when considered with regard to long-term consequences. Reification thus appears as a process by which human beings become the objects for a "process" which is governed by

[77] Habermas, *Technik und Wissenschaft*, p. 117.

technological and economic tendencies inherent in the social and economic system. In order to overcome reification it is necessary that by means of democratic decision-making processes man defines his own goals and consciously directs the ways of achieving these goals, thus becoming master of his own fate. As an ethical and political point of departure this demand must become central, even if its realization appears difficult as all other alternatives appear to be worse.

THE PSYCHOLOGICAL PROCESS OF REIFICATION

So far we have tried to analyze the process of reification on a sociological level and have only occasionally referred to the psychological consequences. Within a social system reifying processes lead to the domination of things over human beings. We have also tried to show that human beings are transformed into objects, into production and distribution factors. This is made possible especially through the location of power in special groups and the corresponding powerlessness of those who do not belong to these groups. As a consequence of the power distribution and the distance and invisibility of decision-making bodies, we hypothesized the depersonalization of human relations and the perception of their asymmetry. Combining depersonalization and asymmetry we postulated a dehumanization of social relations in which man becomes a means in the basic economic processes. What effect does such a process have on man's self-image and self-evaluation? In order to answer the question, let us for a moment return to Marx's definition of man: "The real nature of man is the totality of social relations."[78] This statement can be interpreted as that man is not the *result* of his social relation but rather that man *is* his social relations. In other words the individual and the group are two aspects of the same phenomenon. Marx's theory is almost completely in agreement with those developed by Cooley and Mead. "Both Cooley and Mead thought that a separate individual is an abstraction; the individual has no separate existence. The individual psychological phenomena, consciousness and the self, are social products. Social interaction precedes consciousness and the self. The social interaction creates the individual's consciousness and self."[79] Thus the individual's self and his consciousness are not *characteristics* but *relations*, between the individual and significant others. Marx states in *German Ideology*[80] that

[78] *Mega I.5*, p. 535.
[79] J. Asplund, "Den symboliska interaktionismens värderelevans," *Sociologisk Forskning* VI (1969), No. 1, 1–26.
[80] *Mega I.5*, p. 20.

"consciousness is therefore from the very beginning a social product, and remains so as long as men exist at all."

We will now combine this basic assumption—and call it the Marx-Cooley-Mead relational interactionism hypothesis—with a second assumption developed by Marx. The basic relations between man are those which exist in the process of production and (we may add after our analysis) in the process of distribution. Thus if man's self, his own image, is the relation between himself and others, and if the most important relations are those occurring in the processes of production and distribution, then these relations may have a profound influence on man. If man perceives himself as powerless in his relations to others, if he perceives himself as an object, then this perception will make him experience reification as the "normal state of affairs"—his consciousness will be a reified one.

But the social interaction will also shape the self-image and the consciousness of those in a power position. The more powerful they perceive themselves to be, the more powerless they will perceive others to be. In addition, since powerful persons are located at the top of hierarchies with a wide social distance between themselves and those in lower positions in the hierarchy, they will interact mainly with persons occupying similar positions. As their social interaction is restricted, they will have no direct and living experience of persons located in lower positions in the hierarchy. This will lead to perception of people in lower positions as objects or as means to be used in achieving their own goals.

That would partly explain the inhuman actions of the power elite during the Stalin period in the Soviet Union as well as the neglect of human rights by those who pursue a ruthless capitalistic exploitation, e.g., as is carried out by corporations and other enterprises in the underdeveloped areas of Latin America.

Perceiving people as means and objects leads to the perception of them as replaceable as labor power. But this perception will lead to actions mediated through persons on lower levels in a hierarchy which, in turn, shapes the self-image of those considered as replaceable. Finally powerful people can exist only *in relation* to powerless people, exploiters only in relation to exploited, bureaucrats only in relation to men as objects. Thus, not only does a reciprocity exist but this reciprocity has a feedback effect: social interaction leads to the strengthening of existing self-images. (In this perspective, however, one must also observe the role of the labor movements, e.g., in Scandinavian countries, in creating a new self-image among workers, accompanied by a new self-confidence.)

It is probably easier to understand that a person experiences himself as an object in a process of production in which he *is* labor power, than in a process of distribution in which he also is consumer, i.e., an acting subject. Therefore, let us take a closer look at the second process.

When does something possess a value for a person? An object *o* possesses value for an individual *i* if *i* wishes to have *o*, to own *o*, to consume *o*, to have a certain relationship to *o* in preference to other *o's*. In other words, *i* prefers *o* instead of wishing to give it up for other *o's*. Now if these preferred objects are preferred to other objects independent of their exchange-value and independent of the social situation (i.e., of social influences) because *i* experiences them as means for satisfying needs, then for him they possess use-value.

One of man's basic needs is the need for self-evaluation and self-estimation. In accordance with the interactionist principles previously discussed, self-evaluation is mediated by being evaluated by others.

If we assume that the process of production is man's most important activity, then work and skills in the work situation should play an important role in a person's self-evaluation. To the degree that labor has become mechanized, the individual has no chances of evaluating himself or being evaluated by others in his work activity. Instead his labor power as a commodity can be exchanged for objects with a certain exchange-value.

Since the need for self-evaluation can no longer be satisfied in the process of production and since outside the labor process people often live isolated lives and have impersonal relations to others, no real basis for a self-evaluation mediated by the evaluation of others exists. Others do not know him and are related to him sufficiently to evaluate his "human abilities and skills." However, one visible basis for evaluation exists: the things he owns or uses may give him status. "Status" means a characteristic which is appreciated by others. These objects which endow status have a certain exchange-value. But by giving status they also acquire use-value, in that they satisfy a basic need of self-evaluation. Therefore one central problem in the consumption society is that objects acquire use-value through their exchange-value. Through this *indirect* use-value, for example, a high-priced car may give greater satisfaction than a low-priced car.

In the affluent consumption society the individual is more than a consuming object to be influenced by those who want to sell objects. He also acquires objects, judges these objects in the first place according to their exchange-value, and tries to use this exchange-value to acquire status in order to satisfy his need of self-evaluation and self-estimation. The satisfaction of this need is mediated by the ownership of exchange-values. As a consequence, individuals evaluate themselves, and are evaluated by others, through visible objects which possess a certain exchange-value and, as a consequence, *indirect* use-value.

Thus, reified existence here in the consumption society can be defined as a situation in which objects acquire use-value because they have exchange-value.

ADDITIONAL REMARKS CONCERNING THE INDIVIDUAL'S RELATION TO OBJECTS

Another hypothesis concerning reified relations to objects has been put forward by Lucien Goldmann.[81] He asserts that in the capitalistic market system man's relation to objects is determined by the objects' exchange-value alone. He points out that the use-value of an object is determined by qualitative characteristics, whereas exchange-value, which is common to all commodities—they can be exchanged for each other—is first and foremost of a quantitative nature. Independent of the stand one takes in relation to such a value theory, there is one interesting idea contained in Goldmann's work; in his relationship to the object the individual has a tendency to allow himself to be governed by quantitative judgments. It is this that Goldmann sees as a consequence of reification; the quantitative value of things becomes dominant. Other authors, Fromm, for example,[82] put forward another aspect of the individual's relation to things, namely, that which is a consequence of the consumption society.

In order to demonstrate the individual's quantitative relation to things, I shall begin with an extreme example. Several years ago while taking a walk in New York, I came upon an art gallery where expensive works of Italian Renaissance painters and Dutch masters were displayed for sale. I inquired if anyone apart from museums could afford to buy such works. The owner told me that among his customers were to be found stockbrokers who, when they had make a profit out of their speculations, came and bought a picture. They saw the pictures quite simply as capital investments. Usually they did not hang them, among other reasons because they had not enough room for them. Instead they locked them in the safe-deposit box at their bank. The art dealer added that his customers' aesthetic interest in pictures was of about the same nature as their aesthetic interest in shares. He meant that if it was considered *comme il faut*, they would be equally willing to hang their shares on the walls. In this case the value of the pictures is purely quantitative —it can be expressed in terms of money. Their aesthetic value, which in a certain sense can be expressed as a qualitative value, has been concealed. In this way, a picture becomes in the first place an object, which

---

[81] Goldmann, *Recherches dialectiques.*

[82] E. Fromm, "The Application of Humanist Psychoanalysis to Marx's Theory," in *Socialist Humanism*, ed. E. Fromm (Garden City: Doubleday & Co.), p. 215.

can be exchanged for money or for other objects, while its aesthetic value makes it into a "picture."

As a contrast to this example, one might take the case in which a person refuses to sell an object, despite being offered a great deal of money for it, on the grounds that it has a "sentimental" value for him.

Instead of placing "use-value" against "exchange-value," one could make the assumption that all objects have both an "exchange-value" and a "use-value." If, as an example of the "use-value" of the pictures, we take their aesthetic value as judged by a connoisseur of art and take as "exchange-value" their value in money, and if for the sake of simplicity we divide both "use-value" and "exchange-value" into "high" and "low," we arrive at the following table:

		Exchange-value	
		High	Low
Use-value	High	1. Collection of an art connoisseur	2. A picture with sentimental value
	Low	4. A picture as an investment	3. A picture of the "pavement artist" type

In the first cell we find objects for which both use-value and exchange-value are high for a given individual. In our society (as in many earlier societies) this relation to things is the prerogative of a small group of people, namely, those who are so rich that they can afford to collect objects which satisfy their highly developed "taste," i.e., their knowledge of the use-value of objects, as defined here.

In the second cell we find objects which have a sentimental value for certain people. If we follow Simmel's analysis (see chapter 5), it seems that this relation has been typical for people in preindustrial society.

At the same time we may ask if technical development has not brought with it the opportunities for people to establish this type of relation to objects on a much wider scale. Take, for instance, the cleverly made reproductions of works of art; i.e., they have a high use-value but sell at a "reasonable" price.

The combination in the third cell is probably also more common in a highly industrialized consumption society than was the case in previous societies. If we forget pictures for a moment and think of the wealth of objects that we use of the "buy-use-get rid of" type, then it seems to be extremely common among people in an industrial society to have the relation as given in cell 3 to a great number of different objects.

Finally, in cell 4 we find the reified relation. Goldmann's contention that this type of relation is very common in capitalist society involves two things: (1) that it is more common as compared to earlier societies, (2) that it is more common as compared to other relations in a given society. Our simple analysis suggests that the latter alternative can hardly be correct. As to the first alternative, we can only say that such theories as Simmel's, for example, could be taken as support that there is something in such a contention.

In summary, we can say that Goldmann's hypothesis—that the individual in the capitalist society has a "quantitative" relation to objects, i.e., a relation in which it is mainly the exchange-value that is of importance, use-value being of lesser importance—seems to be valid only up to a certain point. Such a relation to the object does occur and the importance of reification seems obvious. But, in a highly industrialized society characterized by its orientation to consumption, another factor seems to be of greater importance from the point of view of reification.

In such a social system, consumption often has the character of a fetish. People surround themselves with a large number of things. To buy and own things may be a dominant goal—to use things may be just as much a goal in itself as a means for need-satisfaction. This is especially the case as far as "conspicuous consumption" is concerned. In this connection there is another factor of importance for the theory of reification. It is usually presented in the following hypothesis: An involvement with things, with consumption, with one's own living standard, seems to go hand in hand with a lack of involvement in human problems and relations. To quote a Czechoslovakian sociologist: "Because in the industrialized and highly organized society involvement with things is fairly easy, while involvement with human problems and relationships is very difficult and as a consequence becomes almost completely neglected both in child-upbringing and in social life, so involvement in the acquisition of things becomes a surrogate for genuine human involvement, i.e., both for deeper personal demands and for involvement with other people."[83]

It is perhaps interesting to point out that Machovec is not speaking of the capitalist, but of the industrialized and highly organized society. The question is if in preindustrial society human involvement was greater and had the depth that Machovec sees as a desirable goal.

One may answer with two arguments. In preindustrial society, characterized by *Gemeinschaft*, to use Tönnies's[84] term, there were closer social relations between individuals. These were replaced by the anonymity of industrialism's *Gesellschaft*, where an individual's contacts are

[83] M. Machovec, "Hoffnung und Befürchtung der Annäherung," in *Club Voltaire, Jahrbuch für kritische Aufklärung* III, ed. G. Szczesny (Munich: Szczesny Verlag, 1967).

[84] F. Tönnies, *Gemeinschaft und Gesellschaft* (Leipzig: Buska, 1935).

limited mainly to the small nuclear family. Therefore, goods owned by the family (house, car, summer place, etc.) are given the function of holding together the family, by orienting their interests toward these goods.

The second argument might be formulated as follows: Preindustrial society was characterized by want, poverty, and a low living standard. These conditions affected human relations. Getting rid of the worst hardship and replacing it with a reasonable standard of living for large groups should, then, have meant that there would be an orientation toward human relations and, above all, an interest in the social problems of other people. The latter should especially be so because modern mass media has brought into our homes the problems of others, for instance, the problem of poverty in other parts of the world.

The problem is partly a question of influence. Advertisements and propaganda for consumption, plus the consumption ideology itself, have much greater resources at their command than are available, e.g., for spreading information about underdeveloped countries and their problems.

The orientation toward things can be thought of as having yet another consequence. The individual seldom experiences a situation in which he is able to feel pleased and satisfied. It is a fairly well established fact that the level of aspiration is not constant, but rises when the individual has reached a certain level.

This psychological mechanism seems to show that orientation to things does not become weaker when the individual has reached a certain consumption standard. This also contributes to the fact that new products are continuously being brought out and that advertisements attempt to create new demand.

Through this discussion we have also hinted that the theory of reification—at least the aspects discussed here—builds on definite values. They can be described as being opposite to these values which among Christians are sometimes in a negative way referred to as "materialist orientation." To a large extent this orientation coincides with what has here been called "orientation to things." In contrast the values implied in our theory stress among other things a positive appreciation of human relations of a given type, and a rejection of the "striving after things."

These values can be judged in the light of their consequences for action. Allow me to give an example: In Scandinavian countries there has been an intensive debate about aid to developing countries and the question of whether or not we must relinquish a rise in our own standards of living, how much we must help, and how quickly there is to be an increase in the aid we give. Assume that someone suggested we should halt our own living standard, at least in the case of those who cannot be considered as low-wage earners, in order to make possible a rapid increase in foreign aid. How many politicians in "responsible positions" would consider this a "realistic policy"? In my opinion the fact that they do not do so is connected to the orientation to things that I have tried to describe in this section.

RELATIONS BETWEEN PEOPLE

A thesis about reification concerning social relations is that human relations are changed into thing-relations. "In the course of being made into an object by which the human element is moulded into something foreign to man, into a commodity, all relations between people become dependent on money."[85]

If man is perceived as labor power and transformed into a commodity, his usefulness is often determined on the basis of the contribution he makes, or is capable of making, to economic life—to social production. Take a few examples from the Swedish society: (1) Many small farmers have been "rationalized" out of existence, whether or not they themselves wished to remain farmers, because from the point of view of society's economy, they are not remunerative. (2) The sex-role debate is concerned with the equality of women. But the most effective argument for equality is that women are required on the "labor market," i.e., society needs them as "labor power." (3) Those who have passed a certain age limit are made redundant, or they find difficulties in competing on equal terms with younger people, because in terms of labor power they are not considered to be "as good as young people." These three examples illustrate how human relations are transformed into utility-relations, which in turn build on a definite argument concerning efficiency and formal rationality (also anchored in value).

Preoccupation with the "market" affects another aspect of human relations. Social influence, the transmittal of political information or religious messages, etc., are seen as "marketing problems" or problems concerned with how one can best "sell ideas." As an example I will quote a few lines from an essay entitled "The Church's Crisis—A Marketing Problem."[86] With its grotesque exaggerations it is rather revealing.

In the article it is first maintained that the Swedish State Church, with its $80-90 million of wage costs, is a large enterprise run like a retail

---

[85] A. Cornu, "L'idée d'aliénation chez Hegel, Feuerbach et Karl Marx," *La Pensée*, 1948.

[86] E. Elinder, "Kyrkans kris—ett marknadsföringsproblem?" in *Företag och Marknader* (Stockholm, 1968).

business. The church is said to have "landed in the common dilemma of the old, previously successful industrial enterprise—having a production program which is not suited to present-day consumers . . . in the enormous competition for time and interest the Christian congregations, and not least the Swedish Church, annually lose a very large share of the market . . . what surprises a simple consumer of Christian information is that this takes place without those in responsible positions . . . ever having seen the problem as it really is—a marketing problem."[87]

According to this point of view an advertising agency, used to marketing detergents, should certainly be able to deal with the sale of the Christian commodity, not to people but to "consumers."

In this context human relations are seen in terms of utility—to what extent is it possible to make use of a person as labor-power, and to what extent is it possible to make use of him as a prospective consumer? From this point of view, the statement that human relations are transformed into relations between objects has some meaning. But it is not sufficient to be satisfied with the statement. We have seen that the individual's relations to objects can assume various forms, as shown in the preceding section. If one makes the statement more precise, then it is reasonable to utilize the distinction "use-value" and "exchange-value." The "exchange-value" of a person in relation to other people can be seen as the value the person possesses as the acquirer of consumption goods. The "use-value" of a person in relation to others is harder to define, but it should refer to human capacities which are appreciated due to certain value premises; intelligence, beauty, honesty, tolerance, sympathy, solidarity, warmth, love, etc., i.e., those factors or combinations of factors which are traditionally valued highly in relations between people.

An object-relation to another person can then be defined as a relation in which he is assessed as a commodity with a high exchange-value and a low use-value, and in which human contact is based on this assessment. Could a nonreified relation be defined as a relation in which the opposite obtains, i.e., in which social contacts are established which are based on a person's high use-value and low exchange-value?

Clearly it is rather more complex than that. Among other things it depends on which social relation is in question. In economic life, for example, the individual's exchange-value, i.e., the individual seen as labor-power, is of great importance. But even factors defining his use-value may play a part. He may be appreciated for intelligence, knowledge, the capacity to cooperate, etc. In addition, one may perhaps take another approach. It may not be possible to eliminate the fact that an

[87] Ibid., p. 91.

employee *is* labor power, but it can be compensated for. *One* way of doing this is to give him influence and power, i.e., to introduce a system that may be called industrial democracy. The idea of "democracy in industry" usually builds on notions that information, influence, and the power to make decisions alters the individual's objective situation and his perception of his own role. He is transformed from a passive cog in a large machine to an active, acting subject.

In principle the idea of equality (in the meaning that all persons ought to have the same opportunity to take part in those decision-making processes that are of importance for their lives[88]) means the acceptance of the evaluation that human relations should be symmetrical. In this context, relations built upon equality are at the opposite pole to reified social relations. This may also apply to other relations. Equality, e.g. between men and women, i.e. evening out of sex-role differences, also involves the introduction of symmetrical relations.

BUREAUCRATIZATION

In our previous analysis the process of reification has been hypothesized to occur on a societal level with regard to two main problems: (1) The tendency of the consumption society to make demands independent of the need-structure of the individual, which means that consumption is directed more by the exchange-value of objects than by the use-value. Thus the acquisition of things becomes a major motivation of individuals in the consumption society. On a microsociological level this may lead to a situation in which things rule the individual and consumption becomes a necessary precondition for production on a macrosociological level. Finally we hypothesized that this reifying tendency would affect self-evaluation in such a way that people would experience themselves as powerless, and being unable to evaluate their abilities, learn to evaluate themselves through the exchange-value of the things they possess: they perceive themselves as having use-value as human beings through the exchange-value of the things they own.

(2) The second major reifying process is bureaucratization. In order to discuss this process we must briefly explain the term. In fact, we can distinguish at least *four* usages: (a) bureaucracy referring to the social and administrative structure of organizations, (b) bureaucracy as a *system* of *values*, (c) bureaucracy referring to the *people* who are in charge of or hold power in those organizations or social systems having a

[88] T. B. Bottomore, *Classes in Modern Society* (London: George Allen & Unwin, 1965).

bureaucratic structure, and (d) bureaucracy referring to the ways in which bureaucratic organizations *function*.

The theory of bureaucratic organization has been developed by Max Weber (and is treated in chapter 5). According to him bureaucratic administration is built upon rational-legal authority, where "rational" means "formal-rational." It implies the separation of ownership of means of production and of management, in order to limit the power of bureaucratic administrators. However, as we have pointed out, control over the means of production can be effectively carried out without ownership. For Weber, in addition, bureaucratic administration meant hierarchical organization, authoritarian tendencies (e.g., the emphasis on discipline), the definition of the range of competence of an office, selection according to competence, the chances of a career, etc. Weber's description of the bureaucratic organization is "ideal-typical,"[89] i.e. (without going into details), the description of the "pure type" of bureaucratic organization.

The interesting point in Weber's analysis is that his preoccupation with formal rationality leads to his dealing rather superficially with the negative (from certain value-points of view) consequences of bureaucratic organization. He perceives them as the most effective and rational way of administration, making possible the capitalistic mode of production. But since, according to Weber, bureaucratic administration means the exercise of control on the basis of technical knowledge, all social systems must accept bureaucratic organization. This holds for socialist as well as capitalist[90] systems.

Weber sees the risks. He asks himself whether individual freedom and democratic control could be saved. However, he does not answer the question, maintaining that a third question concerning the inherent limitations of bureaucracy is more important.[91] With regard to the development of reifying processes it more than ever seems necessary to make the first two questions salient ones.

The system of values (in Marxist terminology "the ideological superstructure") of bureaucratization can be depicted by mentioning a few terms: efficiency, formalization of rules, impersonal social relations, and the acceptance of asymmetric personal relations, usually in a more or less authoritarian manner defined in terms of dominance and submission. Thus the value system of bureaucratic organizations, being detri-

[89] See the discussion of this problem by P. Blau, *The Dynamics of Bureaucracy* (Chicago: University of Chicago Press, 1955).

[90] M. Weber, *Economy and Society*, ed. G. Roth and C. Wittich (New York: Bedminster Press, 1968).

[91] See the discussion in chapter 5.

mental to a democratic and equalitarian value-system, may be considered to be a sufficient condition for the establishment of the dehumanized social relations characterizing a reified social system.

The third application of the term referred to the group of people in control of the bureaucratic apparatus. In chapter 8 we briefly presented the analysis put forward by Marcović. He, like some other authors, stresses the fact that bureaucratic groups tend to develop into a new ruling class in the socialist countries in the East, while the military-political-technological elites in the West form a similar class. Again, their power is based not only upon the control of the means of production, but also upon control over recruitment into this class; furthermore, they are able to set the goals for the functioning of the economic and state bureaucratic organization, subject to little or no democratic control.

The dominance of the bureaucratic social structure, the dominance of those values coined as bureaucratic, and the dominance of a bureaucratic class—these three factors taken together constitute what may be termed the "bureaucratization of society"—having the effect that bureaucratic organizations develop their own ways of functioning, independent of, and often in opposition to, the goals created for them, and leading to the rule of the bureaucratic class's holding in its hands the concentration of power with corresponding powerlessness among the rest of the population. Thus we have the basis for one of the main reifying processes in modern society.

So far, the analysis has taken place on a macrosociological, institutional level. However, there is also a microsociological level, namely, the level on which the study of specific bureaucratic organizations is carried out. On this level the fourth way of talking about bureaucracy is used, i.e., the one referring to the functioning or malfunctioning of bureaucratic organizations. In addition to Peter Blau's previously mentioned study,[92] we can look at a few theoretical approaches and start with the analysis presented by Merton.[93]

In Merton's view the functioning of a bureaucracy presupposes standardized behavior. This means demands for discipline and conformity to rules. Behavior becomes rigid, and the individual has difficulties in adapting himself and his behavior to the demands of the job, at which point there occurs what Merton calls "trained incompetence."

The rigid behavior of the individual leads to conflicts with those people who are outside the bureaucratic apparatus, and who are supposed to be served by it. The risk of such conflicts, and the lack of adaptation to the job leads to tightened control and increased demands for disci-

[92] Blau, *The Dynamics of Bureaucracy*.

[93] R. Merton, *Social Theories and Social Structure* (Glencoe, Ill.: The Free Press, 1967).

pline. In the long run, the individual within the organization begins to "behave ritualistically": in order to shield himself from criticism he follows the rules to the last letter. Conformity to rules becomes an end in itself, and this makes the real task of the bureaucracy harder to carry out; thus a vicious circle is created.

One may ask whether a bureaucratic apparatus such as described by Merton can function at all. One answer is that conflicts with the environment force the whole structure to be revised and therefore changed. This may occur in various ways, perhaps by bringing in experts from outside, or by giving the employees in the organization a chance to take part in decision-making processes by delegating parts of this process to lower levels, etc.

Sooner or later a bureaucratic apparatus finds itself in conflict with the outer world—as object of criticism—and is forced to change.

Such changes may affect the tasks or the individuals who carry out the tasks. In the first case emphasis is placed on those tasks the individual is to perform. Either the tasks are changed or the individual is given better training and increased knowledge.

However, if emphasis is placed on the individuals who carry out the tasks, then the starting assumption is often that the apparatus in itself is perfect but that the individual is trying to sabotage it. This may result in a series of dismissals or purge.

The latter method not only presupposes a general ideology with regard to the perfect functioning of the organization, it also requires the presence of power conditions which make possible such dimissals or purges.

Michel Crozier,[94] the French sociologist, maintains that in every bureaucracy there occurs a feedback of information concerning mistakes and an attempt to put this to rights. Serious problems occur if the fault ceases to be corrected. One method of learning by mistakes is not to do away with the rules, but rather to define them more specifically, make them still more detailed, and demand even greater obedience. But this means that several situations are neglected, as it is impossible to formulate rules for all possible situations.

Crozier suggests that one way of solving this problem is the creation of parallel power centers, each formulating its own rules. This conflicts with the principle of power-centralization, by which all decisions for which there are no rules are decided centrally. Centralizing of power means that decisions are made, and rules formulated, at a point remote from that part of the bureaucracy which is to make use of these deci-

[94] M. Crozier, *The Bureaucratic Phenomenon* (Chicago: University of Chicago Press, 1964).

sions or rules. As those who make the decisions lack sufficient information, decisions and rules are necessarily unsatisfactory when they come "from above." The system functions in an impersonal manner, and this often means strict stratification and the isolation of persons within their various strata. This reduces information and feedback.

Crozier completes Merton's vicious circle. For the individual, particularly those who find themselves low in the hierarchy, the consequence of all this is that he experiences himself as a thing, a cog in a machine, and feels that the organization is something quite outside his influence. Consequently be becomes passive and apathetic. This is then taken by the leadership as a sign that the individual is unable to participate in the decision-making process, thereby strengthening the idea that centralization is the best power-form, and also strengthening the leadership's unwillingness to allow those individuals who occupy a low position in the bureaucratic apparatus to take part in decision-making processes. Therefore, many of the problems concerning the bureaucratic apparatus are questions of power and the distribution of power-centralization vs. joint influence, democratic control and joint decision-making.

REIFIED THEORIES

REIFICATION AS A COGNITIVE PHENOMENON

So far, we have discussed reification as a social process and have indicated some of the psychological consequences of these reifying processes. However, there is one problem which we have not treated. Our knowledge of reality is usually organized in terms of theories that try to explain phenomena and to establish laws. Are there theories, in particular sociological theories, which can be characterized as "reified theories"? In order to discuss this problem, we have to make a distinction between "theories of reification" and "reified theories." The first types of theories are those which try to analyze and explain the social process of reification. The theory developed in the previous section is such an attempt.

The second types of theories, however, are such that they can be characterized as "reified theories." Thus we must try to present criteria for the classification of social theories as reified theories. This section, therefore, is concerned with this problem. In other words it deals with a metatheoretical problem, i.e., with theories about theories.

We will start our discussion by referring to an analysis presented by Berger and Pullberg[95] in which they attempt to present reification

[95] P. Berger and S. Pullberg, "The Concept of Reification," *New Left Review* No. 35 (1966), 56–71.

within the framework of the sociology of knowledge. They differentiate between two types of sociological theory. One of them "presents us with a view of society as a network of human meanings as embodiments of human activity. The second, on the other hand, presents us with society conceived of as a thinglike *facticity*, standing over against its individual members with coercive controls and moulding them in its socializing process."[96]

The first type of theory sees man as a social being and society as the creator of man. The second takes society as the independent variable, and examines its effect on the individual.

In Berger's and Pullberg's attempt to create a synthesis of both these types of theories—we return to this problem in the next section—the concept of reification plays an important part. They begin by distinguishing between objectivation and reification, using the former concept in the Marxist tradition.

Objectivation[97] is the process by which man produces objects for the satisfaction of his needs, and by which these objects acquire a meaning, that is, the subjective meaning given to them by man. During this process, in order to become conscious of his own activity, man needs to create a distance between himself and both the product and the production. With the help of language he is able to communicate meaning to other people.

The social process of production takes place within a given framework or within a given social structure, which is itself part of, and produced by, the process of production. The whole process, i.e., the method by which material and nonmaterial products acquire a meaning that can be communicated, is reflected in the consciousness of man. It is understood and comprehended. It is this cognitive process, i.e., the knowledge and understanding of how the human world is created, that Berger and Pullberg call objectivation.

The next step is to distinguish between reification and objectivation. Reification is a specific type of objectivation. As the unity of product and production is broken down by one means or another (we need not discuss this any more closely at this point), the objects that are produced may not appear as a human product. Instead, the objects may be seen as "real," in the sense of possessing a reality of their own, which exists independently of the creative activity of man and the meaning he has given to the object. This specific, own-reality has the character of a thing.

[96] Ibid., p. 56.

[97] Berger and Pullberg differentiate between "objectivation" and "objectification." With regard to our aim, however, it is not necessary to follow their suggestion. I do not take into consideration their distinction between "alienation" and "reification," since it differs from the definitions used here.

As here defined, objectivation and reification are both cognitive processes. Objectivation is a general anthropological phenomenon, that is, it occurs in all societies however simple their techniques of production. Reification, on the other hand, is not a necessary process. The conditions under which it occurs is another problem. According to Berger and Pullberg,[98] reification is the alienated method of becoming conscious of man's activity, and the products of this activity. We will now present two diagrams, Figures 11 and 12.

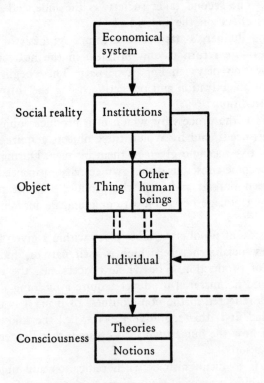

Figure 11.   Reified processes.

As a starting point we will take the Marxist distinction between "social reality" and "consciousness." A broken line separates these two phenomena. The economic system influences the social institutions, for example, production, social organizations, the market, the bureaucracy, etc. The institutions are the framework for the production of objects seen as "things" by the individual. These institutions function in such a way that

[98] Berger and Pullberg, "The Concept of Reification."

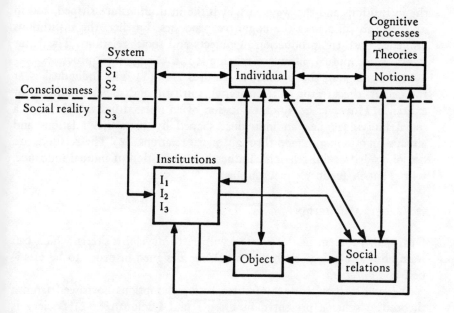

Figure 12. Nonreified processes.

man also appears as an object. Certain definite relations exist between the "object level" and the individual, and they express themselves in the previously mentioned ideas about thinglike relations. These ideas are part of the "consciousness" of the individual, which in the diagram is divided into two levels, theories and nontheoretical notions.

Finally, there is a direct influence from the institutions to the individual. In Figure 11 the sign of reification is that all relations are presented as proceeding in one direction (with the exception of the relations between the object and individual, as these are concerned with ideas). This means that the theory is concerned with causal relations, in which the economic system is the "basic" causal factor.

In the second diagram, Figure 12, we have attempted to present a theory of nonreified processes.

Here, too, there is a dividing line between "consciousness" and "social reality." The individual is at the center—he both creates the various systems and produces the cognitive processes. The various systems S1, S2, S3 are found partly on the "consciousness level" and partly on the "social reality" level. This corresponds to the Marxist division into "basis" and "superstructure."

The individual is the creator of social institutions, which are also influenced by the various systems. In addition, theories and ideas affect the institutions and the ways in which the institutions are shaped, and in its turn this influences the cognitive processes. Further, the institutions influence both the production of objects and social relations. The latter stand in a mutual influence-relation to the cognitive processes.

In this diagram the significant features are: (1) The individual is at the center, the creator of his material, spiritual, and social conditions of existence. However, it is not a question of an isolated individual but of a social individual, i.e., an individual shaped by his social relations and always functioning in, and through, social relations. (2) The relations are not one-sided causal relations. Rather it is a question of mutual influence, with built-in feedback mechanisms.

SOME BASIC ASSUMPTIONS

Our main problem in this section will be to develop criteria which can state how a sociological theory should be designed in order to be classified as *nonreified*.

We will start with a set of three basic assumptions borrowed from a theoretical scheme presented by Berger and Luckman.[99] (1) Society is a human-product. (2) Society is an objective reality. (3) Man is a social product.

These three basic assumptions state, first, that man in his social interaction with other men creates his own social environment, i.e., the conditions for his own life. These conditions are institutionalized and therefore become social facts. They exist before and after man is "born into his world." However, these social facts are continuously altered in the basic process of production in which man objectifies—in the Marxian sense—his own nature. However, "human nature" is conceived of as historically determined and continuously changing phenomena. It is altered through the influences which social institutions have on the individual. These three basic assumptions or postulates assert certain causal relations: man is shaping his own world and is in turn shaped by the products of his own creation.

Thus, the three basic assumptions can be conceived of as constituting together a *causal scheme* which states the type of causal relations to be *necessary* and *permitted* as well as the direction of these relations in a sociological theory to be classified as nonreified.

Together these three basic assumptions form a dialectical system. A sociological theory based upon them can take its point of departure in any one of the three postulates. If it starts with the first, the theoretical

[99] Berger and Luckman, *Social Construction of Reality.*

interest will be focused on historical conditions and the development of different societal types, e.g., characterized by a specific mode of production. Taking the second postulate as a point of departure, a sociological theory can take "society as an objective reality" as the independent variable, whereas man as social product becomes the dependent variable. In this case the emphasis is on processes of socialization and the exertion of social influence.

The important point is that in a theory based upon these three assumptions there are no built-in postulates either implicit or explicit, concerning *one-sided causal determination,* i.e., assumptions concerning determining factors and resultant determined effects. Instead, a dialectical relation is assumed between man as both creating his world and being influenced by the products of his own creation.

The consequence of such a basic approach can best be determined by stating which theoretical approaches are dismissed by such a causal scheme. To begin with, theories of ecological determinism are excluded, insofar as they assert that man is the sole product of his ecological environment. However, theories asserting that man's potential in a given historical epoch may be limited by the factors of his ecological environment are not excluded.

In the second place, theories are excluded which insist on biological determinism, assuming a fixed human nature, as being the determinant of social behavior. Excluded also are psychoanalytical theories asserting "one year of age" determinism, i.e., the assumption concerning the inevitable and unchangeable human personality as formed in early childhood. (However, the influence of childhood experiences is not denied.)

Third, theories of evolution, which assume that there is a process of evolution independent of human action and the effect of the environment created by man, are excluded.

Fourth, all theories of economic determinism are excluded. We will return to this point in the next section.

The important feature of a nonreified theory, then, is the basic postulate that society and its existing conditions have to be explained in terms of human activity, that they are created by man and therefore can be changed by him. This does not exclude assumptions concerning "autonomous effects," i.e., effects which have not been foreseen and therefore can create consequences that may be in contradiction to original intentions. However, the existence of such autonomous effects does not imply the existence of "objective," in the sense of thinglike, nonhuman factors operating independently of human action. They imply only a lack of human foresight, intelligence, and motivation.

Finally, nonreified theories imply not only dialectical relations between man and his environment but presuppose also a rationalistic image of man. Thus, the idea that man is the victim of his blind and unconscious impulses and instincts is not acceptable, but is replaced by an image of man as rational, reasonable, intelligent, being capable of consciously directing his actions and taking the responsibility for them.

The basic image of man implied or explicitly stated is of great importance, since theories about man and about society have an effect on our actions. They may have a "super-personal, alienating, collectifying power over the consciousness."[100]

SOCIOLOGISM AND PSYCHOLOGISM

A sociological theory which ignores the first postulate and in principle makes of society (seen as an objective reality, with emphasis on institutions and social structure) an independent variable, is the expression of sociologism. To the extent that in these theories the social system and the social structure assume a thinglike character, sociologism is an example of a reified sociological theory. The risk of such a reified theory occurring is a consequence of the fact that the first postulate has been neglected.

Much of present sociological theory can be categorized as sociologism. In fact, the study of the growth of social systems, social structures, and institutions is less comprehensive than the study of their effect on social behavior. The social structure is often presented—and indeed experienced —as a phenomenon which exists outside of the individual. The individual is not presented and experienced as an integral part of the structure. A social structure is often both experienced and presented as if it possessed the coercive power over the individual, so "society constrains, controls and may even destroy the individual. Through its agencies of social control, society surrounds the individual at each turn. But through its agencies of socialization, society also penetrates into the consciousness of the individual, molding the latter into a socially desired shape," say Berger and Pullberg,[101] joining Durkheim in their choice of words to demonstrate sociologistic assumptions.

The characteristic feature of the social structure is that it stands above the individual, has coercive power over him, and is characterized by automatically functioning influence. Such ideas regarding the social structure are based on actual social conditions. But, as Berger and Pull-

---

[100] Hofmann, *Universität, Ideologie, Gesellschaft*, p. 58.
[101] Berger and Pullberg, "The Concept of Reification," 63.

berg point out, a social system exists only as long as man sees it as a part of his world.

It could be experienced *a priori* as "an open horizon of possibility for all its members, a medium for the production of a world while at the same time it is itself a produced moment of that world."[102]

Such a point of view presupposes an attitude to sociology that differs from the present widespread attitude. Presumably, it would lead to another type of theory, and emphasize problems other than those which are at present considered to be interesting or important from the point of view of research.

Psychologism is the opposite pole of sociologism, as a reified sociological theory. One type of psychological theory tries to trace all human social activity to man's psychological mechanisms, for example, to his individual motivation. Psychoanalytical literature abounds in examples of psychologism. I shall mention only one example. A psychoanalyist points out that aggression in women is often a reaction to sexual frustration: "I would venture the guess that this kind of aggression has provided a substantial part of the fuel for carrying through the high degree of woman emancipation in Sweden, which would be one example of a constructive channelling of aggressive impulses."[103]

As an analogy, one could maintain that the struggle of the labor movement at the beginning of the century received its impetus from the fact that Swedish workers were sexually unsatisfied, and *therefore* frustrated. This type of explanation tries to reduce sociological phenomena to psychological, and therefore uses an inadequate level of explanation. Here we would like to restate Durkheim's basic rule of sociological method: "the explanation of a social phenomenon by another social phenomenon, the explanation of a mass phenomenon by another mass phenomenon, rather than the explanation of a social phenomenon by individual phenomena."[104]

Popper, who consequently has emphasized an antipsychologistic methodological line, stresses the autonomy of sociology by asserting that this science can make itself independent of psychology, and should do so to a very great degree. One reason for this is that sociology must explain undesired and unacceptable consequences of human action. This can be done only by reference to social conditions. If one wants, for ex-

[102] Ibid.

[103] T. Sjövall, "Sex and Human Relations," in *Sex and Human Relations*, Proceedings of the 4th Conference of the International Planned Parenthood Federation (Amsterdam: International Congress Series No. 102, Excerpta Foundation, 1965).

[104] Quoted after R. Aron, *Main Currents in Sociological Thought*, Vol. II (London: Weidenfeld & Nicolson, 1968).

ample, to explain undesired consequences of competition, this phenomenon cannot be explained in terms of psychological characteristics.[105]

Psychologism as sociologism builds on two definite postulates. They can be formulated as follows: (1) All human social activity is psychologically caused activity. (2) All psychologically caused activity can be traced back to definite mechanisms in the psyche of the individual. Psychologism involves a determinism that excludes a two-directional influence, social conditions being seen as dependent, not independent, variables. While psychologistic theories have the same drawbacks as sociologistic theories (they do not allow the construction of system having mutual influence and feedback mechanisms), the two differ from each other. While sociologistic theories are type-examples of *reified* theories, psychologistic theories are examples of *anti-reified* theories.

Psychologistic theories, however, can easily become reified theories. This occurs through reductionism whereby the two psychological meta-theoretical postulates are replaced by the following two: (1) All human social activity can be traced back to the methods of functioning of human nature. (2) Human nature is defined by definite, unchangeable biological circumstances. We talk about physical reductionism (as, for instance, in "hard-core" behaviorism) or biological determinism. It reduces the individual to a "thing"—a physiological organism whose reactions are determined by chemical processes.

There are several variations of this biological determinism, but they have one thing in common—they consider that social conditions do not influence, or influence very little, man's biological nature. As human nature is to a great extent, or "deep down," considered to be unalterable, how social conditions are organized is not important, or at least matters very little. From a social point of view the consequence of biological determinism is usually conservatism.

Furthermore, it is considered to be a task of the greatest importance to insure that social conditions are so organized that "dangerous" tendencies (for example, aggression), which are seen as a part of man's biological equipment, can be enclosed so that they do the least possible damage.

As it is often difficult to support these theories with data from human behavior, analogies are usually employed, for example in ethology.[106] The behavior of ducklings, mice, and, at best, baboons is often used to support theories of human social behavior. One forgets that if one requires an analogy-model for human behavior then mice, ducklings,

---

[105] K. Popper, "Die Logik der Sozialwissenschaften," *Kölner Zeitschrift für Soziologie und Sozialpsychologie* XIV (1962), 233–48.

[106] E. Hess, "Ethology: An Approach toward the Complete Analysis of Behavior," in *New Directions in Psychology* (New York: Holt, Rinehart & Winston, 1962).

baboons, and their behavior are less suitable than, for example, the system constituted by a computer. The latter is able to store information and produce it on the "right occasion," i.e., make highly complicated choices and carry out very complex operations. As we know, all this is normal everyday activity for a human brain, but hardly for a mouse or a baboon.

Man is characterized by the fact that inborn, biological tendencies— "instincts," if you like—play a very small part in human behavior, when one considers the enormous learning capacity possessed by humans. Instinctive behavior in man, as compared with other higher mammals, is underdeveloped.

IS THERE A REIFIED VERSION OF MARXIST THEORY?

A dogmatic-Marxist conception would certainly call reified sociologism "bourgeois sociology," seeing it as a typical product of the capitalist class society. It would be seen as an "ideology" in the Marxist meaning of the term, which means a theory whose job it is to legitimate the capitalist class society and its power structure.

Therefore, it is interesting to point out that a common interpretation of Marxist social theory can also be seen as sociologism, and therefore as a reified theory. Marxism, as economic determinism, also operates using only the second and third of the three postulates we mentioned at the beginning of the foregoing section. In short, economic determinism means that it is the social, above all the economic, conditions which are the determining factors, and that man and his behavior are determined by these conditions. Such a thesis must be complemented by the notion that man creates and changes the social and economic conditions, if it is not to be called a sociologistic theory.

Sociologism in Marxism is expressed in the way in which the relation between the base and the superstructure is seen.

The economic base is usually thought to consist of four categories of phenomena:

(1) *The basic process of production.* In this process one can distinguish between:
(a) agents of production
(b) means of production
(c) products created

(2) *Productive forces*, which consists of 1a (at least those agents who actively participate in the process of production) and 1b. 1b comprises *natural resources*, e.g., land and minerals; *production resources*, e.g.,

machines tools, the total technical apparatus; and *scientific resources*, i.e., the results of science as applied, e.g., in technology.

(3) *Relations of production*, which are relations between the agents participating in the process of production. These relations are based upon (a) power and control over the means of production as well as over the product (Marx speaks about "appropriation" with regard to the means of production and the result of production) and (b) ownership relations which are determined by power relations.

(4) *The mode of production*, which comprises relations between the three categories of phenomena making up the first category, i.e., the process of production. Thus the mode of production comprises relations between agents of production, i.e., (3), relations between agents and means of production, between agents and the result, and between means of production and the result, expressed in the technology used. Thus this fourth category summarizes the three first.[107] Built upon this economic basic, the ideological superstructure is hypothesized, consisting of science, law, politics, philosophy, morals, and art.

There are two problems of interest in this context, which are intimately related to each other. The first is: How can one determine the way in which a certain phenomenon or class of phenomena is referred to the base or the superstructure, when this category is on the borderline between base and superstructure? This holds, e.g., for science. The other and more important problem concerns the relationship between base and superstructure.

As an example of the first problem, let us discuss the place of science and technology. Both are productive forces and therefore should be placed within the economic base. Scientific activity, however, is a cognitive process, and, as such, it should be placed in the superstructure. One possible means of solving the problem is to make a distinction between scientific activity as a *process*, and the *results* of these activities. The results of scientific activity, especially those which can be 'applied to the process of production, can be placed within the base. On the other hand, scientific activity as a cognitive process could be placed within the superstructure. However, science is a process of production, namely, of ideas, theories, and the transformation of these theories. As a process of production, it should be classified within the economic base. (In fact, scientific-technological research and its application is an outstanding example of our first postulate that society is a human product.)

If one considers scientific activity (and why not all cognitive and artistic activity) as processes of production, then one has to relinquish

[107] Ch. Groth, "Den historiske materialismes metode og hypoteser," *Häften för kritiska Studier* I (1968) No. 4, 6–16.

the sharp distinction between base and superstructure. In fact, one could consider material, scientific, artistic, and other types of production as subsystems belonging to a larger system and influencing each other. This type of analysis is presented by Althusser, who differentiates five levels: economy, law, politics, ideology (e.g., religion and ethics), and science. Within each level there occur different types of production. For example, within the scientific level various branches of science may be differentiated. In addition, each level is characterized by a different process of production specific for the given level.[108]

The analysis of base and superstructure in terms of different levels with specific processes of production, and science being the process of producing knowledge, not only changes the categorization of social phenomena but also implies that certain solutions concerning the relation between "base and superstructure" are excluded. One of them is that which transforms Marxistic theory into reified theory. This interpretation considers the superstructure to be a reflection only of the basic economic conditions. Thus the superstructure is conceived of as "mirroring" basic "material conditions." This mirror-theory is usually combined with concepts concerning economic determinism. (As pointed out in chapter 4, Marx himself rejected the idea of a one-sided economic determinism.)

Such a theory asserts that the economic conditions are determining factors and human behavior as well as ideas, etc., are the determined factors. The question then becomes: Who creates the economic conditions?

The relationship between base and superstructure is in this case a simple causal relation, the base being the cause and the superstructure being the effect, where in addition the cause-effect relation is thought of as a "reflection." Berger and Luckman assert that the "mirror-theory" is a faulty interpretation of Marx's own thinking: "What concerned Marx was that human thought is founded in human activity ("labor" in the widest sense of the word) and in the social relations brought about by this activity."[109]

THE RELATIONSHIP BETWEEN SOCIOECONOMIC
CONDITIONS AND COGNITIVE PROCESSES

Reified theories have earlier been characterized as cognitive processes whereby human activity and the products of human activity are not experienced as typically human, but as having their own reality. Reified

[108] This short presentation is based upon R. Fjellström's outstanding presentation of the theories developed by L. Althusser and his coworkers (mimeo, 1968).

[109] Berger and Luckman, *Social Construction of Reality*, p. 6.

theories are a peculiar phenomenon: "Even while apprehending the world in reified terms, man continues to produce it. That is, man is capable paradoxically of producing a reality that denies him."[110]

One of the reasons for such reified theories is to be found in ideas concerning the relationship between actual social conditions and cognitive processes. In Marxist thinking this problem is dealt with on different levels. One, which concerns a metaphysical and therefore not particularly interesting problem, is the relationship between materia and consciousness or knowledge. One answer given, e.g., by Engels is that consciousness reflects materia. Thus correct knowledge is considered to be a mirror of materia. However another and more important thesis is the one asserting that it is social existence which determines consciousness. This implies an influence–relationship different from reflection or "mirroring." A similar problem on a more abstract level, then, is the relationship between base and superstructure.

There are several solutions to the problem of the relationship between material base and ideological superstructure. One is presented by Goldmann, another by Althusser, and a third by Lucien Sebag.

Modern society is basically an economical society, says Hofmann.[111] The position of man within society is determined by his function within the economic processes, and economical processes are basic to the existence and development of societies.

Lucien Goldmann[112] therefore presents a hypothesis that the dominance of economical factors is historically determined.

In the passage of history, man, because of the ever-present scarcity, has been forced to devote the greatest part of his energies to "solving the problem of production and distribution of material goods, i.e., solving the economic problem."[113] It follows that the quantitative dominance of economic conditions in the thoughts and behavior of the individual can remain only as long as this scarcity exists. In a world which is able to assure the individual of sufficient need-satisfaction, economic conditions will no longer play an important part.

Goldmann adds that in a world so fiercely dominated by economic problems, the mirror-theory (i.e., the theory that man's consciousness and the cognitive products he creates—justice, morals, art, etc.—are only a reflection of the economic conditions) is a reality, the "mirroring" itself being an expression of reification.

Althusser's analysis[114] is more complex. His basic thesis is that social

110 Ibid., p. 83.
111 Hofmann, *Universität, Ideologie, Gesellschaft*, p. 117.
112 Goldmann, *Recherches dialectiques*, p. 74.
113 Ibid., p. 75.
114 L. Althusser, *Pour Marx* (Paris: Librairie Maspero S.A., 1965).

and historical events are overdetermined, a term he has borrowed from Freud and psychoanalysis.

In 1890 Engels wrote a letter to J. Bloch in which he emphasized the following points: "According to the materialist conception of history, the *ultimately* determining element in history is the production and repro-duction of real life. More than this neither Marx nor I have ever asserted. Hence if somebody twists this into saying that the economic element is the *only* determining one, he transforms that proposition into a meaning-less, abstract, senseless phrase. The economic situation is the basis, but the various elements of the superstructure . . . also exercise their influ-ence upon the course of the historical struggle and in many cases preponderate in determining their *form*. There is an interaction of all these elements in which . . . the economic movement finally asserts it-self as necessary."[115]

At the end of the same letter Engels gives reason for the misunder-standing concerning economic determinism. Saying that Marx and he himself are to blame, he adds: "We had to emphasize the main principle *vis-à-vis* our adversaries, who denied it, and we had not always the time, the place or the opportunity to allow the other elements involved in the interaction to come into their rights."[116]

Althusser takes the quoted sentences as his point of departure. He then asks himself whether it is possible to explain concrete historical events, e.g., the Russian revolution, with the help of a simple principle: The revolution was a consequence of class-antagonisms having their basis in the contradiction between the level of development of the pro-ductive forces and the relations of production. Althusser denies that such an explanation is sufficient. In the case of Russia it does not explain why the revolution was successful there but nowhere else in Europe, where similar antagonistic conditions were prevailing. Althusser asserts that there are many conditions, which are neither independent of each other nor of basic antagonistic states, but which are not simply an expres-sion of these states. These other factors which have to be used in explain-ing a historical event or a certain social situation can have an autono-mous status as causal factors. They can be a part of the superstructure. They can be, for example, traditional value- and norm-systems, as the family structure, certain institutionalized conditions within the state or law. They may even be geographical conditions.

A social situation, an event, a historical process can therefore never be explained in terms of a simple principle. Every such event is "overdeter-mined." What Althusser introduces here is the notion of multiple causal-

[115] K. Marx and F. Engels, *Selected Works* (Moscow: Foreign Publishing House, 1949) Vol. II, p. 443.

[116] Ibid., p. 444.

ity or the principles concerning mutual influence with built-in feedback mechanisms.

Like Engels, Althusser asserts that only in the "last instance" are economic conditions decisive. Everything depends on what is meant by the "last instance." One reasonable interpretation is that the expression refers to *necessary* but not *sufficient* conditions.

A third approach is demonstrated by Lucien Sebag.[117]

He maintains that an ideology is a system of thought. It has a certain structure conceived of as a principle of organization. It is this structure which has to be discovered before any conclusions can be drawn regarding the relationship between the system of ideology and the economic base. There could be at least three different relations: (1) *Reflection*: in this case ideology reflects the economical base. (2) *Transposing*: in this case ideology expresses in *a specific language* human relations which originate in conditions of the process of production. (3) *Actualization* of a certain structure in a given area or subsystem, a structure, however, which is common for the totality of society.

Sebag asserts that there are two basic errors in an analysis which hypothesizes causal relations between base and superstructure. One concerns the fusing of a structural with a historical analysis. In the terms of structuralism, synchronic and diachronic relations are mixed together. Since cause-effect relations presuppose a time dimension (the effect comes in time after the cause), such a diachronic analysis is possible only if one refers to concrete events which are related to each other. However, "ideology" and "mode of production" are totalities and, as such, models of thought. As such, an analysis has to be synchronic: it has to discover how both subsystems belonging to the same total system express the same structure, i.e., a certain order combined with rules of combination and permutation.

Thus, one wishes either to establish relations between *events* in a *diachronic way* or to try to find a *common structure* for *models* of *thought*, which means to carry out a synchronic analysis. A theory postulating a causal relation between base and superstructure tries to carry out a diachronic analysis on the abstract level of models. This is not possible.

Sebag illustrates his thesis with reference to two examples borrowed from an analysis of the French philosopher Garaudy.[118] There a relationship between Thomas Aquinas's *Summa Theologica* and the social structure of a feudal society is postulated. Briefly the analysis asserts that hierarchical relations between God and man, as Thomas conceives of

[117] Sebag, *Marxisme et structuralisme.*
[118] Ibid., p. 124 ff.

them, reflect the actual hierarchical conditions in the feudal society. The latter, then, is seen as the *cause* of the theological system, which reflects actual social conditions.

Sebag's objection is that possibly the work of Thomas transposes a special social content to the language of theology. However, this transposition is done neither willingly nor consciously. Nothing more than an analogy can be used. Furthermore, the relationship between the theological thought-system of Thomas and the model of the feudal society has to be seen on a synchronic level: the task is to discover rules of transformation and a structure common to both.

The second example is built upon a book by Montalambert, written in 1848, in which he writes that religion is the only means by which the continued existence of the present social order can be assured. Therefore it should be spread among the people in order to counteract revolutionary activities. Here a relationship between social oppression and a religious ideology can be established. Montalambert is conscious of the possibilities of using religion in order to legitimize existing conditions. The causal relationship established between two concrete events is maintained at all times on a conscious level.

Thus, the central thesis in Sebag's analysis is that the relationship between socioeconomic conditions and cognitive processes—both considered as totalities and, as such, models of thought—has to be made on a synchronic level. On such a level it is meaningless to talk about causal relations.

In the description of a society one can delimit different totalities or subsystems, for example, "economic relations, kinship relations, language or the elements of aesthetics. . . . These phenomena are structured, and the linguist, the ethnologist or the economist try to make these structures clear. In principle these structures do not correspond to real relations, which are richer, much more complex, and are the products of varying influences, which emanate from other sectors of social life."[119]

Thus structures are models with the help of which one can discuss and reveal the principle of organization "ruling a totality of elements which define each other mutually."[120] They define relations between elements and also contain rules for transformation when two subsystems are compared with each other.

Lévi-Strauss[121] exemplifies structural analysis by comparing kinship conditions and language in a given culture. Studying various cultures, he

[119] Ibid., p. 156.
[120] Ibid., p. 119.
[121] C. Lévi-Strauss, "Sprache und Gesellschaft," *Kursbuch* No. 5, (1966), 178–89.

found a definite structure as far as the kinship relations and marriage rules of these cultures are concerned. Among other things, the structure is characterized by certain exchange and mutuality relations. Lévi-Strauss sees the kinship system and the rules regarding marriage partners as a definite type of communication. The "information" is represented by women who can be exchanged between various families and tribes. But Lévi-Strauss goes a step further and compares the communication system formed by kinship relations with that system formed by the language. He hypothesizes that, within various areas, there exist similarities between the structure of kinship relations and the structure of the language.

EPILOGUE

Sociology and the social sciences, on the one hand, and the natural sciences, on the other hand, differ in several ways. One difference concerns the effect of predictions. In the social sciences the very act of predicting future events may effect the occurrence of these events. This is not the case in the natural sciences. Second, in the social sciences one usually studies purposive behavior, i.e., events progressing from certain starting points, e.g., value assumptions of an ethical nature and directed toward certain goals. This does not hold for the natural sciences.

The third difference is the most important. It concerns the field or area of investigations. For the natural scientist this area is clearly separated from the social environment in which he lives and works. His field of investigation is *outside* his social environment. This is not so in the social sciences. The social scientist lives and works *within* the field or area of investigation. Science can be viewed as a social institution and the scientific community as a subsystem of the society in general. Thus, scientific behavior is governed by rules and norms, and the scientist has certain roles bestowed upon him by the social system of which he is a member. These rules and norms, as well as certain values, affect research activity. We can divide these values into *intrascientific* and *extrascientific*. The intrascientific values concern the ways in which research should be carried out. Intrascientific values affect social scientists as well as natural scientists. Intrascientific values can systematically be arranged into a metascience or philosophy of science. The dominant philosophy of science is the one which may be called *positivism* or *empiricism* (sometimes with the attribute *logical*).

But positivism or empiricism is not only a philosophy of science. It can also be considered as "*an articulated ideology*, as an instrument to

343

establish and consolidate a way of thinking about and experiencing the world."[1] To the degree that is a *Weltanschauung* it introduces extra-scientific values into scientific research. Again, that may not particularly concern the natural scientist. However, it should concern the social scientist for two reasons. The first reason is that this ideology may affect his view concerning those phenomena which are a part of his own field of investigation.

The other reason has to be explained in more detail. Human behavior can be studied in two ways: First, it can be studied as factual events, i.e., whether these events occur or not and the conditions under which they occur. "On the other hand one can ask whether human meaning or notions are true, whether human actions are right, whether human institutions are just." [2]

If social science is concerned with the *actual occurrence* of human ideas or human behavior, it usually follows the value-system of positivistic metascience. If it is concerned with social phenomena from the point of view of whether they are true, right, and just, certain standards are applied which may be part of a *critical theory*.

"A critical theory has a legitimating function. It gives a positive or negative sanction to that which is."[3] The phenomena of natural science do not need legitimization. They *are*. Human behavior, however, is not only a fact but also has definite consequences. Therefore human behavior has to legitimize itself. A positivistic metatheory also has a legitimizing function, though such a function is usually denied.

But denying such a function does not abolish it. If sociology and the social sciences assert that they are a positive science and that they therefore are nonpolitical, this assertion that they are nonpolitical is a legitimization built upon certain values—e.g., that of being nonpolitical. These values may have a direct effect. They may contribute to the conservation of existing social conditions, since the social scientist does not in this case use other critical standards which may tell something about the consequence of human action and the consequences of the functioning of human institutions. Thus, the question is whether the monopolistic demand of positivistic science to consider its own metatheory as the only one, should be rejected for the social sciences. Instead one should assert the necessity of supplementing a *positivistic* and *empirical social* science with a *critical* social science.

---

[1] R. Fjellström, "Anteckningar om positivismen," *Häften för kritiska studier 1* (1968), No. 4, 6–16.

[2] H. Skjervheim, *Vitskapen om mennesket og den filosofiske refleksjon* (Oslo: Johan Grundt Tanums Forlag, 1964), p. 123.

[3] Ibid.

Let me argue this point from another angle. Society and language have one thing in common: One cannot study them without knowing them in advance. Thus, in order to understand society one requires a preexisting knowledge about it.[4] However, sociology which explains social phenomena from its own preexisting knowledge may develop a theory that is different from the way in which members of a social system experience their own social reality. One solution may be the development of an "understanding sociology," i.e., a sociology which tries to understand society by studying the notions of social reality held by members of the society and the ways in which these notions affect their behavior.[5]

One could raise the objection that if one requires preexisting knowledge about society in order to understand it, why do we need a social science at all? However, just as one can talk a language without knowing its grammatical rules, people can function within a society without knowing its rules. In fact, we know how to follow a rule without knowing what "following a rule" means.[6] An understanding sociology then could be a sociology which studies the meaning that social phenomena have for the members of society. Thus the ideal of such a social science would be linguistics.[7]

Habermas has an important objection against an "understanding sociology." If language and meaning are taken as central phenomena in the study of social events, one may forget that language and meaning in turn are affected by certain facts forced upon them: The linguistic infrastructure of society is a phenomenon within a context, which is determined by two types of reality: nature and its laws, and the power conditions existing within a given society. Thus we may speak about "outer" and "inner" forces affecting meaning and language. In fact, they affect the rules of language. Therefore, all social acts should be understood from *three different constituent* conditions: language, the basic process of production by which "nature is transformed," and social power relations.[8]

For that reason Habermas differentiates between three types of sociology centered around what he calls the three main media necessary

---

[4] J. Habermas, *Theorie und Praxis* (Neuwied: Luchterhand Verlag, 1967).

[5] P. Winch, *The Idea of a Social Science* (London: Routledge and Kegan Paul, 1965), and P. Berger & T. Luckman, *The Social Construction of Reality* (Garden City: Doubleday & Co., 1966).

[6] Ibid.

[7] C. Lévi-Strauss, *The Savage Mind* (London: Weidenfeld & Nicolson, 1966).

[8] J. Habermas, "Zur Logik der Sozialwissenschaften," in *Beiheft 5 zu Philosophischer Rundschau* (Tübingen: Mohr, 1967).

for the maintenance of a social system: *work* (in the sense of the basic process of production), *language*, and *power*. Connected with each of these three media, there are three types of *interests* motivating research and guiding it. These three types of interests are *technical* interests, *interpretative* (Habermas uses the term *hermeneutical*), and *emancipatory* interests. These three types of interests in turn are related to three types of knowledge: *information, interpretation*, and *criticism*. Finally, to make the paradigm complete, the three types of media, motives for research and knowledge, give rise to three types of social scientific ideals: the *natural science-ideal* as presented by positivism, the *hermeneutic ideal* as, e.g., presented by structuralism, and, finally the ideal of a *critical social science*.[9]

What, then, is the task of a critical social science? "It studies society as a totality and in its historical setting from the viewpoint of criticism and socio-political practice, i.e., not merely with a view to making visible what in any case *happens*, but rather with a view to making us aware of, and keeping us aware of, what we must *do*, viz. the planning and shaping of the future, which we cannot avoid being engaged in. For instance, if critical sociology shows us that, say, social emancipation bought at a price of increasing regimentation is not freedom, that prosperity bought at a price of objectification of enjoyment is not affluence, etc., then such a check upon the results of social planning is its contribution to preventing the society from becoming a closed society. *Such a control* has the explicit political aim of keeping our society an open society."[10]

A critical sociology may thus be seen as a necessity in order to counteract reifying tendencies in society by revealing them. It may also counteract the risk of developing theories which do not try to "understand" society or to view it critically but which want to establish social facts without seeing that such facts are usually a consequence of historically determined social conditions, e.g., the typical mode of production.

Thus sociology should be more than just a positive science. It should be more than an "understanding" science. It should be more than a critical science. It ought to combine all these three aspects, and all of them ought to be acknowledged as *legitimate methods* of scientific undertaking. No one should have the right to make monopolistic demands of representing the "correct" science. This, however, also means that sociology has to substitute the ideal of being like natural science with the ideal of recognizing different research motivations and therefore also different approaches.

[9] Habermas, *Theorie und Praxis*.
[10] G. Radnitzki, *Contemporary Schools of Metascience* (Göteborg: Akademiförlaget, 1968); and Habermas, *Theorie und Praxis*.

It is my firm belief that in the long run it is only this "multivaried" sociology that is of any value to society and its development—a development which may bring with it deadly risks for mankind. To counteract such a development must be a central task for all of us today. Social scientists are not excepted.

NAME INDEX

Abendroth, W., 269 n.
Adler-Karlsson, G., 275 n., 278 n., 304
Adorno, T. W., 13 n., 150 n., 175 n., 206
Allardt, E., 7, 15 n., 214 n., 226-34, 259
Almasi, M., 67, 242, 244-45
Althusser, Louis, 3 n., 63 n., 79, 337-40
Anderson, Perry, 247
Andersson, Bo, 233
Arendt, Hannah, 72 n.
Aron, Raymond, 132, 141 n., 333 n.
Asplund, J., 103 n., 150 n., 313 n.

Baczko, B., 21 n., 71
Bell, D., 71 n.
Berger, P., 81 n., 83 n., 269 n., 284 n., 326, 332
Blackburn, R., 225 n., 226
Blauner, R., 205 n., 207, 215-26; alienation theory summarized, 221-22; on orthodox Marxism, 223; work process description in, 219
Bottomore, T. B., 33 n., 196, 322
Buckley, W., 86, 181 n.

Castro, Fidel, 250, 251 n.
Cooley, C. H., 313-14
Coser, L., 9
Crozier, Michel, 325-26

Dahlström, E., 207, 209, 212 n., 213, 293 n.
Dahrendorf, R., 56 n., 299
Dawydow, J. M., 78 n., 263
Durkheim, E., 7, 15, 211, 233-34, 333; alienation in, 97; anomia and, 134-48; antiindividualistic view of, 147-48; "collective conscience" of, 141-42; cultural-lag hypothesis of, 143; on division of labor, 144; and history of ideas, 134-35; image of man in, 145-48; on industrialized society, 137-38; Marx and, 136-37; on social facts, 145; on suicide, 138

Engels, Friedrich, 2, 82, 90, 91 n., 96 n., 162 n., 241, 339-40
Etzioni, A., 59, 213

Feuer, L., 205

Feuerbach, Ludwig, A., 31, 56, 65
Fichte, Johann Gottlieb, 24
Fjellström, R., 75 n., 337 n., 344
Frank, G. A., 307 n., 308
Freud, Sigmund, 12, 147, 155, 176-77, 179, 181, 182
Friedman, George, 252
Fromm, Erich, 15, 68 n., 69, 76, 125 n., 149, 184 n., 243 n.; alienation theories of, 151-62; ego theory of, 157; Marxist approach of, 150; on mental health, 160-61; personality theory of, 158-62

Gabel, J., 81 n., 90 n.
Galbraith, J., K., 109 n., 110 n., 195 n., 198 n., 273, 278, 282, 300-1, 303-4, 310
Goldmann, Lucien, 271, 282, 316-18, 338
Goldthorpe, J. H., 215-26
Gouldner, Alvin, 144
Guevara, Ché, 249

Habermas, J., 111 n., 169 n., 173 n., 310 n., 312 n., 345-46
Hegel, Georg Wilhelm Friedrich, 3, 18, 51, 72 n., 129, 156, 162; alienation in, 26-29; on labor, 37; Marx on, 30-31; state vs. society in, 33; theory of state in, 34-35; on work, 27
Heiman, E., 45 n., 170 n.
Hess, E., 334 n.
Hofmann, W., 277, 332, 338 n.
Homans, G. C., 227 n., 255
Hook, Sidney, 27
Horkheimer, M., 149 n., 163
Hume, David, 72 n.

Israel, Joachim, 6 n., 9 n., 94 n., 119 n., 150 n., 187 n., 206 n., 215, 256 n., 275 n.

Jahoda, M., 9 n.
Johansson, S., 103 n., 215

Kant, Immanuel, 23-24
Keynes, John Maynard, 276
Kolakowski, L., 65, 66 n., 238 n.
Kolko, G., 64, 299 n.
Kornhauser, W., 199 n.
Kosik, K., 278 n.

SUBJECT INDEX

Abstraction, in capitalist society, 156
Abstract labor, 265
Acquisition, production as, 268
Action, value-rational, 101-2
Activity: self-realization and, 260; transformation of into products, 287; use-value of, 288
"Alienated existence," Marcuse on, 173
Alienated labor, private property and, 49
Alienation: Allardt's theory of, 226-33; as anomie, 258; atomic energy and, 246; of artist, 173; bureaucracy and, 60-61, 240, 248; capitalism and, 216, 257; class-consciousness and, 254; concept of before Marx, 18-29; concept of in Marx's early writings, 2-5; in Cuba, 249-54; definitions of, 5-6, 269; diagrammatic representation of, 54; discarding of as term, 259; as discrepancy in social ideals, 151; discrepancy-theories of, 15, 203; division of labor and, 25, 44-45; double meaning in, 5-6; double root of, 256; economic, 36-62, 217; emancipation and, 3; in empirically oriented sociology, 205-37; empirical theory and, 215; as estrangement or detachment, 26; "exteriorization" and, 51; false consciousness and, 80-96; false needs and, 157; family and, 240-42; five psychological divisions of, 208-15; Fromm's theory of, 151-62; frustration and, 6-7; in history of ideas, 18-19; human nature and, 219; ideology and, 93-95; of intellectuals, 192-94; isolation and, 212; in large organizations, 216; in Marx's early theory, 2, 11, 256; Marx's theories of, 30-62, 256, 290-91; mass society and, 200-4; meaninglessness and, 210; in mental hospital, 215; mental illness and, 81; Mills on, 185-204; in modern industry, 215-26; Nisbet's concept of, 97; norm-lessness in, 211-12, 259; objectification and, 51, 121-34; objections to use of term, 259-60; as objective phenomenon, 7; observable behavior and, 7; in other theories, 97-148; "peak condition" and, 161; political, 33-36; "positive" and "negative" types of, 234; powerlessness and, 208-10, 226-33, 259; preliminary analysis of, 15-17; private ownership and, 48-50, 239-40; production and, 4, 43, 53,

216; psychological, 5, 80-81; psychological conditions in, 207; range of meaning in, 259; as reification, 57-61, 266; rejection of term, 259, 266-67; and "relations of production," 4; religious, 31-33; Rousseau on, 19-23; ruling class and, 196-200; Seeman's theory of, 208-15; self-detachment and, 28-29; self-estrangement and, 212-13, 224; Simmel on, 121-34; social character and, 156; social conditions causing, 53; in socialist countries, 239-40; as social process, 51; society-oriented, 136; sociological approach to, 5, 11, 16, 149-204; stages in, 6; subjective experience of, 208; technical development and, 165-66; technology and, 168-72, 216-17; theoretical problems in, 213-15; as theory of fetishism of commodities, 3; totality and, 29; types of in reference to uncertainty, 229; "unconscious," 81; usefulness as concept, 258-69; use of term, 5-7; value premises and, 260-67; in *Veräussering*, 51; in white-collar workers, 189; work and, 27, 252-54; *see also* Alienation theory
Alienation theory: ambiguity and vagueness of, 258-59; assumptions in, 8; classification in, 14-15; conflict and antagonism in, 11-12; in German Romanticism, 23-26; in Hegelian philosophy, 26-29; human behavior and, 13; human nature and, 8; individual-oriented, 13, 19; individual-society relationship in, 11; preconditions for, 7-10; vs. reification theory, 268; society-oriented, 13; as sociological theory, 11; two classes of, 12; usefulness of concept in, 258-69
American dream, anomie and, 235
American power structure, 194-200
American society, alienation in, 149
Anarchy of production, 119-20
Animal-activity, vs. work-activity, 73
Anomie (anomia, anomy), 7; alienation as, 258; class belongingness and, 236-37; class structure and, 233-37; cultural lag and, 144; defined, 135; Durkheim on, 134-48; educational lack and, 235-36; evil of, 137-38; income level and, 236-37; normal vs. disrupting, 143; suicide and, 138-39
Anthropological-philosophical vs. sociological theories, 78